SERVING THE NATION

New Directions in Native American Studies
Colin G. Calloway and K. Tsianina Lomawaima, General Editors

Serving the Nation

Cherokee Sovereignty and
Social Welfare, 1800–1907

Julie L. Reed

University of Oklahoma Press : Norman
Published in cooperation with the
William P. Clements Center for Southwest Studies,
Southern Methodist University

Parts of chapter 5 have been previously published as "Family and Nation: Cherokee Orphan Care, 1835–1903," *American Indian Quarterly* 34, no. 3 (2010), and are used here with permission.

Library of Congress Cataloging-in-Publication Data

Name: Reed, Julie L., 1976–   author.
Title: Serving the nation : Cherokee sovereignty and social welfare, 1800–1907 / Julie L. Reed.
Description: Norman: University of Oklahoma Press, 2016. | Series: New directions in Native American studies; volume 14 | Includes bibliographical references and index.
Identifiers: LCCN 2015034585 | ISBN 978-0-8061-5224-0 (hardcover : alk. paper)
Subjects: LCSH: Cherokee Indians—Social conditions. | Cherokee Indians—Politics and government. | Cherokee Indians—Government relations. | Sovereignty.
Classification: LCC E99.C5 R359 2016 | DDC 975.004/97557—dc23 LC record available at http://lccn.loc.gov/2015034585

Serving the Nation: Cherokee Sovereignty and Social Welfare, 1800–1907 is Volume 14 in the New Directions in Native American Studies series.

The paper in this book meets the guidelines for permanence and durability of the Committee on Production Guidelines for Book Longevity of the Council on Library Resources, Inc. ∞

1 2 3 4 5 6 7 8 9 10

In memory of
Rachel Johnson Quinton
and dedicated to
Lilith Selu

Contents

Illustrations

Acknowledgments

To suggest that I am the sole author of this book is fiction. It is the fiction of individual accomplishment that denies the importance of *gadugi* and family, erases the contributions of those who paved the way for me, and ignores the people behind the scenes who inspired me, advised me, loved me, listened to me, made me listen, and who someday deserve all that they have given to me returned to them tenfold. So it is in these acknowledgments that I hope to recognize the nameless contributors to this book's authorship.

This book exists because institutions and the people within those institutions educated and sustained me long before my return to graduate school. To start, I want to take a moment to honor the lives of the men I met at the Methodist Warehouse in Dallas and the students I served at Hillsborough High School and Memorial Middle School in Tampa and at East Bay High School in Gibsonton, Florida. Your lives and spoken and unspoken dreams inspired, educated, and transformed me. You prepared my soul for what has followed.

Upon returning to graduate school and entering academia, institutions have continued to support my research and writing. Financially, the UNC Graduate School's Sequoyah Dissertation Writing Fellowship, the American Philosophical Society's Phillips Fund for Native American Research, the Newberry Library's Francis C. Allen Fellowship, and the Cherokee Nation Foundation's Nell Brown Memorial Scholarship supported the project. I offer special thanks to the current and former staff and administrators including Sandra Hoeflich, Leslie Kan, Dianne Dillon, Scott Stevens, Heather Sourjohn,

Shelley Butler Allen, and Kimberly Gilliand, who administered these fellowships and awards. More recently, Alessandra Jacobi Tamulevich at the University of Oklahoma Press patiently worked through the publication process with me and identified readers, including Cathleen Cahill, whose generous and critical reader's report improved this project in its final months. I am honored that Colin Calloway and Tsianina Lomawaima chose to endorse the book's inclusion in their New Directions in Native American Studies series. Ernie Freeberg, my department chair and mentor, deserves special thanks for his generosity before, during, and after my arrival at the University of Tennessee, as do my colleagues in the history department.

The archivists and volunteers at each of the libraries and archives I visited welcomed and aided me in countless ways. Tom Mooney, who has since retired from the Cherokee Heritage Center, risked being late to Cherokee language class to make sure the records I needed were accessible. Nancy Calhoun and the volunteers at the Muskogee Public Library shared Crock-Pot soup while I worked through materials in the Grant Foreman room. At Northeastern State University, Delores Sumner, in addition to letting me pillage the vertical files and make copies, is a resource and archive in her own right, someone I have appreciated listening to and getting to know over the last eight years. Through a fortuitous Facebook comment by the great-granddaughter of John Duncan, the last high sheriff of the Cherokee Nation, and what was probably perceived as a bizarre private message from me to her singing the praises of her forebears, I was able to locate John Duncan's papers at the Talbot Museum and Library in Colcord, Oklahoma, where Donna, Teresa, and Grace all welcomed me and encouraged me to return.

My time in Oklahoma continues to be personally and professionally inspiring as a result of the relationships I have because of this project. Current and former staff members of the Cherokee Nation Cultural Tourism Division, the Cherokee Nation, and Sequoyah Schools deserve my gratitude, including Cady Shaw, Travis Owens, Catherine Foreman Gray, Lauren Jones, Donetta Johnson, Ben Elder, Lisa Rutherford, and Don Franklin. I would be remiss if I did not also offer thanks to Julia Coates, Jack Baker, David Hampton, and

Candessa Tehee, all of whom through conversations and emails have supported my work.

North Carolina institutions and the people within them also nourished me as a scholar. Western Carolina faculty Anne Rogers, Hartwell Francis, and Tom Belt all enabled me to begin my Cherokee language study. Tom and Hartwell have indulged my linguistic questions regarding health and well-being as has Ben Frey at the University of North Carolina. I am grateful to my dissertation committee members, Clara Sue Kidwell, Valerie Lambert, and Kathleen Duval, who have continued to support me beyond my time at UNC.

Theda Perdue and Michael Green served as my co-advisors at UNC, and without them this book truly would not exist. Theda and Mike were my harshest critics and my most enthusiastic cheerleaders. Unfortunately, Mike past away in 2013. Mike—I mourn that I will never drink bourbon and eat M&M's with you and Theda as the three of us argue about what I did right and wrong with this book. Theda—thank you for devoting your career to ethnohistory and your scholarship to American Indians of the Southeast. You have consistently reminded the academy of its merits and encouraged us to do the same. Without a doubt, your commitments to Native American studies and your mentoring of Native American scholars has opened doors for Native academics and has fueled discussions of the Native South at institutions across the United States. Because of you, I am able to continue walking the right path. The heart of this project beats because of the two of you. *Wado.*

During the 2013–14 academic year, I received the David J. Weber Fellowship from the Clements Center for Southwestern Studies at SMU in Dallas. While in residence, I received significant feedback from Clyde Ellis, Katherine Osburn, Ed Countryman, Sherry Smith, Crista Deluzio, Dave Edmunds, Scott Cassingham, John Gram, and Margaret Neubauer on an early draft of the manuscript. I am in awe of the intellectual generosity that was shown to me at that workshop and in the many conversations that followed. I am grateful to Carole Weber's presence at Clements Center events. This served as a testament to David Weber's career at SMU and the Webers' commitment as a family to the next generation of historians. To my fellows Bill DeBuys, Neel Baumgardner, Max Krochmal, and Ben Francis Fallon, and to Andy Graybill and Gammy Ruth Ann Elmore— I am enriched by the scholarly journey we traveled together that year. But of immeasurable value, you are my friends. That friendship means I can pin your names to stuffed animals if I am alone at a happy hour, I have someone I can buy that concealed carry class Groupon with, my child has an emergency contact in Texas, and I will know which button on the microwave to push to reheat my beef rib. If you ever need a cat to attend your book readings or a v-space to store your furniture in, I got you covered.

Friendship is one of the greatest gifts life has bestowed upon me. How I have come to deserve so many of you at life's various mile markers I will never comprehend. So let me say to Michelle Alvarez, Lynn Burke-Bogner, Valerie Lopez-Stern, Deb Langshaw, Beth VanDyke-McCormack, Lisa Parker, and especially to you, Stewart Slayton—you who have walked and run with me through the joys and heartaches of childhood and adulthood—you remain my kindred spirits who light my way.

I have almost never felt prepared for the trials and tribulations of graduate school and academia, but I always felt inspired to face them because I have been joined by Courtney Lewis, Karla Martin, Mikaela Adams, Katy Smith, Crystal Feimster, Jean Denison, Fay Yarbrough, Lisa King, Jill and Miguel LaSerna, Marina Maccari, Brandon and Eboni Winford, and Steve Chin and Shellen Wu. Rose Stremlau and Malinda Maynor-Lowery, as the keepers of inordinate wisdom and strength—please tell me when it is time to get the tats on my biceps.

In 1999, my Uncle Jay gave me a copy of Angie Debo's *And Still the Waters Run*. In it, he inscribed, "May your search for knowledge bring you home." It has, Uncle Jay. And it will again and again and again. My uncle is only one member of my family who has enabled me to come home and to leave again in order to search for knowledge. To my parents, Doug and Marti Reed, there are no words to say thank you for the earliest lessons on history and family each of you imparted and the continued ways you support me as a daughter, a mother, and a scholar. To my Aunt Joan, thank you for the thirty-one-year conversation on our history as Cherokee women that I suspect will never end. To Chad, Kyle, Shane, and Dwight, thank you for sharing your parents. The loss I felt by never meeting Nelson has waned because of the presence, stories, and history I have received from the four of you and Uncles Jay and Frank, Aunts Cordelia, Charlotte, and Cindy, and from all of my ornery cousins. And Pauline—she made sure I received the love. To my Quinton, Smith, Duffield, Reed, Dabb, Haas, and Hardee families—all of you have shaped the person I was, am, and will become. My partner, Nick Thompson, has uprooted his life countless times so that I could pursue my professional goals. He experiences my wrath and bears witness to my greatest weaknesses and successes with more regularity than anyone. For the past eighteen years, he has had my back. Nick—I have not said it enough, but I am grateful for the consistency, humility, and stability you bring to this relationship. And to Lilith Selu—you are still and always will be the most delightfully beautiful and joyful creation that I was able to coauthor. I remain in awe of the book of life you are now authoring and the perfect serendipity that led me to be a character in it.

A Note on Language

As an ethnohistorian, I am sensitive to the language I use in describing the actions of individuals and the Cherokee Nation, as well as the events that transpired. Scholars and communities often rely on the language of blood (i.e., full-blood, mixed-blood, thin blood) to define concepts and explain orientations that were not shared by non-Indians and Indians. Blood quantum (which was assigned quite problematically at allotment) as well as the terms "full blood" and "mixed blood" are fraught with problems. Scientific racism imposed blood quantum on Indian people to systematically separate them from communal landholdings, tribal governments, and their own institutional social services. At the turn of the twentieth century, blood quantum provided a mechanism for land speculators and lawyers to obtain "guardianship" rights of Indian people, especially orphans, and their property, thereby exploiting the economic "rights" of "wards."[1] It also provided reformers and social workers the ammunition to forcibly remove Indian children and those with (dis)abilities to boarding schools and institutions outside of their communities, those the universe had tasked with their care.[2]

Blood quantum was and is the language imposed by a colonial power to racialize and control the political, economic, and personal lives of Indian people. That said, it was a rhetoric adopted and adapted by Indian people to explain and defend their lives to non-Indians. The terms "full blood" and "mixed blood" as used by Cherokee people, more often than not reflect cultural orientations related to traditions, language, lineage, and degree and types of institutional interactions, though they are sometimes used as a way to discuss race. These terms map closely onto the social service system people adhered to from the early nineteenth century forward. Particularly in the period after the Civil War, when Cherokee people began using the terms more frequently, they reflect political, social, and economic cleavages that existed within the Nation and say much less about degrees of Indian ancestry. In fact, these terms say more about individual, familial, and local adherence to traditional versus national social services; as such, institutional affiliations and their durations are far more powerful tools for understanding Cherokee people's actions and identities than the language of blood quantum. Therefore, I will avoid use of the language of blood unless my sources deploy it themselves.

Nineteenth-century institutional language also comes with its own share of problems. An asylum defined by early nineteenth-century standards was a place of refuge, sanctuary, and security.[3] Now we hear the term in horror movie titles or as locations for ghost-hunting reality TV series. In the popular imagination, people equate asylums with places where the former residents never found peace or rest. Institutional death rates and these institutions' declining conditions over time explain these associations, but they do not reflect the possibilities of reform and care intended or the lived realities of many institutional residents. The Cherokees referred to their institutions most often as the Cherokee National Prison or Jail, the Cherokee Orphan Asylum, and the Cherokee Insane Asylum or Asylum for the Deaf, Dumb, Blind, and Insane. The latter is the most problematic institutional name readers will encounter. We no longer use the term "dumb" to refer to those unable to speak, and, unless used within a quote, I avoid the term entirely. Throughout the book, I will use "orphanage" interchangeably with "orphan asylum" and use "asylum" to refer to the institution that served individuals with (dis)abilities or mental illness. I offset the prefix "dis-" in "(dis)ability" to answer the call made by those in (dis)ability studies who ask us to consider the ways "(dis)ability" has been constructed over time and in different societies and how that construction blinds us to the presence and contributions of the differently abled.

As my language applies to social services, I make distinctions between traditional social policy and national social policy. I define traditional social policy, what I refer to as *osdv iyunvnehi*, as a system that traced its origins and guiding principles to matrilineal kinship systems, egalitarianism, gadugi, and communal landholdings. Lastly, throughout the book, I use the term "social policy" to describe the rules and regulations that governed the distribution of services administered by the Cherokee Nation or were accessible only to large groups of people based on citizenship. These include corn distributions, poor relief, orphan services, medical care, educational services, and services for Cherokees with (dis)abilities. However, the book primarily focuses on the services and provisions distributed to those perceived as vulnerable in some way by community and national authorities.

SERVING THE NATION

Introduction

In 1893, public intellectual Walter Adair Duncan, arguably the father of Cherokee national social services, declared in an editorial in the *Cherokee Advocate*, "For my part I am not prepared for citizenship in the United States. I do not want it."[1] At the time of his letter, Duncan had twice witnessed the destruction of the Cherokee Nation and had twice participated in its rebuilding. An elder in the Methodist Episcopal Church South, he had served multiple roles in his nation's government and administration: as a senator from the Flint District, as an executive councilor to Principal Chief John Ross, as president of the Cherokee Board of Education, as superintendent of the Cherokee Orphan Asylum, and as a board member for the Cherokee Insane Asylum. He was versed in Latin and English, somewhat conversant in Cherokee, well-read, and well-spoken.[2] If anyone in the Cherokee Nation was prepared for citizenship based on the standards expected by U.S. officials, it was Walter Adair Duncan.

Yet Duncan argued in his letter that Indian Territory should not become a territory or state of the United States, grounding his objections to U.S. citizenship in morality, treaties, history, and the law, but also rooting his argument in elements of a traditional Cherokee social welfare system, which included kinship obligations and *gadugi*— coordinated work for the social good. This ethic required the stronger and more talented to "help their brother[s]," an approach that he said trumped a system of individualism intent on "rob[bing] the poor at its footstool." For Duncan, theology and morality required that the poor receive preferential treatment. He argued that U.S. policy

3

diff between U.S. and cherokee

produced the conditions that led to poverty, and yet it failed to "condone the woes that follow on its footsteps." The Cherokees' inherent sovereignty and the treaties forged between the United States and the Cherokee Nation, he wrote, validated the Nation's historic and legal right to exist and its right to set its own social policy that protected communal landholdings. For Cherokee leaders and Cherokee social reformers like Duncan, history and comparative study affirmed the advantages of the Cherokee Nation's use of communal landholdings. He mocked the idea that individual land-ownership was the superior system by pointing to its current failures for Indians as well as for non-Indians who were "clamoring for bread."[3]

In contrast to the individualism and private property ownership promoted by the United States, Duncan continued, communal land-holdings coupled with a communitarian ethic served as Cherokee social welfare safeguards to prevent a deluge of orphans, poverty, and starvation. To be a successful U.S. citizen required "greed," and Duncan "was not raised to indulge in such practices." He rejected eating "the flesh and bone of his fellow citizen" and taking the "skin from the poor and improvident." He predicted that if Indians became U.S. citizens, they "would be classed with the poor and down-trodden of citizens"; the full-blood would be left "without home, without money . . . scoffed, abused, and plundered."[4]

A common fear

By the time Duncan wrote his letter, the cultural and legal changes leading up to the forced removal of Cherokee people from their southeastern homelands as a result of the Indian Removal Act in 1830 as well as civil wars had required the Cherokee government to provide social provisions for its citizens for decades. Changing family structures endorsed by the U.S. government's "civilization policy" in addition to the coercive and violent policies of the removal era had led Cherokee people to debate and the Cherokee Nation to legislate its first codified social policies. The move by Cherokee people from an exclusively matrilineal kinship system to a nation comprised of citizens and governed by written laws complicated access to and delivery of social provisions.

Trans to thesis

Serving the Nation examines the origins and development of the Cherokee Nation's social welfare policy and the reforms the Nation

Promise to quote

(handwritten margin note: ↗ Create a hybrid system)

enacted from the removal era through Oklahoma statehood in 1907. In the intervening years, the Cherokee Nation created a hybrid system of social welfare that merged key features of its traditional matrilineal social welfare system, universally available to all based on clan and kinship, with its national system, which offered social protections and provisions to those defined as Cherokee citizens. The hybrid system embedded its traditional community ethic, which privileged the needs of the many over individuals, and its system of communal landholdings into its national social policy. As a result, the Cherokee Nation's social policy provided a more expansive and universally available cadre of social provisions and institutional services to its members than those administered by the United States to its residents. Even though it was more expansive, the Cherokee Nation's system still produced social welfare inequities based on race, gender, and class, albeit with some similar and other acute differences in outcomes than those produced by state and federal systems.

(handwritten margin note: Still not equal)

Regardless of the negative economic and social outcomes that allotment and statehood ultimately produced for the vast majority of Cherokee citizens, the Nation's social welfare debates and its ability to determine when and whether it enforced its stated policies within the Nation produced a less coercive and more culturally responsive social provision delivery system that remained intact for Cherokee citizens over the course of the nineteenth century. However, there is no denying that gaining citizenship equaled improved social welfare. The Duncan family provides a case in point. Just as Cherokee citizenship improved conditions for individuals, the federal government's acknowledgment of tribal sovereignty provided greater social welfare protection to groups of Indian people. The Cherokee Nation's advocacy for social welfare provisions for Indian people at the federal level throughout the nineteenth century advertised the social welfare needs and expectations of American Indians to U.S. politicians and reformers as they considered significant policy changes. *Osdv iyunvnehi*, roughly translated today as welfare, but more adequately defined as the continual act of perpetuating positive well-being for the community, is the term I use throughout the book to indicate a preference for an older Cherokee social policy predicated

(handwritten margin note: → Def of Osdv iyunvnehi)

on matrilineal descent, matrilocal dwellings, egalitarian relations among all members of society, gadugi, and a commitment to communal landholdings to sustain everyone. What follows is a description of how that system operated before 1800 and the ways Cherokee people interpreted and responded to the social welfare concerns Euro-Americans would impose on Cherokee people in the decades that followed.   → Method statement

Osdv iyunvnehi

Throughout the eighteenth century, gadugi and kinship obligations at the familial and national level weaved together a web of social welfare fail-safes.[5] Individuals locally and nationally ensured that Cherokee people never faced chronic individual poverty or spiritual, physical, or familial crises alone. Cherokee people did not view individual want as a failure of the individual in need; it was a failure of the entire community at the micro level and clan networks at a macro level to respond to the need as required by gadugi and the rules of kinship. Families and communities used the resources provided by communal landholdings to fulfill those obligations.

Matrilineality and gadugi joined with communal landholdings to shield Cherokee families from long-term individual suffering. Immediate families emanated out from elder women whose daughters passed the family's clan to their children; sons did not pass their clan to their children. A son's biological children resided with their clan kin—their mother's clan. Clan kin provided care, intimacy, protection, food, and education to other members. A woman's unmarried brothers resided with the family and served as lifelong father figures to their sisters' children. Husbands of daughters became temporary to permanent fixtures in the home depending on how long a marriage lasted. If either the husband or wife was unsatisfied, the husband returned to his clan kin's home.

A Cherokee's extended family included all other clan members whose kinship obligations included the same hospitality ethic offered to neighbors at the local level and the protection, care, and affections offered within one's immediate family, regardless of where one lived.[6] Euro-American outsiders regarded this system as a "petticoat government" controlled by women. It offended their patriarchal and patrilocal sensibilities because it privileged the social and economic rights of women at the familial and national levels.[7]

Membership in a Cherokee clan made a person a Cherokee, so clan identity provided a national identity. Clans prevented children *Orphans* from becoming orphans in Cherokee society. Maternal aunts acted as mothers, providing a home, food, and education as well as linking motherless children to their clan network. Any woman of a child's clan had maternal responsibilities for that child just as any male member of the clan offered protection, mentored older boys and young men, modeled appropriate behaviors and obligations, and assumed other masculine roles in the family. Even if a child were a stranger to these clan relatives, the mutual obligations defined by clan and kin ensured familiarity and security. These rules of kinship, rooted in the clans, provided a vast network of family to guide and care for children in the event of a biological mother's death.[8]

Communal landholdings provided Cherokees equal access to the material resources of the land, to fresh water flowing through the rivers for drinking, performing daily purification rituals, and fishing. They also provided land for women to plant the three sisters—squash, corn, and beans—the staples of a Cherokee's diet, and forests in which older children and women would gather herbs, nuts, berries, and medicinal plants. Communal landholdings afforded materials for home building, as well as access to the hunting grounds that supplemented food stores with deer meat and small game, and they provided materials for clothing. Although men and women often engaged in labor related to the land separately, everyone's labor was equally valuable in ensuring that basic necessities were available to all.[9] Communal lands along with matrilineal kinship responsibilities protected families and equalized the place women, men, children, and elders occupied in relationship to each other.

Agricultural endeavors reinforced gadugi, kinship responsibilities, and the importance of women's control over their homes and the fruits of their agricultural labor, all of which benefitted social welfare. Together, men and women cleared community fields. Elders, children, and women maintained the fields, and the surplus was placed in a community coffer that any family in need could pull from if hardship arose. Women also maintained secondary kitchen gardens that provided food for their family's everyday use. However, when a neighbor visited the family, a hospitality ethic dictated that some of what families produced would be offered to guests. Other towns and communities replicated the system; this ensured that even if a failed crop harmed an individual family, the community could respond. At the local level, this social service system prevented one seasonal drought or one flood from reducing the community to starvation—collective privation, yes, individual or community starvation, no. Individuals never suffered unduly and communities prospered and conserved together.[10]

The oldest members of matrilineal households were held in high regard. Elders comprised the leadership of the white councils, or peace councils, and facilitated the everyday decision-making processes. Cherokees designated elder men and women who had distinguished themselves as leaders as beloved men and women.[11] Elders were the historians, teachers, and healers. Their labor also contributed to child rearing and farming. All of these contributions centralized their place in Cherokee communities. The same kinship responsibilities that prevented children from becoming orphans respected and revered elders.[12] Without the contributions of elders and children, a community risked upsetting cosmological balances.

Throughout the eighteenth century, a sophisticated legal system existed within Cherokee society. Like other matrilineal tribes living in what is now the southeastern United States, the Cherokees privileged the local community and the decision making of a victim's clan to determine the appropriate punishment for a wrongdoer of another clan. When an individual committed a wrong against the community, leaders selected a group of individuals to carry out penalties, including executions in cases of arson, treason, and witchcraft.[13] If the deviation harmed another clan, wronged clan members determined the penalty, and a clan agent, usually a brother, inflicted those penalties, including death in cases of incest and homicide. Cherokees employed ear cropping, insult, public disgrace, and stoning as penalties for crimes against the community or an individual.[14] Cherokees understood that another clan member or the entire clan could suffer on account of the actions of an individual. Spiritual deviations could result in the punishment of the entire community. Rather than meting out justice, penalties for clan or community violations aimed to restore temporal and cosmic balance.

Legal obligations were clear. Town elders publicly announced the law that reminded all people of their duties and responsibilities to each other at annual ceremonies. Clans and towns had until the time of the Green Corn ceremony to administer punishments in all cases except homicide. Preparations for Green Corn required purifications. Men hunted and gathered wood; women prepared food; everyone fasted, including children. Members of the entire community immersed themselves in the river and received medicinal roots to continue purification rituals at home. Men sang, women danced. Buildings were repaired. Homes were cleaned. The Sacred Fire polluted by the wrongdoing of the previous year was reignited. All was made anew. This renewal included restoration of Cherokee people to one another. No one could participate in the ceremony if anger or hostilities remained.[15] Cherokee livelihood, food, homes, and communities depended on the ability of Cherokee people to pardon offenses and move into the future restored.

Community ceremonies reinforced the value of restoration. Daily responsibilities and ceremonial preparations balanced the labor and contributions of men and women, old and young; everyone had an equal responsibility to the health and well-being of the entire community. Oral traditions reinforced an egalitarian view of community and valued the contributions that all Cherokee people had made and should continue to make, regardless of age or gender. It was the young water beetle, not her grandfather, the beaver, that carried mud to the surface of the watery world so animals would have a place to live.[16] It was the elderly buzzard whose flapping wings dried the mud. It was Kanati, the first man, who rolled the stone away from the cave and released deer and game for Cherokee people to hunt. It was Selu, the first woman, who produced the corn that nourished her family. It was also Selu, not Kanati, who sacrificed herself, so that Cherokee people would have food supplies readily available to them after her death.[17]

Traditional Cherokee social services rooted in matrilineality and a hospitality ethic did not create utopian conditions, but they did mediate chronic poverty and prolonged social isolation and affirm the equality of all people in maintaining cosmological balance. Like Euro-American systems, Cherokee systems used social and familial ostracism to coerce socially acceptable behaviors. However, annual ceremonies ensured shameless reentry to the community on the part of wrongdoers and placed equal responsibility on the wronged to restore balance to the community. Holding a grudge or allowing hostilities to linger for more than a year threw the world out of balance as much as the original wrong committed. Osdv iyunvnehi did not prevent local vulnerability in the event of a drought, pestilence, or flood, but kinship ties prevented other communities from turning away from the needs of clan relatives, even if kin were only acquaintances or even strangers who sought aid during times of displacement or distress. Every community, family, and individual, regardless of age or sex, had the power and authority to aid or harm everyone else.

This perspective led Cherokees to assign human beings responsibility for illness. According to oral tradition, disease entered the world because Cherokee people had failed to adhere to ceremonies and prayers that maintained a delicate balance between humans and the cosmos. In response to overhunting caused by population increases and the failure of Cherokees to offer prayers and thanks to the game they killed, the animals held a council and determined that each animal would create a disease to afflict the people.[18] In this instance, the entire community suffered because of their collective actions, but failure to adhere to the rules of kinship that maintained balanced relationships also brought disease and illness to the clan or to the individual.

In addition to the failure to maintain cosmological order through group or individual ceremonies, illness was also believed to emanate from ghosts, spirits, or witches. Witches presented a particularly troubling situation because they preyed upon vulnerable populations, particularly the sick, infants, and women in labor.[19] Witches took aim at the old and the young, those who connected Cherokees to their past and to the future. Besides inflicting illness and death, witches could evoke the name of an individual or clan during an incantation to produce insanity.[20]

Instead of restoring balance, witchcraft disrupted society by causing those who committed egregious acts to prosper and those who
followed established rules to suffer.[21] Accusations of witchcraft coincided with an individual or group's unwillingness to fulfill their
family and community obligations. For all of these reasons, witchcraft
was a capital offense. For traditional Cherokees, (dis)ability, insanity,
and disease originated from their failure to perform appropriate ceremonies to maintain cosmological order or as a result of the practice
of witchcraft. Therefore, treatment addressed the spiritual causes as
well as the physical symptoms, and medical practice centered on the
use of healing herbs and sacred incantations.

Osdv iyunvnehi rooted in kinship responsibilities, gadugi, and
communal landholdings contrasted with the systems practiced in the
seventeenth and eighteenth centuries by Euro-Americans along the
Eastern Seaboard. Puritan New England families relied on a fear-
based theology centered on God as father to reinforce fathers' patriarchal authority. Fathers in turn used inheritances of land and material
wealth to coerce the behavior they expected from their children.
Indentured servitude and family fragility were two key features of
life in the early Chesapeake region to the south. African slavery replaced
the indentured servitude experienced by European immigrants, and
the rise of the planter class that followed only served to reinforce
patriarchy and patrilineality and a gendered hierarchy.

Rather than the rigid discipline that marked Puritan New England
approaches to girls' and boys' child-rearing, education, and employ-
ments, planters indulged their male sons' childhood pursuits; this
contrasted with the violence inflicted on men and women of African
descent in the South to maintain plantation slavery. By the mid-
seventeenth century, northerners and southerners implemented laws
that—though enacted in different ways—privileged the legal and
economic power of white men at the expense of the political and
economic independence of women and children. Relief for the poor
was provided for women and children as an act of a patriarchal
benevolence to reinforce the power of systems designed by and primarily benefitting men. By the mid-eighteenth century, southern
colonies encouraged slaves to marry and reproduce. Slave owners

recognized that women's reproductive labor maximized their profits; this also enabled slave owners to use threats to family stability to maintain control.[22]

Eighteenth- and early nineteenth-century changes impeded traditional Cherokee social service systems. Two waves of smallpox outbreaks resulted in significant population losses.[23] From 1721 to 1798, the Cherokees signed thirteen treaties, resulting in sixteen land cessions. The rise of the deerskin trade in the early eighteenth century led the Cherokees to shift from the Cherokees' mixed subsistence-based economy, which blended women's gathering and agricultural production and men's hunting and fishing, to a market-connected economy dependent on men's hunting expeditions to procure European trade goods.[24] The subsequent decline of the deerskin trade by the 1760s and the decreasing demand by Cherokee people for European trade goods led traders to ramp up their distribution and sales of alcohol to Cherokee people. Traders realized the demand for alcohol, unlike that for kettles, cloth, or guns, would remain high. Colonial officials recognized that debts, even those of individual Cherokee people, could be used to leverage land cessions from the larger community.[25] Cherokee leaders appealed to colonial officials and Indian agents to rein in the exploitative practices of traders engaged in the most egregious practices.

A shrinking land base, exploitative trade practices, and the increase in violent altercations as a result of illegal settlement and activity by Euro-Americans led Cherokee people to reconsider how to best protect their communal landholdings, which were essential to national and local social welfare. Britain's Proclamation of 1763 extended legal recognition and protection of Cherokee national borders and led Cherokees to ally with the British during the American Revolution. In response to this, colonial militias targeted densely populated Cherokee towns during the war, burning homes, community fields, and community food supplies. Familial and local social service fail-safes were the strategic targets of colonial forces. Many families dispersed onto individual homesteads and away from more populated towns to avoid the Euro-American tactics, which included massive warfare aimed at heavily populated village centers. Even as towns dispersed, intergenerational families continued to live together and support each other, but with less organized local support and interaction to aid them in times of need. The treaties for peace that followed the American Revolution resulted in the loss of 100,000 square miles of Cherokee land.[26] The dislocation caused by war coupled with the displacement that resulted from land cessions taxed the resources of kin and communities, resulting in near starvation as kin and towns continued to deploy traditional social service systems to bear the burden together.[27]

The civilization policy introduced by George Washington and Henry Knox in 1789 attacked matrilineality and promoted the creation of agriculturally centered male-headed households steeped in individual male property rights animated by a Protestant Christian work ethic. Beginning in the 1790s, the government funded and employed Indian agents to serve large tribes and set up factories, which were government-administered trading posts, in order to moderate the actions of unscrupulous traders and to distribute the tools necessary for men to become farmers and for women to shift to domestic occupations.[28] These factories also provided a mechanism to increase the debts of individual Indians and local communities. In 1819, the U.S. government began providing funding for missionaries' efforts to promote this scheme, though it had encouraged missionaries' efforts in the 1790s. The policy took aim at women's control of basic resources, including food and household property, but it also undermined the familial, local, and national systems that supported osdv iyunvnehi.

By the beginning of the nineteenth century, the Cherokees had already adapted to numerous demographic, economic, and social changes as a result of sustained contact with Euro-Americans. Even so, Cherokee people expected non-Cherokees who lived among them to fulfill kinship obligations and to abide by a community ethic. Presbyterian minister Gideon Blackburn, who, with the blessing of the Indian agent, established two schools in the Cherokee Nation in 1804 and 1805, discovered that all visitors to the school expected to be fed, an expense that neither he had anticipated nor the Presbyterian Church had budgeted for. In 1804, as a result of drought, local chiefs in the vicinity of Muscle Shoals in present-day Alabama sought bread supplies from Agent Return J. Meigs until future harvests could replenish their supplies. Meigs complied, but kept detailed records of the loans against future payments owed.[29] Meigs failed to abide by a communitarian ethic.

• • • •

My work indirectly joins and benefits from a body of scholarship intent on answering the question, why did the United States develop a welfare system so at odds with other industrialized countries? Why did the United States develop a system of selective entitlements? Instead, I ask the questions, why did the Cherokee Nation develop the social policies it did and how and why did it choose to administer those policies in the ways that unfolded? My work examines the treaty negotiations that not only secured the apparatus and the funding for Cherokee administered social provisions but also obtained federal provisions for Cherokee people. If we imagine the numbers of treaties negotiated, signed, and carried out with hundreds of tribes that each contained community-specific requests for social provision before and after the United States came into being, we have a federal government perfectly comfortable and primed to deliver selective entitlements to other groups.

Most scholars interested in the origins of the U.S. welfare state focus their intellectual energy on the welfare reforms of the Progressive Era.[30] Theda Skocpol's pioneering work on the development and expansion of what both she and Linda Gordon refer to as the "maternalist" welfare state moves the chronology of the inception of the U.S. welfare state earlier by focusing on the expansion of entitlements. Skocpol examines the growth of the federal bureaucracy and budget necessary to administer increasingly generous Civil War widows', orphans', and (dis)ability pensions, thus ushering in an exceptional U.S. system of selective entitlements instead of the "paternalist" (and more universal) policies developed in Europe to support men engaged in wage labor. Scholars interested in gender have also remained focused on the Progressive Era to demonstrate the contributions reform-minded middle-class women made in creating welfare programs that severely hurt poor women. Gwendolyn Mink accepted that "gender difference was the cornerstone of the welfare state" but reached the conclusion that "the social geology of race in America drove the politics of welfare state building." Yet in all of these works on social policy and provision, individual Indians, Native nations, and federal Indian policy are relegated to single sentences, if that. More times than not, those single sentences include the word "expropriation" and ultimately cast Indian people aside as victims of the economic and social carnage created by U.S. expansion. They inevitably become welfare recipients.

By examining the development of Cherokee national social policy, it is impossible to cast Indians aside as victims doomed to an ongoing existence as state and federal welfare recipients.[31] This was not the norm when Euro-Americans came into contact with Cherokee people, and it was not the norm throughout most of the nineteenth century. In fact, Walter Adair Duncan and his brother DeWitt Clinton Duncan pointed out the features of federal and state policy that would create the conditions and construct the "reality" of Indian poverty where it had not previously existed.

With the exception of a few recent works written by historians of Native America, scholars have largely ignored the role and presence of Indian people in shaping what C. Joseph Genetin-Palawa refers to as "viable [federal] policy alternatives." Even fewer works consider the possibility Indian people contributed in any way to the development and construction of a welfare state. Cathleen Cahill's recent social history of the federal Indian Service examines the ways Indian people, including significant numbers of Native women, employed by the federal government attempted to use their positions to better their own economic situation and that of their families and communities. She demonstrates that employees were also in a position to resist or support policies that would directly affect Indian people. Rather than focus my work on Indian interventions on federal policy as Cahill and Genetin-Palawa do, I remain focused on the internal social policies debated and devised by the Cherokee people within the Cherokee Nation.[32]

The Cherokee Nation, to borrow the language used by Kevin Bruyneel, existed in a "third space of sovereignty."[33] Within that actual physical space, Cherokees did not simply imagine a viable alternative to the social policies offered by federal officials and states; they

imagined, created, debated, and reformed their own social policies throughout the nineteenth century. I suggest that this directly
influenced how federal officials approached their delivery of social
provisions offered by Indian Health Services that Cahill describes
in her book *Federal Fathers and Mothers*.

My work is not an examination of the interplay between black-
ness, social policy, and nationhood, though it enters the discussion.
Other scholars have produced a rich conversation on slavery and
race in the Cherokee Nation, Indian Territory, and Native nations, and
their ideas influence my thoughts and conclusions. If anything, my
work examines the interplay between whiteness, social policy, and
Cherokee nationhood. John Duncan's and his sons' trajectories can
easily be read next to Shoe Boots's and his children's lives and experiences. It becomes clear that citizenship paired with whiteness, in at
least this instance, accrued social welfare benefits for the Duncan
family over time not consistently available to Shoe Boots's family.[34]
Throughout this book, the Duncan family provides one example of
a family that benefitted from the protections afforded citizens as a
direct result of the nation-building process. Walter Adair Duncan did
not benefit because the Nation chose to exclude African Cherokees
or their children from the legal and economic protections offered by
the Nation or because it revoked Cherokee women's political rights,
but he inherited and played a role in reforming social policies that
continued to do so. The social policy that protected him and enabled
him to so beautifully articulate what was at stake for most Cherokee
people during the allotment era also crippled his ability to see or
give voice to ways in which it might be modified to protect others.

My work is bookended by examinations of the Cherokee Nation's
influence on federal social policy for Indian people and contradicts
the position asserted by some scholars that the treaty annuities, goods,
services, education, and health care services were "welfare-like dependency" or special entitlements. Instead, they characterize the nation-
to-nation agreements forged by sovereign Native communities
attempting to fulfill their obligations to one another that preexisted the
formation of the United States. The treaty negotiation process, the treaties
produced, and the efforts by the communities that followed the treaties
represent Native nations' efforts to negotiate a process meant to limit

the exercise of their sovereignty, diminish their independence and self-sufficiency, and disable their previous social welfare systems.[35]

In the Cherokee Nation's case, removal treaty negotiators worked diligently to offset the catastrophe that they knew would follow, in part through control of Cherokee Nation social services. Cherokee officials sought to achieve self-sufficiency as they traversed processes that limited the Cherokee Nation's and individual Cherokees' abilities to do so. Nation building, social welfare administration, and institution building took work—physical and intellectual. In the mid-to-late nineteenth-century, when the federal government and states throughout the South lacked the political or economic will to develop universal national- or state-administered welfare services, the Cherokee Nation forged ahead, creating national bureaucracies and professional organizations to administer services to all citizens.

By examining the first steps toward an American Indian welfare state, the social policy designed and administered by Cherokee people, and the services the Cherokee Nation provided, it becomes impossible to simply view Indian people as dependent wards, though within Cherokee institutions some were. Walter Adair Duncan could never be accused of the "moral and intellectual weakness" commonly assigned to American Indians to explain poverty. Cherokee people were both the subjects and objects of these institutions. Institutions affirmed Cherokee sovereignty, exposed the limitations and weaknesses in its social policy, and revealed the weaknesses of the federal government's, states,' and territories' social services. The Cherokees' social welfare efforts provided a counter-narrative to social policy reforms crafted by states and the federal government directed at people of color, immigrants, and the poor. Cherokee people challenged the late nineteenth-century reformers' writings and rhetoric that gawked at American Indian poverty in periodicals and newspapers. They rejected the positions of those who "mobilized sentiment against the undeserving poor."[36] Cherokee leaders, including Duncan, pointed out that once classed as "the poor" within the United States, Cherokee families would be subject to the same scrutiny, coercion, and denial of human dignity and autonomy that those who spoke different languages, structured families differently, or practiced different religions were already subjected to by the United States and its citizens.[37]

Works that examine non-Indian–administered institutions, particularly federal Indian boarding schools, as sites of repression and resistance among Indian peoples have become common in recent years. The earlier scholarly literature treated federal Indian boarding schools as total institutions, mechanisms for the complete assimilation of Indian people, bent on the destruction of Indian children's cultural, religious, and social practices while replacing them with white, middle-class, Protestant American values.[38] Works that have followed highlight the resilience and agency of Native American youth within a system intended to erase the students' tribal identities, languages, family systems, values, and cultures.[39] As these scholars point out, the actions and resistances of institutional residents prevented these institutions from the total recalibration and assimilation they sought to produce.[40] In all their works, residents creatively adapted their responses to forced assimilation and chose to cooperate, resist, or combine strategies of both. Like these other institutions, the Cherokee institutions examined in this book aimed to reorient Cherokee people as well. However, because they operated at the will of Cherokee people and within the boundaries of the Cherokee Nation, they adhered to a system that avoided "instruction through domination" and stood in contrast to what earlier missionaries had offered and what late nineteenth-century reformers proposed.[41]

As U.S. officials debated how to integrate people who were not citizens prior to the Civil War, including Indians and freedmen, the Cherokee Nation reiterated its own statement on this issue. Cherokee people did have the full rights of citizenship—Cherokee Nation citizenship. This granted them access to a range of Cherokee social services that were in place well before their U.S.-run counterparts. The Cherokee Nation's Public Education Act in 1841 predated the development of the Indian School Service by forty-one years. In 1875, the same year Richard Henry Pratt began his educational experiment with Kiowa prisoners, the Cherokee Nation opened its national prison. Thirty-one years before General Samuel Armstrong enrolled Indian students at Hampton Institute in Virginia, the Cherokee Nation established its male and female seminaries. Five years before Hampton accepted Indians, in 1872 the Cherokee Nation opened its orphanage, which provided a home and school for Cherokee children within the boundaries of the Cherokee Nation. Three decades before the Office of Indian Affairs extended employment opportunities to nurses and doctors in the first decade of the 1900s, the Cherokee Nation established its medical association. Twenty-seven years before the Canton Asylum for Insane Indians began accepting patients, the Cherokee Nation provided institutional care to Cherokee people struggling with mental health issues. By the 1880s, when the U.S. Indian Service launched many of its services and incorporated the labor and skills of Indian people, the Cherokee Nation had already provided a blueprint to the federal government for the delivery of these services.[42]

By the time of removal, the Cherokee Nation had already been subjected to thirty years of federally supported agents, institutions, and state systems aimed at reforming Cherokee behavior, remaking their families, and extracting Cherokee people's economic and social resources. A small percentage of Cherokee leaders shared the beliefs held by federal officials, missionaries, and U.S. social reformers that institutions could be used to control social deviance during moments of social upheaval and potentially could bring about change in society.[43] In fact, many of the Cherokee nation's emerging leaders were beneficiaries of educational institutions, yet those same leaders rejected the embrace of education as a signal that they were willing to cede land. For the vast majority of Cherokees, the presence of social services administered by the Cherokee Nation provided a political and social barrier that prevented Cherokee people from being labeled deviants by non-Indians and defended osdv iyunvnehi. Many understood their function to include a defense of two intertwined social welfare structures, osdv iyunvnehi animated by kinship and a national social service system governed by ideas of citizenship. Both systems required the continuation of communal landholdings to operate successfully and both adopted a community-centered ethos.

The Cherokee Nation's social service institutions, like its U.S. counterparts, promoted particular behaviors and ways of thinking, but most Cherokees defined deviance and (dis)ability differently than was the case in the United States. As a result, Cherokee institutions chose to address care, rehabilitation, and education in ways that reflected U.S. practices yet often embedded traditional understandings of medicine, illness, child rearing, gender, and kinship into those services. For Cherokees, institutions provided a suitable mechanism to advertise the trappings of "civilized" thinking promoted by politicians, missionaries, and agents, while maintaining the ability to design and debate institutional purposes and structures palatable to Cherokee people.[44]

Methods and Sources

In order to grapple with the community as well as national and international dimensions of social services, my work employs ethnohistory as its methodology. Rose Stremlau, author of *Sustaining the Cherokee Family*, eloquently defined and described the purpose of ethnohistory as "a disciplinary hybrid, a fusion of historical and anthropological approaches enabling scholars to study American Indian history despite gaps in the documentary record and misrepresentations of indigenous people."[45] Like David Chang, I listened to "multiple tribal voices" to understand how institutions and social services shaped and were shaped by a variety of Cherokee people all committed to defending Cherokee sovereignty.[46]

As a nineteenth-century Cherokee historian, I am fortunate to have a plethora of materials produced by Cherokee people, and I rely heavily on those documents. The *Cherokee Advocate*, the national paper, printed articles related to social welfare policy, published annual reports, and talked back to other papers that reported on crime, poverty, and education in the Nation. Federal pension applications provide tremendous insight into how Cherokee families organized themselves in the aftermath of war. Beginning in the 1850s, the Cherokee Nation periodically printed its constitution and laws in English and Cherokee for distribution in and outside the Nation. The federal government also administered and documented payments to those who were removed for their losses in the East as well as pensions for service to the U.S. military. After the Civil War, the Cherokee Nation agreed to conduct a census every ten years, and these documents specifically identify residents receiving institutionally administered social provisions.

I also draw heavily on the documents produced within Indian Territory. Under Walter Adair Duncan, the orphanage acquired a press and produced a paper with students' writings. Some of these publications have survived and provide a small window into the interests and concerns of a few of the children at the orphanage. I owe a debt of gratitude to the empowered dissidents and success stories who made their voices heard. The *Advocate* published many of the prisoners' confessions from the gallows, one of the few venues where the prisoners' voices can be heard, although it is possible that these were sanitized or edited for national purposes. The documents produced are not perfectly representative. In some ways they represent outliers—the star pupils, or the most deviant. The documentary records often obscure the experiences of monolingual Cherokee speakers, women, Cherokee freedmen, or those with (dis)abilities who lacked the ability or the kin to advocate for them. The voices of dissidents and high achievers cannot provide complete insight into the lives of all Cherokees who passed through the facilities, or contracted with the institutions for services, those "who wasted away" at the asylum, or the family members of those who watched their kin hang on the gallows. Regardless, they represent a large swathe of Cherokee people overlooked by scholars who have emphasized a bifurcation between market-driven "mixed-blood" political elites regarded as indistinguishable from whites and the subsistence-based monolingual Cherokee "full-bloods." The individuals in the pages of this book refuse to conform to the dualisms scholars have long offered to explain difference.

The available sources tell a compelling story of Cherokee self-determination in the face of repeated challenges to Cherokee people's abilities to fulfill their obligations to one another. Faced with removal and civil war, rather than turn its social services over to non-Indians, the Cherokee Nation asserted its right to build institutions within the Nation, administered by Cherokee people, both as an affirmation of its national sovereignty and as a community imperative.

Because these were Cherokee national institutions as opposed to institutions or services administered by the United States or its secular or religious agents, Cherokee people expected leaders, institutional and national, to abide by communitarian ethics when providing services. When necessary, Cherokee people debated the merits, economic viability, and legitimacy of their national institutions. The institutions they created also brought disparate groups within the Nation together in new ways; for instance, through them, monolingual Cherokee and bilingual speakers whose families more closely adhered to osdv iyunvnehi interacted with their bilingual and monolingual English-speaking counterparts more committed and beholden to national institutions.

Like Walter Adair Duncan, other Cherokee social reformers affiliated with social service institutions articulated a cogent defense of Cherokee nationhood grounded in treaties, a Cherokee-centered definition of the responsibility of a guardian to a ward, and a communitarian ethic that stood in contrast to the individual greed and moral and racial superiority espoused by speculators, railroad interests, and "Friends of the Indian." Federal officials and reformers failed to grasp—though Duncan said it repeatedly—that the federal government could not adequately care for individual Indians; rather, tribal communities and nations possessed this inherent right and critical task. It was the federal government's job as a guardian to perform its legal and economic obligations as defined by treaties. But it was up to tribal governments and Indian people to wrestle with how best to use their resources to care for the impoverished, orphans, and the (dis)abled as well as to manage the punishment of criminals. When William Penn Adair, a Confederate Cherokee and ardent Cherokee nationalist, described Cherokee social services as "ten times better" than those of Arkansas at the 1878 Indian Agricultural Fair meeting, he reflected a belief shared by several of his predecessors: Cherokee people were capable of the innovation necessary to improve their lives and build their self-chosen institutions.[47] Cherokee social services were "ten times better," not because the systems were perfect, but because, as I argue, Cherokee people devised, built, supported, and contested them.

CHAPTER 1

Taking Care of Our Own, 1800–1829

In February of 1806, when a smallpox outbreak struck the Chicka-mauga towns around present-day Chattanooga, Tennessee, Cherokees Pathkiller, John Lowery, and intermarried white trader Daniel Ross asked U.S. agent to the Cherokees Return J. Meigs to "procure some of the cowpox" and obtain the services of a local doctor to administer the inoculations.[1] When Dr. McNeil of Maryville, Tennessee, arrived in the Cherokee Nation, however, he put forward a less-than-favor-able assessment of the cowpox vaccination, which was relatively new. Instead, he offered to provide smallpox variolation, an older tech-nique, which involved lancing the pustules of a smallpox-inflicted patient and then placing the infected material in the arm of a healthy person. The community rejected the treatment and sent McNeil away.

As the fledgling United States extended its civilization policy and dangled the possibility of "citizenship" just out of reach of Indian people, Cherokees chose to debate social and public health policy internally as community rules dictated. These debates occurred as U.S. officials and citizens grappled with the Enlightenment beliefs shared by many of the founding fathers suggesting that Indians could be equal in all things. Cherokees further had to contend with growing romantic nationalism that espoused a racial and intellectual superiority of Euro-Americans relative to all people of color. The latter movement denied the intellectual equality of Cherokees and African Americans. The former placed a series of moral, intellectual, gender, and religious roadblocks on the road to citizenship. U.S. rep-resentatives, particularly those most covetous of Indian-controlled resources in the South, backed away from the civilization policy, which at least in principle conceived of the possibility of Indian equality in the United States, and moved toward removal policy, or what today would be termed "ethnic cleansing."

This chapter explores a moment when federal policy held out the future possibility of Cherokee peoples' full inclusion in the United States. However, everyday U.S. settlers and state governments made clear what the prevailing attitudes and interactions that governed Indian-white relations would entail. Professionals like Dr. McNeil would flaunt their perceived cultural, racial, and intellectual superiority over Cherokee people and engage in price gouging to provide the social provisions that community ethics required Cherokee people provide for one another. Most Cherokee people never seriously considered second-class citizenship in the United States; instead, they debated and adjusted their social policy to determine how best to care for one another in an altered international landscape.

The community's rationale for rejecting treatment, outlined in several follow-up letters to the agent, provides insight into the debates waged within the community during this transitional period in federal policy. In a subsequent letter, Cherokee local chiefs The Glass, Dick Justice, and John Bogs, writing through interpreter Charles Hicks, who would later serve as second chief, asked the agent to pay the doctor's $150 fee and "charge it to the nation." The letter stated that the chiefs "had not expected to see the doct[o]r here, as [they] had never sent for one." As the letter makes clear, neither Pathkiller, nor Lowery, nor Ross shared their request, nor did they seek the consent of the other local chiefs before making a unilateral decision to secure medical services. The Glass, Justice, and Bogs described Cherokee people's resistance to the services offered by Dr. McNeil not as arising from suspicion of new treatment but "owing to the impossibility of the patients attending to the doctor's directions."[2]

In a follow-up letter, Daniel Ross offered additional reasons that led the community to decline McNeil's services. Ross voiced his personal disagreement with Dr. McNeil's views on cowpox vaccination, a technique that Edward Jenner had developed in Britain and that Harvard professor Benjamin Waterhouse and Thomas Jefferson had endorsed.[3] The inoculation required an incision to be made in the arm and infected material from cowpox placed in the incision and covered. Jenner's "Instructions for Vaccine Inoculation," published in England in 1801 and in Philadelphia in 1807, described an eighteen-day process that required keeping the vaccination site open to the air, yet clean.[4] Both Waterhouse and Jenner promoted a vaccination process burdensome to those who worked and spent a significant amount of time outdoors, as Cherokee people did. If Dr. McNeil had outlined a similar treatment, Cherokee people might have rejected it for quite pragmatic reasons.

Ross asked the agent to locate and acquire the cowpox vaccine as Pathkiller had originally requested.[5] Even as Ross offered legitimate reasons for the community to refuse vaccination, he distanced himself from the community's decision. By doing this, he suggested that people who failed to accept the services of doctors or abide by their instructions (even if the instructions were at odds with the reality of one's condition) were irrational.

Ross also cited the unreasonable $150 charge for services. The demand of set fees by professional doctors for medical services provided was a relatively new concept, even for U.S. citizens. For Cherokee people, charging fees for services stood in direct opposition to the practices of local *adonisgi*, local healers who diagnosed and treated individual physical and spiritual conditions and carried out community ceremonies. They expected no compensation for fulfilling a community obligation, though Cherokee people offered generous gifts ranging from agricultural products, baskets, jewelry, pigs, or horses in gratitude for their aid. This monetary expense for McNeil's medical services compounded the view that treatment was more costly than bypassing vaccination.

If one considers Ross's and the local chiefs' letters in their entirety, the community offered a rational and diverse critique of the public health services secured by the agent and offered by Dr. McNiel. The local chiefs rejected the treatment based on the paternalism exercised by Ross, Lowery, and Pathkiller, who sought services without informing the community. The community "had never sent for [a doctor]."[6] The three men made a public health decision without the rest of the community's consultation and consent. As even Ross acknowledged, the doctor charged unreasonable fees. Finally, Dr. McNeil was not providing the services Pathkiller had specifically requested, and "some of the chiefs did not appear willing to introduce the usual mode of [i]noculation," the usual mode being smallpox vaccination.[7]

In light of hardening racial attitudes in the South, U.S. politicians advertised removal as a more humane and economical answer to the violence and border skirmishes that already raged between tribes and settlers. This shift in policy and the events it triggered led Cherokee people to debate strategies to defend their continued ability to fulfill their social service obligations to one another; it is these events and the corresponding debates and Cherokee policies enacted that this chapter will focus on. The decision to variolate or vaccinate paled in comparison to the social welfare emergencies potentially created by the loss of Cherokee homelands.

Nevertheless, public health concerns and the louder removal debates that would physically and politically divide the Nation derived from the same central question facing Cherokee people. Who has the responsibility, the rights, and the ability to assume care for others? Within a traditional social service system, the community's spiritual, economic, and social health and well-being trumped an individual's personal autonomy. Community decisions came about through consensus building, not the acts of a small, consolidated group of men assuming the right to speak for all. As Daniel Ross explained to Agent Meigs, he did not think it "proper" to introduce variolation "without [the local chiefs'] approbation."[8]

From 1800 to 1829, Cherokee people moved from a nation made up of autonomous towns governed by the rules of kinship and connected together through seven matrilineal clans to a constitutional republic comprised of citizens operating under a constitution that administered pensions from a national treasury. The decisions that led to institutionalized centralization occurred in tandem with the shift in U.S. policy. This chapter traces the social protections and provisions that federal officials, state governments, and the centralized Cherokee nation presented to Cherokee people during this period and the choices different groups of Cherokees made in response. As demonstrated by numerous scholars, class differences, racial demarcations, and political schisms informed the decisions that groups pursued. However, different means did not imply different ends. As

Cherokee society and families underwent uneven changes, all Cherokee people remained committed to fulfilling their social obligations
to their families and kin. However, the changes taking place meant
that not all Cherokees had the same social protections and provisions available to them within or outside the Nation; this led families to choose options that sometimes undercut the social provisions
and protections available to other Cherokee people.

As the vaccination/variolation debate illustrates, Cherokee people
showed an openness to new medical concepts, but remained reluctant to abandon their own medical practices completely. Even though
John Lowery, Pathkiller, and Daniel Ross clearly embraced the services of medical doctors, the majority of Cherokees continued to seek
the services of local adonisgi for treatment. Adonisgi approached
illness and its treatment holistically. Physical and psychological illnesses were not mutually exclusive and one could manifest itself as
the other. Regardless of how symptoms manifested, adonisgi sought
to restore balance, and as a result community ceremonies and medical treatments included similar components. Both included medicinal
remedies and purification rituals. Adonisgi identified young people
who proved particularly adept at skills and ceremonies necessary
for apprenticeships. Healers emanated from the community and
proved their competence over long periods of time.[9] Their position
differed greatly from that of outsiders like Dr. McNeil, who had little
medical authority among community members when he arrived to
administer the smallpox vaccination in 1806.

For Cherokee people, using the kinepox (cowpox) vaccination, a
treatment derived from an illness caused by animals, probably made
far more cosmological sense than treating a disease with the disease.
Cherokee cosmology readily accepted a world where animals could
aid or hinder the lives of humans.[10]

Within the community, missionaries introduced Euro-American
medicine to Cherokee people and offered alternative ideas about
psychic and physical illness and treatment. Cherokee people continued to apply traditional remedies while seeking additional sources
of healing power. In 1810, for example, the paternal uncle of Tlaneneh,
a student at the Moravian Springplace Mission, asked the missionaries for medicine for Tlaneneh's father Suakee. Despite their reluctance

to provide medicine when they were unable to examine the patient "because he seemed already to be in the hands of an Indian doctor," the missionaries decided that they "could not refuse since he was our friend." Three days later, the missionaries reported that Suakee was on his way to recovery.[11] In 1814, Dawzizi, another pupil at the Springplace Mission, returned to school after an absence due to illness. Dawzizi reported to his teachers that "an old Indian doctor had scratched his whole body [with a saw-shaped lower jaw of a fish] and rubbed it with the juice of certain herbs. . . . The doctor extracted a little horn of blood from his forehead and back of his head, which provided him with the desired proof against headaches."[12] The process described bore remarkable resemblance to the preparation for traditional ball play, which the missionaries discouraged. It is possible that Dawzizi misrepresented his absence, but it is equally possible that he described receiving "medicine" before the ritual cycle of ball play and the missionaries misunderstood his meaning. It is also possible that a healer used scratching as a means to administer medicine directly to Dawzizi's blood and the horn of blood was an attempt to draw out impurities causing his affliction.[13]

Most missionaries had little formal training as physicians, but their position required them to fill many roles. Perhaps the first recognized Euro-American physician to live in the Cherokee Nation was Congregationalist missionary Elizur Butler, who had studied medicine, anatomy, diseases, and surgery under another physician, not unlike the training of Cherokee medicine men. He arrived in the Nation in 1820.[14] Unlike Dr. McNeil, missionaries lived in the community, were willing to defer to the care of traditional healers, based their actions on a community ethic, and provided ceremonies, albeit in the form of Christian prayers, with medicinal herbs. During the first three decades of the nineteenth century, between the medical services offered by missionaries and the continued access to traditional healers, most Cherokee people neither desired nor required national officials to institute services for individual and family health matters.

Just as community members integrated some aspects of Euro-American medicine and rejected others, three prominent Cherokee leaders—John Ross, Sequoyah, and The Ridge—identified with and ˙˙˙ˑᵈ the elements of the civilization policy that proved useful for them even as they discarded others. Ross, Ridge, and Sequoyah all rose to prominence because they embodied a mix of traditional Cherokee values and "civilized" skills and abilities. All three lived in close proximity to the U.S. Indian agent and benefitted from institutional services provided by the agency. All three came of age in an era of nation building and anomie, and over time they came to represent the growing class divides evident in the Nation. Also, they each benefitted from the increasing influence and official political authority that men were acquiring within and outside the Nation.

John Ross, future principal chief of the Cherokee Nation, was born a member of the Bird clan in 1790 near Turkey Town on the Coosa River, near present-day Center, Alabama. His mother was Mollie McDonald, a Cherokee and the daughter of Anne Shorey and the granddaughter of Ghigooie. His father was the white trader Daniel Ross, a Scottish immigrant who was "left an orphan" in Baltimore, Maryland.[15] While working as a trader, Daniel Ross met McDonald, whose father was also a trader among the Cherokees.[16] John Ross received an English education that surpassed that of most U.S. citizens of his day. His father employed private tutors for him, and later he attended an academy in Tennessee. He owned stores and operated ferry crossings, including Ross's Landing, in present-day Chattanooga.[17] With the profits from these businesses, Ross established a plantation in 1827, near what is today Rome, Georgia. The plantation was made possible by the labor of enslaved people, an endeavor viewed by other elite southern whites as the most civilized and profitable pursuit for men.[18]

Sequoyah and The Ridge never spoke English and had very different educational experiences from Ross's. Sequoyah's childhood combined many elements of traditional matrilineal Cherokee life with features that accompanied living in close proximity to Euro-Americans. A member of the Red Paint clan, he was born in approximately 1767 and was raised by his Cherokee mother, Wuh teh. He grew up in the Tuskegee community of the Overhill Towns along the banks of the Little Tennessee River, near what is today Vonore, Tennessee. His father's identity is debatable and within a traditional matrilineal Cherokee worldview not relevant in determining kin ties. His mother operated a trading post and had a small farm. Like many Cherokee women, she stepped forward as the rightful vendor of the products of her agricultural labor and the rightful caregiver and guardian to her child. Sequoyah aided his mother on her farm. As he grew older, he developed skills as a silversmith and a blacksmith, two skills encouraged by the civilization policy, and he married and became a father.[19]

Rather than invest in English-language pursuits, Sequoyah devised a system of writing for the Cherokee language brought into use during the second decade of the nineteenth century. He believed that innovation could come from within the Nation. Additionally, a written language afforded the Cherokees advantages that they otherwise lacked.

Sequoyah sequestered himself away for close to a year to devise the syllabary at the expense of his familial and community obligations. Rumors spread that he was possibly engaged in witchcraft.[20] Frustrated with Sequoyah's failure to fulfill family and community obligations, his wife threw early drafts of his invention into a fire.[21] Many people were aware of Sequoyah's efforts and likely discounted the possibility that he was engaged in witchcraft, but the rumors and his wife's frustration both originated because he isolated himself from his community and failed to fulfill his obligations.

Ultimately, his daughter—his first student—gave public demonstrations of the syllabary, and, beginning in 1821, it would offer many Cherokee people who were ambivalent toward the Christianity embedded in missionaries' educational offerings access to literacy.[22] Nonetheless, Sequoyah's experience provides one example of the suspicions cast on individuals as people negotiated the changes wrought by the civilization policy.

Unlike Sequoyah, The Ridge—earlier called Nung noh hut tar hee and later known as Major Ridge—worked to obtain English education for all of his children, both boys and girls. The Ridge enrolled his son John and his daughter Nancy in the Moravian Springplace Mission in 1810. He also encouraged his nephew's education at the mission. In 1821, John commended his parents' efforts and commitments to education in a letter to President James Monroe.[23]

Though he would later support a policy of peace and the economic pursuits encouraged by the civilization policy, in his early life The

Ridge followed a very different path. He was born near the Hiawassee River in what is present day Polk County, Tennessee, in about 1771. When he was a small child, his village was laid to waste, forcing his family to relocate to Walden Ridge in the Sequatchie Valley, which stretches along the Cumberland Plateau.[24] The Ridge was a member of his mother's and his grandmother's Deer clan.[25]

Throughout the 1780s and into the early 1790s, The Ridge participated in raids and skirmishes with the renegade Chickamauga band, led by Dragging Canoe, even after the majority of local Cherokee chiefs concluded peace treaties with the United States. It was during one of his absences with the Chickamauga band that both of his parents died. Although his maternal aunts likely provided daily care and sustenance for his younger siblings, if he and his siblings lacked maternal uncles, clan law obligated him to hunt for and protect them. In order for him to continue participating in skirmishes that kept him away for weeks at a time, kin and community were essential support systems for his siblings.

Chickamauga actions forced The Ridge to wrestle with the need to balance individual actions with the good of the larger community. In 1793, The Ridge and other Cherokee warriors killed two white men. In response, the Tennessee militia attacked Pine Log, a Cherokee town in present-day Georgia committed to peace. Rather than blame the militia, the town placed blame upon the actions of The Ridge's party and shunned the warriors. The families of the deceased demanded the lives of the Cherokee warriors to fulfill blood vengeance. Supported by one conjuror in Pine Log, The Ridge's party offered to seek vengeance against the militia. What followed was the attack on an extended Tennessee family of mostly women and children who occupied a small outpost. It was likely during this period that The Ridge recognized that if he hoped to elevate himself in Cherokee society, he could not pursue war indefinitely. The Pine Log community reminded The Ridge that he was answerable to the grievances of kin and communities and that a warrior's life was unsustainable and inappropriate in a world that sought to be in balance. The Pine Log community objected to the actions of the warriors because they undermined the ability of community members to fulfill their obligations to protect and care for each other. After a Chickamauga defeat at Etowah in what is now Georgia in 1793, The Ridge chose to relinquish his role as a warrior.[26] Over the course of their lives—as I will show in subsequent chapters—Ross, Sequoyah, and The Ridge would represent different approaches to the institutions that impacted how Cherokee social policy moved forward and faced alteration in the years ahead. The three men would come to sometimes similar and sometimes profoundly different answers to these challenges, but all three shared a continuing struggle with their obligations of care to their families and to Cherokee people. These debates would impact the generation that followed.

An 1807 execution marks an important turning point in the administration of social services within the Cherokee Nation, as it was the first time the Nation took on what were formerly clan responsibilities. The executed man, Doublehead, had been The Ridge's former fellow warrior and chief of the Lower Towns, and he became speaker for the Nation in 1796. In the postrevolutionary era, leaders young and old debated the merits of additional land cessions and their impact on all Cherokee people. After Doublehead enriched himself through 1798 treaty negotiations, Cherokee people questioned his worthiness as a leader. Cherokees The Ridge, James Vann, and Charles Hicks understood the designs of the United States on Cherokee lands and the danger that Doublehead's actions could have on communal landholdings. It is likely that all three men also worried about their own financial interests if individual Cherokees could dispose of land. Less clear is how Cherokees who were not leading men viewed Doublehead's actions.

In 1807, a group of Cherokee men, including The Ridge, executed Doublehead. Cherokee officials ordered the execution as a result of another land cession by Doublehead that included lands north of the Tennessee River, including the last of the hunting grounds located along the Cumberland Plateau and into Kentucky and stretching southwest to Muscle Shoals. Leaders deemed Doublehead's actions "contrary to the commonwealth of the people" and for "his own private advantage."[27] Protecting the communal land base became a national social policy priority. The imposition of a national death penalty on an individual who sold communal lands easily fit into Cherokee legal theory because Cherokees understood that individual actions could devastate the larger community's social and spiritual well-being. It was the community message clearly conveyed to The Ridge when he entered Pine Log in 1793. In these situations, it became imperative that penalties restored order and balance. Cherokee officials defended the execution to U.S. officials based on the fact that Doublehead's execution fell under new legal provisions that forbade local chiefs from making land cessions. However, those same leaders likely realized that national agents might face repercussions from adherents of clan law. Therefore, the agents who carried out the execution justified their actions to the community because it also fulfilled ancient clan obligations.

The execution party literally and symbolically merged the traditional functions of law with newer national laws. Doublehead, whose wife was the sister and clan kin of James Vann's wife, had earlier beaten his wife to death while she was pregnant. In response, Vann's wife, fully within her matrilineal rights, called for the death of Doublehead and joined the party to carry out the execution. Internally, although she did not perform the execution, Vann's wife's presence likely dispelled the opposition of adherents of traditional clan law to a centralized body's action. Externally, The Ridge's action as a national agent affirmed the execution's legitimacy to non-Indian settlers and politicians who viewed revenge killings as backward and savage. The execution met both Euro-Americans' criteria for civilized state-sanctioned killings and fulfilled clan law's requirement that wrongdoers restore balance to the world for the sake of the larger community. Whether it was pragmatic, cynical, or shrewd political decision making, officials successfully carried out a sovereign national execution that met the traditional social welfare expectations of the vast majority of Cherokee people.

The execution of Doublehead exposes the gendered differences between the trajectories and rationales for the United States and Cherokee people in regard to national social policy. All Cherokee people needed land, albeit for different reasons. Women who continued to engage in farming and gathering needed access to land, as did men who were cultivating farms, but as U.S. officials acknowledged and hoped for, farming took far less land than hunting. The land cessions that led to significant upheaval were those that resulted in the loss of hunting grounds.[28] Unlike the Euro-American system, which articulated an imagined equal economic independence for propertied men, Cherokees recognized the equal vulnerability of all people and responded in this case to the need of its men, particularly its young men, who without access to vast hunting grounds lacked access to economic resources and the ability to fulfill their gender-specific social welfare responsibilities.

Euro-American authorities wed to systems privileging men's economic independence spent sizeable amounts of colonial and state budgets on poorhouses and poor relief, but aimed the bulk of that benevolent relief at economically and legally vulnerable widows and orphans. The same system that simultaneously limited the legal and political rights of women, children, and the aged and then judged them for their economic helplessness resisted acknowledging the economic and social vulnerability of able-bodied men. In response to the loss of hunting lands, Cherokee officials focused on the economic, legal, and social vulnerability of men. Certainly, land cessions threatened the economic interests of a small but growing Cherokee elite, but a contracted land base threatened young traditional Cherokee men with social and economic displacement far more than it did Cherokee women.

Doublehead's execution served as a basis for the Nation's usurpation of kinship responsibilities both as a protection of the larger community and as an instrument to fulfill specific clan functions.[29] In the aftermath of Doublehead's execution, his family failed to seek clan vengeance and national authorities moved forward with a more aggressive agenda. There are several plausible explanations for Doublehead's clan's decision. Clan vengeance was unnecessary if members believed Doublehead violated clan law by killing his wife or if they recognized the corporate harm land cessions presented. However, the first written Cherokee law, passed in 1808, also introduced a national barrier to Doublehead's family's exercise of clan vengeance. The law barred the use of clan vengeance when national agents carried out a killing. The law also authorized use of a light horse brigade, an early version of a police force with limited scope, paid out of a national annuity to police and adjudicate property crimes. This began the shift

Doublehead → Execution set up shrugging clan responsibility

from restorative balance to punishment and from clan to national authority.[30] Doublehead's execution, coupled with the 1808 law, provided the centralizing Cherokee government with a clear precedent to assume clan and familial responsibilities if officials deemed that it served the best interests of the entire nation.[31]

That same 1808 law passed by the national council also redefined responsibilities to children under newer minority family structures, those reflected in many mixed-descent families. The law gave men the right to pass property to their children and to their widows in the event of their deaths.[32] The law expanded definitions of children's kin to include fathers who, under traditional rules of kinship, were not the clan kin of their children and had no long-term obligation to provide support or security for them; that had been the responsibility of their mothers' brothers, who were their clan relations. The changes to the law suggest that the wives of a particular subset of Cherokee men no longer asserted their matrilineal and matrilocal authority or that some Cherokee men were engaging in subterfuge to undermine the traditional legal and social influence of their Cherokee wives. As in John Ross's situation, this privileged men who descended from Cherokee mothers and intermarried white fathers. They stood the most to gain from a law of this nature.

Additionally, the law provided a new legal justification for Cherokee family members to shirk their responsibilities to kin, but not a justification from the perspective of traditional rules of kinship. Perhaps this older responsibility to matrilineal kin led John Ross to mentor and support his sister Eliza's son William P. Ross, who was born in 1820.[33] The law also suggested that Cherokee children whose biological mothers were dead were orphans. Within traditional Cherokee families, as long as a child had any living female clan relatives, he or she was not an orphan. If children without biological parents were "orphans" and dependent on patrilineal lines for financial support and care, men like The Ridge, as the oldest surviving brother of his siblings, would not have been able to continue war activities that lasted weeks to months at a time after his parents died. This law failed to acknowledge the roles and responsibilities of Cherokee kin embedded in traditional social welfare systems. From a legal standpoint, it suggested a preoccupation of mixed-descent families with an economic and social vulnerability that likely did not exist in most Cherokee families.

Missionaries encouraged the reconfiguring of Cherokee families after they first entered the Cherokee Nation in the 1760s. Their efforts gained a foothold only after 1800 as a result of some Cherokees' desire for educational opportunities and the simultaneous implementation of the U.S. civilization policy. In keeping with federal policy, missionaries endorsed nuclear, male-headed families that pushed men to become the primary financial providers for their children and ignored the economic contributions of women who supported their efforts.[34] The family structure endorsed by Christian missionaries also limited the number of adults responsible for children and made "orphans" more likely. By the time of removal, Moravians, Baptists, Methodists, and the American Board of Commissioners for Foreign Missions supported missions in the Cherokee Nation.[35] All except the Methodists operated residential schools. The 1808 law suggested that "orphans" needed economic protections, and yet the records of missionaries indicate the opposite. Kin continued to provide for children as traditional social welfare systems dictated. In fact, the children who did attend the mission schools tended to be those of well-to-do and politically prominent Cherokees rather than impoverished orphans. The children of Chiefs Charles Hicks and John Ross and the children of The Ridge, for example, attended mission schools for the advantages an English-language education conveyed rather than out of material necessity. Matrilineal authority over their children's activities sometimes undercut missionaries' and Cherokee men's attempts to secure educational services for their children. On numerous occasions, mothers arrived at the mission schools to lay claim to children brought by other family members, often "half-breed [fathers] of some education" who ignored the matrilineal authority of mothers.[36]

Few families needed to surrender children, but if they did, they reluctantly turned them over to missionaries. In 1818, for instance, a "poor Cherokee woman" took her eight-year-old daughter to the Presbyterian's Brainerd Mission in Tennessee to acquire the food, clothing, and education that the school offered. Despite assurances from the mother that she would not remove the child from the mission, eight days later she returned and did exactly that.[37] Missions, therefore, might serve as an occasional safety net for children, but they were not orphanages. Women's continued access to land for subsistence-level farms, the continued protection of women's property rights, and the continuation of extended networks of matrilineal kin to care for, educate, and protect Cherokee children left little need in the pre-removal period for children's services.

Traditional Cherokee men faced a more precarious situation as they attempted to fulfill their responsibilities within a traditional social service system. U.S. officials and a growing number of Cherokee authorities expected Cherokee men to economically provide for nuclear families and cared little about the men's traditional kinship obligations they were also expected to fulfill. Cherokee women, meanwhile, could maximize social service options, including traditional kin networks and the services offered by agents and missionaries who viewed women as vulnerable and in need of care.

With hunting grounds depleted, Cherokee men lost access to the products of their labor and sought out appropriate men's activities to continue fulfilling their community and kinship obligations. By the early 1800s, some men, including The Ridge and John Ross, turned to plantation slavery. Other men resembled yeoman farmers. The labor provided by enslaved people and men's agricultural endeavors undermined some women's spiritual and economic authority.[38]

When Agent Meigs faced a shortage of blacksmiths in the Nation, it did not occur to him that Cherokee men were in a position to perform the duties. Rather than use the blacksmiths to offer apprenticeships to Cherokee people, the agency controlled the services of blacksmiths. When the blacksmiths' services failed to meet the demands, the agent and Cherokee leaders offered other non-Cherokee blacksmiths work permits and land use for cultivation in exchange for services. In 1816, Meigs reported the presence of fifteen blacksmiths, "5 of which are Cherokees, self taught." Only after Cherokees taught themselves the skills did it occur to the agent to use a tinplate worker in a teaching capacity. By earning a living as a self-taught blacksmith, Sequoyah decreased his local communities' dependence on the labor of and exploitation by non-Cherokees.[39]

The loss of hunting grounds that occurred in treaties that followed the American Revolution and ended with Doublehead's 1806 deal led men to turn to a burgeoning market in stolen horses. Because the changing system did not provide avenues for all men to immediately access the economic promises of civilization policy, some men engaged in horse theft. Horse theft enabled them to reclaim the lost wealth of their families and communities due to theft carried out by illegal settlers and the horse syndicates operating on boundaries of Indian and white communities. For others, horse theft connected Cherokee men to another lucrative, albeit illegal, market economy. For still others, it was a means of expressing their discontent with the changes thrust upon them by U.S. policy and their anger toward illegal encroachment.[40] Cherokee men struggled to find a place in a system that expected them to disrespect the rights and privileges of their grandmothers, mothers, and sisters. Horse theft provided them with a means to avoid the domestic economic violence that was necessary to that process. If men took up farming as the civilization policy dictated, they usurped their mothers' and sisters' rightful economic and symbolic place in Cherokee society, thereby undermining their ability to fulfill social service obligations.

Within Euro-American and Cherokee worldviews, participation in war offered Cherokee men a socially acceptable masculine activity in order to fulfill their obligations to their kin, communities, and their increasingly centralized nation. During the War of 1812, most Cherokees chose to side with the young United States. The reasons for this alliance were many, most of which supported traditional social safety nets and kinship obligations and attempted to circumvent Euro-American warfare's likelihood to create impoverished conditions for tribal communities. Cherokee people feared the potential depredations of volunteer militia and federal troops as they marched through Cherokee lands, potentially destroying crops, stealing food, depleting herds, and assaulting Cherokee women. In theory, a Cherokee alliance with the United States during the War of 1812 acknowledged and protected Cherokee communal landholdings and boundaries. Even though over six hundred Cherokee soldiers in the War of 1812 aided General Andrew Jackson in the Red Stick Revolt, a Creek civil war, he demanded land cessions from Cherokee and

Chickasaw allies.[41] In reality, an alliance did nothing to prevent any of these abuses, but it did provide soldiers and Cherokee leaders a legal recourse. In 1814, six weeks after the Battle of Horseshoe Bend, Agent Meigs wrote to Washington, D.C., and sought funds for depredations committed by Tennessee militia and deserting soldiers traversing Cherokee lands.[42]

Cherokee society and the United States rewarded men's participation in war, and both served to support national and traditional social welfare systems. Like their U.S. counterparts serving in the War of 1812, Cherokee men were in a position to contribute to their families through the bounties and pay they received. In 1816, capitalizing on U.S. regard for military personnel, Cherokee chief Pathkiller sent six Cherokee delegates and war veterans to Washington, D.C., to seek pensions on behalf of invalid warriors and deceased soldiers' families and to advocate for spoliation claims.[43]

As part of the negotiations that cost the Cherokees more land, Cherokee leaders capitalized on the expanding "socioeconomic reach" of federal pensions, and the Cherokee nation set a precedent of using treaty negotiations to advocate for federal entitlements to aid Cherokee people.[44] Pensions of U.S. soldiers in the War of 1812 had been subject to legislation that governed Revolutionary War pensions. Initially, only (dis)abled officers or their widows received pensions. Through a series of acts between 1789 and 1806, the federal government expanded access to (dis)ability and widows' pensions to include rank-and-file soldiers and the state militia. In 1816, Congress raised the pension rates for invalid soldiers from five dollars to eight dollars for privates. The legislation also extended half pay to widows and orphans of deceased soldiers for five years.[45] In order to qualify for pensions, soldiers applied to the federal pension office. Due to the sheer number of claims, the absence of a federal bureaucracy to evaluate claims, and the lack of documentary records for many soldiers, the federal government required district courts to evaluate claimants' applications, their affidavits, and their perceived needs.[46]

As Cherokee leaders unsuccessfully staved off additional land cessions, they used the process to capitalize on access to federal entitlements for Cherokee people. As a result of the Cherokee Nation's 1816 delegation to Washington, D.C., President Madison authorized the federal agent for the Cherokees, Return J. Meigs, who was housed at the Tennessee Indian Agency in what is present-day Kingston, Tennessee, to establish a board to evaluate claims for pensions of indigent Cherokees. The participation of Cherokees in the War of 1812 resulted in thirty-six deaths; fifty-one more were wounded. Eighteen of the deaths occurred at the Battle of Horseshoe Bend. For most Cherokees who sought pensions, Meigs became the arbiter of their claims. How Meigs and the board determined pension allocations is unclear. Meigs periodically distributed blankets, merchandise, and occasionally cash payments to Cherokees in need. These early distribution records do not record whether the recipients solicited the items they received or whether the agent unilaterally made distribution decisions. Meigs provided multiple distributions to widows and "guardians" of minor children. For instance, he distributed money to the guardian of Killer's child and cloth and a blanket to the widow of Woman Holder.[47] In 1815, Meigs gave the widow Chenowee ten dollars' worth of merchandise due to the loss of her husband at Horseshoe Bend.[48] Meigs's distributions appear arbitrary, despite the fact that pensions at the federal level were fairly uniform.

Pension laws conformed to the federal government's gendered ideas about family relationships intended to support patriarchal nuclear family configurations, ideas that failed to consider the absence of formal marriage among even U.S. soldiers, and certainly did not represent Cherokee practices and Cherokee economic systems.[49] This did not stop Cherokee leaders or Cherokee people from negotiating access to and, in many cases, advocating for entitlements for family members who fell outside the definition of family dictated by federal pension law. U.S. federal pension distributions threatened to divert resources from a Cherokee soldier's clan to that of his wife's. Children's pensions did the same.

Within a matrilineal society, widows' and orphans' pensions should have been mothers', brothers', sisters', nieces', and nephews' pensions, but since they were not, traditional Cherokee people attempted to adapt pensions to meet their families' needs. For example, Two Killer's wife adopted a boy and girl "to be the descendants of Can naw wes o ske, who fell in battle" and "who left no relatives in his descending line." The children were Tau clan tauh's children, Can naw wes o ske's older brother. Within a traditional matrilineal welfare system and according to Cherokee law operating at the time, women determined who was Cherokee. When Two Killer's wife adopted the children, they became members of her clan and her family. The only way the adoption could make the children members of her clan and that of Can naw wes o ske's clan was if the woman was clan kin to Tau clan tauh and Can naw wes o ske.

This adoption and the request for the pension tried the definitions of family imposed by federal pension law. Meigs had to sort out who was entitled to whose pensions. Two Killer and Can naw wes o ske were both eligible for pensions. Were the children entitled to Two Killer's pension as a result of this legal adoption within Cherokee society, or were they entitled to Can naw wes o ske's pension as a result of this adoption? If the pensions had been distributed based on Cherokee family law, the children were entitled to Can naw wes o ske's pension. If the federal government respected Cherokee matrilineal adoption laws and Cherokee marriages, but applied its pension laws, then they were entitled to Two Killer's pension based on its patrilineal definitions of family. What Cherokee people fully understood is that Two Killer and Can naw wes o ske had family that they were obligated to support, regardless of whether one applied U.S. patrilineal definitions of family or Cherokee matrilineal definitions. Based on their service to the war, someone should receive those resources.[50]

Because federal pension law defied matrilineal welfare systems, when traditional Cherokee people attempted to adapt federal entitlements to meet their needs they may have unknowingly undermined others who adhered to the same system. Another request coming for the full pension of Can naw wes o ske came from his "aged father and mother" based on the fact his wife had "deserted him" and his "child had died." Although the request was made on behalf of both parents, which suggests a possible bilateral or patrilineal family structure, the letter listed the mother singly, and then the author added the word "father" in the margins before the word "mother," suggesting that including the father was an afterthought.[51] Within a matrilineal social welfare system, Can naw wes o ske's mother, as clan kin, had an absolute right to the spoils of war and decision-making authority related to his death. It is unclear whether Two Killer's widow and Can naw wes o ske's mother knew of the other's request for the pension. If they did, it is plausible that they used multiple strategies to gain access to their clan kin's resources. Because the agent never saw fit to record the name of the women involved, it is entirely possible that Two Killer's widow and Can naw wes o ske's mother were the same person.

Cherokee men also stepped forward to object to pension distributions based on their matrilineal understandings of family. In 1819, Deer-in-the-Water objected to Woman Killer's widow, Wattee, receiving his brother's entire pension. Deer-in-the-Water was Woman Killer's clan kin; Wattee was not. Deer-in-the-Water fails to mention if Woman Killer left behind his mother or any nieces and nephews, for whom, in the event of his brother's death, he now had additional responsibilities.[52] Even though pensions introduced an unfamiliar social service system and complicated the economic rights of matrilineal kin, matrilineal kin attempted to claim pensions in order to fulfill their traditional social welfare obligations.

The expectation on the part of U.S. officials for men to act as guardians for widows and orphans provided another mechanism for the federal government to undermine the traditional roles and responsibilities of women and matrilineal kin and exposed a willingness by some Cherokee men to participate in the process. The pension process introduced the concept of legal guardianships to Cherokee society based on the assumption that women and children operated at a diminished political and economic capacity without husbands and fathers. The civilization policy aimed to reorder men's responsibilities to children from their matrilineal kin to their biological children, who were not clan kin.

Pensions created a situation where children became the legal and economic pawns of Cherokee men who favored men's economic dependence and potentially shared no social or familial responsibility for the children. After determining the whole claim submitted by Two Killer's wife "fraudulent," second chief and former interpreter Charles Hicks recommended diverting the orphan pensions appropriated for Can naw wes o ske's children to the orphaned daughter of Katehee of Ellijay and the "boy son of Woy a ga gis kee," whose

"father[s] acknowledged them in their lifetime."[53] In September of
1819, three months after Deer-in-the-Water objected to his brother's
widow's pension, Chief Pathkiller granted a guardianship for Woman
Killer's children to John Miller, a mixed-descent Cherokee who often
served as an interpreter. The records offer no explanation for the
choice of John Miller. This letter contradicted Deer-in-the-Water's
earlier letter that there were no orphan children entitled to the pension.
However, within a matrilineal context, none of the widow Wattee's
children were Woman Killer's responsibility. If Wattee had other
children from a previous relationship, Woman Killer still bore no
long-term responsibility for them. Deer-in-the-Water had stated that
there was one child who had died, so it is possible that Deer-in-the-
Water accepted the bilateral descent of a child between Woman Killer
and Wattee but was not willing to concede that his family had no
claim on some portion of the pension.[54] If pensions were for the
family of the deceased, Deer-in-the-Water was well within his rights
to make a claim.

Whatever the reason for the contradictions in the documents, Deer-
in-the-Water was struggling to assert his rights based on matrilineal
definitions of family that were under attack. He was trying to claim
an entitlement due to families based on an imposed understanding
of family that devalued the specific roles and responsibilities that
maternal brothers and uncles played within a larger kinship system.
In spite of social and legal barriers to pensions for matrilineal families, it was the duty of matrilineal brothers and uncles to step forward and claim the compensation attached to their kin's life. Guardianships, in theory, offered a means by which matrilineal kin could
continue to assert their rights as caregivers and legal and pecuniary
agents for widows and minor children. Guardianship terminology
was foreign to people who, as a result of a community ethic, had
responsibilities to anyone in need but whose everyday responsibilities were to matrilineal kin.

Men who favored patrilineal families, many of whom focused on
amassing private property, exhibited a willingness to use pensions
to reward those with similar family configurations. However, the
disconnect between the rules governing pension applications and
Cherokee family systems led many of these men to serve as community

advocates for traditional social welfare policies. When Allbones died in the War of 1812, he left behind two wives and children from each wife. After the Treaty of 1817, one of his wives removed west to Arkansas with her son, but some of the children from his other wife remained in the East. Instead of advocating for the wife and child who moved to Arkansas, Chief Hicks attempted to secure funds for Allbones's sister's "oversight" for the children who remained in the East.[55] In this case, Charles Hicks exhibited a willingness to acknowledge women's guardianship claims to children, albeit for the benefit of patrilineal family members. In 1819, Paw yus skee (sp?) of Turkey Town complained to Hicks that he had not received any compensation for his service in the war. Paw yus skee was told by the interpreter for the agent that the money had been paid "by his power of attorney" to Timothy Meigs, the agent's son.[56] By 1820, several Cherokees entitled to pensions had secured lawyers to intervene on their behalf. Lewis Ross, the brother of John Ross, intervened on Walkingstick's widow's behalf. The families of Ne caw wee and Allbones secured Elijah Hicks and Richard Taylor as attorneys, respectively. Both of these cases involved men who had more than one wife.[57] Lewis Ross and Richard Taylor were both veterans of the Red Stick Revolt. That at least some Cherokee people turned to veterans familiar with governmental affairs, the English language, and the ability to legally act on their behalf suggests that Cherokee people did not trust the federal government or the Indian agent to dispense pensions fairly when it involved traditional Cherokee family systems.

In at least one pension case, men favorable to patrilineal family systems showed far more interest in debating the appropriate legal and economic guardianship of an orphan than in her actual care. A debate ensued over who should serve as Elizabeth Hildebrand's guardian after her non-Cherokee father, John Hildebrand, was killed in the War of 1812.[58] In 1819, Charles Hicks recommended that Elizabeth Hildebrand's paternal half-brother, Michael Hildebrand, serve as her guardian. Within a matrilineal system, Michael was not related to Elizabeth, yet Hicks believed that Michael would have no problem giving her the pension to which she was entitled when she turned seventeen or married. Hicks acknowledged him as her brother based on a patrilineal definition of family. A year later Hicks wrote to Agent

Meigs to discuss the possibility of placing Elizabeth with Mr. and Mrs. Gambold, Moravian missionaries who operated a boarding school. Over the next several months Gideon Morgan's and Lewis Ross's names were listed on drafts of guardianship paperwork instead of her brother's. Finally, in September of 1820, Lewis Ross was listed as the guardian and the recipient of the funds owed to Elizabeth Hildebrand. This suggests that a small number of Cherokee men conceived of their social service obligations as fiduciary agents only, and to some of those men residential schools served as a necessary social provision even when funds were available to support a family's care of a child.

The federal government's shift from a civilization policy, aspects of which many Cherokee leading men agreed with, including the presence of mission schools—to which Elizabeth Hildebrand's situation attests—to a removal policy coincided with another legislative move by Cherokee officials toward centralization. Cherokee leaders were well aware that bribery had been the norm to coerce local chiefs to sign earlier land cession agreements. Centralization undercut these strategies.[59] Some intermarried Euro-American men sought to capitalize on land deals and removal schemes. Writing from Washington, D.C., in 1814, during the War of 1812, intermarried white John D. Chisholm wrote to Agent Meigs soliciting an opportunity to move west to Arkansas with his family.[60] The Treaties of 1817 and 1819 cost the Cherokee Nation an additional 2.2 million acres of land, and they contained additional provisions to induce Cherokee families, including families headed by men like Chisholm, to remove west of the Mississippi. The provisions enticed others with patrilineal control of private landownership complete with U.S. citizenship. In 1817, the Cherokees formed a bicameral legislature that included a standing national committee comprised of thirteen members who initiated law and the Cherokee National Council of headmen from the fifty-four towns who affirmed or rejected the laws.[61] They had already established a national treasury into which annuity payments for ceded lands were paid, but the 1817 reforms took control of the funds away from Agent Meigs and placed it with the Cherokee National Committee.

This move not only enabled the Cherokee governing body to better manage attempts to dislodge all Cherokees from their lands through removal but also transferred the distribution of poor relief from the federal agent to the Cherokee Nation. Without a standing committee to oversee Cherokee annuities, pensions, and funds from the national treasury, Agent Meigs had arbitrated many of the financial transactions for the Nation. He had negotiated and controlled the payment of debts to traders and purchased corn when needs arose. The redistribution of extended families onto individual homesteads away from town centers, coupled with a severe drought in 1816 and the near-constant assaults and theft of food supplies committed by white settlers in the Lower Towns near Alabama, in particular, had led to significant requests to the agent for relief. Simultaneously, the pressures placed on Cherokee people to remove increased. As the distributor of relief, Meigs had been in a position to coerce removal by administering or withholding funds. The 1817 reforms placed social welfare responsibilities for Cherokee people with an institutionalized Cherokee Nation, not with the federal government or its agents.

These negotiations point to considerable Cherokee acumen in the semantic gymnastics necessary for equitable treatment under U.S. law. Meigs recorded Cherokee men's legal capacities as "guardians" to women and children and "lawyers" to men. This conformed to gendered legal understandings in the United States. From a legal standpoint, women and children operated at a diminished legal, economic, and intellectual capacity and were in need of men's guardianship and protection. In theory, men did not need guardians because they were equal participants under the law. Instead, they needed the professional services provided by other men—lawyers. Yet for practical purposes, the activities these men performed in both capacities were the same. U.S. officials and some Cherokee men resisted acknowledging that women and minor children could act as autonomous legal and economic agents. Cherokee officials understood these semantic distinctions and adapted to them in order to gain access to the resources Cherokee families were entitled to. It is safe to assume that in the minds of many Indian people, guardians and lawyers served identical functions; they were responsible for informing Cherokee people about the funds to which they were entitled and for advocating on their legal and economic behalf, inside and outside of their communities.[62]

By 1820, the increase in the number of Cherokee leaders raised by non-Cherokee fathers versed in U.S. property laws coupled with the numerous means by which the U.S. government and its citizens sought to undermine women's rights left women vulnerable to legal, social, and economic exploitation that had been rare fifty years earlier. In contrast to their U.S. counterparts, Cherokee women exercised autonomy as it related to their sexual decision making and marital choices, which in turn led to intermarriage with white and black men. But as Cherokee people quickly realized, women's relationships with men of African descent left their children susceptible to enslavement within the United States with very little legal recourse.[63]

As Cherokees underwent centralization, new governmental structures limited women's formal political participation. This process likely made Euro-American men far more comfortable in their dealings with Cherokees, but it also led Cherokee women to increasingly rely on men to guard their internal legal rights in external negotiations. For years, Cherokees had complained that the federal government placed unscrupulous white men in the Cherokee Nation and encouraged them to marry Cherokee women. For example, Pathkiller wrote to Agent Meigs in 1806 and requested that he remove the teacher who was "guilty of all the charges given against him . . . and more too," including "impos[ing] on John Lowery . . . to give him his Daughter in Marriage" and abandoning a wife and three children in North Carolina.[64] Another letter described the teacher as a "madman and imposter" and his behavior as "reprehensible."[65] Nine years later, a man from Tennessee entered the Cherokee Nation and confiscated the property of his intermarried brother's widow. U.S. common law and a lawyer hired to act on the widow's behalf failed to protect her rights.[66]

As one means to erode the land base even further, the United States used provisions of the Treaties of 1817 and 1819 to exploit the economic and political rights of Cherokee women for the benefit of intermarried Euro-American men.[67] Both treaties provided 640-acre tracts of land to individual male heads of families who desired U.S. citizenship. The Treaty of 1819 required those taking advantage of the provision "to be persons of industry, and capable of managing their property with discretion."[68] Many of the individuals who accepted citizenship and reserves in Georgia and Tennessee were Euro-American men who claimed through the "right of wife."[69] Agent Meigs recorded at least seventy-two intermarried white men exercising their claims to land through "right of wife"; an additional six claimed reserves through "right of children."[70] Twenty five percent of the total number recorded acquired lands through this means. The records suggest that none of these women exercised those rights in person; and Meigs only recorded the name of one of these women. These men subverted their rights as Cherokee residents at the expense of their Cherokee wives. Both states operated under coverture laws that denied married women property rights. As late as 1849, officials in the state of Tennessee claimed that women lacked independent souls and were therefore unable to own property.[71]

By contrast, Beloved Woman Nancy Ward and others exercised their matrilineal rights as Cherokee women and in 1818 sent a petition to their "Beloved Children," specifically objecting to "some white men among us who have been raised in this country from their youth, are connected with us by marriage, & have considerable families," who were encouraging Cherokee immigration and who were only "concerned how to increase their riches, but do not care what becomes of our Nation, nor even their own wives and children."[72] As Cherokee women deftly pointed out, the individualism and patrilineal pursuits that motivated many intermarried whites trampled the rights of the Nation and the rights of wives and children within the Cherokee Nation. Less than a year after the women's petition and in recognition that the right of wife provisions and removal inducements butchered the Nation's land base and compromised all Cherokee people's abilities to care for each other, the Nation in 1819 passed legislation that recognized "the improvements and labors of our people by the mother's side [as] inviolate during the time of their occupancy," a confirmation of matrilineal descent and communal landholdings.[73] The law also nullified intermarried men's citizenship if they divorced their wives.[74] Right of wife had its limits.

The individuals who took these reserves did so for several reasons. The Cherokees who accepted lands in North Carolina under these treaties tended to be more culturally conservative than their Cherokee counterparts to the south, and their remote mountain homes lacked

the same economic appeal to federal and state officials and speculators clamoring for removal in order to gain access to lands.[75] These
families form the nucleus of those who have come to be known as
the Eastern Band of Cherokee Indians.[76] It is reasonable to assume
that some of the individuals who signed did not appreciate or understand the legal ramifications of what they were signing given the fact
that personal landownership was a foreign concept to most Cherokee people.[77] Other men hoped to sell their land for a profit and
return to the Cherokee Nation. And others planned, as the treaty
offered, to relinquish their political ties to the Cherokee Nation and
exercise their rights as citizens of the United States.

Several individuals and families took reserves in what became
Hall County, Georgia; the events that followed offer insight into how
these groups navigated the process. One of the extended families
that chose to take advantage of the reserve provision was the Duncan
family. Dorcas Lightfoot Benge Duncan, Walter Adair Duncan's grandmother, was a member of the Deer clan. She married at least twice.
The first marriage resulted in the birth of her son Edmond Benge.
Her second marriage to Scottish immigrant Young Charles Gordon
Duncan resulted in the birth of six more children, three boys and
three girls. The Duncan family, including Dorcas Duncan, Edmond
Benge Duncan, John Duncan, and Charles Gordon Duncan, secured
four 640-acre reserves on Wau hough Creek, located about twenty
miles north of present-day Gainesville, Georgia, as a result of the
Treaty of 1817. Dorcas Duncan claimed a total of three members in
her family, and these were likely her daughters. Her son John also
claimed three in his family, presumably his wife, a South Carolinian
named Elizabeth Abercrombie, and their two oldest children. Dorcas
Duncan (or her sons) later sold her reserve for $1,600, and she relo-
cated back within the boundaries of the Cherokee Nation.[78] By 1825,
the same year Dorcas Duncan's grandchildren became eligible for
citizenship in the Cherokee Nation, John Duncan had also relocated
back into the Nation and was serving as a judge in the Hickory Log
District, now located within Georgia. In 1826, he served as delegate
to the Cherokee's constitutional convention.[79] By 1834, he would have
a total of ten children, including sons Walter Adair Duncan and DeWitt
Clinton Duncan. Whether the Duncan family members intended to

become citizens of the United States when they accepted reserves is unclear. Regardless, as members of the Deer clan, Dorcas Duncan and her children could continue to benefit from communal land-holdings if they moved back into the Nation.

John Duncan's children represented the traditional/national social provision divides in the Nation that federal officials hoped to tear wide open to bring about removal. At the time they took reserves, Dorcas's son John's children lacked a clan and they lacked citizen-ship in the Cherokee Nation. They were locked out of traditional social protections and provisions provided by a clan. It is possible that this informed John's decision to take a reserve. It is also likely that the possibility of citizenship for his children led him to return to the Cherokee Nation. His sons and his daughters would benefit from Cherokee Nation citizenship in a way only his sons could in the United States. With the passage of an 1825 law that granted citizen-ship to the children of non-Cherokee mothers, Walter Adair Duncan and his siblings became the first generation of Cherokees in his family to be Cherokee citizens, but not clan members.[80] They had a family, but no kin. They were eligible for national benefits, but not those available only to kin. Even though only his sons could vote and hold office, his sons' and his daughters' property rights were protected by the Cherokee Nation. Cherokee society also offered the Duncan daughters far more sexual freedom and family decision-making authority. Many of the intermarried white men and their progeny used the right of wife provision to maximize the political and eco-nomic standing of their children and by doing so undermined osdv iyunvnehi tied to communal landholdings and matrilineality. They intended to be citizens tied to a nation, rather than kin connected to clans. The question was, which nation? John Duncan hedged his bets.

The land cessions that followed the War of 1812 also led some Cherokees, often referred to as the Arkansas Cherokees, or Old Set-tlers, to remove west. Unlike those who sought U.S. citizenship or those who chose isolation in the mountains through stipulations in the 1817 and 1819 treaties, 200 families, comprised of 870 Cherokees, faced displacement as result of those same treaties' land cessions. Some families relocated onto the more retracted Cherokee land base and struggled to fulfill their traditional social service obligations.[81]

Others chose removal and the theoretical refuge it offered in the West. Separated from his childhood home, his traditional classrooms, and the laboratories of his intellectual breakthroughs, Sequoyah removed west of the Mississippi to the Arkansas Territory around 1822.[82]

Because the federal government targeted "poor warriors" for removal in the Treaties of 1817 and 1819, many of those who removed west over the next ten years articulated men's social welfare concerns.[83] They rejected new laws that forbade clan vengeance. They resented land cessions that limited their ability to hunt. They objected to official laws that stymied and in some cases criminalized men's traditional social service obligations. Although not a single man, Sequoyah was one of those who espoused what William McLoughlin describes as a Cherokee Separatist Nationalist belief system.[84] Cherokees, including Sequoyah, believed that Cherokees were better equipped to guide the social, economic, and political course of the Nation. Given the violent and coercive tactics used by U.S. officials and citizens to claim Cherokee lands, Cherokee Separatist Nationalists increasingly favored removal west to better care for one another.

As the centralized government passed laws that protected Cherokee women's economic rights, conferred citizen-making status on intermarried white women, and granted limited economic rights and privileges to intermarried Euro-American men, the Cherokee government left some Cherokee people and their African-descended family members without the same level of protection. Highly respected War of 1812 veteran Shoe Boots recognized the inadequacies of new laws to protect his children. In 1824, Shoe Boots successfully petitioned the council to acknowledge the free status of his children with Doll, his African Cherokee slave. Rather than use this as a moment to expand the protections offered by the Cherokee Nation to all of its families through citizenship, three weeks later, the council closed legal loopholes and outlawed citizenship for the children of Cherokee parents and African Cherokee slaves.[85] As Tiya Miles contends, this support for "antiblack racism" by Cherokee political leaders did not express admiration for Americans; it expressed their desire to be rid of them.[86] Despite the desire to create a parallel and yet alternative system that protected Cherokee people, this new bilateral and racialized understanding of citizenship and parentage affirmed a truncated view of matrilineality and introduced measures that complicated the traditional social service systems that had historically guided clan members' responsibilities to one another.

The Cherokee Nation missed an opportunity to expand the reach of the social protections offered to its families. Citizenship laws strengthened the ability of white Cherokee men and clan members with clanless wives like John Duncan to care for their children, yet undermined the ability of Cherokee fathers who had children with African-descended mothers to protect their children. Cherokee law barred some Cherokee fathers from passing citizenship rights to their children, and if the children lacked a matrilineal clan they were without access to traditional social protections and provisions as well. Neither traditional matrilineal kinship responsibilities nor new laws extended social provisions or protections to African-descended mothers and their children residing in the Cherokee Nation. Cherokee law codified protections for some families and left others without; this occurred at the same moment threats to Cherokee people and residents in the Nation increased.

In the minds of many southern settlers, Cherokee lives and property did not have to be respected. State and territorial courts resisted filing charges against settlers who committed crimes against Cherokees. During the second decade of the nineteenth century, Agent Meigs expressed his frustration at the neighboring states and their courts' unwillingness to hold whites criminally responsible for their actions. If charges were filed, state and county laws prevented Cherokees from testifying against whites, and local juries were not inclined to find whites guilty of crimes against Cherokees. The federal government used cash payments, referred to as "peace offerings" when applied to murder cases, as an attempt to ameliorate families' legitimate hostility when southern states proved averse to holding their residents accountable for criminal activity.[87] However, the patrilineal definitions of family that guided restitution payments on the part of federal officials failed to address the spiritual and legal dimensions of traditional or legislated Cherokee jurisprudence. For traditional Cherokees, no amount of money silenced the crying of the blood of the deceased. Distributing payments to pay individuals who were not clan kin offered no recompense to those who were. In 1816, for example, Meigs paid fifty dollars to Yellow Bear as a "peace offering . . . for a child that was killed in his arms by a white man" after the local state court acquitted him of the crime. Fifty dollars could not have provided solace to the child's mother, and it certainly did not assist the child in passing on to the darkening land.[88] Moreover, the money was paid to Yellow Bear and not to the child's mother, although it was mothers who traditionally adjudicated and determined the fate of those who took the lives of their clan kin.

For Cherokee families who adhered to traditional social service practices, these payments were spiritually and economically bankrupt. Although Meigs often investigated and sought remuneration, his ability to provide justice or restore balance was impotent. The misguided payments to Cherokee families depended on the War Department's budget and the agent's due diligence. The government ended the practice in 1820. In these death transactions, or "murder-compensation payments" as William McLoughlin describes them, the agent became the judge, jury, and evaluator of claims.[89] Cherokee husbands and fathers became the recipients of these payments. To what degree these patrilineal transactions encouraged Cherokee fathers to assume economic and social responsibilities to care for their wives and children as opposed to supporting a view of fathers as those responsible for external business transactions is debatable.[90]

The Cherokee National Committee passed far fewer criminal laws by the 1820s relative to the number of civil laws; yet criminal law, as Doublehead's 1807 execution suggests, had entered Cherokee legal thinking. In 1810, the Cherokee Nation universally outlawed clan vengeance and acknowledged instances of justifiable homicide.[91] That law also permitted a man to be prosecuted for his brother's murder, a crime previously left up to their clan to adjudicate.[92] The court's ability to pass judgment on a sibling exposed an increasing emphasis by the national government on the harm to individuals and the Nation as opposed to harm to a specific clan. By the 1820s, new civil and criminal laws affected relationships between individuals, clans, communities, and the emerging national government.

These laws were the culmination of more than twenty years of legal change. Beginning in the late 1790s, centralized national authorities established new legal frameworks and bureaucratic processes for what had been clear Cherokee legal theory. Traditionally, the responsibility for seeking vengeance fell to the injured party's nearest relative, usually the maternal uncle or eldest brother.[93] The 1808 law had established a police force "to suppress horse stealing and robbery of other property." Major Ridge had advocated the development of the light horse brigade and served as a captain.[94] The light horse also adjudicated internal matters and reported non-Indian crimes to federal authorities.[95] Communities and clans continued to handle all other matters under traditional legal theory. The light horse gained prominence when the Cherokee Nation sanctioned the police force to address legislated crimes. Their status as judiciaries remained primary until the council established district courts in 1820 and then the positions of marshal, district sheriffs, and constables.[96]

The district court model remained the skeleton of the Cherokee national courts from the centralizing process of the early 1820s until the dissolution of tribal government in the early twentieth century. The legislation divided the Nation into eight districts and designated five days in both May and September for each district to hear its cases. To manage increasing responsibilities, the national council often relegated matters of stolen property to the courts. In 1822, the national committee and council established a superior court to handle appeals from the district courts.[97] Council actions reflected the nebulous relations that the courts, light horse, and national council had to one another in the first third of the nineteenth century. In November of 1824, the council required lighthorsemen to serve as jurors in the respective districts. In a move that limited the possibility that clan or kin might make legal decisions impacting an accused individual, the council rescinded that act and instead required the district courts to secure "five disinterested men" to serve as jurors by October of the following year. At the same national committee meeting, legislation established the courts as a separate and independent branch of government.[98]

Throughout the pre-removal period, the national committee and council passed legislation to streamline the courts and develop a system that could manage the cases presented. The 1827 Constitution reaffirmed the judicial branch and specified the selection of judges,

clerks, justices of the peace, the rights of the accused, and the responsibilities and makeup of the district, appeals, and supreme courts.

The court's development coincided with the rise of assault, theft,
and murder on the Cherokee Nation's borders. For years, Indian
agents had served as the main adjudicators of crime between settlers and Cherokees. Meigs often expressed frustration at his inability
to sort through property crimes committed by settlers, Cherokees,
or other parties. By administering its own courts, the Cherokee Nation
lightened the federal agent's caseload and freed him to focus on
adjudicating cases involving settlers' criminal wrongdoing.

The court's necessity arose, in part, from the more dispersed living
patterns of Cherokee people. People could no longer appeal to local
councils who were more likely to know the townspeople and the
status of the property involved. Most of the court's activity reflected
elite Cherokees' relatively new preoccupation with private property.
Citizens increasingly filed complaints against Cherokee neighbors
on matters of property theft. The court's actions over property matters included women as defendants and plaintiffs, thus reaffirming
women's traditional rights as property holders.[99] Horse theft presented the greatest problem due, in part, to the rise of organized
syndicates outside of the Cherokee Nation targeting livestock.[100] The
court system replaced clans as arbiters of property disputes. Previously,
the wronged clan had the right to demand restitution for property
theft or damage but that authority now passed to the courts.

Within a traditional social welfare system, homicide, regardless
of intent, distorted balance in the world. In 1828, when the national
council turned its attention to homicide laws and mandated the death
penalty for anyone found guilty of "willful murder," it created a
legal scenario at odds with traditional law that sought restorative
balance.[101] The legislation created written criminal distinctions between
types of homicide and exempted those who killed another in self-
defense "or by accident," an outcome that meant some homicide cases
would result in the world remaining permanently out of balance.
Legislation of this kind motivated some of the Old Settlers to remove
west. Assaults committed in the progress of another crime resulted
in a fine of up to fifty dollars and fifty stripes or less, at the discretion

of the jury.[102] Local chiefs had mediated accidental homicide cases in the past, but these formalized measures removed the possibility of local town mediation and placed the cases with the district courts.[103] Many of these laws responded to increases in crime as a result of national instability as a result of civilization and removal policies, but they also denoted a willingness by the Cherokee Nation to adjudicate crimes within its borders to stand against the systems beyond the Nation. The activities of Cherokee courts made the absence of favorable actions on behalf of Indian people in the Southeast that much more obvious.

Cherokee people were not alone in debates over who should be treated as criminals and who should not and what the community's responsibility to those people should be. By the 1820s, a growing number of reformers in the United States questioned the use of prisons and poorhouses to attend to the needs of various classes of people, including elderly, deaf, blind, and insane people. Counties established poor farms to serve the impoverished, and cities and states assumed more control of institutions to deal with the growing number of displaced workers and immigrants who needed temporary relief.[104] In 1826, the Cherokee National Council passed legislation that protected "lunatic[s]" or a "person insane without lucid intervals" from prosecution or a guilty verdict for a crime committed "in the condition of such lunacy or insanity."[105] Localities in the United States embraced reform for reasons related to economic disparity, emigration, and population density, but these reasons fail to explain fully why the Cherokee Nation turned its legislative energy to the mentally ill and (dis)abled people and whether in fact these changes were necessary.

Acknowledging insanity through legal codification challenged Cherokee ideas about the insane and reflected the desire on the part of Cherokee officials to protect individual citizens from inappropriate judgment under the law. Within Cherokee society the law represented codified legal protection for people traditionally cared for by kin. However, this desire to protect citizens was a work in progress. Without clearly defined definitions of insane behavior, the legislation did not preclude witchcraft or spiritual imbalances as plausible causes of insanity. The law, even without any additional protocols or institutions to manage the mentally ill, moved the Nation toward national public health policies and gave some legal authority to the courts to deal with the criminally insane; yet it also maintained traditional systems in which kin and local communities cared for and treated mentally ill family members.

While it was increasingly accepted that mental illness could exempt some whites from punishment for criminal behavior, including violence against Indian people, the same protections were more elusive for Indians. Cherokee leaders had already confronted the U.S. legal implications of an insanity defense for non-Indians in 1819. Agent Meigs had excused the murder of an "insane soldier with a long knife [who] killed an Indian and wounded several others." The agent made sure to explain that it was "derangement," not the soldier's "former prejudices" toward Indians, that was the cause of the attack. The man escaped from prison and the impending trial, but that did not preclude the possibility, Meigs said, that he was at times "actually a madman."[106]

Regardless of whether the 1826 legislation helped prevent mentally ill individuals from being wrongfully convicted in the Cherokee Nation, the acknowledgment of insanity as a mental condition that could afflict Cherokee people and the presence of an "insanity" defense within the Nation signaled to non-Cherokees the viability of the condition and this defense for Indian people more broadly. The new law affirmed that if U.S. citizens could escape criminal responsibility through insanity, Cherokees could too.

Cherokee people did not uniformly support all of the legislative changes taking place within the Nation that led up to its call for a constitutional convention in October of 1826; some publicly rebelled against the changes. The record of grievances does not exist, but historians have put forth a variety of plausible objections including traditional leaders' opposition to the imposition of "Christian morality," concerns over more rigorous enforcement of new laws that compromised traditional social provisions, and the move from a "noncoercive political system" to one with elected delegated authority based on citizenship.[107] The variety of grievances begged the question: what did this proposed constitutional republic offer to the mass of Cherokee people who continued to abide by a traditional social welfare system or were casualties of the social provision drift encouraged by federal policy and supported by laws proposed by largely white mixed-descent Cherokee men? The convention proposed a government less committed to individual rights. In fact, the Cherokee Nation's constitution lacked a bill of rights. This enabled the national emphasis to remain on the community's protection, instead of on individuals, which may have reassured those wed to osdv iyunvnehi. Others consented because they knew states could not guarantee their economic, political, or social rights. In sum total, the Cherokee Nation's social policy offered more to Cherokee people than the alternatives available.

In 1829, two years after the Cherokee Nation's adoption of its constitution, the national council granted a one-dollar monthly payment to Kahateehee "to take good care of an old blind man, named Big Bear." This payment marked the first documented time the Nation assumed fiscal responsibility for one of its citizens. In exchange for the financial support, Kahateehee consented to "supply [Big Bear] with food, wash his person and clothes, and keep him in a decent condition at his house."[108] Kahateehee's request for financial assistance pointed to the tears in the traditional social service safety net weaved together by the kinship system, communal landholding, and redistribution in providing for all Cherokee people. As Big Bear's case illustrates, individual poverty had become a real possibility, but one a centralized Cherokee government was willing and able to respond to if necessary.

From 1800 to 1829, as the Nation consolidated authority and faced a removal threat, Cherokee men and women grappled with how best to fulfill their social welfare obligations to one another. Federal pension laws had ignored Cherokee mothers', sisters', brothers', and uncles' roles as providers and facilitators of their kin's needs, but national officials attempted to mediate the exclusions these laws created. Cherokee women's formal political rights and the symbolic associations between women's life-giving power through agricultural endeavors waned. But women's traditional rights within Cherokee society and Euro-American views of women as vulnerable and in need of men's beneficent care in the United States still left most Cherokee women in a better position to fulfill traditional social welfare obligations within the Nation. Men had continued access to a formal political voice through voting and political office, but those who adhered to traditional matrilineal social welfare practices also faced challenging social and economic conditions. By 1829, commitments to citizenship by some Cherokees and the continuation of a matrilineal system by others marked a clear change in how Cherokee people negotiated their social service responsibilities. Yet, all of these negotiations were Cherokee attempts to respond to Euro-American systems that simultaneously sought to create dependency while maiming traditional social service systems in order to coerce conformity to U.S. civilization policies or bring about Cherokee removal. The mass of Cherokee people navigated conditions as they always had; they relied on communal landholdings, extended kinship systems, and a communitarian ethic to provide for each other. Just as osdv iyunvnehi dictated that Cherokee people take care of one another, the nation-building process established institutions to advocate on behalf of and take care of Cherokee citizens.

CHAPTER 2

The Crises of the Removal Era, 1830–1860

A year after the Cherokee National Council granted its first pension to Big Bear to care for Kahateehee, the Cherokee Nation's legal battle against removal began in earnest. The legislation Georgia had passed in 1828 became effective June 1, 1830; it nullified the Cherokee government, extended Georgia's laws over Cherokee citizens, and prohibited Cherokees from testifying in state courts.[1] In November of 1830, Georgia authorities tried, convicted, and condemned Cherokee Corn Tassel for the murder of another Cherokee, Sanders Ford. Although the Corn Tassel case did not directly relate to federal removal efforts, it represented an institutional strategy by the state of Georgia to stamp out Cherokee sovereignty within its claimed boundaries and served as a means to coerce removal. The case also represented the legal and personal challenges that the Nation and individual Cherokees would face in their efforts to resist removal, and it informed their responses to it. John Ross, by then principal chief, employed former U.S. attorney General William Wirt to bring the case before the U.S. Supreme Court on the grounds that the state of Georgia lacked jurisdiction in a case involving two Cherokee citizens. The Supreme Court issued a writ of error. To avoid a possible judgment that might limit the exercise of state sovereignty, Georgia expedited Corn Tassel's execution, hanging him before the Supreme Court hearing could be held.[2]

The Corn Tassel case served as the first of the three test cases to assert Cherokee sovereignty and resist Georgia's strong-arm tactics, yet this case, more than the other two, represented the "justice" individual Cherokee people could expect when subjected to southern states' laws—no ability to bring Cherokee witnesses, a jury of non-Cherokee peers, and an undermining of a higher court's ruling on their behalf by a state court.[3] The Cherokee Nation argued that its rights as a sovereign nation included the ability to administer justice based on its laws and on behalf of its own citizens. Tribal judicial sovereignty had national implications. For the families of Corn Tassel and those who had taken 640-acre reserves in Hall County, Georgia, under the Treaty of 1819 where Corn Tassel was incarcerated, tried, and executed, the implications were far more ominous. Removal policy induced individual Cherokees to accept individual land allotments that threatened the foundation of Cherokee social welfare—communal landholdings—and then Georgia attacked individuals. The Corn Tassel case tied the sovereign rights of the Nation to the social well-being and the very lives of everyday Cherokee people.

In this chapter, I examine the coordinated offensive on the part of the federal government and state officials in order to induce removal, Cherokee people's responses to those attempts, and the long-term social, economic, and political consequences that reverberated through the period leading up to the U.S. Civil War. State officials intended to use the laws and institutions at their disposal to create socially and economically unbearable conditions for the Cherokee Nation and individual Cherokees in order to coerce removal. Rather than examine Cherokee resistance to removal through the actions of elected officials and courts within and outside of the Cherokee Nation, I expand my view to consider removal's impacts on the ability of the Cherokee Nation and Cherokee people, regardless of their relationship to the Nation as matrilineal clan kin or as citizens, to fulfill their social welfare responsibilities to one another. Removal attacked Cherokee national sovereignty and Cherokee families' economic, communal, and psychological stability. The instability discouraged families' long-term planning and their short-term ability to plant crops and share agricultural resources. Impotent to defend their families from the brutality and loss of removal, post-removal Cherokee men turned on one another. Removal introduced the possibility that long-term poverty might haunt Cherokee people. Yet national leaders, extended families, and local communities still mustered the collective will to obtain the resources and enact laws to care for vulnerable Cherokee people.

The federal Indian Removal Act passed in 1830, but the threat posed by removal did not begin then, or even with Andrew Jackson's election in 1828. By then the threat was more than two decades old. In 1806, Thomas Jefferson had proposed to the Cherokees that they remove west of the Mississippi, the same year Doublehead and a small group of Lower Town chiefs had signed a treaty with the United States ceding the last of the Cherokee hunting grounds and securing themselves financial favors. Through secondhand accounts, Cherokee leaders received word that Jefferson suggested running up individual Cherokee debts to force land sales and removal to fulfill the debt.[4] In response to these threats, Cherokees centralized power, challenged the legality of treaties forged without the consent of the full council, and passed legislation to protect the most coveted national asset for Cherokees and U.S. citizens—land.

Jefferson's proposal came in the midst of land cessions that, over the period 1794–1808, severely compromised the Cherokee land base. Cherokee leaders made political decisions with defense of homelands as the goal. As mentioned above, when the War of 1812 broke out between the United States and Britain, the Cherokees allied with the United States and Upper Creeks under Andrew Jackson against the Red Stick Creeks. Cherokee leaders raised troops to avoid the wrath of armed frontiersman and potential treatment as enemy combatants.[5] Despite the alliance; the military service of numerous Cherokees including The Ridge, John Ross, Sequoyah, and Junaluska, a prominent chief among the Cherokees who remained in North Carolina; and the deaths of thirty-six Cherokee soldiers, the United States and General Jackson exacted additional land cessions totaling 2.2 million acres from the Cherokees and the Creeks, their neighbors to the west, through treaties that followed the war.[6]

The Treaties of 1817 and 1819 demonstrated to the Cherokee Nation that the decision of individual Cherokees to enroll for emigration to the West threatened common title to land, which had served as a bulwark against widespread poverty. As removal pressures loomed in the 1820s, the Cherokee Nation passed legislation to protect communal landholdings from loss when individual

Cherokees chose to emigrate west. In 1821, to discourage emigration, the Nation had imposed fines on any emigrant selling his or her improvements.[7] Instead, those improvements reverted to the Nation. The Nation took coercive steps to limit the ability of individuals to harm the entire community. Four years later, the council forbade any sale of improvements to citizens of the United States and made clear that "the legislative council of the Nation shall alone possess the legal power to manage and dispose of . . . the public property of the Nation."[8] Those who chose to emigrate or move beyond the boundaries of the Cherokee Nation, the council decreed in 1828, "forfeit[ed] all right, title, claim and interest that he, she, or they may have or be entitled to as citizens of this Nation."[9] Had this law been passed fifteen years earlier, the Duncan family would not have been able to so easily resume their place within the boundaries of the Cherokee Nation. Through financial penalties and citizenship limitations, these laws discouraged removal, but they also reiterated the social and economic importance of common landholdings to the larger body of Cherokee people.

Federal and state officials stepped up their efforts to use or withhold state power and employ their institutions to force the Cherokees into submission. During and following his governorship of Tennessee, Joseph McMinn had served as an agent to oversee removal treaty negotiations with the Cherokees. In that capacity, he had threatened in 1818 to unleash lawless whites and illegal settlers on the Cherokees to coerce removal and force submission. In 1829, fellow Tennessean President Andrew Jackson's secretary of war turned over the policing of intruders on Cherokee lands to the state of Georgia.[10] After a group of Cherokee lighthorsemen, its early police force, removed illegal U.S. settlers from their lands in 1830, a mob of twenty-five whites returned and beat four of the light horse officers, killing one. The Georgia mob then placed the three Cherokee men they assaulted in the penitentiary near the state capital at Milledgeville, which at the time was under the governor's direct administration.[11]

Despite class divides and citizenship laws that excluded residents based on race, Cherokees and their non-Cherokee allies, particularly Presbyterian and Methodist missionaries, experienced the intimidation and violence that accompanied removal policy in similar ways.

In 1831, Georgia established the Georgia Guard for the express purpose of policing Cherokee borders, but in particular to prevent
anyone, including Cherokees, from mining gold on Cherokee lands.[12]
Throughout the year, missionaries James Trott, Dickson McLeod,
Samuel Worcester, and Elizur Butler all faced arrest and incarceration when they violated a Georgia law that required non-Cherokees
to obtain a permit to preach and live among the Cherokee. The Georgia
Guard arrested intermarried printer J. F. Wheeler, employed by the
Cherokee Phoenix, which impeded the newspaper's publication and
thereby prevented the Cherokee Nation from pleading its case to
the U.S. public more broadly.[13] In 1833, the state of Georgia confis-
cated Joseph Vann's plantation based on a trumped-up labor violation.
That same year, Principal Chief John Ross lost his Georgia home.[14]
From 1830 to 1835, as William McLoughlin summarizes, the Georgia
Guard "became a prime source of Cherokee destabilization."[15]

The state of Georgia left little formal recourse for Cherokees. In
fact, by 1830 southern states had made it clear that Indians who chose
to remain in the South did so as second-class citizens.[16] Georgia
law required those who objected to the Georgia Guard's abuse to
file civil suits and thereby shielded the state from any legal or economic responsibility for the guard's actions.[17] In September of 1831,
missionaries Elizur Butler and Samuel Worcester were sentenced to
four years of hard labor at Milledgeville Prison for their failure to
abide by the Georgia law requiring all whites residing among the
Cherokees to swear an oath of allegiance to the state.[18] Although
the law never went into effect, in 1831 the Georgia state legislature
briefly debated abolishing its prison as a result of inmate resistance
coupled with the prison's failure to be economically self-sustaining
as promised, but the proposed legislation required the continued
imprisonment of all Indians.[19] Legislation of this kind sent a clear
message to Cherokee people that, regardless of the economic hardships created by the prison and its willingness to shut an institution
because white *prisoners* objected to its existence, it would continue
to use state institutions to control and coerce the behavior it expected
from Indians.

Although federal officials avoided the use of physical force to
coerce removal, the state officials were more than willing to use their

institutions to assault individual Cherokees' liberties and Cherokee national sovereignty to achieve their ends. As stated earlier, the Duncan family sold their homes within the boundaries of the Cherokee Nation in advance of the land lotteries, and in 1834 the family relocated to the Arkansas Territory, without Dorcas Duncan, before the signing of the removal treaty and forced removal. In 1835, as the Cherokee Nation continued to resist removal, the Georgia Guard also crossed into Tennessee's jurisdiction to arrest Chief John Ross and his guest, U.S. citizen John Howard Payne. The guard marched the men twenty-five miles in the rain to the Cherokees' Springplace Mission (also confiscated by Georgia). The guard placed the men in a log cabin prison with the chained son of Going Snake, a veteran of the War of 1812. Ross was held for nine days and Payne for nearly two weeks.[20] Officials refused to tell Ross why he was being held. Emboldened Georgia settlers confiscated the property and homes of Cherokee people and assaulted Cherokees, regardless of class.[21]

While Georgia deployed physical coercion, the federal government under southerner Andrew Jackson's leadership focused on economic coercion in order to undermine the Cherokees' financial stability and bolster Georgia's offensive. In 1830, the federal government, in violation of agreements with the Cherokee Nation but in compliance with Georgia's laws that disbanded the Cherokee government, refused to pay the annuity due to the Cherokee Nation into its national account. It used the laws passed by Georgia to argue that the Cherokee Nation ceased to exist and instead insisted on paying the money due to each individual Cherokee at the Tennessee agency. Some Cherokees would have to travel up to 180 miles to claim their forty-six-cent per capita payment.[22]

This move by the federal government stood in contrast to the changing impulses of U.S. social reformers at the time. U.S. reformers increasingly distrusted the financial decision making of those in need of aid. As a result, reformers discouraged local governments from providing cash payments or store credits to individuals to support themselves as they had in the past. Instead, reformers advocated institutional residential services for the poor, (dis)abled, and deviant. Even Georgia increasingly favored institutions to serve the poor.[23] In irony not lost on the Cherokee people, federal officials in favor of removal argued that educated mixed-descent Cherokee men could not be trusted to act in the best interest of monolingual full-blood Cherokee people as one justification to turn to individual per capita payments. The same traits that non-Indians had celebrated as evidence of Cherokee people's civilized status and that had qualified individual people to receive 640-acre reserves now worked to disqualify them as untrustworthy.

The per capita distribution and the attacks on Cherokee leaders undermined Cherokee sovereignty. Because the Cherokee Nation used its national treasury to finance its legal battles, administer its courts, and publish its national paper, which served as a vital mouthpiece for arguments against removal and a corrective for misinformation circulating in the wider press, the distribution of individual per capita payments starved the Cherokee Nation. For average Cherokees, the payments offered little, if any, long-term relief and they did nothing to bolster traditional social provisions that hinged on communal landholdings, stable farming conditions, and functioning kinship systems.

By 1830, when the federal government refused to pay the annuity into the national treasury, Cherokees were familiar with the economic hegemony at work and had devised a range of intertribal, national, and individual strategies to resist. In 1823, John Ross had publicly exposed to the Creek council attempts by Creek general William McIntosh to bribe him with funds from the federal government to negotiate a treaty to cede more Cherokee lands. Cherokee leader John Ridge, like his father Major Ridge before him, and David Vann served as secretaries to the Creeks from 1826 to 1827. In their official capacity, the men advised Creek officials of Cherokee affairs and discussed shared concerns. They also provided the Creeks with their English-language and literacy skills. Agent to the Creeks John Crowell described the Creek Upper Towns as "under the immediate guardianship" of John Ridge, a guardianship Crowell intended to end.[24] This "guardianship," as Crowell described it, stemmed from Ridge's service as an advisor to Creek headman Opothle Yoholo. In his secretarial capacity in 1826, Ridge recommended that the Creeks, whose annuity payments were even larger than the Cherokee

Nation's, form a national treasury to finance their own legal defense.[25] William McKenney, head of the Office of Indian Affairs, exploited this information to raise suspicions among Opothle Yoholo's political rivals that Ridge and the Cherokees planned to use Creek money for their own devices. The ploy worked and undercut a potential Creek/Cherokee economic and legal anti-removal defense.

The Cherokee Nation used its national paper the *Cherokee Phoenix*, which began publication in 1828, as a mechanism to remind Cherokee people of these tactics and to inform U.S. residents of these earlier ploys. Editor Elias Boudinot, John Ridge's cousin, reported on the bribery, the false accusations lodged at Cherokees by federal agents, and the attempts by federal officials to hold negotiations at locations that hindered the participation of most Cherokee people.[26] This longer recognition of the coercive practices deployed by federal and state officials to coerce treaties favorable to the United States probably informed the decisions by many Cherokees to refuse to claim the per capita payments that should have been placed in the national treasury.[27]

National and individual starvation and induced dependency developed as tools to coerce removal. These strategies were not new; officials had used them at various points over the previous decades to coerce acceptance of their policies and programs. McMinn, in his capacity as an agent to negotiate a removal treaty, withheld annuity payments to the Cherokees in 1817 in order to strangle the Cherokee Nation's ability to pay its debts and to keep poor relief in the form of corn distributions coming squarely from federal officials.[28] In 1827, Alabama passed legislation prohibiting Creeks from hunting, trapping, or fishing within the state of Alabama or on recently ceded lands from where Creeks were still relocating. Alabama followed Georgia's lead and extended laws over the Creek Nation that dissolved its government and subjected Creek people to the "whims of the state."[29] Conditions in the Creek Nation deteriorated quickly. Whites confiscated Creek homes and farms. Some Creeks fled to the Cherokee Nation. Many of the most vulnerable were reduced to begging. Though not passed, state legislation to seize the meat from Indians who engaged in hunting to feed themselves was proposed by Mobile residents.[30] As editor, Elias Boudinot regularly reported instances of Creek suffering in the *Cherokee Phoenix*, which he renamed the *Cherokee Phoenix and Indians' Advocate* in 1829, the year after it began publication.

Although Georgia's execution of Corn Tassel aborted the possibility of a ruling from the Supreme Court in 1830, Supreme Court chief justice John Marshall's January 1832 *Worcester v. Georgia* decision upheld tribal sovereignty and the validity of nation-to-nation treaties forged between the United States and the Cherokee Nation. It also committed the United States to the protection of tribal nations. The case centered on the constitutionality of a law passed by Georgia in 1830 requiring whites, including missionaries, living in the boundaries of the Cherokee Nation to swear an oath of allegiance to the state of Georgia or face removal from the state. The 1831 arrests and convictions of Presbyterian missionaries Samuel Worcester and Elizur Butler provided another legal opportunity to test Georgia's sovereign claims against those of the Cherokee Nation's. The decision vindicated the Cherokee Nation and determined that it retained exclusive jurisdiction over its land and citizens. Yet, the decision described the nation-to-nation relationship between the federal government and tribes as one that resembled "that of a ward to his guardian," an analogy that would be perverted during the allotment era. As Marshall reasoned, the United States built the relationship through its earlier treaties forged with a "dependent ally, claiming the protection of a powerful friend and neighbor." "Protection," however, did not imply the sovereign "destruction of the protected."[31] Even though Marshall used the guardian/ward relationship as a metaphor to describe the legal and political responsibilities between the two national bodies, he did so at a moment when the definitions and uses of guardianship were changing for Americans and Cherokees. Noah Webster's 1806 dictionary described a guardian simply as "one who has care of another."[32] By 1828, the same year educational reformer and Massachusetts legislator Horace Mann described the relationship of the insane to the government as "wards of the state," Webster defined a guardian in two ways: (1) "a warden; one who guards, preserves or secures; one to whom any thing is committed for preservation from injury," and (2) a vague legal definition, "one who is" a guardian.[33] The rise in the use of institutions and institutional administrators to differentiate social provisions to vulnerable populations directly contributed to the more thorough first entry in the 1828 dictionary.

Most Cherokees were probably not aware of Webster's efforts to nationalize language usage and fix its meanings, but leading men, in particular, were grappling with and interpreting the legal concept of guardianship within their communities and how it would be applied to them.[34] Within Cherokee communities, the term had limited applications. It continued to describe the leading men who acted on behalf of women and children to obtain the federal benefits to which they were entitled. Yet, its usage was expanding. In 1826, for instance, Creek agent John Crowell had cast John Ridge's "guardianship" to the Creeks in negative terms.[35] In that instance, federal officials actively undermined and challenged the ability of Indians to serve as guardians to other Indian groups. As part of their attack on tribes to coerce removal, southern judges ruled that Indians were too savage and racially inferior to govern themselves.[36] By extension, no Indian person was intellectually fit to act as a guardian within a southern Euro-American worldview. There was more at stake for Cherokee people in the *Worcester* decision than communal landholdings and tribal sovereignty; the decision could affirm or further compromise the ability of Cherokee people to perform their traditional social service responsibilities and to serve as guardians to one another.

As men tasked with diplomatic affairs and international defense, Boudinot and his cousin John Ridge had unique experiences leading up to and following the *Worcester* decision. Both were in the North on business for the Nation when Marshall issued his ruling. Elias Boudinot's tasks, as editor of the *Phoenix*, were to present the Cherokee Nation's position on removal and report news to Cherokee people. Boudinot rhetorically linked their Indian neighbors' experiences to their own. He chronicled Creek resistance to removal and "their degraded state" and "rapid decline" under repressive conditions. He also reported on the Choctaw's removal experience.[37] Privately, he also wrote a letter to his brother Stand Watie, which revealed that he was ecstatic over the decision. Meanwhile, writing from Washington,

D.C., John Ridge informed cousin Stand Watie of the Creeks' "foolish" removal treaty.[38] This treaty left the Cherokee Nation pinned in on all sides by white settlers who were unrestrained by any legal forces.[39]

As a result of their positions, Boudinot and Ridge knew before other Cherokees that President Jackson had no intention of enforcing the Supreme Court's decision. In his letter referencing the Creek Treaty, John Ridge warned Watie a month after the decision that "the contest [was] not over" and the Secretary of War was "exceedingly anxious to close a [removal] treaty" with factions of the tribe if necessary.[40] The cousins returned to the Cherokee Nation prepared to debate the merits of removal in the pages of the *Phoenix*. The family, including Stand Watie and his uncle, Major Ridge, shared the men's new skepticism that the Nation could not survive in the East subject to the whims of settlers and the laws of southern courts.[41]

By July of 1832, the prominent political guardians of the Nation who shared so many views on the political future of the Nation, including the public endorsement of many features of the civilization policy—including increasingly patriarchal and hierarchical gender norms and the merits of Euro-American education and economic development—now disagreed over how best to preserve the Nation and how to protect one another. Boudinot planned to use the *Phoenix* to begin discussing removal, which was not the official position of the Nation. Principal Chief John Ross censored Boudinot's editorial efforts to discuss removal, and Boudinot protested by resigning his position as editor in August of that year.[42] Ross believed that publishing a public debate in the paper distributed to Cherokees and non-Cherokees weakened the Nation's official position and provided another opening for federal manipulation. Given the numerous ploys used by federal officials to divide and undermine the Nation's position, this was a legitimate concern.

The political turmoil created by removal revealed the extent to which egalitarian systems and matrilineality had been internationally suffocated in favor of the positions and personalities of an elite group of Cherokee men. Elias Boudinot and John Ridge were two of the most educated men in the Nation as a result of mission schools in the Nation and additional education at the Foreign Mission School in

Cornwall, Connecticut. Both men had met and married their non-Cherokee wives at Cornwall.[43] The 1825 marriage law that usurped the ability of Cherokee women alone to determine rightful heirs to the Nation protected the interests of the children these marriages produced. Ridge and Boudinot also belonged to a wealthy slave-holding elite. Many of these men, especially those most educated and Christianized, saw themselves as the rightful guardians of the Nation. Yet, what that guardianship entitled them to do without the consent of the community continued to be debated and contested. Ross, even as the first elected principal chief of the Cherokee Nation under its constitutional republic, did not believe he had the authority to usurp the will of the majority of Cherokees, many of whom were traditionally minded Cherokee people who believed in lengthy public proceedings to reach community consensus.

In December of 1835, while Principal Chief Ross was away in Washington, seventy-five signatories, including Major Ridge, Elias Boudinot, John Ridge, and Chief Ross's brother Andrew, appointed themselves the rightful guardians of the Cherokee Nation and signed an unauthorized treaty that exchanged Cherokee communal land-holdings in the East for lands west of the Mississippi and stipulated a five-million-dollar payment to defray the cost of removal and reimburse individuals for property losses. As a result of its earlier advocacy for removal, the national council had removed John Ridge and Major Ridge from their official offices. By Cherokee law, only the full council and the chief were in a position to authorize a treaty.[44] The treaty signers lacked the authority necessary to make this agreement. In carrying out this act, they assumed the right to speak on behalf of the sixteen thousand Cherokees who remained in the East.

Treaty Party signers disagreed with Ross's resistance to removal and what they saw as dictatorial leadership. For example, Treaty Party signers objected to Ross's decision to bypass national elections based on the emergency created by removal. John Ridge had also planned to run against him. The Treaty Party had already drafted one treaty before the December 29 version, which Major Ridge, John Ridge, and Elias Boudinot refused to sign because its provisions for education and a total land base were inadequate.[45] John Ross, in his earlier attempts to stall for time and consider the Nation's options, had proposed a twenty-million-dollar price tag (a price closer to the actual cost), which Congress rejected for its exorbitance. Congress countered Ross's offer with a five-million-dollar maximum payment.[46]

The removal treaty signed in December of 1835 at New Echota included provisions predicated on the poverty, loss, sickness, and death that removal was guaranteed to create; yet this knowledge also led the Removal Party to lay the financial groundwork for a social service system controlled by Cherokee people. In exchange for removal and the lands it gained, the United States, as it had with the other southeastern tribes, agreed to provide a year's worth of rations to Cherokee people, thereby giving them time to reestablish their farms and yield crops.[47] Unlike the other tribes' treaties, it required that a doctor be provided for each removal detachment. The treaty stipulated a payment of $100,000 "for the benefit of the poorer class of Cherokees" and included a provision for an increase in the school fund investment from the $50,000 provided by earlier treaties to $200,000, the annual interest on these investments, which would be set aside to establish a common school system and a "literary institution of a higher order." These goals were long shared by many leaders who were now bitterly divided over removal. Of the $200,000 school investment, $50,000 "constitute[ed] an orphan fund" for the "support and education of orphan children as are destitute of the means of subsistence."[48] The treaty placed fiscal control and implementation of education and orphan projects with the Cherokee Nation rather than with the missionaries or the federal government, as was the case in the Choctaw and Creek treaties.[49] It also protected the federal pensions secured by the Nation in 1816 for Cherokee soldiers and their families who had fought in the War of 1812.

As the preamble to the Treaty of 1835 stated, the removal treaty signers agreed to remove beyond the boundaries of the "state sovereignties" in order to "establish and enjoy a government of their choice and perpetuate such a state of society as may be most consonant with their views, habits and condition; and as may tend to their individual comfort and their advancement in civilization."[50] Treaty signers believed removal offered Cherokees an asylum in the West and the peace they needed to affirm and foster traditional social policy even as it acknowledged through its economic provisions that removal would paralyze families' and communities' abilities to fulfill those obligations.

All of the removal treaties affirmed tribal sovereignty, and most pointed out the failure of the United States in its duties as a guardian of tribal communities even as federal officials and Congress sought to sanitize the treaties of their culpability. The treaties expressed a desire by the tribes to escape the jurisdictional authority of federal and state officials. Rather than face oppressive laws in the states and submit to this "great evil," the Chickasaws agreed to move west. A section of the removal treaty with the Choctaws that Congress failed to ratify read,

> WHEREAS the General Assembly of the State of Mississippi has extended the laws of said State to persons and property within the chartered limits of the same, and the President of the United States has said that he cannot protect the Choctaw people from the operation of these laws; Now therefore that the Choctaw may live under their own laws in peace with the United States and the State of Mississippi they have determined to sell their lands east of the Mississippi.[51]

By the time the Cherokee treaty was signed, removal treaty templates existed and the consequences of removal were known. The Choctaws, Creeks, and Chickasaws had all signed removal treaties under similarly coercive and unrepresentative circumstances.[52] In 1833, a flood had destroyed the homes and provisions of Creeks who had removed west, leaving even more well-off Creeks facing starvation.[53] Provisions of the Chickasaw treaty placed numerous Chickasaws on individual parcels of land until removal. Chickasaws later contested this on the basis that it made no provisions for orphans, and as a result of these objections they were able to secure half-sections of land for orphans. However, Alabama and Mississippi courts assigned "guardians" to Chickasaw widows and orphans in their respective states, leading to rampant exploitation.[54] All but approximately seven thousand of the Choctaws had removed in 1831, and an additional group of Creeks had removed in 1834; thousands had died as a result. The Cherokees and missionaries who had already removed to the West described the sicknesses that awaited those who would remove later.[55] Through news and editorials in the *Cherokee Phoenix* and firsthand accounts, the Cherokee people had already witnessed the death, disease, exploitation, and despair that removal would entail.

The vast majority of Cherokees represented by John Ross objected to the Treaty Party's paternalism and the treaty's legality. In 1835, unlike what had happened twenty-nine years earlier, when local people rejected the public health services a few leaders had thrust upon them, they could not simply send removal away as they had Dr. McNeil. Even though Ross may have personally supported removal, he continued to work to delegitimize the treaty.[56] Perhaps he believed, as his father had thirty years earlier, that it was not proper to do otherwise without his constituents' approbation.

In 1836, the approximately fourteen thousand Cherokee men and women who chose not to remove with the two thousand Treaty Party members submitted a petition to Congress voicing their opposition to the treaty.[57] Their opposition represented a national effort by Cherokees to defend their traditional social service systems in the Southeast. One missionary, paraphrasing the prophetic and well-informed rationale articulated by one Cherokee, recorded, "If we leave this country, these hills and valleys and this mountain air, we shall sicken and die. What can we have in exchange? Perhaps war on our arrival, or . . . a few years of peace, and [we may] cultivate the land, [but] again the white man will trade our rights. Where can we find rest or protection?"[58]

In the Cherokee Nation's search for redress and its willingness to suffer abuse, usurpations, and oppressions, it exposed the United States' untenable commitments to equality, rights, and the pursuit of happiness if it could not uphold the legal and economic responsibilities it agreed to in its treaties with Native nations.[59] The United States risked becoming the tyrant it had railed against and not a "guardian" tasked with guarding, securing, and preserving the tribal nations as the *Worcester v. Georgia* decision resolved was the United States' legal obligation. Although Jackson was not in office when forced removal took place, he owed much of his political support to those engaged in the legal and economic tyranny against Indian people that culminated in state-supported and federally sponsored ethnic cleansing.

Individual experiences of confinement within Georgia and Tennessee's jails from 1820 to 1835 served as a precursor to the mass incarceration felt by the "Nation of prisoners," as one female missionary put it, during removal.[60] When the Senate ratified the treaty by a single vote in March of 1836, it turned the entire Cherokee people into prisoners.[61] In his 1838 orders to oversee removal, General Winfield Scott recognized that troops "will probably be obliged to take prisoners and to march or to transport the prisoners, by families" to the emigration centers. He presumed the prisoners would be men who resisted; to deal with this anticipated resistance, he gave orders for men's guns to be taken and their families held hostage, but he discouraged violence on the part of the military personnel. In a society based on kinship systems and responsibilities to one another, Scott misunderstood what violence was and how it was perpetrated. This was neither the first nor last time that imprisonment and familial isolation would be used as tactics to compel submission to policies viewed by Cherokee people as illegal and immoral. Scott also identified the groups who might require "peculiar attention," including "infants, superannuated persons, lunatics and women in a vulnerable condition."[62] The removal process and Scott's own words reveal how quickly self-sufficient people could be rhetorically transformed into deviants and vulnerable dependents.

As anticipated, the removal process, which began in 1838 and took two years to complete, presented substantial challenges to osdv iyunvnehi. Forced to leave their homes, often without adequate clothes or provisions, and interned in stockades for months to await removal, Cherokees indiscriminately suffered disease and death. The cramped conditions at the camps caused or contributed to dysentery, fevers, whooping cough, and measles. People slept on the ground, exposed to the elements. Whiskey peddlers abounded, which led to instances of violence, especially against women.[63] After four months in stockades, the first group traveled west, many on foot, during the winter.[64] The food that the army and then federal agents supplied was unfamiliar to most Cherokees and contributed to their illness. Even though physicians accompanied each detachment, they often served as disbursing agents. Additionally, Cherokees faced language barriers and preferred their own medical practitioners who relied on the use of plants common to their ancestral home, one of the most botanically diverse ecoregions in the world, to concoct medicines.[65] Internment, followed by a nine-hundred-mile journey to an unfamiliar geography inhabited by other Indian peoples, compromised traditional healers' abilities to gather the necessary medicines to administer to the sick. More than 30 percent of the plants Cherokees relied on for medicines, food, and other "culturally salient practices" in the East did not grow naturally in the West.[66] Removal not only separated Cherokee people from their land but also denied them their pharmacopeia.[67] It compromised the ability of Cherokees to heal themselves through the ceremonies and medicines that sustained them in the East at least in the short term.

As the Choctaws', Creeks', and Chickasaws' removals and the Treaty of 1835 foreshadowed, by the end of 1839 the Eastern Cherokees arrived in Indian Territory widowed, orphaned, indigent, sick, weak, exploited, grieving, and politically divided. The best estimates place the number of Cherokee deaths at approximately 25 percent of the total population.[68] Those numbers suggest that every Cherokee family lost a family member or a neighbor as a direct result of removal. They were most likely to lose their traditional healers, the adonisgi. The loss of elders cost Cherokee people their historians, those best equipped to put trauma and loss in historic perspective and remind Cherokees of their resiliency as a people and their ability to fulfill community responsibilities in the face of adversity. The removal era also cost many white Cherokee families the mothers and grandmothers who tied their sons' families to matrilineal kin and traditional social service systems. Cherokees lost their children and babies, the hope of the next generation and a reminder of whose lives and futures were at stake if they did not fulfill their responsibilities to one another. The uneven family systems created by the civilization policy along with the political rifts created by removal challenged Cherokee people's ability and faith in one another to fulfill their responsibilities at the familial, local, and national levels. The social safety net created by kin, communities, and a community ethic was in tatters, though not destroyed.

The loss of the land, which had been able to support the people, and the death and division of families, who had taken care of one another, meant that the specter of long-term collective poverty gripped Cherokees. The food rations provided by the federal government after removal proved to be substandard, and privation compounded the mental anguish removal caused. Unscrupulous federal agents and contractors short-weighted promised corn, delivered flour ruined by water, and charged excessive prices for meat. Distributions occurred once a month, a schedule that required food-storage facilities Cherokee families did not have. On some occasions, the rations were not available at all, and agents issued credits in hopes those denied would not return to claim their rations.[69] These frauds made the difficult first years in the West unnecessarily severe, particularly for Cherokee citizens who continued to value living simply and had the least material wealth when they left the Nation. The implements for farming guaranteed by the treaties did not arrive. Deprived of their guns, Cherokee people were unable to hunt.[70] Whiskey peddlers near Fort Smith were more than willing to offer solace through their wares, and, desperate for a temporary escape from the nightmare removal had wrought, Cherokees imbibed.

Removal reunited groups of Cherokees who had made different choices about how to govern themselves and manage social provisions. Politically, the Nation had two governing bodies—the Old Settlers, who had reorganized in the Arkansas Territory after the Treaties of 1817 and 1819, and who had since drafted laws to govern themselves, and the Eastern Cherokees, forced to remove under the Treaty Party's 1835 Treaty.[71] Treaty signers had joined the Old Settlers in advance of the Eastern Cherokees' arrival.

The absence of a legal consensus and a national government acceptable to all led to rampant violence motivated by political loyalties, personal grievances, the presence of alcohol, and the absence of legal restraint. Though there is no evidence to suggest his personal involvement or sanction, there is no doubt that John Ross's supporters planned coordinated executions of removal treaty signers Elias Boudinot, John Ridge, and Major Ridge in June of 1839.[72] John Ross's son, whose mother and clan kin, Quatie, died during removal, aided in planning the attacks, but remained with his father while they were carried out. Stand Watie, through advance warning, escaped execution.

Over seventy-five men participated in the executions, more than the total number who had signed the contested removal treaty. The executioners saw themselves as enforcers of the national law that barred individual Cherokees from ceding land.[73] The meeting that led to the executions, however, also hearkened back to more traditional Cherokee legal practices when individual Cherokees, not national officers, enforced the law.[74] Although the executions may have quieted the blood of the deceased, they stymied a political, legal, and social reunification amenable to all.

As a result, elected officials focused on the most pragmatic concerns first. In order to reestablish their lives and their nation, the Cherokees needed to negotiate with the federal government. The July 1839 Act of Union and September 1839 Constitution brokered by key Old Settler leaders, including Sequoyah, Tobacco Will, and John Drew along with members of the Eastern Cherokees, only partially solved the social, political, and economic divisions. Under the Act of Union, each group could continue to negotiate "all unsettled business" with the federal government based on their "respective treaties."

Leaders also focused their reunification efforts on the matters for which they had majority support. The Act of Union reiterated that the "title to public Cherokee lands shall henceforward vest entire and unimpaired in the Cherokee Nation."[75] To avoid any ambiguity about ownership of their territory, Article 1, Section 2 of the 1839 Constitution designed to govern the Old Settlers and the Eastern Cherokees confirmed that "the lands of the Cherokee Nation shall remain common property."[76]

As a result of the removal era's turbulence and the post-removal violence exasperated by alcohol, the merged Cherokee Nation reached legislative consensus on the need to regulate it. Pre-removal alcohol laws had targeted the actions of non-Cherokees, but post-removal laws focused on the actions of Cherokee Nation citizens.[77] In September of 1839, the national council outlawed drinking in public places, imposed fines on those found guilty, and authorized public agents to destroy confiscated whiskey.[78] The conditions became so severe that the Nation imposed complete prohibition in 1841.[79] Violence, sparked by removal and fanned by alcohol, challenged the Cherokee Nation's efforts to rebuild in the West.

The Cherokee Nation also reached legislative majorities on racial discrimination and redoubled its efforts to limit the rights of slaves and "free negro[es] or mulattos." At the time of the 1835 removal census, 200 families owned 1,600 slaves. The labor provided by enslaved people enabled slaveholding families to rebuild. The Nation passed increasingly severe slave codes in the years following removal. In 1842, during the post-removal violence, a slave revolt occurred that involved at least twelve slaves, most of whom were from Joseph Vann's plantation near Webbers Falls in the Cherokee Nation. The presence of free African Seminoles removed from Florida who resisted relocation to the Creek and Seminole Nations by remaining near Fort Gibson in the Cherokee Nation likely influenced the slave revolt. Considering the larger context of violence among Cherokee men and the more repressive slave codes, the revolt and escape suggests that the treatment of slaves—the most legally, economically, and socially vulnerable—deteriorated as well.[80] The events also underscore the impact of race relations in Indian Territory and the region on the Cherokee Nation.

From 1839 to 1846, discerning between criminal activity and political violence became difficult. In 1843, Stand Watie killed Cherokee James Foreman, who was linked to the killing of his brother, cousin, and uncle. Watie stood trial in the Arkansas district court and was found not guilty on the grounds of self-defense. In 1845, Watie's brother Thomas was killed during ongoing reprisals.[81] Because of the violence, the council had reestablished the light horse, which Treaty Party members saw less as a police force and more as an arm of the executive branch to put down political detractors.

This distrust in national authority by members of the Treaty Party made judicial reform impossible. The 1839 Constitution left pre-removal criminal procedures intact. The Nation continued to use guards to maintain custody of offenders, but the council began to tighten rules governing this practice. The Cherokee Nation relied far more heavily on corporal punishment and executions than it had in the East. Local sheriffs carried out corporal punishments immediately after the sentencing, and the guilty then returned home. For capital offenses, each of the nine districts established an area for hangings in its courthouse yard.[82] This system provided a continuity of older systems that privileged the town's ability to administer punishments for wrongs committed, but it also provided districts with residents more wed to national social policy the ability to administer justice as they understood it. The problem, of course, was that Cherokee people who held different views resided in all districts.

An ostensibly minor law passed by the national council in 1843 at the height of post-removal strife limited the ability of two classes of citizens from eight of the nine districts from fully exercising their rights and fulfilling their responsibilities as citizens. The law made it illegal for guards to board prisoners at the public houses during the session of the national council.[83] Guards had previously chosen where to board prisoners, and many of them took their charges along to Tahlequah when the council was in annual session. Since citizens from throughout the Cherokee Nation poured into the capital when the council was in session, accommodations in Tahlequah were at a premium. For the Nation, boarding the guards and the prisoners was an unwarranted expense. Guards who lived in Tahlequah profited from the law in two ways. They could board prisoners who needed to be in the capital at their homes during council sessions while increasing their income.[84] They also remained connected to political affairs. For guards serving in other districts, this new law created a barrier to their participation in the national sessions.[85] It prevented those who stood accused of crimes from accessing legal and political information as well as the ability to debate the merits of pending legislation. A prison would have alleviated questions of where to house prisoners and would have increased access to political participation for guards, but political violence prevented its consideration.

Even as violent reprisals continued and Cherokees resisted judicial reform, the Nation began administering formal social provisions through its educational institutions. In December 1841, Principal Chief John Ross approved the Public Education Act to establish a national school system. The common schools served younger children and were the modern equivalent of elementary schools. This legislation expanded the educational opportunities Old Settlers had provided. They had established a few schools and after moving west in 1822, and Sequoyah had taught the syllabary to students in community school settings.[86]

The introduction of public schools answered a social provision grievance, albeit delayed, voiced by traditional leaders leading up to and during their opposition to the 1827 Constitution. In theory, secular public schools offered the educational option many Cherokees had desired for their children in the pre-removal period. Some had tentatively accepted education from Christian missionaries, but remained dissatisfied. Others had rejected any education administered by missionaries in residential facilities. They objected to the moral judgments of the teachers and the insistence by many missionaries and elite Cherokee leaders that "religious ceremonies and political authority" were disconnected. They resented children's education occurring away from their communities, homes, and their traditional religious and political settings.[87]

Although some Cherokees had never supported missionary activities, other Cherokees' attitudes toward missionaries had also shifted in the era of removal. In 1839, the Nation passed legislation that prohibited missionaries from entering the Nation without first obtaining a license.[88] This act responded to pre-removal appeals by administrators of traditional social provisions to limit and control the activities of missionaries within the Nation.[89] But it also pointed toward some Cherokee leaders' dismay at the close relationship between members of the Treaty Party and some missionaries, particularly the Moravians, who were close to the pro-treaty Ridge family. After removal, the Nation thwarted attempts by the Moravians to establish a mission school by opening a public institution "at [their] door."[90] Many of the missionaries had left the Nation in anticipation of removal. Other missionaries abandoned the Cherokees as a result of the harassment they faced from Georgia. Only four missionaries participated in forced removal.[91] This abandonment soured public sentiment toward missionaries among Cherokees broadly, but elevated the status of individual Presbyterian, Baptist, and Methodist clergymen who in various combinations already served Cherokees in the West, had participated in removal, and had embraced the conversion experiences and endorsed the ability of Native Cherokee preachers.

The Public Education Act also provided a vehicle for delivering the social provisions for orphans funded by removal treaty provisions. It offered financial incentives to Cherokee families to care for each other and gave families an alternative to the education and services previously offered by missionaries. The act provided monies for orphan children in each school district, who were provided for in a "good steady family convenient to the school."[92] Initially, every common school received a $200 allocation for its orphans. In 1842, the total amount was $2,200 for the eleven schools in operation.[93] As the number of schools expanded, so did the budget. By 1847, the annual appropriation for orphan care had reached $3,600.[94] More well-off families were in a better position to support local schools and were therefore more likely to benefit from the supplements to their incomes by taking in other children.

Those Cherokee leaders who believed in the promise of universal public education soon confronted the same barriers faced by missionaries in the East in their efforts to provide Cherokee children with an English-language education. Initially, the Cherokee Nation faced teacher shortages. Rather than commit their skills to educating others, many of the young men from mixed-descent patrilineally oriented families with the skills and abilities to teach often chose to engage in other types of professional pursuits to increase their personal wealth. They engaged in cattle herding, owned mills and taverns, and served as store clerks. Many studied the law. Missionaries often volunteered to provide personnel for schools (and denominational teachings), but this replicated the problems associated with mission schools in the East and was what many Cherokees hoped public schools would counter. In addition, post-removal Christian Cherokees expressed denominational loyalty and refused to send their children to schools taught by missionaries from other denominations. Without a ready supply of Cherokee teachers, the Nation was forced to hire teachers from the East at competitive salaries. As a solution to this professional deficit, the Nation in 1847 allocated funds to build male and female seminaries modeled on elite schools in the East. The seminaries would open in the early 1850s and provide a high school curriculum and preparation for professional work or university training outside the Cherokee Nation.[95] This approach

appealed to many of the elite and middle-class Cherokees who benefitted from a free prep school education, but it also integrated the
philosophy of Cherokee Separatist Nationalists, who believed that
Cherokee people were better equipped to serve other Cherokee people.

Although Separatist Nationalist Sequoyah likely dreamed of a
Cherokee Nation with Cherokee as its official language, the merged
Cherokee Nation never considered using Cherokee as the official
language of the public schools. However, officials continued to discuss the need for bilingual teachers and texts.[96] In the 1850s, Walter
Adair Duncan proposed bilingual education as one means to bridge
the language divides in the schools and as a means to encourage
more traditional monolingual families to send their children.[97] Sequoyah's invention of the syllabary remained a symbol of Cherokee
advancement to all. But the embrace or rejection of its use and
dissemination became a powerful indicator of the degree to which
Cherokee people adhered to traditional social welfare systems.

In light of the very real needs of Cherokee people, the council
attempted to administer social provisions that blended the desires of
families who adhered more closely to osdv iyunvnehi with those who
desired institutionally delivered provisions. The Cherokee Nation
considered institutional services for children in need, but as in the
pre-removal period, most Cherokee people remained reluctant to turn
their children over to institutions. In 1842, the Cherokee Nation considered a partnership with the Methodist Episcopal Church (MEC)
to establish a Manual Labor School for the "exclusive" use of orphans.
Two years after the proposed partnership, the MEC established the
Indian Mission Conference to serve all of Indian Territory, a measure
that provided a greater voice to Indian Territory in the national MEC
structure.[98] Although a committee comprised of both Cherokees and
Methodists drafted a plan for an orphanage in 1849, the Cherokee
National Council rescinded its collaboration until a more suitable
plan could be developed.[99] Institutional changes in the Methodist
Episcopal Church, including a split resulting in the formation of
the Methodist Episcopal Church South over the issue of slavery,
likely impacted these negotiations. For their part, missions and missionaries cared for orphans only by individual arrangement.[100] For
example, from 1852 to 1861, missionary Jerusha Swain would house

a succession of four young women in her home, including ten-year-old orphan Nancy Watts, whose uncle arranged for her care.[101] Furthermore, fellow missionary Elizur Butler housed "one orphan Cherokee girl, who ha[d] learned to read and write."[102] Entrusting orphans to missionaries, however, was not national policy, nor did most Cherokees desire it to be.

In the aftermath of removal, Cherokees preferred that Cherokee families care for orphans, and the Nation financially supported these efforts. Ideally, the superintendent of schools distributed orphans equally over the common schools, but in actuality the number of orphans assigned to each school varied. Occasionally, school district budgets failed to meet the needs of the families caring for orphans. In 1843, for example, two families that boarded orphans attending the Skin Bayou School, taught by Robert Benge, requested additional funds from the national council. John Benge, who had served as a leader for a removal detachment, boarded two orphans, and Michael Waters, a judge in the Skin Bayou District, kept one.[103] Both men requested additional support in order to care for these children, and the council authorized twenty-four dollars and twelve dollars, respectively, for the men.[104] The council also moved to make those caring for orphans more fiscally accountable to the Nation and specified that the cost to board an orphan could not exceed four dollars per month.[105] This amendment to the Public Education Act required the superintendent to include the "names and condition of the orphan children" in the annual reports.[106] The superintendent, a paid employee of the Cherokee Nation, became a quasi-social worker whose responsibilities now included monitoring the orphans funded by the Nation.

Throughout the 1840s, the Nation continued to expand its involvement in and commitment to its children's lives. Traditional Cherokee family practices required extended matrilineal kin to care for children in the event of the mother's death, but the council deviated from this practice when it made either surviving parent the guardian of the children in the event of the other parent's death. In the eyes of the law, a father's legal responsibilities to his motherless children trumped those of matrilineal kin. The council further specified that if a parent "shall be incompetent to discharge the duties devolving upon them as guardian, then the children shall be dealt with as the law directs."[107] The council asserted a right to intervene in matters of guardianship and assumed the responsibilities of parents by assigning children without competent parents to families who "regularly sent [them] to school."[108] These changes represented practical responses to the family disruptions and dislocation created by removal. Nevertheless, they also reinforced ideas about patriarchy endorsed by the federal government and adopted to some degree by elite Cherokee men.

In 1841, the council formally acknowledged the presence of Cherokees with (dis)abilities when it passed legislation to provide twenty-dollar annual pensions to "all blind persons . . . those who may be maimed, crippled, or disabled . . . destitute of the means of subsistence" or without relatives "materially" able to care for them. Though requests were infrequent, the council followed through, approving, for example, a thirty-dollar pension for Ke ti ke ski, who was destitute, in 1843 and a twenty-dollar annual payment in 1849 for Big Dollar, who was crippled.[109] If necessary, the law required the council to assign guardians to individuals who could not care for themselves. As a protection to (dis)abled persons, the council mandated appraisals of their property to be performed by two "disinterested" parties and required guardians to account for all "moneys, property, and other effects" belonging to them. The law mandated that guardians post bonds, double the value of the property, with the district judge.[110] Even though the Nation passed laws to govern guardianships, the council did not assign guardians to Ke ti ke ski or Big Dollar.

Within the Cherokee Nation, the expanded and codified roles and responsibilities of guardians acknowledged a transformed Cherokee society. The legislative energy attached to guardianship laws for the (dis)abled within the Nation marked a clear shift from the pre-removal era when clan kin performed these duties and when guardians served as legal and economic mediators on behalf of a limited group of women and children with the U.S. agent to the Cherokees. Guardianship laws granted the Cherokee Nation the legal authority to determine the competency of guardians. The Cherokee Nation could have used its authority to undermine biological parents' rights, but in many instances it enabled the Cherokee Nation to validate traditional kin ties and respond to the new realities of a post-removal Cherokee Nation.

Despite resistance to missionary activities, national social policy and denominational activities both provided opportunities and spaces for those who were Cherokee citizens to come together with those who were both citizens and clan kin. After they arrived in the West, Walter Adair Duncan's family settled in the Goingsnake District in the Cherokee Nation. From 1845 to 1854, Duncan served as a Methodist Episcopal Church "missionary to his people" within the Indian Mission Conference. His itinerancy included the Webbers Falls area near the Arkansas and Canadian Rivers, Sallisaw, and the Flint District. It was "almost entirely new work . . . among the most wild and unsettled parts of the Cherokee Nation." In other words, Duncan worked among more traditional, monolingual Cherokee people who adhered to osdv iyunvnehi. The Indian Mission Conference operated a wide range of seminaries, manual-labor schools, and academies throughout Indian Territory.[111] Duncan married seminary graduate Martha Bell, the sister of Sarah Bell Watie, Stand Watie's wife. The Bell-Duncan children benefitted from the educational and professional opportunities provided by Cherokee Nation and Christian institutions operating in the Nation. These same institutional experiences placed Walter Adair Duncan in regular and sustained interactions with traditional and oftentimes monolingual Cherokee people. Although he may not have had a clan or kin, his wife and children did; he also worked closely with Cherokee people who did, and he still lived in a Nation that abided by a communitarian ethic.

The rising generation of Cherokee people moved forward after removal by living, loving, and aiding each other; those entrenched in the political, economic, and social divides deepened by the removal era required institutionalized measures to be assured of their protection and security moving forward. The Treaty of 1846 had resolved the pecuniary and legal disagreements between the Eastern Cherokees, the Treaty Party, the Old Settlers, and the United States. It had granted general amnesty to all Cherokee people in addition to providing a blank slate for the criminal justice system. The proceedings, overshadowed by the presence and interventions of U.S. officials, produced a tentative truce. Cherokee men lined up and shook the hands of the other Cherokee men assembled, a symbolic act meant to resolve political hostilities and end the violence.

This event shaped the direction of social welfare reforms moving forward and marked the distance from where Cherokees had come. Cherokees no longer gathered collectively for annual social welfare ceremonies, including the Green Corn ceremony, that all members of the community, regardless of age, race, class, and gender, had to participate in for community restoration and balance to be achieved. In contrast to earlier community events, the men assembled, under the watchful eyes of federal officials. Federal officials and the men gathered hoped to accomplish the same purpose achieved by Green Corn, but the ceremony failed to include the entire community and suggested that those not present bore no responsibility for osdv iyunvnehi.

These proceedings enabled men to carry out the judicial reform previously impossible. In 1851, the council allocated $1879.00 for the construction of a national prison. The proposal highlighted the arguments for its construction: "The system of imprisonment renders the escape of offenders against the law less liable to take place; will have a great tendency to deter from crime, and will afford a means to enable us to discriminate by law between the different degrees of man-slaughter, and better to proportion the punishment in all cases to the degree of the offence."[112] Unable to construct the prison in 1851 due to financial difficulties and objections of the guards, who worried their incomes might suffer, Principal Chief John Ross six years later called for renewed efforts to construct a prison on the grounds that "[homicide] . . . [and] violent assaults, have been committed with impunity for the want of some measure of punishment that does not exist, and which cannot be had without a prison."[113] For Ross, the construction of a prison fulfilled the responsibility of a nation to protect its citizens.

Despite the political and social violence, the Cherokee Nation had experienced remarkable growth in the years immediately after removal. In addition to the development of its common school system and its orphan services, which received dividends from investments of the Cherokee School Fund and Orphan Fund, the Nation built a courthouse, reestablished its national newspaper, opened its male and female seminaries, and developed three bustling towns. The expansion of government services, coupled with the financial losses resulting from removal, taxed the Nation's resources. The Nation relied on credit secured by the anticipated payment of funds owed under the removal treaty. However, until the Eastern Cherokees consented to the terms of the removal treaty in 1846, the money could not be released. When the funds were finally dispersed in the early 1850s, most of it paid back the loans amassed in the years following removal. Although the Nation attempted to sell the Neutral Lands, a small strip of land between Indian Territory and Kansas, to stave off financial problems in the 1850s, negotiations repeatedly broke down, first among Cherokee officials and then between Cherokee delegates and Congress.[114] Financial ruin threatened.

In the face of the financial crisis, the Cherokee Nation also began to cut back on services to children. Privileging the education of those with less familial material wealth, in 1856 the Cherokees made the decision to close their seminaries in order to protect the funding for their common schools. The same year, the national council required parents or guardians to pay the cost of food for students in the public schools, but it did not ignore the Nation's responsibility for orphans. Accepting its obligation to the most vulnerable, the council emphasized the "duty" of the board of directors for each school district to request funds from the council for the costs of food for "orphans or of children or youth whose parents are very poor." Nevertheless, the council mandated that Superintendent of Schools Walter Adair Duncan reduce the number of orphans to eighty-three and allocate them equitably among all the public schools.[115] Throughout the 1850s the number of orphans served under the law fluctuated between 110 and 120, but this mandate reduced services to thirty-four children. The council did not advise Duncan how to make these reductions. The next year Duncan reported a decline in services to orphans, but he explained that at "some of the schools the people agree among themselves to put in more orphans than are required by law, and for four of them to be reported and paid for as the law provides, and the money to be divided pro rata among all the orphans at the school."[116]

These communities agreed to suffer the economic effects together as required by a communitarian ethic rather than allow individual children to suffer. Children denied services or relocated for the purpose of equalization almost certainly faced disruption of their daily lives. Despite the council's attempts to operate a family-based system of care amenable to the Cherokee majority and administered by public officials, budgetary constraints hindered its ability to act as surrogate kin, but it did not prevent some schools from doing what the national budget could not—fulfilling social welfare obligations to all children.

Budget concerns and cuts to internal social provisions coincided with new threats to the Cherokee Nation's land base and sovereignty. In his 1857 annual message, Ross condemned Kansas governor Robert J. Walker's inaugural address, which celebrated the removal of Indians from Kansas and his suggestion that Indian Territory, "valueless to [Indians]," should be sold and opened up to "us" as a state as well as for railroad development. Walker aligned Kansas's economic interest in the breaking up of Indian Territory with Louisiana, Texas, and Arkansas. Walker aimed to link each of the states' the economic markets through railroads.[117] In official correspondence in the years that followed, Ross lambasted Kansas's audacity to include Cherokee-owned lands in its application for statehood.[118] The land in question, called the Neutral Lands, was a parcel little used by the Nation, which it had repeatedly tried to sell after 1846 to decrease its debts and infuse cash, but the federal government rejected at least two offers from the Cherokee Nation. For Kansas to claim land that the Cherokee Nation had offered to sell to the federal government frustrated Ross and the council.[119]

In the same address, Ross emphasized the national and international importance of the Cherokee Nation's institutions: "To accomplish [civilization], upon which depends such great interests, it becomes the duty of the national council to sustain and strengthen our institutions within our own limits, and to guard against every untoward encroachment." At the time, the Nation's institutions consisted of the public school system, the national court system, including its supreme court, its male and female seminaries (despite their temporary closure), and its national press. Ross also envisioned the addition of a national bank, a prison, and a library. For Ross, "the rights of soil and self-government, of free homes and self-chosen institutions" were worth the "struggles of the past," and he committed the Nation to its "defense and continuation" for the future. For Ross, institutions functioned on two levels; they were a manifestation of Cherokee sovereignty, and they fulfilled the obligations of the Nation to "establish justice, ensure tranquility, and promote the common welfare."[120]

Ross articulated a clear commitment to a "civilized" Cherokee Nation, but of equal import to Ross was the Nation's sovereign right to dictate from within the community what that civilization might look like. Ross's national vision faced significant roadblocks in the years that followed. With the seminaries closed, debts unpaid, orphan care reduced, and Kansas coveting Cherokee lands, the Cherokee Nation faced another crisis. The outbreak of the U.S. Civil War in 1861 would erase the short-term peace and prosperity achieved by the Treaty of 1846 and would reopen the old wounds and divisions connected to removal. It also ushered in a new era of Cherokee national social reforms.

CHAPTER 3

The Civil War and
Reconstruction Treaty, 1860–1868

Just fifteen years after the internal civil war that followed removal reached a conclusion, Cherokee families yet again faced the harsh realities of a divided nation and a widespread internal suspension of communitarian ethics. Forced removal survivors Turnip Vann and his father, Jim Vann, joined the Union forces. The family members of Turnip's wife, Martha, who had belonged to the Treaty Party, made different choices; her father and uncle joined the Confederates under Stand Watie. Both families replicated their removal allegiances. The two families faced each other in battle at Honey Springs.[1] Hannah Hicks, daughter of missionary Samuel Worcester and wife of Abijah Hicks, a Cherokee man, described the suffering of those who remained in the war-torn Cherokee Nation. In 1862, Pin Indians, those aligned with the Union sympathizers and committed to osdv iyunvnehi, mistakenly killed Hicks's "beloved husband." This act left her a widow with five children at the age of twenty-eight. Then Confederate soldiers arrested her brother and left her with "[her] house . . . burnt down, [her] horses, taken," and the youngest of her five children desperately ill. Her suffering was not unique. "William Spears was killed some weeks ago," she wrote in her journal. "His wife has been searching, until yesterday she succeeded in finding part of the bones and the remnants of his clothing." After Union soldiers robbed Hicks, she lamented, "I begin to think we have no true friends at all. The Federals come and give us good words, then pass right on & leave us to a far worse fate than would have been ours if they had not come." Hicks also feared an escalation of violence as rumors spread that the

Confederates "have begun to kill women and children." As the war ground to an end in the Cherokee Nation, she bemoaned conditions in the Nation: "It is pitiful, pitiful to see the desolation and distress in this Nation. Poor ruined Cherokees."[2]

The Civil War challenged Cherokee people's faith in one another and their social safety nets. The war and the treaty negotiations that followed expose the continuing consequences of colonial policy on Cherokee people. This chapter briefly outlines the events of the war itself and the social conditions in the Nation. It delves into the complex and contested treaty stipulations that resulted from internal divisions that lingered from the removal era. These negotiations served as a final moment for tribes to moderate the terms of their relationships with the federal government through treaties and to negotiate for the economic and legal apparatus to continue administering their social policies. Instead of examining the Treaty of 1866 for its political implications, though I do address those, the chapter reassesses the treaty's impact on social policy in the Nation, including the imposition of a national census, the social policy implications of adding new groups of citizens, the Nation's ability to experiment with social policy reform, and its ability to carry out unrealized social policy agendas. I pay particular attention to the selective entitlements and social provisions issued by the Cherokee Nation and those available in the form of federal pensions as a result of the Treaty of 1866. Regardless of the treaty features that diminished aspects of its sovereignty, the Cherokee Nation's leaders exacted the political, economic, and legal machinery to once again secure a "third space of sovereignty" for Cherokee people within the United States and yet outside it.[3] Within this space, the Cherokee Nation existed as a viable political entity to shape the implementation of those treaty provisions and to continue governing social policy. Additionally, individual Cherokee people were able to continue fulfilling their social welfare obligations to one another, albeit some with more social provisions available to them to do so.

Other scholars have examined the events that led to the Cherokees' participation in the Civil War. Briefly outlined, Principal Chief John Ross hoped to avoid participation in the war. Pressure mounted early when Texas and Arkansas seceded from the Union in February and

May of 1861, respectively. The federal Indian agent resigned his post and joined the Confederacy. Then the Confederacy appointed Albert Pike, an Arkansas attorney who had represented the Creek, Choctaw, and Chickasaw Nations, as its commissioner of the Office of Indian Affairs; it then authorized him to negotiate generous treaties with the tribes. When the federal government withdrew troops from Indian Territory and sporadically paid its annuities, it left tribes militarily and economically vulnerable. The Creek, Choctaw, and Chickasaw Nations all signed treaties in early July of 1861, and the Seminoles signed their treaty on August 1. Stand Watie viewed an alliance with the Confederacy as an opportunity to supplant Ross's leadership. When the Confederacy commissioned Watie as a colonel, it undermined the Nation's ability to maintain its official neutrality. In October of 1861, the Cherokee Nation was the last of the Five Tribes to conclude an alliance with the Confederacy.[4]

The U.S. Civil War destroyed the unity Ross sought to maintain. The Confederate Cherokee units segregated into Ross and Watie supporters.[5] As one of their first actions, Cherokee soldiers were ordered by the Confederacy to pursue Creek leader Opothle Yoholo's group of loyal families making their way to Kansas. Cherokees had agreed to fight Union soldiers threatening the Cherokee Nation, but they did not anticipate attacking their Indian neighbors. Consequently, many Cherokee soldiers switched sides or deserted, which plunged the Cherokee Nation into its own civil war.[6] When federal troops returned to the Cherokee Nation in 1862, they arrested and escorted Principal Chief Ross out of the Nation. Once removed, they paroled him so that he could travel to Washington to meet with President Lincoln. While away, he organized funding for Indian Home Guard units to defend Indian Territory from Confederate troops. However, during his absence elections were held. Southern Cherokees held a council in Tahlequah in August of 1862 and elected Watie principal chief. Home guard regiments unable to reenter Tahlequah until February 1863 reelected Ross and chose Lewis Downing to serve as acting chief in Ross's absence.[7]

Neither the Union nor the Confederacy provided Indian Territory soldiers with adequate provisions, which forced soldiers to pillage and steal food, equipment, and supplies. Civilians who chose not to seek refuge in Texas or Kansas as others did faced the depredations of the soldiers. Although soldiers directed physical violence toward men, they stole food and clothing from women and children, rustled livestock, laid waste to farms, and burned houses. Southern forces shot Cherokee soldiers found guilty of desertion, and other Cherokee men were wounded or killed in battle. As early as 1862, superintendent for Indian Affairs for the southern superintendency, W. G. Coffin, reported that two thousand men, women, and children were "entirely barefooted, and more than their number have not rags to hide their nakedness."[8] Food was soon in short supply, and people turned to seed corn for food, a decision that left women without seed to plant for the next year. During the war, women who adhered to subsistence-based farming and more traditional understandings of gender probably felt less disruption to their daily lives than women who engaged in domestic pursuits and whose husbands controlled agricultural pursuits and participated in a market economy.[9] However, all women feared for the lives of their male relatives and struggled to provide adequate food, shelter, and warmth to the family members who depended on them. These anxieties cut across political, class, racial, and gender boundaries.

Unlike most Cherokee men who wound up serving one side or the other, neither Walter Adair Duncan nor his brother DeWitt Clinton Duncan fought in the war. Walter Adair Duncan's wife, Martha, had died around 1858, leaving him "three little orphans."[10] Although he briefly lived in the Chickasaw Nation during the war, he later sought refuge in Rusk County, Texas, with his wife's kin, Sarah Bell Watie, a woman obligated to his children. In Rusk, he taught school, and this likely allowed him to provide for his children. Given the death the Watie family had already faced and the further losses the war promised, it is possible that Sarah Watie insisted they come; it is just as possible that he offered to bring his family there. DeWitt Clinton was attending Dartmouth at the outset of the war, and, after graduating in 1861, he moved to Wisconsin to teach before moving to Iowa where he served in local office.[11] Just as their family had done in the removal era by joining the Old Settlers in the West in 1834, Walter Adair and DeWitt Clinton escaped the brunt of the political violence that followed by leaving the Nation. John Duncan's sons, whether by design or chance, remained out of the political fray yet again.

The close of the Civil War left the Nation in nearly the same state it had been in after removal, but with new groups of citizens to care for and govern. The war left 1,200 children orphaned, ten times more served annually in the common schools between removal and the war.[12] Population losses within the Nation during this period ranged from 25 to 50 percent, mostly comprised of men.[13] Regardless of whether Cherokee families continued to adhere to a traditional social welfare system or whether they had shifted toward the use of national social provisions, sons, brothers, uncles, fathers, and husbands were (dis)abled, deceased, or suffering from the trauma associated with warfare. Unlike removal, when disease disproportionately claimed the lives of the old and the young, the Civil War ravaged all age groups, particularly Cherokee men, who served on both sides in the conflict as well as in irregular units at home.[14] In 1864, Stand Watie had passed a conscription law for boys and men between the ages of sixteen and thirty-five.[15] His oldest son, Saladin, enlisted at the age of fifteen.[16] It wasn't only combat that led to causalities; that same year, John Ross's son died in a Confederate prison.[17] A year later, Colonel George Harlan reported, "Marauding parties . . . murdered all the old men and boys large enough to aid their wives and mothers in raising a crop whom they could catch, and threatened the women with a like fate if they did not abandon their crops."[18] Soldiers were not the only causalities; famine, disease, and dislocation, as well as violence, took a heavy toll on noncombatants.[19]

By war's end, Cherokees needed desperate relief, but they were politically and geographically divided. As a result of the elections held by Confederate Cherokees in 1862 electing Stand Watie and the 1863 election that reelected Ross, two leaders claimed the right to represent the Cherokee people. Many Cherokees loyal to Chief Ross and the Union had fled to Kansas; Confederate Cherokees and their families had fled to the Chickasaw Nation and to Texas. Despite the Cherokee Nation's initial treaty with the Confederacy, more Cherokees fought with the Union in part because a significant number fought for both based on their commitment to Ross's leadership. The competing delegations arrived in Fort Smith in 1865 and again in Washington in 1866 to meet with federal officials to renegotiate treaties.

The two delegations arrived with different goals—goals that had significant implications for the social welfare provisions that would be available to Cherokee people in the years that followed. Lincoln's assassination, internal divisions, and the initial treaty signed by the Cherokee Nation, which committed its support to the Confederacy in 1861, gave U.S. officials the ammunition it needed to play one delegation against the other. This undermined the headway Ross had made the previous three years while living in Philadelphia and traveling to Washington to negotiate with President Lincoln.[20] Confederate Cherokees proposed a separate nation and were willing to concede any number of financial and legal matters to the United States to accomplish those ends.

Elected Cherokee officials and delegates to Washington recognized that railroads were coming to Indian Territory with or without their consent. The only option was to negotiate the best terms for Cherokee people. During the negotiations, members of the Southern Cherokee delegation, including Stand Watie, were willing to concede sizable right-of-ways to the federal government for railroads in their treaty proposal. Ross and his delegation actively worked to limit railroad right-of-ways in theirs.[21] Railroads, the laborers, employees, and the riffraff that came with them posed serious threats to the Cherokee Nation's jurisdictional authority and made it imperative that the federal district court adequately police Indian Territory and remove intruders, which it never did.

Union-aligned Cherokee officials responded by devising a plan to influence and benefit from railroad development. In 1866, the Cherokee National Council unanimously passed legislation to invest $500,000 in the Union Pacific Southern Division (UPSD) railroad stock and to seek two director positions on the UPSD board. The railroads would receive a one-hundred-foot right-of-way and access to timber within the Nation at a cost to be paid in cash and additional railroad stock. Profits from the investments would benefit the Cherokee Nation's treasury and infuse the Nation with the services it provided as well as with money and salaries; profits would be redistributed into national institutions. Given the fact that the Treaty of 1866 tied a proposed orphanage's budget to annuities on railroad investments, the Cherokee Nation had an even greater incentive to oversee railroad development and its success.[22]

No doubt leading men in the Nation, including William P. Ross, John Ross's nephew, planned to personally invest and benefit, but this plan ensured that the Nation would benefit as well. Elias Cornelius Boudinot, Elias Boudinot's son, who had witnessed his father's execution as a boy, was orphaned as a result, and had been raised in the northeastern United States by his non-Cherokee stepmother, also served as a treaty delegate for the Southern Cherokees. He objected to his father's political adversaries' personally profiting from the Cherokee Nation's railroad plans. Instead, Boudinot actively worked against this process in Washington. The commissioner of Indian Affairs never approved the Cherokee Nation's measure. In 1868, with the Cherokee Nation's contract with UPSD dead, Elias C. Boudinot intro- *Personal* duced a bill to create his own railroad company and incorporate "a Central Indian Railroad Company to be owned and operated by the Indians of Oklahoma."[23] Boudinot represented a group of Southern Cherokees willing to carve up the Nation's communal landholdings essential to the welfare of all Cherokee people, especially to those most tied to traditional social welfare systems, to achieve the Southern Cherokees' larger political aims. Dividing up the land, the same proposition that emerged after removal to resolve divisions, ultimately brought Southern Cherokee representatives and Union-aligned delegates together against these measures.

The prolonged negotiations that eventually favored Ross's leadership and the Union-aligned Cherokees prevented those most desperately in need from receiving aid; nonetheless, the negotiations demonstrate the continued efforts of a sovereign Cherokee Nation to maximize its ability to rebuild and to reestablish long-term safety and security for Cherokee citizens. The Treaty of 1866's final provisions had important implications for the economy and the future distribution of social provisions for both Southern and Union-aligned Cherokees.

The unequal balances of power between the Cherokees and the federal government during treaty negotiations forced Cherokees to concede aspects of its sovereign authority in order to preserve other features of it. In addition to railroad right-of-ways, another area of concession was its acquiescence to new groups of citizens. In exchange, it secured federal entitlements for Indian Home Guard veterans, maintained its ability to continue administering social provisions to vulnerable groups as it had in the post-removal era, and expanded financial provisions for education and institution-building projects.

The Cherokee Nation agreed to allow "civilized" Indians from other tribes and those tribes "friendly" to the Cherokees and the neighboring Native nations to be relocated to the Cherokee Nation and receive citizenship in the Nation. However, it specified additional financial and legal criteria that supported the Cherokee Nation's existing and planned social welfare provisions. If a group relocated as a corporate body and chose "to maintain their tribal laws, customs, and usages, not inconsistent with the constitution and laws of the Cherokee Nation," the Cherokee Nation agreed to establish a distinct district for this purpose. This scenario provided the relocated tribe with a communal land base not to exceed 160 acres per person. The provisions also permitted individual Indians to become citizens of the Cherokee Nation. In either scenario, the Cherokee Nation would receive deposits into its national fund to cover the costs of the additional social services the Nation would need to administer.[24]

These provisions shed important light on the competing aims of the Cherokee Nation and the federal government during the negotiations. The Cherokee Nation acknowledged the importance of traditional social and legal welfare systems of Indian peoples and created a geographic and legal space for those systems to operate. The 160-acre-per-person land designation signaled the next phase of the federal government's Indian policy, breaking up communal landholdings into individual allocations of land.

The negotiations and provisions for Indian citizens shared some of the same language of citizenship as sections related to freedmen, but the freedmen's provisions did not come with the same financial contributions to its national fund or any legal accommodations for traditional social welfare practices. In essence, the Cherokee Nation developed a system of social citizenship that accommodated and funded provisions for different groups in different ways. According to the treaty, Indian citizens would "be incorporated into and ever after remain a part of the Cherokee Nation, on equal terms in every respect with native citizens." Cherokee freedmen, similar to any new Indian citizens, received "all the rights of native Cherokees" in the treaty.[25] The treaty extended citizenship to those who previously had been slaves of Cherokee citizens and who were living in the Nation at the outbreak of the Civil War. If they had left the Nation, as many were forced to do when those who owned slaves fled to the Chickasaw Nation and Texas, they had to return within six months of the war's end to establish their citizenship. They then became subject to the laws of the Cherokee Nation like other Cherokee citizens.

However, the Cherokee Nation and the federal government disagreed over who would decide issues of citizenship. In 1869, the national council passed legislation empowering the Supreme Court to determine Cherokee citizenship claims. The Cherokee Nation would ultimately establish a citizenship committee in 1879. These citizenship decisions determined which government, that of the Cherokee Nation or of the United States, governed and had the social, legal, and economic obligations to the individuals. Freedmen residing in the Cherokee Nation who did not qualify for Cherokee citizenship became subject to federal law.[26] Given the lack of federal social provisions offered by the U.S. government, for practical purposes any freedmen ejected from the Cherokee Nation relied on the rights available to and social provisions offered in the state they chose to reside in. If the Cherokee Nation admitted individuals to citizenship, in theory, they gained access to national social provisions including communal landholdings and public education. Because article 13 of the treaty guaranteed the Cherokee Nation "exclusive jurisdiction in all civil and criminal cases" that only involved Cherokee citizens, determining rightful claimants to freedmen citizenship was critical. Article 7 established a federal district court in Indian Territory to manage cases involving non-Indians, a provision the Cherokee Nation favored. Cherokee officials believed the court's presence enabled the federal government to fulfill its legal responsibilities as guardian to the Cherokee Nation. The federal government had a legal obligation to protect the Cherokee Nation from "foreign enemies" and "against interruption and intrusion from citizens of the United States,

who may attempt to settle in the country without their consent."
The United States consented to remove "all such persons . . . by order
of the President."[27] The federal government's selective enforcement
and inadequate funding of this provision had major implications for
the Cherokee Nation's ability to administer social services properly
in the years ahead.

There is no doubt that those vying for political leadership in the
post–Civil War era included the distribution of social provisions into
their political calculus.[28] John Ross's death in August of 1866 and
Stand Watie's advanced age provided an opening to reconfigure the
political parties based for the first time in thirty-five years on something other than removal era divides. When Ross died, Downing, as
acting president of the council, temporarily assumed the office of
principal chief. Then, in October of 1866, the council chose Princeton-
educated William P. Ross, John Ross's nephew, to replace his uncle.[29]
This provided a short-term continuity of John Ross's policy, but
offered little assurance to Southern Cherokees or to more traditional
Cherokees, who had less confidence in the nephew than the uncle,
that reunification with the Nation was possible.

Downing demonstrated the ability to merge osdv iyunvnehi with
prudent national concerns. During treaty negotiations with the United
States, Downing had opposed exclusion of either Southern Cherokees or freedmen. Downing sought to restore balance to the community through consensus building. In advance of the 1867 election,
he reached out to members of the Southern Cherokees in order to
move beyond the internal hostilities that had embroiled the Nation
since removal and no doubt because he needed their support for his
candidacy against William P. Ross. In his view, institutional opportunities provided one means of bringing Southern Cherokees back
into the national fold.[30] He insisted that Reconstruction institutions
promised to blot out "every line of distinction. . . . We should be one
in our laws, one in our institutions, one in feeling and one in destiny."[31]

In 1867, the Nation's voters elected Lewis Downing as their new
principal chief. In keeping with the sentiments of John Ross and
Treaty Party leaders, Downing, a monolingual Cherokee speaker, a
Baptist, and a lawyer, put his faith in the ability of national institutions to secure and protect the Cherokee Nation and its people. He

would oversee efforts to ameliorate relationships between Southern Cherokees and the National Party through institution building. In order to accomplish his reunification goals, he selected individuals who were amenable to members of both parties to lead these efforts. Downing chose Walter Adair Duncan to serve as the first superintendent of the orphanage. Duncan occupied a politically moderate and conciliatory space as a result of his service to Ross's executive committee in 1855; his ministerial service to rural, traditional, and monolingual communities in the Nation; his absence from Civil War service; and his ongoing commitments to education. As a result of his experiences, Duncan was able to clearly articulate why be believed that all Cherokee people should support institutions, and this clear articulation would serve the Cherokee Nation in the years ahead.

Downing's intention to use institutions to deliver social provisions as one means of national reunification set it apart from the federal government's post–Civil War approach to social provision. The Civil War had been devastating to both North and South; at least 620,000 men in the United States lost their lives through disease, battle, and infection while others were left maimed and (dis)abled.[32] By 1866, U.S. public officials, women's auxiliaries, and military personnel worked together to establish federal soldiers' homes to care for (dis)abled veterans. The following year, three regional branches had been established, the eastern branch at Augusta, Maine, the central branch at Dayton, Ohio, and the northwestern branch at Milwaukee, Wisconsin.[33] By 1888, the federal government would operate sixteen homes that served sixteen thousand men.[34] The selective criteria for pensions excluded Confederates. Confederates also lacked access to the residential services provided by the national homes for veterans throughout the final two decades of the 1800s.[35]

The federal government's limited foray into federal provisions, with the exception of military pensions, left most families to rely on states, mutual aid societies, and private individuals to provide resources for recovery.[36] With the exception of federal pensions, which would comprise 40 percent of the federal budget in 1893, the federal government limited postwar social provision to land grants, a small number of asylums, and the relatively short-lived Freedmen's Bureau. This would remain the case until the New Deal.[37] Within states, state, private, and local agencies provided social services to veterans, children, the (dis)abled, and the poor.

Institutionally administered social provisions appealed to Cherokees, especially elite and middle-class Cherokees, but the federal pensions available to Union-aligned Cherokees as a result of the Treaty of 1866 also ensured financial resources for Cherokees most committed to osdv iyunvnehi. Like their Union counterparts, Cherokees who fought for the Union qualified for federal pensions that aided their recovery, but neither states nor the federal government considered Cherokee people citizens; they therefore lacked eligibility for the institutional services available outside the Cherokee Nation.

The national social provisions available for Confederate families and southerners followed a more complicated trajectory. Despite the Confederate states' purported opposition to an overreaching centralized government, over the course of the war the Confederacy provided extensive poor relief to soldiers' families after a public outcry, particularly from yeoman farmers whose families depended on them and whose wives could not sustain farms without them.[38]

During Reconstruction, Confederate poor relief suffered. The percentage of spending from southern state budgets on social services for veterans and their families would remain minimal from the 1870s to the 1880s, even as Union states' budgets for pensions increased significantly. When former Confederates regained control of their state legislatures, they began allocating resources to Confederate Veterans through widows' and soldiers' pensions as well as through the construction of Confederate soldiers' homes. Governors appointed the state officials who evaluated claimants and distributed poor relief. In Florida, every governor from 1885 to 1900 would be a former Confederate, and the state would fund its services through property taxes on landowners. African American landowners, who owned relatively small amounts of land, contributed taxes to the state services that they were systematically denied.[39]

The unraveling of Reconstruction efforts dismantled many of the social provisions available to African Americans and poor whites in the South at the national and state levels. Even though African Americans obtained history-making political representation during the Reconstruction era, "nowhere did blacks control the workings of state government" and nowhere did representation reflect total populations.[40] After the Freedmen's Bureau ended in 1868, which had provided legal services, employment negotiations, and medical services, African Americans relied far more heavily on one another, churches, privately funded institutions, and white benefactors to provide social services. For example, the Jenkins Orphanage, which would open in 1891 in Charleston, South Carolina, provided a home, a school, and "reform" to African American boys.[41] The end of the Freedmen's Bureau, with the exception of educational services, left African Americans at the mercy of the southern courts, peonage labor, and the uneven beneficence of their white southern neighbors. At the same time, selective entitlements to Union-aligned white men and their families and a limited number of African American veterans in the North expanded.

Though Downing intended to "blot out all distinctions" among Cherokees through institutional social services, the institutional services offered and those necessary for different groups of Cherokees were not the same. He faced the reality that the types and amounts of economic support within and outside the Nation were not universally accessible to all Cherokees. As spaces for reunification, institutions could provide services and employment to Cherokee people regardless of wartime affiliation.

Downing also faced the reality that the desire or lack of desire for national social provisions and prewar social policies had a direct bearing on Cherokee people's access to opportunities for newly available social provisions after the war. Employment opportunities created by institutions required a range of skills, not all of which every Cherokee possessed. Regardless of wartime affiliation, Cherokee families who were former slaveholders possessed far more wealth and had far greater institutional and educational access before and after the war than many of their nonslaveholding counterparts, and this afforded them many of the skills and experiences necessary to serve as institutional administrators and employees. The Cherokee Nation had denied enslaved African Cherokees access to the public schools before the war, and sympathetic missionaries and individual families had provided limited educational opportunities to slaves. This limited the professional opportunities for most African Cherokee citizens. The availability of federal pensions for many people who abided by osdv iyunvnehi supplemented the incomes of many families and decreased their need for institutional provisions.

Because Cherokee families had failed to conform to the definitions and expectations imposed by the federal government's pension laws, some Cherokee families had lost access to War of 1812 pensions, a circumstance the Cherokee Nation sought to avoid after the Civil War. The Cherokee Nation recognized that (dis)abled and deceased soldiers had familial and community obligations regardless of whether the federal government acknowledged the legitimacy of those responsibilities. Rather than allow the monies of heirless deceased soldiers to be lost, the Treaty of 1866 directed deceased soldiers' bounties and back pay into its orphanage fund. The Nation may not have been able to force the federal government to acknowledge its family systems, but it could at least secure funds to support those without families. This provision meant that those Cherokee Union soldiers' deaths without families would benefit all Cherokee orphans. This was consistent with a community ethos that spread resources around to minimize the negative impact to a single individual. In this case, the children left behind were Cherokee children, and wartime affiliation bore no consideration when it came to their care.

This provision was a significant step toward national reunification and restorative balance through the use of the Nation's institutionally administered social provisions, but it also marked a departure from the previous system, which preserved families as the primary unit of care and conceivably gave matrilineal, bilateral relatives, or the people they trusted who were "convenient to a school" the ability to step forward as caregivers. In 1866, the council appointed a committee to "arrange and negotiate" with churches to establish an orphanage as it had tried to do and failed to accomplish in the prewar era.

In order to comply with treaty obligations and in an effort to assess the true needs of its children for the purpose of establishing the Nation's orphanage, the national council authorized its first nationally administered census to determine the number of orphans between the ages of five and fifteen.[42] The time-consuming nature of the census that took place in 1868 prevented any immediate action, but it secured the necessary information for the development of the orphanage. In the meantime, the council continued to appropriate funds for clothing and boarding orphans through the common schools even as it moved forward with its plans for an orphanage.[43]

James Scott posits the introduction of a census is a key step in modern statecraft. It represents the efforts of national authorities to attempt to exert power and influence over people; in a sense, the Cherokee Nation's implementation of a census fits his model. Federal officials had imposed numerous censuses on Cherokees over the years to better understand who Cherokee people were, what resources they possessed, and to whom the federal government needed to pay for certain expropriations of property. These censuses never represented the full diversity or richness of Cherokee society. Cherokee people realized the limitations and often-nefarious purposes attached to census data. In light of this, the Cherokee Nation used its 1866 treaty negotiations to claim control of the census process. Cherokee control of the census enabled Cherokee officials to obfuscate information that might limit its sovereign authority or hinder Cherokee people's continued abilities to perform their social welfare obligations. But the census still performed a statecraft function for the Cherokee Nation. It still provided details that enabled it to "monitor, account, assess, and manage Cherokee people" in a way that it had not before.[44]

Census takers also created a new category for understanding who Cherokee people were and what their needs were. The 1867 census identified what Scott would call "heretofore unknown truths" when some census takers recorded different categories of Cherokees with (dis)abilities, though it was clear that a standard terminology did not exist to document these individuals. One district's census documented "unfortunates." The Illinois District reported one blind, one "dumb alone," and two people who were both hearing impaired and unable to speak living in the district. The Third Educational District counted two blind, two hearing and speech impaired, and one unable to speak.[45] It is unclear whether these numbers included only children or children and adults, an important distinction necessary in considering how those Cherokees tasked with completing the census defined dependency in this period. Many districts failed to report any "unfortunates," but if the two districts are representative and the average was 4.5 per district, the total number of "unfortunates" in the nine districts totaled slightly over forty. If these numbers only accounted for school-age children, and did not include adult populations, the actual numbers would have been higher. The inconsistency of the data provided suggests that census takers disagreed over the relevance of the data and the task to which they were assigned.

These designations suggest that either individual census takers or national officials directing census takers viewed Cherokees with physical differences as (dis)abled and in need of special care or services not provided by families. This belief mapped on to larger reform agendas in the United States that sought to provide individuals with (dis)abilities educational opportunities that would enable them to gain skills and possibly pursue employment.[46] The inconsistency in reporting suggests that some census takers chose to report based on personal understandings of the reform efforts needed as opposed to a simple counting of children residing in the Nation.

The recording of this data by census takers also likely stemmed from knowledge of the Nation's distribution of Cherokee national pensions, which resumed in 1866 and increased in the years ahead. From 1866 to 1876, the Nation distributed pensions to persons labeled "crippled," "blind," "elderly," and "infirm." The council authorized at least one payment to a widow, but the vast majority of recipients who received pensions had some form of physical (dis)ability.[47] The absence of women's widows' pensions suggests that becoming a widow produced different economic outcomes for Cherokee women. These requests indicate that Cherokee people's expectations of the roles and responsibilities of the Nation were expanding to include care for people who had previously been served by osdv iyunvnehi.[48]

In contrast, federal policy offered no provisions for civilians. It provided military pensions to veterans with (dis)abilities based on the belief that a man's (dis)ability prohibited the individual from contributing to the economic life of the family by working. In theory, because federal policy makers viewed men as the breadwinners, (dis)abled married men warranted financial support more than (dis)abled women, who officials presumed had a father or husband responsible for their care.

Beginning in 1829, the Cherokee Nation had signaled a willingness to provide civilians with pensions. The post–Civil War national pensions as well as other onetime social provisions mark a continuation of that earlier tendency by the Nation to provide care and assistance to Cherokee people in need. The number of people seeking national assistance documents the effects of the Civil War on traditional social welfare. The war likely weakened functioning kinship systems for some Cherokee families and certainly compromised the spirit of gadugi that encouraged Cherokee people to care for one another before the war. In two instances, the Nation paid for funeral expenses. One of these funerals in 1870 was for "Wah la ne da, a stranger, who was temporarily in Tahlequah" and for whom there was no one "present to take charge of the corpse."[49] The deceased's family was unable to assume responsibility for burial, so the Nation stepped in. However, economic realities limited its ability to expand the distributions as far as it might have otherwise. Instead, individual national pensions and select social provision expenditures served as a limited response to the exigencies created by war.

Even as the Cherokee Nation under Principal Chief Downing's leadership experimented with expanding selective entitlements to other classes of citizens, federal selective entitlement policies influenced the availability and access to selective entitlements within the Nation. Downing's tenure overlapped with efforts to secure the selective entitlements granted to Union-aligned soldiers that were not available to other Cherokee people.

Since their 1816 negotiations for War of 1812 pensions, Cherokee leaders had paid attention to federal pension law in order to advocate on behalf of Cherokee people. In the post-removal era, Cherokee national officials and citizens had aided each other in applying for or revising federal pension applications. The Cherokee Nation had modified its guardianship laws and procedures in order to streamline the federal pension process for those entitled to War of 1812 pensions and to better enable Cherokee Nation officials to act on an individual's behalf. For example, Principal Chief Ross submitted a list of soldiers entitled to pensions and the estimated amount they were owed to federal authorities. In 1843, Ross served as a witness to The Blanket's service and injury during the Battle of Horseshoe Bend. When The Blanket died, the Cherokee Nation had appointed Thomas Wolfe the guardian of The Blanket's children. Wolfe filed an application on the children's behalf for their pension as minor dependent children.[50] In 1851, William Barnes, an intermarried white citizen of the Nation, also filed an application to modify his partial (dis)ability from a gunshot wound to a total (dis)ability.[51] Ross had also urged federal officials to provide pensions as "early as practicable."[52] By the time the monies were finally distributed in the 1850s, many of those entitled to payments were dead, including The Blanket and The Beaver, who had died during removal.[53] When the Nation received the funds, Ross distributed them to living veterans, widows, and their heirs. In some cases, Ross personally benefitted from the distributions. Ross and his business partner had advanced many families store credit in anticipation of the payments.[54] It is unclear from Ross's records, how much, if any, interest he charged. Regardless, the securing of modified federal pensions represented a tangible way for the Cherokee national government to protect and serve citizens when national funds tied to removal had remained frozen.

In the post–Civil War era, Cherokee political leaders once again mediated the challenges that federal pension law created for Cherokee people. Other than eliminating Confederates, federal pension laws lacked any inherently discriminatory stipulations based on race or ethnicity. However, a new generation of Cherokee people had to navigate the same gendered economic practices that privileged male heads of households and required Cherokee people to legitimize their social and familial practices to non-Cherokee agents. This complicated the pension process for many families. Widows had to prove the legality of their marriages, and children had to prove they were legitimate heirs.[55] In spite of an 1855 Cherokee Nation law that required Cherokee couples to marry and divorce before a recognized authority that could document the actions, Cherokee people had continued to abide by traditional laws and make and break unions without government sanction. Within the Nation, violating the law had very few consequences. As tradition dictated, married couples commonly had different surnames or no surnames at all.[56] Despite the difficulties of securing petitions under these circumstances, an 1866 list of eligible pensioners submitted to the Department of the Interior included Akego, widow of Swimmer; Betsey Glass, widow of Henry Morgan; Ca her kah, minor of Middlestriker; and Grass, an invalid.[57]

Moreover, others may not have applied as the expenses related to pension applications proved prohibitive to many Cherokees. In 1867, for example, Betsey Still, widow of Cook Still, made five separate trips to Fort Gibson, a distance of fifty miles from her home, to attend to her application. Applicants also presumably had to bear the cost of witnesses who appeared on a claimant's behalf. When, on one trip to Fort Gibson, Mrs. Still presented herself to collect the money she was due, the attorney handling the claim asked her "to go and get two loyal men" to verify her husband's enlistment. She secured witnesses, but instead of asking them any questions, the attorney informed Mrs. Still that her husband was a deserter and that she was not entitled to payment.[58] Like many Cherokees, Still had probably returned home to help with his family without a formal discharge. Another challenge for many petitioners was access to a board of physicians to validate injuries related to service.[59]

The daunting pension process led many people to rely on the services of attorneys, notaries, and claim agents who filled out the paperwork and forwarded it to Washington, D.C., to be processed.[60] Non-Indian claim agents and attorneys proved to be problematic. As Theda Skocpol's work documents, fraud would become a political talking point for the Democrats during the 1880s. It was difficult to determine how deep and wide the problems of pension fraud ran. It was up to investigators to identify fraudulent cases, and commitments to careful audits waxed and waned based on political and economic supports for investigations. However, Skocpol points out that investigators honed in on the applications of particular groups, including "'cowardly veterans,' blacks" and especially widows.[61] Though Skocpol makes no mention of Indians as prime suspects of pension fraud, Indian people also faced scrutiny.

However, the Cherokee Nation's intervention shielded many Cherokee people from the targeted investigations aimed at politically vulnerable pensioners. In 1872, for example, the federal government launched an investigation into the activities of attorney John W. Wright. In 1865, Wright had presented himself to the Office of Indian Affairs on behalf of the Cherokee Nation and Cherokee Nation citizens to collect bounties, back pay, and pensions due them. He posted bond in the amount of $100,000. Seven years later, federal authorities suspected Wright of fraud in excess of $150,000. Such claims agents often preyed upon legitimate claimants. Even more unscrupulous men sought to increase payments to claimants and therefore their share, which was a percentage of the lump sum.[62]

Fraud exasperated an already-challenging pension process given the failure of pension laws to match the realities of Cherokee society. William P. Ross, who by 1874 was again principal chief, petitioned Congress that year to challenge the large numbers of Indian soldiers marked as deserters and denied pensions as a result. Ross pointed out that many soldiers possessed "a very imperfect knowledge of the English language," and that when they requested short-term leave to care for family or to be treated for illness, white officers marked them as deserters. Furthermore, Cherokees did not normally receive medical treatment from military hospitals, so there was less documentary record of their illnesses as there would be for white soldiers.[63] The investigation into Wright's fraudulent activities, for example, acknowledged that the "peculiar habits of the Indians, the character of their marriage laws, and the difficulty of settling questions involving the legitimacy of their children" prevented many Indians and their families from receiving the pensions to which they were entitled.[64] Cherokee soldiers represented a broad cross section of Cherokee society, and no one group was spared the difficulties of receiving their pensions. As late as 1882, the war records and pay of former Principal Chief Lewis Downing, by then deceased, would remain contested.[65]

To combat the potential for fraud by the influx of non-Cherokee people seeking to capitalize on Cherokee pension claims, the Cherokee national press assumed responsibility for disseminating important information regarding pensions. In January of 1871, the *Cherokee Advocate* printed a comprehensive list of the names of pensioners who had received payments in order to determine whether payments went "to the rightful claimants or not." A secondary list of claimants who had filed applications in the Washington, D.C., pension office but who had not yet been evaluated also appeared.[66] In 1873, to aid Cherokees in gaining access to the "Examining Surgeon for Pensions," the *Advocate* published the name and location to "all concerned" for the newly appointed physician.[67] The role of the Nation's newspaper as well as the national council in seeking pensions for and preventing swindling of Cherokee Nation citizens followed the tradition, dating to the pre-removal period, of concern for those unable to care for themselves. What had changed was the scope of the problem. The Civil War had left so many Cherokees widowed, orphaned, (dis)abled, and impoverished that public efforts to secure individual pensions became a national cause.

Federal pension law ultimately adapted to meet the needs of diverse family systems and their economic realities. The federal pension modifications, which would be approved in June of 1874, included several sections aimed at nonwhite pensioners; two of the provisions applied specifically to Indians. The first one, which concerned "widows of colored and Indian soldiers," recognized undocumented marriages of couples who "were joined in marriage by some ceremony deemed by them obligatory, or habitually recognized each other as man or wife, and were so recognized by their neighbors." Another section, "Indian claims," extended the application period for two years and validated documentation by Indian agents or an "officer of any tribe, competent according to the rules of said tribe to administer oaths."[68]

This last provision mandated what was already common practice on the part of Cherokee national officials. Petitioners for pensions in the Cherokee Nation often relied on the assistance from other Cherokee Nation citizens to aid them in the process. In her 1867 application for a widow's pension, Betsey Still sought the aid of Spencer Stephens, a graduate of the male seminary and a public schoolteacher to "make out the necessary papers."[69] She later called upon "Allen Ross and Hendrix" to act as witnesses on her behalf.[70] James Hendricks, a Cherokee judge, likely the same Hendrix to whom Still had appealed for help, kept records of Cherokee pensioners and copies of federal pension laws in his files.[71] Stephens and Hendricks [Hendrix] acted as good neighbors and fellow citizens, but they also were employees of the Nation, which gave their support of Still an official imprimatur.

The Civil War pension process had become a truly national effort on the part of the Cherokees. At the local level, Cherokees joined together to help their fellow citizens secure the support to which they were entitled. In 1865, Captain Christie submitted affidavits for James Shave Head's widow, Watty.[72] The same year, Captain Spring Frog supplied affidavits for Go ne chu squah le's widow, Tah nee, and Ske no yah's widow, Too kah.[73] Lewis Downing and Joshua Ross also furnished affidavits for widows. In 1873, Walter Adair Duncan provided the evidence of marriage for Polly Downing.[74] Tu ta Big Talker testified the same year that Downing performed the marriage ceremony.[75] Cousins and brothers of deceased soldiers provided affidavits for family members. Military officers, national officials, ministers, family members, neighbors, men, women, Cherokees literate in English, Cherokee, or both, and the illiterate all provided affidavits, interpreted, and served as witnesses to aid other Cherokees in obtaining pensions. Indeed, drawing the line between official and individual actions is almost impossible, a circumstance that demonstrates how embedded personal notions of helping the unfortunate were in national government.

As they had after the War of 1812, Cherokee national officials lobbied the federal government on behalf of veterans and their families and pressed the federal government to acknowledge a range of social practices. The Cherokee Nation's willingness to recognize the continuation of traditional marriage practices at odds with its own national laws provides evidence that the Cherokee Nation had in fact perpetuated, as the 1835 Removal Treaty stated, "a state of society as may be most consonant with their views, habits and condition."[76] The Cherokee Nation used national institutions to encourage elements of Euro-American "civilization," but it was reticent to use its legal apparatus to coerce changes in families that did not threaten the economic or sovereign status of the Nation. Even though the United States distributed pensions based on the imagined and endorsed male-headed household, once Cherokee families received the funds they could choose to use them to support the family systems they chose.

From the Cherokee Nation's perspective, pensions supported the economic well-being of the Nation.

Despite the systematized ways pension distributions undermined matrilineality and supported the reordering of Cherokee families, pensions sustained diverse family systems and the traditional social services present in the Cherokee Nation in the post–Civil War period. Even though post-removal guardianship laws favored biological fathers' rights over matrilineal kin and gave the Nation the authority to privilege patriarchal and patrilocal families and guardianships if it chose to, it did not. For instance, in 1865, Jane See Kee Kee was appointed guardian of Moses Vann's children.[77] In 1868, Jane Path Killer acted as William Bump's four children's guardian.[78] John Tadpole took in his brother Crossing Tadpole's children.[79] Frog Sixkiller, a neighbor, took in Jackson Rail's children after Rail's wife Anna died in 1868.[80] The Nation could have used this as an opportunity to turn to missionaries to act as guardians, but it did not. Cherokee courts granted guardianships not based on gendered legal norms or family structures represented by Cherokee elites or U.S. officials, but based on families' or an individual's willingness and commitment to care for the children. Instead of radically re-altering Cherokee families, pensions and guardianships reflected the practical demographic realities of the postwar period and supported a range of family structures through the community ethic still present, though recovering, in the Cherokee Nation.

The Treaty of 1866 did not include all of the possible social protections the Cherokee Nation had hoped to obtain. It contained provisions that undermined aspects of its sovereignty, including its ability to determine its own citizens without duress and its ability to exercise control over railroad corporations entering the Nation and the corporate policies that would severely impact life in the Nation in the years ahead. Yet, the Treaty of 1866 sustained the communal land base, secured funding for long-discussed reforms in national social policy that would develop in the years ahead, and secured access to federal military pensions for Union-aligned soldiers. Despite the fact individual Cherokee people experienced hardships in obtaining the pensions to which they were entitled, the Cherokee Nation's initial

advocacy for pensions after the War of 1812 and its continued lobbying efforts on behalf of Cherokee people after the Civil War resulted
in equitable access to pensions for all Indian soldiers. New federal
pension laws extended legal protections and recognition of Native
nations' family laws that federal pension law had previously disregarded and villainized.

CHAPTER 4

Strengthening Our Institutions, 1869–1877

The Treaty with the Cherokee in 1866 reestablished a nation-to-nation agreement between the Cherokee Nation and the United States. It also ushered in a new stage in Cherokee national social policy. The treaty provided the economic provisions necessary to rebuild the Nation after the Civil War. Specifically, it provided funds to support residential institutions for orphans and (dis)abled Cherokees. However, Cherokee people had also long debated (and at times approved) the need to build a national prison. The Cherokee Nation constructed these new institutions at the same moment new groups of citizens sought access to social provisions. Agreeing to, designing, constructing, and administering new social policies, especially establishing institutions, were not easy tasks. However, given the foreboding territorialization provisions contained in the Treaty of 1866; the arrival of railroads; and another shift in federal Indian policy to the reservation system, confining tribes to bounded spaces controlled by often-corrupt U.S. military personnel, the vast majority of Cherokee people recognized the need to sustain the Nation. Serving the Nation required a careful negotiation between the needs and desires of the community and pragmatic realties of operating under an increasingly menacing federal system. Because of their successful efforts to maintain the sovereignty of the Nation, Cherokee leaders were able to look within the Nation to identify those who could lead their social reforms.

This chapter outlines the social policy changes that followed the Treaty of 1866. It examines new legal and bureaucratic mechanisms

introduced under the auspices of public or social welfare and considers their political and economic purposes and results as well—in
particular, I focus on the New Codes, legal reforms prompted by the
need to manage residentially administered social provisions. The
New Codes included laws that governed the Nation's new Cherokee Medical Board and impacted the practice of medicine in the
Cherokee Nation. The Nation also introduced institutions to protect
groups of Cherokees classed as especially vulnerable, orphans and
Cherokees with (dis)abilities or mental illness, *and* to protect Cherokee people from other Cherokees. It acquired, remodeled, and built
structures for its Cherokee Orphan Asylum, Asylum for the Deaf,
Dumb, Blind, and Insane, and National Prison. This simultaneously
represented the continuation of proposed, yet unrealized, social policy
reforms and the possibility of serious rupture with adherents of osdv
iyunvnehi, who would likely object to overly coercive social policy
measures. Because of this, Principal Chief Lewis Downing's role in
institution building becomes even more significant when one considers that his political support included those more committed to
traditional social welfare practices.

Because a social policy existed to guide the care of orphans and
Cherokees reached relative consensus that children were a social
service priority, services to orphans resumed quickly under the Nation's
old policies. Chief Downing had used the data from the 1867 children's census and the collaboration with the Methodist Church to
develop a plan for its orphanage. In the meantime, by 1871 the superintendent of the common schools reported, "There are now 236
orphans provided for in private families by means of the orphan
fund."[1] That figure accounts for only 20 percent of the 1,200 children
made orphans by the war, and, although five years had passed since
the children's census, it suggests that orphans were being neglected
by the Nation's orphan services. However, because families, census
takers, Cherokee officials, and federal authorities likely defined orphans
differently, the figure of 1,200 may have been problematic to begin
with. By 1871, it is more than likely that extended families took a
portion of those children in, as kinship dictated. It is improbable that
all of the children counted were in fact orphans based on traditional
kinship practices. Because schooling was not compulsory, other

children were likely in families, but not attending school. Some families that took in orphans may not have sought funds for their care. It is almost certain that not all those children classified as orphans were equally in need, but certainly more than the 20 percent receiving orphan educational services were. The orphanage could address this outstanding need.

Rather than turn control of its social policy administration over to the Methodists or any other denomination as federal Indian policy dictated for tribes being confined to reservations, the Cherokee Nation profited from the presence of Native preachers with the professional experiences to administer services.[2] As planning for an orphanage progressed, the Nation selected Walter Adair Duncan to continue charting a course for institutional development.

The choice of Duncan represents a symbolic moment in Cherokee nation-building efforts meant to create a hybrid social service system. In a sense, Cherokee national social policy and Duncan had developed in the same womb and had matured side by side. Duncan had borne witness to unspeakable tragedies in his lifetime, but he had placed those events in a historical context and committed himself to national service. He was the fourth of ten children born before removal around 1823 in the Old Nation, in what is today Georgia. His birth nearly coincided with the Cherokee Nation's adoption of its constitution in 1827, and his father John Duncan signed that document.[3] Duncan's parents' firsthand knowledge of the failure of the United States' earlier allotment schemes, and of Georgia's dereliction of its duties to protect residents' life, liberty, and property, informed their decision to remove to the West in 1834, when, as a teenager, Duncan and his family had joined the Old Settlers. As a young man, he had witnessed the post-removal Cherokee Nation tear itself apart through violent civil strife as Cherokees sought solace for the countless family members lost as a direct result of forced removal. Duncan had served as an itinerant minister for the Methodist Episcopal Church throughout the 1840s.[4] He would never turn away from Methodism, but, like many Cherokee Methodists, "Cherokee nationalism" was as potent a force as "Cherokee Methodism."[5]

Despite Duncan's close associations with the Southern Cherokees, his wider experiences connected him to Cherokee people from every background; this and his professional experiences made him an ideal candidate to act as the orphanage's first superintendent. For example, Duncan had served as superintendent for the Methodist's Honey Hill School in 1871.[6] As an ordained elder and former president of the Cherokee Board of Education, Duncan understood the financial strains faced by church schools, management challenges within national schools, and the responsibilities heaped on superintendents in their roles as "farmers, contractors, government agents, sawmill builders and operators, log cutters and haulers, blacksmiths, carpenters and general mediators between the Indians, their chiefs, and the United States authorities, both civil and military."[7]

As a Cherokee citizen and official, he understood the political, social, economic, and educational concerns of monolingual subsistence-based farmers, western-educated Cherokee elites, Cherokees who had owned one slave, and those who had managed plantations with fifty or more slaves. With the exception of his one term as senator from the Flint District in the 1850s and his service as a member of Ross's executive council in 1855, Duncan remained outside the political mainstream. When the common schools faced economic shortfalls in 1856, as the superintendent of schools, Duncan was assigned the task of reducing orphan services. Even if he had no hand in the decisions by some of the schools to maintain services to all the children at reduced, but equitable amounts, he had witnessed gadugi in action. Duncan's service to the Methodist Indian Mission Conference suggests that he was at least knowledgeable about and more than likely closely connected to earlier efforts to contract orphan services with the Methodist Church in the post-removal era.

In March of 1872, the orphan asylum opened at the Cherokee Male Seminary building, a temporary location until the seminary could reopen and a permanent location could be selected. It opened with fifty-four male and female students. Given the familiarity with missionary boarding schools within the community, it is not surprising that the Cherokee Nation's orphanage superficially fit patterns of institutional orphan services that emerged in non-Indian communities. The first North American orphan asylum had opened in New Orleans in 1739, but the growth of orphan asylums exploded in the period after the Civil War even though many social reformers had become skeptical of institutional outcomes.[8] Civil War deaths, particularly of soldiers, forced states, communities, and organizations to rethink their responsibilities to orphans and half-orphans, children with only one living parent. The loss of husbands, fathers, and brothers or those who returned with physical (dis)abilities after the war required many women to work outside the home for the first time. Families with less material wealth had often relied on the income of all family members. Mothers in these circumstances faced a precarious employment situation, and domestic service, one of few opportunities for poor urban women, often required live-in arrangements that kept mothers away from their children.[9] Soldiers' orphans' homes emerged in the Civil War era to aid the large number of children left half-orphaned by war.[10]

Industrialization, urbanization, and immigration exacerbated the problem of children's services even for two-parent families, many of whom became incapable of providing for their children as a result of dislocation and poverty. From the 1830s to the 1880s, orphan asylums constituted the most popular means to care for children whose parents could not raise them, whether as a result of death or circumstance.[11] Trustees, reformers, and social workers aimed to create homelike institutions based on the middle-class cult of domesticity. The cult of domesticity privileged the importance of the domestic sphere and the role of mothers in establishing a proper environment in which children could develop into productive citizens.[12]

Orphan services also raised new political and bureaucratic questions within the Cherokee Nation. The male seminary provided a temporary site for the coeducational orphanage, but only until a permanent facility could be located.[13] The politics behind this decision slowed the process down and converged with other questions raised by the push to build institutions.

Even though it had been envisioned by Ross and had been debated legislated, and budgeted by council in the pre–Civil War period, the Cherokee National Prison's future remained uncertain in the postwar period. A national prison was the one institution the Nation had not provided funding for in any of its treaty provisions, and the project, though a part of older social reform agendas, had not moved forward since the financial crises of the 1850s. In December of 1871, the Cherokee Senate failed to pass a jail bill that would have begun construction on the jail proposed by John Ross two decades earlier. The main objection was the expense, although the guards opposed the measure out of concern for their salaries.

There may have been other reasons for the bill's failure. Incarceration stood at odds with the freedom of movement and autonomy Cherokee people prized. For the Eastern Cherokees, who had been subjected to imprisonment in Georgia or Tennessee or had experienced the stockades before forced removal, imprisonment represented the worst experiences with "civilized" society the Cherokee people had faced. Elite Cherokee men like John Ross had embraced its place in the Nation as a marker of civilization and its sovereign responsibilities to protect Cherokee people. Ross's adversaries may have opposed it over concerns that they would find themselves locked in it.

In the postwar years, resentments lingered between members of the Keetoowah Society, a traditionalist group that had supported Chief John Ross and fought for the Union, and Southern Cherokees. Intermarried white citizens who had aligned with the Southern Cherokees were more than willing to take advantage of the antagonistic federal court in Arkansas to exasperate attempts by the Nation to reestablish jurisdictional control over citizens. In April of 1872, five months after the jail bill failed, federal marshals arrived at the Goingsnake District courthouse to take custody of Cherokee citizen Zeke Proctor, a Keetoowah, who was accused of the attempted murder of an intermarried white Cherokee citizen who had fought for the Confederacy, a case over which Cherokee courts claimed jurisdiction. Two marshals accompanied by family members of the victim interrupted the proceedings of the court, and a shootout ensued, which resulted in the deaths of the defense attorney, a deputy marshal, and seven others.[14]

This incident highlighted jurisdictional conflicts and exposed the overreaching actions of federal agents within the Cherokee Nation. From the Nation's perspective, "U.S. Marshals should have respected the legal proceedings of the Cherokee Nation." Sovereignty demanded jurisdiction over a nation's citizens and required that such cases be handled bureaucratically rather than by a "Marshal's *posse.*"[15] This incident pointed to both the physical and legal intrusions into the

Cherokee Nation that frustrated Cherokees and had deadly consequences. It also provided media fodder for U.S. homesteaders,
speculators, and railroad companies more than willing to depict
the Cherokee Nation as a lawless place incapable of policing its
citizenry. The Goingsnake tragedy, however, served as an impetus
for elected officials to fund the construction of the national prison.
Within a year of the incident at Goingsnake, the council not only
passed an act to build a jail but also allocated $4,000 more than the
$1,879 allocated in the 1850s.[16]

In 1873, Cherokees began work on the New Codes, which have
primarily been treated by scholars as legal reforms.[17] Given that the
bulk of the changes covered criminal law, this is not entirely untrue.
However, this interpretation of the New Codes misrepresents the
full scope of the reforms enacted. The New Codes spell out the
Cherokee Nation's national social policy. They covered all aspects
of the bureaucratic procedures governing the Nation's proposed
social welfare institutions. The New Codes addressed the acquisition
of properties, selection of personnel, administrators' roles, procedures
for becoming a resident in the facilities, and services that would be
provided to residents. The New Codes also confronted older policies
that clearly discriminated against new groups of citizens—freedmen.[18]

The New Codes centralized control of the courts, eliminated aspects
of the law that provided room for local communities to administer
justice based on more traditional understandings of the law, and
usurped control of the death penalty's administration from local
communities. The codes provided specific definitions of crimes,
distinguished between felonies and misdemeanors, and provided
sentencing guidelines to the courts. The New Codes provided the
specific criteria for capital offenses and established prison terms for
lesser offenses.[19] Treason, first degree murder, the rape of a child
under the age of twelve, and arson resulting in death were the only
capital offenses, although some repeat offenders of lesser crimes could
be subjected to the death penalty.[20] Second-degree murder and first-
degree manslaughter both carried sentences between five and twenty
years. The codes distinguished between burglary, robbery, and larceny, and penalties relative to seriousness of the offense ranged from
a single month to fifteen years and required fines to be paid double

the amount of the damages. The changes created by adding new degrees of crime erased the former features of the Cherokee legal system that had led a jury to find Zeke Proctor not guilty. The Cherokee Supreme Court acquired the power to determine the legality of lower court decisions and to require them to follow precedents.[21] The New Codes eliminated overtly racist laws, including a law against intermarriage between Cherokees and African Cherokees, as well as a law that assigned the death penalty to African Cherokees convicted of raping Cherokee women (though it assigned a lesser penalty for Cherokee men convicted of the same crime).

Although it centralized the location of hangings, the New Codes reflected little interest on the part of Cherokee people to engage with discussions outside the Nation to abolish the death penalty, which had by the 1840s included a serious push for abolishing capital punishment. Among the Five Tribes, acquiescence to a death penalty by the wrongdoer and his or her kin fulfilled their traditional social service responsibilities to restore balance to the community. A death penalty quieted the blood of the victim and restored balance to the community, though so much death followed removal and the civil wars that it may have seemed as if balance could never be restored. The Choctaws, like the Cherokees, established a gallows as a central location for their hangings and continued its use through statehood.[22] The Chickasaws used hanging as well, though they used it infrequently and discontinued its use in 1885.[23] The Creeks and Seminoles and on some occasions the Choctaws used a firing squad in homicide cases. In the Creek Nation, the Creeks assigned the light horse the responsibility of carrying out executions.[24]

Even though Progressive, reform-minded Cherokees tended to give serious consideration to U.S. reform agendas, there is no evidence that Cherokee citizens ever seriously called for abolishing the death penalty. Instead, following the New Codes, the Nation in the late 1870s adopted other features of the United States' penal reform, including the move from public to semiprivate executions.[25] The laws changed the location of executions from each district's courthouse yard to within the "walls or enclosure" of the national prison. New Codes also designated, if "practicable," that the high sheriff should request attendance by a physician, the sheriff of Tahlequah, and "not less than six reputable citizens" at executions. From a symbolic standpoint, officials' presence at executions legitimized them as statesanctioned acts. Counsel, immediate family members, and such others as the high sheriff "may see fit" could also attend.[26] As reformers in the states pushed for the professionalization of institutional service providers, the Cherokee Nation designated the institutional professionals who should be in attendance at executions.

The New Codes, in addition to reworking criminal procedures as well as sentencing guidelines, also outlined the procedures that would govern the orphanage and an asylum. Yet, even before the permanent facilities opened, political controversy arose. In 1872, to expedite the process for opening the orphanage, the national council ordered the board to consider available properties including those owned by Lewis Ross, one of the wealthiest men in the Nation who had died in 1860, leaving behind a three-story brick house and a collection of farm buildings and slave cabins. Officials selected his plantation located along the Grand River in the Saline District as the site of an orphanage. Also in 1872, the board recommended another improvement of Lewis Ross's on which to locate the asylum, located six miles from Tahlequah near Park Hill.[27] Not only did the asking price for both properties exceed the appropriations, but Principal Chief William P. Ross, as the executor of the Lewis Ross estate, stood to profit from the sale of the properties. The price and the political controversy delayed acquisition of all of the properties, but in 1875 officials finalized arrangements for the purchase of the Lewis Ross estate.[28] The New Codes created gendered hierarchical governing bodies at all the institutions. The New Codes specified that the principal chief would appoint boards with the council's approval to govern each institution. This matched the practice of the United States; institutions that provided social provisions increasingly established boards of directors to "secure the greatest degree of usefulness at the least expense."[29] The boards appointed the superintendents of the orphanage and the asylum, and the high sheriff, which meant that, in contrast to district sheriffs, who were popularly elected by residents of the districts, the high sheriff's position was tied to political patronage.

As appointees, board members faced replacement when a new chief was elected. The Cherokee Nation never appointed women to any of these positions.

The New Codes also introduced a medical board and adopted rules related to public health and medical needs that, on the surface, responded to concerns generated by the war.[30] The war had made many Cherokee families, particularly those committed to Victorian values, acutely aware of the lack of institutional medical services in the Nation to adequately deal with war-related injuries and disease. After losing her husband during the Civil War, Hannah Hicks watched her infant grow ill. Hicks lamented the lack of physicians "to tell [her] what to do to relieve [him]."[31] The end of the war brought further health crises for Hicks and others in the Nation. Hicks remarried the assistant post surgeon, Hitchcock, at Fort Gibson, and, along with other Cherokee refugees, she and her children took shelter there. In 1867, cholera broke out at Fort Gibson, and, despite having given his wife instructions for his care, Hitchcock died.[32] In less than five years' time, Hannah Hicks was widowed twice. The cholera outbreak created a public health crisis at Fort Gibson and demanded governmental intervention. Soldiers encouraged young Cherokees at the fort to move to Tahlequah. African Cherokees took refuge at Four Mile Creek, where the federal government delivered rations to them.[33] However, potential pensioners, many of whom were adherents of osdv iyunvnehi, had also needed access to trained medical professionals in order to document the impact of their war-related injuries and illnesses.

U.S. citizens who suffered the physical and mental devastation of the war also realized the insufficiencies of their own medical care. The era ushered in by Andrew Jackson's meteoric rise to the presidency bore responsibility for some of this. In the early nineteenth century, medical training and services underwent some professionalization. Dr. McNeil's exorbitant charge for vaccination services to Cherokees in 1806 was one manifestation of the changes taking place. During the War of 1812, the federal government established the office of physician and surgeon general and the position of apothecary general. Army doctors gained valuable individual insights into disease and treatment, but lacked any formal channels or organizations to gather and share information. Jacksonian democracy, also referred to as the "era of the common man," supported the belief that any man with common sense, a satchel, and whiskey could treat patients. By the early 1830s, the fifteen states that had required practicing physicians to be licensed repealed those requirements. By the 1840s, "anyone was free to practice" medicine.[34]

Physicians had worked to combat this trend. In 1845, New York physicians unsuccessfully proposed a national medical society. Two years later, the American Medical Association (AMA) formed in Philadelphia with representatives from twenty-eight states.[35] In the association's earliest years, Cherokees appeared at these meetings as objects of study only.[36] Dr. Robert Ross, John Ross's nephew, began attending the association in 1855. He attended every year from 1855 to 1860, when the Civil War discontinued the AMA's meetings. The meetings resumed in 1864, as did Dr. Robert Ross's attendance.[37]

The pension process, in addition to reminding Cherokee people of the economic exploitation and moral judgments they faced navigating the systems devised by the United States, had required access to medical professionals to validate injuries and deaths. Cherokee officials read annual reports and were well aware of the requests made by federal officials on behalf of the other Five Tribes as well as tribes confined to reservations. For example, in 1872, the U.S. Indian agent requested that the federal government provide funds for a hospital and appoint a physician to the Seminoles. The agent to the Cheyennes and Arapahos requested similar funds. By 1878, the Kiowas and Comanches had an agency physician. Many of the agencies requested additional funds for medicines.[38] The Cherokee Nation knew the federal government had a long history of using social service emergencies to exert its will over Indian people and officials' willingness to extract financial gain when people were compromised.

The legislation passed governing the practice of medicine was as much about the Cherokee Nation's control of its own territory and who should benefit from it as it was about public health and wellness. The legislation empowered the Nation to monitor and profit from non-Indian doctors seeking employment in the Nation. Legislation required Cherokee citizens to pay bonds for the non-Indians they employed and for those workers to secure one-year permits.

The medical board evaluated the credentials of doctors seeking work in the Nation. The Nation collected their licensing fees.[39] The legislation exempted Cherokee doctors and intermarried white doctors from the fees and professional scrutiny. Most of the institutionally trained medical doctors in the Nation were intermarried whites, and they therefore stood to benefit the most in the short-term from participation on the board. In 1874, Dr. E. Poe Harris, an intermarried white, served as the president of the examining board with Dr. Walter Thompson Adair, a Cherokee, as a board member.[40] The medical board controlled access to the practice of profit-seeking medicine and ensured both the appearance and enforcement of professional medical standards. At the same time, the legislation entirely ignored the presence or practices of traditional medical practitioners.

Rather than simply an effort to professionalize doctors or control the exploitation of citizens from quackery, a national medical board provided another institutional safeguard to prevent intruders from undermining the Nation's sovereignty and by extension Cherokee people's abilities to care for one another. The board evaluated applicants' credentials and issued medical certificates to non-Cherokees who wished to practice medicine in the Cherokee Nation. In 1878, for example, the executive council granted a permit to Dr. D. A. Corner, a U.S. citizen, after Drs. Walter Adair and L. M. Cravens certified his credentials.[41] The next year the principal chief issued a public notice for all physicians "not citizens of the Cherokee Nation, desiring to practice the profession of medicine" to appear before the board "without delay." If they failed to report, they would be classified as intruders, and the Nation would take measures to expel them.[42] The irony of the intruder problem in this case was that it was one of the Nation's own making. If Cherokee people with the economic resources to pay desired the availability of institutionally trained doctors, they had to recruit doctors from outside the Nation.

Until the community could supply its own medical school graduates, it had few options. The same families who wanted the services of doctors trained at medical schools personally supported efforts in their own families to achieve that expertise. John Ross had supported his nephew's medical training before removal. Joseph L. Thompson attended Princeton and later graduated from medical school in

Philadelphia. He practiced medicine until his death in the 1870s.[43] However, medical training took time. The war had suspended most Cherokee common schools' operations, and the seminaries had remained close. The seminaries would not reopen until 1872. The Nation needed functioning schools in order to prepare students for medical school. By 1880, the census noted the presence of eight doctors and physicians, including Drs. Cravens and Adair. Of the eight, seven were intermarried whites who had been accredited; Walter Thompson Adair was the only Cherokee physician listed.[44] The desire of many Cherokee families for doctors trained in medical schools and the Nation's desire to provide professional medical services through its national institutions informed medical legislation, but it also provided the greatest benefit to an elite group of Cherokee people.

The New Codes resolved political and bureaucratic problems related to introduction of residentially administered social provisions and enabled officials to move forward with institutional projects, but the institutional structures also called attention to the class differences that existed within the Nation. The year before it moved to its permanent home in Salina, the orphanage had served ninety students. The Lewis Ross property located on the Grand River totaled 340 acres, a sufficient acreage for a working farm capable of supporting manual-labor training similar to those operated by the Methodists.

Nevertheless, the structures on the Ross plantation required modification. The redbrick house underwent renovations that added first an east and later a west wing. The west wing addition alone cost approximately $8,000.[45] Construction included accommodations for staff: the matrons' quarters ranged from "small but comfortable" to "large" and "fine."[46] The impressive façade conveyed a sense of permanence and attested to the high priority the Nation assigned to the care of its orphans, but it was atypical compared to most Cherokee peoples' homes. Pillars framed the front of the house, and a granite porch lined the exterior. Workers converted the former slave quarters into a blacksmith's shop.[47] A granite springhouse, the only trace of the facilities that exists today, provided water to the orphanage. In 1877, officials installed a pump with the ability to supply water directly to the main building. The amenities the orphanage offered far exceeded

Cherokee Orphan Asylum, ca. 1875. Photograph by Jack Hiller. Courtesy Dr. C. W. Kirk Collection, photographs, box 1, Research Division of the Oklahoma Historical Society, Oklahoma City.

those of most Cherokee families, but the model for the orphanage, as Walter Duncan articulated it, remained the family.

This emphasis on family was critical in interpreting the orphanage as a home and a school to everyday people. In most families, members had to work together to support themselves, an economic reality that formal education often jeopardized. School separated children from their families if they did not live locally and placed an economic burden on families. Even parents living within the vicinity of a school often sent their children sporadically because they needed their labor. The educational effects of children's labor had long been a source of debate among missionaries and common school officials, but both acknowledged the economic need.[48] Presbyterians and Baptists had chided the Methodists' use of day schools instead of boarding schools in the pre-removal period, but when the Nation established

Students and springhouse, Cherokee Orphan Asylum, Salina. Courtesy the Thomas Lee Ballenger Papers, 1730–1968, photographs, ca. 1866–ca. 1904, box 4, folder 75, Newberry Library, Chicago.

its schools, it followed a model similar to the Methodists.[49] Many officials understood that children's lives remained rooted in the home, and the needs of the household came first. For the orphanage to resonate with Cherokees, it needed to replicate the activities and relationships of home as well as the value placed on the community rather than the individual.

The Cherokee family life that the orphan asylum tried to emulate remained centered on the household and continued to emphasize a community ethic in the post–Civil War period. Some men wholly adopted agricultural pursuits or cattle grazing as a legitimate means of supporting their families; others hired laborers or rented their lands. For those unwilling or unable to hire non-Indian laborers, hunting and fishing—certainly not the mainstay they had been in the seventeenth and eighteenth centuries—still contributed to family and community well-being. In most families, the entire family and community participated in planting and harvesting, but the daily maintenance continued to be a pursuit of mothers, children, and any elderly family members living with them. For instance, when Rachel

Lane was a child in the 1860s and 1870s, her grandmother took in two orphans. Lane hauled two or three buckets of water a quarter mile from Butler Spring to her home in the Delaware District. In the spring and summer, she helped the family hoe the corn and vegetable gardens. She also aided her grandmother in gathering herbs and roots. Her aunts sewed her clothes by hand.[50]

Walter Adair Duncan recognized that the orphanage would need to "supply the place of home and parent to the orphan." Duncan's philosophy reflected the fact that both he and the Cherokee Nation believed that families were more than simply close biological kin. In his philosophy of education, Duncan linked agricultural labor, academic endeavors, and nationalism, but these pursuits rested on the family. "In the order of nature, home precedes the school," Duncan wrote in the mid-1870s. He continued, "Society has always adjusted itself in accordance with those conditions, and by consequence, as a general rule, the sphere of the school works entirely outside the circle of home." But Duncan saw no reason why this should be the case. Duncan envisioned the orphanage as a place where orphans found a home, parents, and the affection that emanated from the family as well as the responsibilities that family entailed.[51] Duncan's philosophy reflected a middle ground between the industrial labor model proposed by elite men like William P. Ross and a bilingual common school system proposed by Baptist missionary John Jones.[52] The orphanage under Duncan would be a home that included labor, Cherokee-speaking staff, a common dwelling, and shared meals as well as a school where children received an academic education.

These features mirrored other manual-labor schools in both Indian Territory and the United States, but of critical importance was the orphanage's place in the Cherokee Nation and its control over staffing. Not only did the orphanage's buildings reside within the Cherokee Nation's borders, but also the Cherokee National Council and its appointed officials managed the orphanage's operation. The orphanage also fulfilled the Nation's long-term goal of controlling educational projects and keeping children rooted in the Nation. If the Nation failed to take care of its orphans, others might usurp the right to do so. In 1855, the New York State Legislature had incorporated the Saint Thomas Asylum for Orphan and Destitute Indian Children, located on the Cattaraugus Reservation in New York; it admitted Indian children from across the state.[53] Given Cherokee officials' close readings of annual reports to the commissioner of Indian Affairs, it is likely that Cherokee officials were aware of this institution.

As a superintendent employed by the Nation, Duncan controlled the orphanage's day-to-day operations. With the input of the orphanage board of directors, Duncan assessed the expenditures and sought budgetary approval from the council. Negotiations over curriculum, finances, and authority took place within the Nation, not between the Nation, mission boards, and Indian agents. The Cherokee Orphan Asylum was truly a public institution and an expression of Cherokee nationalism.

The children's education at the orphanage offered curricular features similar to the Cherokee common schools and the seminaries. In 1878, Duncan placed an order for arithmetic, grammar, and geography books as well as for slates, crayons, and pencils.[54] By that point, students studied English grammar, geography, arithmetic, algebra, history, and physiology, and a few students completed Robinson's geometry.[55] In the mid-1880s, the orphanage employed a music teacher.[56]

Like the common schools, the orphanage hired qualified teachers who passed the necessary examinations administered by the Cherokee Teacher's Institute held annually at one of the Cherokee Nation's common schools. The three-day teacher's institute featured lectures and discussions from members of the Cherokee Board of Education and school personnel. The orphan asylum's superintendents also participated in the institutes. Most teachers in the nation's schools were Cherokee. Although the seminaries often selected teachers recruited from the eastern schools. This stemmed from the desire on the part of elite Cherokees to have their children receive education in the Cherokee Nation on par with the finest institutions in the United States.[57]

The orphanage also hired staff and teachers from the East throughout its operations, but it eventually employed more graduates from its own seminaries than from eastern colleges. In its first year of operation, the orphanage employed three teachers, two of whom were Cherokee, and one matron, who was a widow from Delaware.[58] By 1876, teachers and matrons totaled seven, the majority of whom were

Male faculty and students, Cherokee Orphan Asylum, Salina. Seated at center is Joseph Franklin Thompson. Courtesy the Thomas Lee Ballenger Papers, 1730–1968, photographs, ca. 1866–ca. 1904, box 3, folder 51, Newberry Library, Chicago.

Cherokee.[59] Other staff, who included cooks, farmers, and washer-women, were Cherokee.

The more rural location of the orphanage, sixty miles from the capital in Tahlequah, led officials to adjust housing accommodations at the institution to meet employees' needs over time. Most of the employees lived on-site, which established the orphanage as a home to its employees as much as its residents. In 1881, while employed as a teacher, John Henry Covel's wife, Elizabeth Mayes Covel, gave birth to their first child Ella Mae at the orphanage. The orphan asylum added a small house for the medical superintendent's exclusive use in the 1880s. In 1885, as compensation, Secretary of the Board of Education J. L. Adair offered Iowa teacher Emma Dunbar "fifty Dollars per month, board, lodging, washing, and room furnished free."[60] As was the case with the orphans, the orphanage provided its employees and their children with a home, employment, and a community. Little evidence exists that suggests Cherokees opposed the presence of an orphanage or the benefits it offered. The Cherokee Nation avoided coercing matrilineally oriented families who might have had orphans in their home into using the facility, but it was available to them if they chose to receive care, and this likely minimized discontent.

The Committee to Build the Jail reflected attempts by the Nation to circumvent political discontent as well as the ability of Lewis Downing to bridge political divides in support of new unproven institutions. The committee included Riley Keys, who had signed the Act of Union between the Old Settlers and the Eastern Cherokee and who was an official in the Cherokee national government during the Civil War as well as a judge.[61] One of its other members, John Lynch Adair, had been born in the East to an intermarried white father and Cherokee mother. When his parents died, he was raised by relatives residing on the Arkansas border, was educated at the Moravian mission, and was later taught by missionary Cephas Washburn in Arkansas. He fought for the Confederacy during the war before serving in Lewis Downing's executive cabinet.[62]

Built as part of the Cherokee Nation's post-removal "endeavor to preserve and maintain the peace of the country," the penitentiary answered the cries of those who objected to outcomes similar to those in Zeke Proctor's trial, those who desired sentences that differentiated between the severities of crimes, and those who sought to reduce the use of corporal punishment.[63] The penitentiary also allowed Cherokee officials to maintain physical control of their own citizens who committed crimes and prevented them from escaping Cherokee jurisdiction to Arkansas, Texas, or elsewhere. Incarcerating prisoners forced the federal court to abide by the Cherokee Nation's bureaucratic procedures to gain access to Cherokee citizens if they were incarcerated and to wait its turn to prosecute them at Fort Smith. The prison served as a symbol that the Cherokee Nation was able to provide protection and security to Cherokee people. Its construction served as physical testament to the Cherokee Nation's intention to deliver justice within its borders and redirected the hostility of Cherokee people toward the U.S. district court into a pride in its own institutions.

By the time construction began, Cherokees seemed to accept the prison as a necessary evil. During the post-removal civil war in the

Cherokee Nation, federal officials had used the perceived turmoil and lawlessness within the Nation as an argument to exercise its authority over the Cherokees. The Treaty of 1866 had confirmed the United States' respect for the Cherokee Nation's jurisdictional rights over its citizens. But railroad right-of-ways added a stream of noncitizens into the Cherokee Nation's midst. If the Nation expected the newly formed federal court in Arkansas to handle its jurisdictional responsibilities, it behooved the Cherokee Nation to do the same.

The Nation located its prison a block from the epicenter of the Cherokee national government in Tahlequah, the Cherokee Supreme Court building, and the Cherokee capitol. In February of 1874, the *Cherokee Advocate* published a call to contractors for bids to construct the prison. By July, four months before the Nation needed the penitentiary for use, "the foundation of the National Prison [had] been dug out" by local citizens hired by the contractor, including African Cherokee Harry Starr.[64] With the basement complete, "the laying of the stone" for the exterior walls began. Once completed in 1875, the sandstone national penitentiary, including its basement, stood three stories tall. The Nation added a ten-foot fence for security two years later and a gallows where all executions in the Nation subsequently took place.[65]

On December 4, 1875, Samuel Sixkiller posted his bond with the Cherokee Nation to serve as the first high sheriff of the newly erected Cherokee National Prison.[66] Sixkiller's experience, like that of Zeke Proctor, whose trial was at the center of the Goingsnake massacre, highlights how quickly Cherokee people's status in the eyes of some Cherokees and many non-Cherokees could move from law abiding to criminal and back again.

Samuel Sixkiller grew up in a family attuned to stockades, courts, prisoners, nuanced understandings of "justice," and jurisdictional questions. His father, Soldier Sixkiller, had removed west on the Trail of Tears at the age of eleven and was present at the Goingsnake massacre. His large, extended family lived close to one another in Watts, a town in the Goingsnake District. Soldier Sixkiller had served as a council member, read Cherokee, kept the Nation's law books in his library, and, like many Cherokees, had served in both the Confederate and Union armies.[67] He had owned slaves and engaged in farming and cattle raising. Soldier offered the use of his property to U.S. marshals and sheriffs transporting prisoners to the court in Arkansas or to the courts in the Cherokee Nation. Yet, the family kept a picture of Cherokee Zeke Proctor hanging on its wall. The 1872 criminal trial of Proctor, who had served as a district sheriff before his arrest for murder, had come to symbolize the importance of jurisdictional integrity to Cherokees. Many non-Cherokees viewed Proctor as an outlaw; for most Cherokees, however, Proctor symbolized patriotism grounded in traditional social welfare obligations.

Samuel Sixkiller himself would be charged with the murder of Cherokee Jeter Thompson in 1879 and would abruptly lose his tenure as high sheriff as a result. Both Sixkiller and Proctor illustrate the ambiguous place where many officers of the law resided, regardless of where they served in Indian Territory. Their experiences also point to the vulnerable place that all Cherokee people risked occupying if jurisdictional disputes arose.[68] Although Sixkiller was ultimately cleared of the charges, he never resumed his position as high sheriff. In 1880, the Union Agency, the recently consolidated agency to the Five Tribes located in Muskogee, Creek Nation, tapped him to serve as the first captain of the U.S. Indian Police, a position he held until his death in 1886.[69] Samuel Sixkiller received his professional preparation for his employment to the U.S. Indian police, not from training delivered by the United States, but from his family, his community, and his tenure as the first high sheriff of the Cherokee Nation.

Although he only served as high sheriff for three years, Sixkiller set the precedent for the obligations and responsibilities of the role. In addition to his primary task as the warden to the inmates, Sixkiller served as an accountant, a construction supervisor, a bookkeeper, and a citizen. The *Cherokee Advocate* chose to emphasize Sixkiller's skills as "a natural and cultivated Mechanic," as opposed to his skills as a lawman.[70] The high sheriff also served as the guardian of the public grounds that included the capital building, the supreme court building, and the square. This responsibility required not only his oversight of the construction of a prison wall but also the removal of "stumps and undergrowth" from the capital square and the addition of shade trees.[71] In 1877, the council passed legislation that aimed to make the prison self-sufficient. The legislation mandated the addition of mechanics' shops on the prison grounds and required every prisoner to learn a trade.[72] This drew on Sixkiller's skills as a mechanic since he had to oversee farm production and the implementation of the manual-labor training provided to prisoners.

The New Codes had provided the legal guidelines for sentencing a citizen to prison. Although the code was set to take effect November 1, 1875, publication delays pushed its implementation back a year.[73] Despite a requirement that the laws circulate publicly in Cherokee and English ninety days in advance of their application, some judges implemented the New Codes. The legal controversy surrounding the New Codes' public circulation limited the number of individuals who arrived at the prison after having been accused or convicted of violating one of the provisions in the codes. In October of 1876, Charles Clark, sentenced to five years for resisting an officer, was the prison's lone resident.[74] Six months later, the prison housed six prisoners serving sentences that ranged from four to fourteen years.[75]

The crimes Cherokee men committed differed little from those involving non-Indians tried at federal court in Fort Smith. Men stole whiskey, hogs, and money.[76] Theft led to most incarcerations. Some Cherokees used horse theft as "a means for physically able-bodied men to earn a living,"[77] In the pre-removal era, emboldened by the knowledge they could commit crimes against Cherokees with impunity, horse theft syndicates had operated on the borders of the southeastern tribes and targeted Indian people. Under traditional law, Cherokee men engaged in horse theft to recover property or perform their societal responsibilities to vindicate kin and restore lost wealth.[78] The problem of horse theft escalated in the post–Civil War era, a pattern replicated across tribes in the region during the decades of the 1860s and 1870s. Tribes relocated to reservations in Indian Territory faced declining access to buffalo herds as a result of the non-Indian trade in hides that threatened buffalo populations and the increased pressure on herds as a result of settler intrusion into the West. Indian men across the region increasingly turned to horse theft to procure goods and provisions previously unnecessary as a result of the availability of buffalo. The federal government criminalized the acts and prosecuted the men for carrying out their traditional roles, what Jacki Rand Thompson cites as another example of "state criminalization of tribal practices" among the Kiowa. In the Kiowa's situation, the men's "dangerous" labor helped the community manage food scarcities, and it provided a defense against the Indian agents and federal officials who withheld rations owed under treaties to "coerce . . . compliance" from Kiowa people.[79] At the same moment, the Cherokee Nation practiced its own form of state criminalization; after 1875, horse theft landed Cherokees in the national prison.

On the surface, this parallel event appears to be the Cherokee Nation expanding the reach of its own coercive state. In a sense, it was. Those incarcerated for horse theft lost freedom of movement and their personal autonomy for a period of time. However, it also provided the Cherokee Nation with the means to protect the greater body of Cherokee people from the same coercive policies facing other Indian peoples. As other tribes faced confinement to reservations, military oversight, an increased dependency on federal annuities, and the theft of annuities by Indian agents, the Cherokee Nation maintained control of its land base, and the Cherokee people were able to exercise more autonomy in their everyday choices as it related to their families' social welfare needs.

Cherokee officials also exercised discretion as it related to sentences. By statute, prison sentences at the national penitentiary could range from a month to twenty years. This had been a point of contention among some Cherokees who worried about the impact of long sentences and hefty bails on Cherokee people.[80] One year was a common sentence for misdemeanor offenses, whereas felony convictions usually resulted in sentences of five or more years or, in some cases, the death penalty. However, there is little evidence that men ever received sentences longer than ten years. Commutation and pardon applications resulted in far less time spent for many sentenced to longer periods of time.

Because circumstances of arrest and prison sentences varied widely, various categories of prisoners arose. The presence of the prison in Tahlequah allowed the sheriff to take someone into custody immediately for a crime committed. Therefore, the institution served as both a jail for temporary incarceration following arrest and a prison for the convicted serving sentences. In 1877, for example, "a disorderly negro called Willis fired his pistol off in town . . . close to the jail, and in the course of a few minutes took up his lodging there for the night." The man, an African Cherokee whose full name was Willis Petit, was ultimately convicted of the misdemeanor crime of disturbing a religious meeting while intoxicated; he served a one-year sentence in the national prison.[81] The need to provide the services of both a jail and a prison led the national council in 1879 to propose building a separate log house inside the prison walls to confine "intoxicated & disorderly persons who may be arrested for disturbing the peace and quiet."[82]

The need for institutions to serve people with varied needs guided approaches to the asylum as well. Rather than build a soldiers' home for the families of people directly impacted by service in the war, as many states did, the Cherokee Nation had decided to set up a more comprehensive institution. It would allow the Nation to serve a variety of people with the (dis)abilities identified through the 1867 children's census. The asylum's creation also led the Nation to suspend its national (dis)ability pensions in 1875. After January 1, 1875, the Nation required those seeking national pensions to reside at the asylum.[83] Providing institutional facilities to each specific (dis)abled group was an economic impossibility. An institution that could serve multiple categories of residents was not only reasonable, but, given the number of pensioners, also presented the possibility of economic savings.

The national council required the board of trustees to visit the asylum at least once a month, to hold quarterly meetings at the facility, and to keep a "fair and full record" of the business of the asylum.[84] One of the early duties of the board of trustees at the Cherokee Asylum for the Deaf, Dumb, Blind, and Insane was to appoint a medical superintendent for the facility. In general, the board answered to the council; the steward and the medical superintendent governed the institution based on the bylaws determined by the board. The board, the steward, and the medical superintendent all submitted annual reports to the national council.

The Nation expected all those employed to provide an established standard of care to the individuals housed at the asylum. Despite its governing function, the board also had the responsibility to furnish bedding and clothing, secure food, and purchase "medical supplies as may, from time to time, be required for use at the asylum."[85] The "general superintendence" of the grounds and facilities fell to the steward. Legislation mandated that residents should be bathed regularly, provided clean clothes as needed but minimally once a week, and furnished "wholesome food, warm clothing, and bedding."[86] As for the facilities, the law required the steward under the direction of the medical superintendent "once a week [to] have scoured and cleaned up the building, and have it kept in a healthful condition."[87]

When unexpected events occurred, the board of trustees secured from the council the necessary monies and provisions for the successful management of the asylum. In 1879, for example, a tornado struck the facility, tore off the roof, demolished the third floor, and destroyed the southeast corner of the "fine building." Principal Chief Dennis Bushyhead, in his capacity as president ex officio of the asylum, relayed damage reports from the medical superintendent and the steward to the national council so that the council could appropriate funds for repairs.[88] Officials temporarily suspended admissions and relocated the residents without family to take them in to the prison until the building was repaired.[89]

Initially, the medical superintendent shared responsibility with other institutional officials to provide care to residents at the asylum; however, his authority increased over time. The earliest rules assigned most medical care not to the superintendent but to the steward, who administered the treatments "under the direction" of and "prescribed" by the physician. As already mentioned, the steward also maintained the grounds and farm, and in addition kept an accounting of payments, purchases, and inventories; maintained records with each resident's name, age, sex, district, date of arrival and departure, death date, and any known cause of death; and temporarily admitted potential residents until the board evaluated their applications for admission.[90] To aid the steward in meeting the daily needs of residents, the board of trustees eventually added staff and changed its policies.

As ideas about public health and medical care changed in and outside the Nation, medical professionals took on a more prominent

Cherokee Asylum for the Blind, Insane, and Deaf, near Tahlequah, Oklahoma, ca. 1921. Courtesy Margaret Hill Collection, photographs, box 1, Research Division of the Oklahoma Historical Society, Oklahoma City.

role at the asylum. Two years after the Cherokees established their medical board, the American Public Health Association was organized. By 1872, three states and the District of Columbia had established boards of health. In 1875, the American Neurological Society formed.[91] These new U.S. organizations established standards, regulated practitioners, and disseminated public health and medical information to practitioners; they also addressed areas of concern not only for northern cities but also for the South and Indian country.

Nurses were a late addition, both to the Cherokee Asylum and to the institutions in the states. It was not until 1882 that any permanent institution in the United States existed to train nurses.[92] During the 1870s, the Cherokee Asylum did not employ any nurses. In 1885, however, the asylum employed five nurses in title; none of them were women. Several were former prison guards. Although institutions in the states separated female and male residents, the caregiving staff at U.S. institutions tended to be male. Not until 1879 did Pennsylvania require the hiring of a female attendant at any institution that served male and female residents.[93] In 1891, the Cherokee medical superintendent recommended that the national council allocate funds for the addition of "a good and efficient female nurse."[94]

These centralizing processes and legislative changes bolstered the Nation's larger efforts to provide quality health services to Cherokee people through its institutions. By 1880, the national council would establish the official position of a medical superintendent not only at the asylum but also at the male and female seminaries, the orphanage, and the prison. The council funded the position from the school fund, the asylum fund, and the general fund. It set the salary at $1,500 annually, but the act required that the superintendent purchase his own medicines and "medical apparatus." The 1880 law removed the selection process from the board of trustees and instead required a joint ballot with the national council.[95]

The increased opportunities and demand for medical professionals in Indian Territory coupled with an explosion of medical schools in closer proximity led to an increase in the number of doctors trained in medical schools in the post–Civil War period. At least three graduates of the male seminary attended medical school at Missouri Medical College after the Civil War, including Walter T. Adair, William W. Campbell, and Felix McNair. The Nation added citizens Jesse C. Bushyhead, Charles M. Ross, Emmett Starr, Bartow Fite, R. L. Mitchell, and Claud Thompson to its list of Cherokee Nation citizen doctors.[96] Drs. Adair, Fite, Ross, and McNair all benefitted from the professional opportunities these institutions created when they received appointments as medical superintendents.

The economic opportunities provided by institutions were not limited to professional staff. The institutions created a demand for goods and services from a wide range of Cherokee citizens. All residents had to receive food, bedding, and clothing. Stapler & Son, a Cherokee-owned sundry store near the prison in downtown Tahlequah, filled the bulk of the orders for materials and supplies, including fabric, material for the prisoner's uniforms, shoes, calico, shovels, spades, axes, and ax handles throughout the prison's operation. Stapler & Son also served as a bonding agent, and several high sheriffs, including Charles Starr and Robert M. French, paid their surety bonds to the national treasury with the aid of Stapler & Son.[97]

Because of the proximity of the prison to the store and the economic and social relationships that developed, the high sheriff often called on Johnson Thompson, who worked at Stapler & Son, to serve as a temporary guard and witness the signing of warrants.[98]

In addition to Stapler & Son, hundreds of individual Cherokees sold fresh produce or provided skills to the institutions. The asylum employed a matron, often the wife of the steward, to assist with care of residents. Through the years, the asylum also employed farmhands, cooks, teamsters, laundresses, and sick nurses. In addition to the fulltime employees, the asylum, like the prison and the orphanage, often paid for the services and commodities from individuals who provided periodic labor, eggs, meat, and seamstress work.[99] David Rowe, who served as a judge of the Cherokee Nation's Northern Circuit Court in 1875, benefitted from a contract with the orphanage to furnish beef and pork.[100] The institutions' purchases continued for decades. At the close of the fiscal year 1886, for instance, the high sheriff made 123 cash payments to individuals for goods and services. Although a few individuals received multiple payments, most were onetime payments.[101]

Although the public—and highest paying—positions exclusively benefitted men, other opportunities available to women supported aspects of the traditional social welfare system that privileged and protected women's economic rights. Women, who were the prison's only seamstresses, made the prisoners' uniforms, mended their clothes, and sewed suits for each man's release.[102] The ability to sew, which the federal government's early nineteenth-century civilization policy endorsed, and which missionary schools and the Cherokee Female Seminary provided instruction in, was intended for women's domestic use. The skills flourished in the Cherokee Nation and, inadvertently, with the rise of national institutions provided women with a marketable skill. Culinary skills also opened up an economic opportunity for women at the prison. In its early years, the job fell to the high sheriff's wife and further compensated his family, but over time the high sheriff hired women related to the guards and others living in the community.[103] Most payments made to women, however, were not for sewing and cooking but for produce and livestock. Women exercised their rights to sell their agricultural products and use their domestic skills to contribute to their families.

The Nation's control of institutionally administered provisions ensured that the economic opportunities they provided to the Nation benefitted Cherokee people. Cherokee people, whether residents of the facility or not, became tied to the institutions for their economic livelihood. The institutional demand for goods and services provided thousands of Cherokee citizens professional employment and access to cash for the few store-bought goods they might need. The sheer number of economic, professional, and personal connections with institutions forged ties between the Nation and citizens that were unprecedented just fifty years earlier.

Cherokees would soon face the same economic, personnel, socioeconomic, and political challenges that institutional services across the United States faced. They would also face unique challenges: once Reconstruction ended in southern states, federal policy did not threaten to dismantle the states' land policy or subject white citizens to second-class citizenship. Instead of being able to debate, strengthen, and improve institutions, Cherokees were informed by threats of allotment and territorialization in the reforms they might otherwise freely consider. These threats also caused critical economic resources to be diverted to national defense instead of domestic reforms. These concerns did not stop Cherokees from debating the merits of their institutions; they simply bound those conversations to the larger threat of allotment and U.S. territorialization.

CHAPTER 5

Institutional Lives, 1877–1880

Catcher Rock was born in 1877 and grew up in the Saline District, the same district as the Cherokee orphanage, at the peak of Cherokee institution building, which began in 1868 with the completion of the children's census and ended in 1880. As Catcher Rock's life demonstrates, not everyone had a reason or the need to interact with the institutionally administered social welfare provisions offered by the Nation. As U.S. Indian reformers shifted their approaches to coerce assimilation of Indian peoples, the Cherokee Nation modified its institutional practices to meet the new threats to its sovereignty. Yet, despite these changes, when he was interviewed in the 1930s, Catcher Rock recalled a childhood of plenty. His parents, "full-blood" Cherokees, emigrated to the Cherokee Nation in 1838. They later separated and, as was the case among traditional matrilineally oriented families who married in the "common" way, his mother and grandmother raised him. His maternal grandfather, Kingfisher, died shortly after his participation with the Indian Home Guard in the Civil War. When he was ten, Catcher moved with his grandmother and mother to the Tahlequah District. His grandmother traded a "small pony" for a place in Peggs, near Tahlequah. This trade was possible because of the Nation's communal landholdings; the land itself added no additional cost.[1]

Despite the presence of twenty-four stores throughout the Cherokee Nation, including at least six in nearby Tahlequah, Catcher Rock "seldom went to these places because [his family] did not have any money to spend." However, Catcher Rock's lack of money did not constitute an impoverished condition. Instead, it highlighted basic features of late-nineteenth century agrarian living. People worked hard, produced what they consumed, and used their marketable skills to earn a few dollars for the scant items (coffee, sugar, and nails) a store might provide. Catcher Rock's daily diet consisted of "bean-bread, dried pumpkin, hominy, sweet potatoes, and wild meats." He helped his mother and grandmother farm; he hunted and his grandmother smoked the venison; and he fished in nearby rivers. Catcher Rock received a traditional Cherokee education, which for most Cherokees by the 1870s included attendance at Cherokee public schools for varying lengths of time. Rock described a life supported by communal landholdings, traditional matrilineal kinship networks, his maternal relatives' property rights, and a system that protected his family from needing residential institutions to supplement his care when he had family able and willing to care for him, a situation that stood in contrast to the situation faced by many single mothers in the United States.[2]

Despite the presence of new institutions, most Cherokees including Rock continued to live lives that resembled those of the majority of nineteenth-century rural Americans and Cherokees of varied social strata. Catcher Rock's childhood illustrates the continued presence of functioning osdv iyunvnehi. His life resembled the lives of count-less other Cherokee people, many of whom, as result of slightly different circumstances, however, did interact with the nation's social welfare institutions as residents, inmates, administrators, farmers, guards, staff, or cooks. Yet, his childhood would increasingly become illustrative of the dysfunction U.S. reformers would rail against in their attempts to undermine Native nationhood and communal landholdings.

This chapter attempts to paint a picture of life at each of the social welfare institutions introduced into the Cherokee Nation after the Civil War. By focusing mainly on the years 1877 to 1880, I am able to capture institutional life when institutions were no longer in their infancy, still received adequate funding, and grew at a time when administrators were not caught up in debates over institutional missions and purposes that occurred under the dark shadow and dwindling budgets created by the fight to resist allotment and terri-torialization. These descriptions enable comparisons of Cherokee institutions with those operating in the United States as well as those being developed by federal officials for Indian people described in this and later chapters. The chapter will demonstrate that people who entered the institutions impacted the institutions. The administrators selected to lead the institutions mattered; each brought different skills, abilities, and philosophies of care to the facilities they governed. Every individual housed in the facilities lived there as an individual and as a member of a larger community. For their part, employees arrived with potentially similar, dissimilar, or diametrically opposed views, as did those who received services, education, or punishment. Institutions formed new spaces for Cherokee citizens with different prior experiences, from different ages and stages of life, to interact with one another across lingual, familial, racial, and class divides. And yet the institutions occupied community spaces in the Cherokee Nation, and Cherokee people treated them as such. Whether an institution and its employees fulfilled its community responsibilities, more than anything else, determined how Cherokee people evaluated each institution's contribution to the Nation.

As stated above, Catcher Rock's childhood shared the features of many children's lives, including Cherokee children living at the orphanage as well as non-Cherokee children in other regions of the country. Children whose pioneering parents set out for the West were expected to contribute to their families' livelihoods. They tended cattle, gathered wood and water, cooked, and, if they were older siblings, they assisted with younger children. In many respects, they were miniature adults.[3] Poor immigrant children residing in northeastern urban centers of the United States often lived in small one-room tenements with extended family groups. The family members all pieced together odd jobs to contribute to the family's existence. Men found jobs on the docks, boys sold newspapers, and many girls and women became domestic servants.[4] Most children labored in some form or another, but it was the middle-class families who were able to offer a childhood for their kids and shelter them from the work that most people of all ages contributed to in order to sustain their families. In most areas of the United States, if a man died or abandoned his family, the wife and children faced even greater legal and economic insecurity. Parents in the East who could not sustain themselves financially, emotionally, or structurally turned to institutions to aid them when burdens became too great. The same was true in the Nation. For example, when Cherokee Narcissa Owen's former railroad company president husband died after the Civil War, leaving the family in challenging economic straits in Virginia, she returned to the Cherokee Nation in 1880 and received employment at the Cherokee Female Seminary.

Cherokee national social welfare policy also provided a secondary barrier of protection from those outside the Nation, including government officials, reformers, territorialists, and penologists more than willing to serve as guardians to and exercise their coercive authority over all Indian people. Cherokee institutions provided what historian Andrew Denson describes as "instruction without domination," as opposed to the benevolent repression offered by many of its U.S. institutional counterparts.[5] By 1880, the Cherokee Nation's population was approximately 20,000, but with the addition of intruders and those seeking citizenship the number was closer to 26,000. The Cherokee Nation's rural locale and its control over citizenship kept institutions from becoming the large overcrowded facilities that were growing in the North to accommodate hundreds, if not over a thousand, individuals.[6]

Even though they were born over forty years apart, Walter Adair Duncan and Catcher Rock described the need for similar skill sets to live in the Cherokee Nation during the course of their lives. In 1877, the year of Catcher Rock's birth, Walter Adair Duncan was beginning his fifth year as the superintendent of the Cherokee Orphan Asylum in the Saline District. The men's writings and interviews confirm the importance of farming and express an appreciation for a rural life. However, Duncan's life intermingled with religious and educational institutions. His educational philosophy combined the best practices of Indian Territory Methodist educational institutions, including manual labor, and those of the Cherokee Nation's public schools with his lived experience as a Cherokee man. Duncan saw no incompatibility in merging the educational aims of the Nation with the skills necessary to live a life similar to the one described by Catcher Rock. As early as 1856, Duncan had vocalized the importance of manual labor for Cherokee people and the realities of work

Reverend Walter Adair Duncan. Courtesy the Thomas
Lee Ballenger Papers, 1730–1968, photographs, ca. 1866–
ca. 1904, box 3, folder 36, Newberry Library, Chicago.

that Cherokee men faced: "All cannot live here without manual labor.
Each cannot be a professor, lawyer, doctor, preacher, school-master.
The means, opportunities, and occasions are wanting."[7] As a facility
superintendent who adhered to this view but was charged with educational goals, Duncan needed to overcome the same challenges
faced by other Cherokee educational settings, such as the common
schools and seminaries.

Language remained a key concern for educational settings. By
1877, the Cherokee Nation common schools had for more than twenty

years attempted to employ bilingual teachers whenever possible to overcome the educational challenges faced by monolingual Cherokee students.[8] Duncan had reported on these concerns to the federal government as early as 1856. The orphanage had by no means resolved the debate, but it had avoided the critiques lobbed at the seminaries for their overt discrimination against Cherokee speakers and at the public schools for the inadequacy of hiring monolingual English speakers or interpreters to provide English-language instruction to monolingual Cherokee children.[9]

The early Methodist missionaries, unlike their denominational counterparts, never tried to translate Cherokee like the Presbyterians had and avoided employing large numbers of interpreters. Instead, they immersed themselves in Cherokee communities and relied on the language skills of bilingual Cherokee people in their congregations.[10] A student's ability to read, write, and speak English made common school education much more accessible to them. Those termed "full-bloods," usually as a result of exclusive command of the Cherokee language, often felt discriminated against in the public schools and even more so in the seminaries, which made few concessions for students who spoke Cherokee as a first language.[11] The language barrier would continue to be a concern; as late as 1900, a little over 17 percent of those designated "full-bloods" in the Cherokee Nation remained monolingual in Cherokee, including Catcher Rock.

The orphan asylum, because of its bilingual staff and its large number of Cherokee-speaking children, employed the Cherokee language with fewer obstacles and less resistance than either the common schools or the seminaries. In its earliest years of operation, many students spoke only Cherokee when they entered the orphanage, so it seems unlikely that all students progressed at the same rate. Rather than deny children their language or shame or degrade its use, as was common practice at federal boarding schools like General Samuel Armstrong's Hampton Institute and the Carlisle Indian School run by Richard Henry Pratt, matrons and staff made regular use of Cherokee language; some teachers employed Cherokee to communicate with students, and students used Cherokee in the classrooms. Even though the orphanage taught and promoted the use of English in the classroom, the orphanage was a home and that home was bilingual in Cherokee and English.

Children on the balcony of the Cherokee Orphan Asylum. Courtesy Cherokee Heritage Center Archives, Tahlequah, Oklahoma.

Language barriers, however, did exist. Emma Dunbar, a white woman recruited from the East, recounted her first experience in an orphanage classroom in the 1880s, remembering one Cherokee-speaking child who "stamp[ed] her foot and exclaim[ed]—'I-tee-see-col-ee' meaning I can't understand you."[12] Since Dunbar lacked fluency in Cherokee, someone translated the phrase for her. Even Cherokee faculty and staff were not necessarily conversant in the language. In an article Duncan wrote for the *Cherokee Advocate* in the late 1870s, he lamented, "I do so much wish that I could speak the Cherokee well enough to converse in it; I could explain many things pertaining to the nature of our public institutions."[13] His statement suggests that his conversational skills were limited, but not his understanding or basic vocabulary. Rather than lament the inability of Cherokee people to speak English, Duncan expressed a humble desire to speak Cherokee. It was his limitation, rather than that of monolingual Cherokee speakers, that needed to be overcome. Yet, Duncan's article illustrates that by 1876 he was aware that some monolingual Cherokee speakers resisted wholly embracing the orphanage based on their perceptions of its goals and purposes.

The issue clearly remained on his mind. A few years later, in 1881, as one means to address inadequate communication with the local community and to reach an international community as well, Duncan acquired a printing press by collecting subscription payments from Cherokee Nation citizens and orphan asylum employees.[14] Duncan's efforts also provided additional skills for the students. The children learned how to set type and operate a press. Under Duncan's direction, the students began to publish the *Children's Playground*, a supplement to Duncan's *Orphan Asylum Press*, which printed Cherokee Nation political news as well as news from the states and from abroad.[15] The *Children's Playground*, which resembled publications of the Cherokee Male and Female Seminaries, featured students' short poems and compositions and charted their academic progress, thus offering a glimpse into the children's world during this period.

Despite Duncan's desire to convey ideas about the nature of public institutions to Cherokee speakers, the paper was not a bilingual publication nor was it strictly meant for Cherokee Nation citizens. The *Children's Playground* circulated widely throughout Indian Territory, but the orphanage also exchanged papers with other institutions, including the Bureau of Education, the Carlisle Indian School, the Vacation Colonies for Sickly Children, and the Department of the Interior's Western Education projects.[16] This exchange of publications was normal throughout the United States. For Duncan, the exchange advertised the Cherokee Nation's sovereignty and its social services to other nineteenth-century reformers, including those at Hampton and Carlisle, who were engaged in similar institutional endeavors.

Though the curriculum and the skills administered at the Cherokee Orphan Asylum were similar to those at federal boarding schools, Cherokee officials did not create the institutions based on the premise that Cherokee people were inferior. Often, they signified the opposite. As reformers pushed to remove Indian children from their communities in order to produce Indians prepared for U.S. citizenship, the articles written by Duncan and the students advertised the children's Cherokee citizenship and their intellectual capabilities without the aid of U.S. reformers. In 1881, Duncan published the complete results of the Cherokee Nation's and the United States' elections. The same year, he and the entire staff issued a circular thanking the Indian-Treaty-Keeping Society, a group that had emerged from the Baptist Women Home Mission's Society in Philadelphia, and that would later be known as the Women's National Indian Association (WNIA), which had recently sent a petition to Senator Henry Dawes objecting to efforts to disregard treaties.[17]

Although the *Children's Playground* likely published the writings of the highest-achieving students, the demographics of the students had not changed much since 1879. In its first publication, editors Lizzie Stinson and William Cobb appealed to the national council to erect a monument to Sequoyah, "the Cherokee Cadmus," as a measure of their love and admiration for Cherokee literacy, the Nation, and its institutions. Another article heralded the orphanage as an "institution . . . founded upon a proper basis. It is as truly a part of the design to teach suitable branches of industry as it is to impart a knowledge of the ordinary academic course. Manual skill is to be made as creditable as it is often more useful than the ability to conjugate a verb or read a line in Greek."[18] The publication attested to the fact that the orphanage had already achieved all of the purposes and more than those proposed by reformers.

Walter Adair Duncan's publication stood in obvious contrast to the publications produced by government-supported manual-labor schools for Indians. Two 1881 issues of Hampton's *School News* included Eastern Band Cherokee children praising white benevolence and questioning the merits of Native languages. A "half-breed Cherokee" wrote, "But now the Indians have a better chance than they ever had before, and have more friends among the white people, who are willing to help the Indians more than before. So the Indians need always to be kind to the people of these United States."[19] Another child wrote bluntly, "The English language is much better than any Indian language."[20] The publications served as political tools. Federal boarding schools intended to use Indian children's voices against other Indian cultures; Duncan intended to use Cherokee children's voices on behalf of Cherokee people.

The Cherokee publication also encouraged the intimacy of the students with one another. Students celebrated dark-skinned class-mates and Cherokee cultural norms such as ear piercing. Each issue of the *Children's Playground* included regular columns "Guess My Subject" or "Guess Who It Is," descriptions of students written by classmates. In one issue, Sallie Walker asked, "Who wears ribbons round her neck and a bow on her hair, and is good-looking? She wears her earrings every day and I think they look well on her. She has black eyes, black hair and dark skin. Her ruffle is lace; her bask is white; her dress-skirt is black. I love to see her with a white bask and a black dress-skirt. Her sleeve ruffles are wide." In another piece, Mary Riley wrote,

> She is a little girl about 12 or 13 years old. She is good and kind to all of the girls and we love her very much. Her complexion is dark. She has black hair and eyes and is about as tall as Ida Langley. . . . She knows a great deal about work to be so small. She has a very sweet voice and sings nicely. She seldom gets scoldings like some of the girls, for she always attends to her own work. She is never idle; she is either reading or employed in something else equally as useful.[21]

This celebration of dark-skinned classmates contrasts with attitudes documented among female seminary students during the same period who demonstrated a preference for "white ancestry."[22] Instead, orphanage residents remarked on appearance without attaching racial meaning and defined beauty in terms of many other attributes celebrated and endorsed by reformers inside and outside the Nation—singing voice, treatment of others, good behavior, and industrious-ness.[23] Furthermore, the guessing games, amusing perhaps to out-siders, could only be played by orphanage residents since they alone would be able to solve the puzzles. The games contributed to a common sense of identity for the participants as both Cherokee children and residents of the orphanage.

Despite efforts to instill national pride in all Cherokee people, at least some of the students endorsed institutional educational achievements as the measure of one's character and reflected the moral judgments endorsed by missionaries and reformers beyond the Nation. Lizzie Stinson contributed a composition entitled "If We Could Mind Our Own Business." In it she rebuked gossip and reminded classmates, "We should all get along much better if we would mind our own business, and escape much trouble and hard feeling. We would make more friends and fewer enemies." She also warned that examinations would expose those who had heeded her advice and those who had not.[24] In 1891, published years after Duncan's tenure had ended, an article warned of the dangers of smoking "the devil's kindling wood."[25] This latter condemnation did not reflect the views of traditional Cherokee men and women, who regularly used tobacco in ceremonies and moderately in social settings. At least some of the lessons the children received from their families or the adults at the orphanage passed judgment on the actions and values of traditional Cherokee families.

The children, however, shared Duncan's and Rock's awareness of the importance of the physical environment to their daily lives. In the May issue, Annie Mills wrote, "Little girls like to play under the trees. The boys like to climb trees. I like to play under trees in summer."[26] In the 1881 issue of the *Children's Playground*, Jennie Duncan mourned the loss of a tree to a storm: "All of the other trees look like they are crying about it. Every body seemed to like to sit under it. I miss the tree very much." M. E. Pitcher, in an article entitled "Country Life," revealed, "Lizzie Stinson and I are going to live in the country, when we leave the Asylum." The children lived and imagined their future lives in rural spaces.[27]

During his entire tenure as superintendent, Duncan worked hard to reassure Cherokee people of the orphanage's purpose and to demonstrate the institution's commitment to gadugi. For example, when the new orphanage opened in 1874, Walter Adair Duncan walked side by side with the children from the temporary facility at the Cherokee Male Seminary in Park Hill to Salina, a distance of just under forty miles. Duncan and the Nation encouraged Cherokees and non-Cherokees to visit the facility. The *Cherokee Advocate* extended

Students at the Cherokee Orphan Asylum, Salina, ca. 1872 Courtesy the Thomas Lee Ballenger Papers, 1730–1968, photographs, ca. 1866–ca. 1904, box 4, folder 74, Newberry Library, Chicago.

an institutional invitation to the orphanage's public examinations. Duncan submitted a series of articles to the *Cherokee Advocate*, wanting the Cherokee people to look upon the orphanage with affection and to "build it up."[28] In 1876, in his article on the "Nature of the Cherokee Orphan Asylum," Duncan rhetorically asked, "What is the real basis of a public enterprise? It should be founded in the affection and confidence of the people. The people are the ultimate sovereigns."[29] Duncan reassured families skeptical of the value of education that the orphanage provided the most important aspects of home as well.

Duncan's work as a Methodist minister opened the facility to another Cherokee audience as well. Every year, the Indian Mission Conference appointed a minister to the facility. In this capacity, weekly Methodist church services were available to local Cherokee people. In his role as superintendent and minister, he drew upon the strengths of Methodism among Cherokee people before and after removal. Although they did not arrive in the Cherokee Nation in the

East until 1822, Methodists secured numerous converts by incorporating traditional features and values of Cherokee society into their missionary efforts.[30] The earliest Presbyterian and Moravian missionaries in the East had focused their evangelizing efforts on mixed white Cherokee families and the families of local chiefs eager to obtain English-language education for their children. Throughout the 1820s, Methodists and Baptists, in contrast, focused their work among everyday Cherokee people who adhered to traditional social service systems.[31] Both the Baptists and Methodists licensed Native preachers and employed interpreters far more than their Moravian and Presbyterian counterparts. Two of the earliest Methodist itinerates, Richard Neely and James J. Trott, both married Cherokee women in the mid-1820s. The Methodist missionaries readily accepted (and as a result of poor funding relied upon) the hospitality ethic of Cherokees, who provided food and lodging during their circuit rides in the pre-removal period. The Methodists' camp meetings, which lasted days, if not weeks, at a time, and love feasts resonated with the political and ceremonial practices of Cherokee people. The Methodists also focused on right action as evidence of salvation rather than on having received God's grace; the latter conversion process left Cherokee people's conversions open to the judgments of other denominational authorities, who were reticent to legitimize the religious experiences of Native Christians.[32]

The most important events at the orphanage were the opening and closing ceremonies in September and May, which resonated with Cherokee traditions and promoted Cherokee nationalism.[33] Summer ushered in a series of key rituals that led to the Green Corn ceremony, the observance of which was widespread in Cherokee society throughout the early nineteenth century and was still practiced in Creek/Cherokee border communities. The Green Corn ceremony celebrated the arrival of the new corn and required a thanksgiving feast, ritual cleansing, and related important cosmological and social lessons. For Green Corn, men and women worked to refurbish and purify public spaces, and people erected temporary structures to accommodate kin who traveled to attend the ceremonies, play ball, and dance. The Green Corn ceremony reconciled and revitalized the community.[34] These rituals brought the community together and reminded kin of their obligations to maintain harmony and right relationships with each other. Although opening and closing events were common in non-Indian schools, the orphanage's opening and closing ceremonies' timing, observance, and duration introduced elements of traditional practices that likely resonated with more culturally conservative Cherokees.

The closing ceremonies lasted for days and provided the time necessary to incorporate events that demonstrated a hospitality ethic and resembled traditional ceremonies. The celebrations that Duncan encouraged in the late 1870s continued in much the same way into the 1880s. In 1878, the principal chief, council members, the U.S. agent to the Cherokees, writers for local papers, teachers from the East, ministers, and Cherokee citizens attended the events, gave speeches, and reported on the festivities.[35] More often than not, "the exercises on the occasion of the opening of the Orphan Asylum occup[ied] the greater part of the day," refreshments were kept on hand, and a basket dinner was provided. Continuing into the 1880s, the

> annual commencement at the Cherokee school was an occasion of absorbing interest. Preparations for the event went on for weeks. From cellar to garret the house was scoured. People came in crowds and stayed for days, many bringing their tents and camping on the grounds. Then there were great barbecues in order to provide sufficient meat for the guests and other provisions in proportion were prepared. It was a time of great merriment.[36]

The orphanage's institutional life opened and closed annually by embodying a hospitality ethic and bringing together all classes of Cherokee people.[37]

At least one post–Curtis Act criminal case that fell under federal jurisdiction suggests the extent to which institutions had fulfilled traditional social service expectations whether they desired to or not. A hospitality ethic required everyone to provide generously to their neighbors. The orphanage's resources often exceeded those available to many Cherokee people. In 1899, the *Indian Chieftain* reported that the commissioner was holding Jack Soldier's boy for committing larceny after he stole a yearling from the orphanage during its commencement. The paper quoted Joseph Franklin Thompson, Duncan's successor at the orphanage, as saying, "If everybody who had ever stolen an orphan asylum yearling had been convicted, the penitentiaries would have to be enlarged."[38] Thompson acknowledged the wrongdoing and its frequency, but simultaneously downplayed its significance. Jack Soldier's boy may have done what many other Cherokee people had since the facility opened in 1872—they took from the institution because it had resources it was obligated to share and the institution rarely sought legal remedy.

Duncan and other national officials remained cognizant of the scrutiny the institution faced from U.S. officials who were engaged in a wider policy of Indian assimilation. Duncan accompanied ten students to the Indian Agricultural Fair in Muskogee in 1876, an event attended by U.S. officials, numerous tribes, elected officials from the larger region, as well as individuals from the United States and the Five Tribes.[39] Duncan's public efforts often tried to balance the expectations of his multiple audiences. In one of his articles to the *Cherokee Advocate*, he celebrated the orphan asylum as a mark of advancement for the Nation.[40] Reinforcing the connection between positive character and educational attainments, orphan asylum officials provided the *Advocate* with the orphanage's Roll of Honor to be published in the paper.[41] The *Advocate* reminded the members of the first graduating class of their responsibilities as they moved forward.[42]

Duncan recognized the need for public goodwill, yet he tempered this with the need to provide practical skills and intellectual stimulation to the residents. Duncan's early life had included pursuits "divided mainly between filial service on the farm and solitary effort in pursuit of mental culture."[43] This was the sort of experience he sought for children at the orphanage, and those he modeled by continuing to labor as well as to teach. When the orphanage's hired farmer left, Duncan assumed his duties, and the council later approved his permanent role as both superintendent and farmer.[44] Duncan maintained membership in the Indian International Agricultural Society and supported the Nation's participation in the Indian Agricultural Fair, an annual event held in Muskogee, Creek Nation, to highlight the "civilization" of the Five Tribes.[45] Therefore, he determined to prepare students to be farmers and skilled workers.

Part of the education the students received was an introduction to scientific agriculture. Beginning in the 1840s, colleges in the United States had begun building science departments devoted to the study of agricultural chemistry, including soil science. The U.S. government formed the Department of Agriculture in the late 1870s.[46] Scientific agriculture endorsed an increasing reliance on farm equipment, rather than animals or people, to produce larger crop yields. Many subsistence-level farmers lacked access to the funds necessary to purchase the equipment recommended, equipment the institutions often introduced. The orphanage, like Cherokee farms, cultivated corn as a staple. Duncan and the hired hands also used the acreage for orchards, grazing, and crops. The fifteen-acre garden also produced "an abundant supply of vegetables, lettuce, mustards, peas, beans, cabbage, parsnips, onions, tomatoes, pumpkins, squash, cucumbers, melons, and turnips."[47] Fruit trees, including the eight hundred ordered in 1880, supplied food as well as writing topics for the children.[48] For the first three-quarters of the nineteenth century, farmers moved from the planting of orchards for cider production and animal feed to the use of grafting to produce varieties of fruits available for human consumption.[49] Despite Duncan's efforts to grow apples, the orphanage supplemented the crop with purchased fruit. Duncan rarely bought milk; presumably the cows maintained by the hired herder provided milk. The orphanage never slaughtered its cattle, so Duncan ordered beef at regular intervals.[50] As of 1877, the orphanage cultivated ninety acres of corn, wheat, oats, and garden crops, which probably explains the absence of recorded payments for such items, since these crops would have fed both animals and people.[51]

Staff members theoretically provided gender- and class-based role models for children as a part of their educational and home life at the orphanage. Duncan provided boys with a male agricultural role model. As part of their manual-labor instruction, boys farmed and cut wood, and the matrons taught the girls to sew using the fabrics, needles, buttons, and pins purchased by the orphanage.[52] One year, Christmas presents for the girls included wax-faced dolls, bought "in vain" since a number of the girls inexplicably chewed their faces off.[53] In the late 1870s, store-bought toys were a relatively new luxury provided

Cherokee Orphan Asylum faculty with Superindendent Walter Adair Duncan, late spring 1875. Copy print of original photography by Jack Hiller. Courtesy Eliza Ross Collection, photographs, box 1, Research Division of the Oklahoma Historical Society, Oklahoma City.

to more privileged children in the United States, and they often served to reinforce "moral values and gender norms" of middle-class Protestants in the Northeast. When Cherokee children did have toys, they were often homemade.[54] Regardless of whether they were Cherokee or not, most rural and working-class children, if they "played" at all, "climb[ed] trees" and "play[ed] under trees in summer."[55]

But eastern urban gender norms, promulgated by U.S. reformers, did not always serve the needs of Cherokees, so there was considerable fluidity at the orphanage. Duncan seemed to assume an almost maternal role, more in keeping with traditional understandings of women's connections to farming and crops. In her description of Duncan's efforts to replace a large tree in 1881, his daughter Jennie said, "There are plenty of little maple trees coming up. Papa is trying to take care of them. In a few years they will be big and beautiful."[56] Both male and female students participated in "almost daily hunting

Kindergarten class of 1886–87. Courtesy Cherokee Heritage Center Archives, Tahlequah, Oklahoma.

exhibitions" for small game. In the early 1880s, even white teacher Emma Dunbar acquired a six-shooter and participated in the hunts.[57] In addition to the women killing game, the men at the orphanage nurtured crops. Unlike the seminaries, founded in the early 1850s and operated intermittently through statehood, which separated male and female students and staff, the orphanage provided a coeducational institution with less rigid boundaries dictating gendered behavior. The orphanage's practices also reflected the realities of living in the West more broadly. Carving out lives in rural western spaces often required the participation of all members, regardless of gendered expectations.[58] The orphanage encouraged gendered divisions of labor, but failed to rigidly apply them in all settings.

Like the other national institutions, the orphan asylum expanded the social and familial relationships of its employees and residents and provided both bilateral and patrilineal family models. The families of employees usually lived with them at the school and set the tone for interactions. Because Superintendent Duncan's own children attended the school at the orphanage, he was, in fact, a "papa," a role he extended to the orphans. In a history of Duncan's life, the anonymous author described how the superintendent "sheltered [the orphans] under the care of a father."[59] Perhaps because the niece of Reverend Joseph Franklin Thompson, Duncan's successor as superintendent in 1884, was enrolled as a student, the children referred to Thompson and his wife as "Uncle Joe" and "Aunt Ellen." Matrons and washerwomen often received the title "aunt," and, with the exception of the teachers, the title of "aunt" or "uncle" applied to nearly all the men and women who worked with the children on a daily basis.[60] The widow Katherine Caleb, who came from Delaware in the mid-1870s to work at the orphanage as a matron, brought her daughter Florence with her. Florence attended the orphanage as a pupil. In 1878, after the death of his second wife, Walter Adair Duncan courted and married Katherine Caleb at the orphan asylum. Reverend Joseph Thompson, after the death of his wife, Ellen, married the widow of orphanage physician Dr. Walter Thompson Adair. The *Orphans' News* included an announcement of baby Ella Mae Covel's first teeth. Ella Mae, whose father, John Covel, was a teacher, became a point of pride for all residents at the orphanage.[61]

All of the relationships and families formed within the context of the institutions ran the risk of being temporary. Throughout his tenure as superintendent, Duncan's annual expenses included the purchase of coffins. In 1876, new student James Burntweed died at the orphanage.[62] The summer of 1877 proved especially deadly. In May, orphan asylum pupil Lewey Downing, son of the former principal chief, died at the home of his brother.[63] Two weeks later, fourteen-year-old Mary Watts died.[64] In September, an accidental shooting at the orphanage claimed the life of one brother at the hands of the other.[65] A year later, Duncan reported two additional deaths.[66] The children also acknowledged the deaths of the students and staff at other institutions. In the wake of James Vann's death in 1879, the "meeting of the officers and pupils" published condolences to the "bereaved relatives and to the teachers and pupils of the Male Seminary" in the *Cherokee Advocate*.[67] The orphanage also faced near-constant threat of disease. In 1874, the *Advocate* reported, "All [orphans] doing well so far," during a measles outbreak.[68] Disease forced quarantines when the community at large or the orphanage experienced an outbreak. No one at the orphanage was immune: in 1876, Duncan suffered the loss of his eldest living son and his second wife while he was superintendent.[69]

Death also revealed the extent to which the institutions fulfilled the social service needs of children deemed "orphans" through definitions of a nuclear family rather than definitions of kinship. Lewey Downing had lost his parents before he died, but other relatives, including a brother, survived him. Nevertheless, the Nation, through the orphanage, cared for and educated him. In 1877, the Orphan Asylum Committee shared the loss of Mary Watts with her "relatives at home."[70] Some students even had a living parent. The death of a classmate in 1878 prompted one student to write, "My Dear Mother, I take my pen in my hand to tell you how I am getting along one of our school mates died here a while a go they will beary him to maraw. . . . Mother ples excuse my bad writeing I feale very sad today about the boy that dide."[71]

Death provided further evidence of the orphan asylum's integration of the hybrid social welfare system, yet it also revealed the ways Cherokee widows, who were the most connected to patrilineally oriented families, received additional protections from the nation's social welfare policies. In 1877, Lizzie Meigs Ross, a well-educated member of two prominent Cherokee families, took the position of matron as a means to support herself and her two children after the death of her husband.[72] When Ross died in 1883, the *Advocate*'s report of her death indicated that she had followed in the footsteps of her mother, who had served as matron at the orphanage earlier in her life after she was widowed. The protections offered to Cherokee women extended, in isolated cases, to non-Cherokee widows from the United States as well. For example, the Cherokee Orphan Asylum provided employment as a matron to Katherine Caleb, which in turn supported her children.[73]

The hierarchical structure of the school and its emphasis on individual achievement and behavior resulted in different dynamics between students and staff. The superintendent and teachers exercised authority over the children in ways that cooks and washerwomen did not. Staff occasionally subverted that authority. Jim Stearns, a cook known for his generosity to both staff and students, packed a sack of food for a child who ran away.[74] On the other hand, attempts by teachers to discipline children sometimes resulted in hard feelings. Right after the orphanage's move to Salina from the male seminary in 1874, when boys became "obstreperous" and refused "to respect the authority of their teachers," orphanage officials reestablished "quiet and control" through the expulsion of the "turbulent and disorderly spirits." One woman suggested to the *Advocate* that the boys' behavior served to undermine the reputation of the institution among the public, so such harsh treatment might have been necessary.[75] Children often preferred the outdoors to the classroom, as was the case with Jack Young Wolf, whom the principal teacher caught "going out the window when he was a student in the 1880s."[76] The orphanage's regimen, which emphasized academics and agriculture for the boys, deviated from traditional expectations of Cherokee men. Traditionally, women controlled the agriculture, and only young children assisted, as was the case with Catcher Rock. Some youths no doubt had difficulty adapting. Expelling students from the school as a means of discipline also points to an unwillingness of institutional authorities to use the orphan asylum as a reform school, which were becoming increasingly common in the United States.[77]

These incidents and others like them suggest that the orphanage served the interests of female students better than those of their male counterparts. In the opinion of a teacher who came from the East in the 1880s, girls "profit[ed]" from their education and became "educators either in the home or school." For her, the orphanage's benefits for boys were less clear: "Some of them engage in active business life, others follow the example of their forefathers, lounge, hunt, and fish."[78] The teacher constructed a binary of "civilized" versus "uncivilized" masculine pursuits similar to those espoused by U.S. officials and reformers—business pursuits on the one side and hunting and fishing on the other.

This critique misrepresented the practical realities of agrarian living and the limited professional opportunities available to Cherokee men that Duncan had discussed for decades.[79] Yet, critiques like this also created unease among Cherokee officials as it related to Cherokee masculine identity. The more elite male seminary struggled with similar dilemmas in the 1880s. National leaders questioned the merits of academics alone for its male seminary students, articulating the views Duncan had expressed in the 1850s:

> Our education is useful, but it does not go far enough. The pursuit of agricultural or other industries and the occupations of domestic life will be the lot of nearly all who are here and to send them forth ignorant of their duties and, many of them, to places not supplied with the abundance, the comforts, and the guardian care thrown around about them, without means and ability to acquire a livelihood, will be an experiment full of trial and danger, to both themselves and their people.[80]

By the 1880s, Cherokees worried that institutional guardians protected seminary boys from the conditions the world would expect them to face.

Too much book learning and not enough manual-labor training did not serve the interests of Cherokee men who chose to make their lives in the Cherokee Nation. The vast majority of Cherokee men found work as farmers and mechanics, not as attorneys and doctors.[81] As one writer wrote to the *Advocate*, "manual labor is honorable" for men and women.[82] Many of the men who had professional jobs also kept farms. Dissonance existed between imparting an academic education to the Nation's young men and meeting the need for farming, industrial, and subsistence skills essential to life in the Cherokee Nation. As they did in the centralization era, Cherokee officials agonized over the economic prospects for their sons. What middle-class reformers and teachers from the East endorsed as respectable professional work did not match the economic and geographic realities of Indian Territory. Educators debated these and other questions at the annual teacher's institutes.

Despite racially segregated schools, teachers, irrespective of race, attended the Cherokee Teacher's Institute held in Tahlequah, but the presence of African Cherokees did not mean that all Cherokee teachers acknowledged the equality of African Cherokee participants. Most Cherokee teachers were graduates of the male and female seminaries, which had long been critiqued for practices and attitudes that discriminated against monolingual Cherokees and those committed to osdv iyunvnehi, let alone freed people and African Cherokees. The seminaries did not encourage students to consider equal those of another class, race, or language. The seminaries educated the most affluent Cherokees, many of whom were the heirs of those who had benefitted from plantation slavery and who most closely adhered to patrilineal systems tied to the market economy.[83] Before beginning her position at the orphanage in 1885, Emma Dunbar, a teacher from the East, attended the Cherokee Teacher's Institute. She observed, "The Indian considers the negro far beneath him. And when a well educated colored teacher rises to make a few remarks, a large majority of the Cherokee teachers leave the building."[84]

A small minority stayed. Whether one of those individuals was Walter Adair Duncan, who served on the Cherokee Board of Education in 1885, is not clear. Despite the presence of a significant subset of Cherokees whose families had benefitted from earlier citizenship laws that privileged white intermarriage, many of these same individuals refused to respect the newest beneficiaries of citizenship laws. The role of the freedmen in the Cherokee Nation continued to be a controversial issue, and the Nation only grudgingly accepted any responsibility for them.[85] The Nation embedded a hospitality ethic into its services, but racism prevented some institutional leaders from expanding its national community ethic to include freedmen.

Eventually, children left the orphan asylum. In his 1877 annual report, Duncan inquired at what age orphans "should be received into the asylum, how long they should remain within its walls, and at what age this connection with the asylum should cease." Age of admission varied from year to year. Some years, the orphanage received students as young as five, and other years, they were as old as seven. Although residence usually ended at eighteen, on rare occasions, students remained until nineteen or twenty.[86] Some graduates married and established their own households; others went to live with relatives. At least one, Taylor Eaton, found employment at the orphanage. Reverend Thompson, who served as superintendent from

1884 to 1893 and again from 1897 to 1907, gave Eaton and his wife, Ida Cornstalk, both graduates of the orphanage, a wheelbarrow filled with provisions, and he continued to provision them in their first year of marriage.[87] The orphanage did not simply release children into the world without resources. During the 1876 school year, the "orphans discharged" totaled twelve, and each received a payment of ten dollars.[88] Whether Thompson provisioned other graduates is unclear.

Although the prison did not provide the home or the English-language education offered at the orphan asylum, officials and private citizens believed that it played a role in helping inmates develop a "good, civil, and sensible disposition." In the late 1870s, prison leaders looked to the New Codes of 1875 and the legal modifications that followed for the theoretical blueprints to accomplish this task. To national officials and reformers more broadly, inadequate job skills prevented men from becoming productive citizens and therefore encouraged recidivism.[89] Based on this belief, the national council in 1878 allocated funds to build shops and to instruct prisoners in a host of "mechanical arts," including blacksmithing, farming, wagon making and shoemaking, all marketable skills useful in Indian Territory.[90] Six months after the act passed, the prison was "rapidly training boarders," and the high sheriff planned to have shops erected "shortly."[91] In an attempt to achieve economic self-sufficiency, the prison sold surplus goods to pay instructors, purchase additional supplies, and enhance the prison coffers. Despite the training provided, blacksmithing remained an annual expense for the national prison.[92]

Cherokee law required that "all convicts sentenced to hard labor [should be] employed as constantly as may be, for the benefit of the Cherokee Nation."[93] Consequently, the high sheriff used convict labor for public works. In 1876, Samuel Sixkiller set the precedent by using prison labor to remove stumps and do weeding at the capitol building in addition to maintaining the grounds of the prison.[94] Prisoners replaced the roof and windows at the capitol and also kept up the outhouses for public buildings.[95] In 1878, Sixkiller oversaw the construction of a "large lime kiln, half a mile from town" that belonged to the Nation.[96] Inmates kept up the roads in Tahlequah and those that led to the male and female seminaries as well as the asylum.

They provided firewood to these institutions as well as to the capitol building, a task that remained constant throughout the prison's twenty-six years of operation.[97]

Although national officials likely conceived of labor as a means for prisoners to fulfill their responsibilities to the Nation for a wrong committed, communal labor was historically a key feature of Cherokee society. Even before written laws, penalties—including banishment—existed for those who refused to work and contribute to the community.[98] Into the mid-twentieth century, ethnographers would continue to document communal labor as a hallmark of Cherokee communities in the Cherokee Nation.[99] Instead of the earlier penalty of banishment, people who broke the law and undermined the community by ignoring their responsibilities faced imprisonment, fines, and manual labor.

To encourage labor projects, national officials incentivized it. The *Advocate* heralded the work performed by prisoners much like it did the educational attainments of students at the orphanage.[100] Because most prisoners were jailed for committing crimes against property, their sentences often combined monetary restitution with incarceration. Prisoners who labored on behalf of the Nation received, at least for a brief period during the 1880s, a one-dollar-per-day payment to aid them in paying fines and making pecuniary amends.[101] The prison only provided coffee and sugar, staples in Cherokee homes, to prisoners engaged in labor.[102] Laboring outside the prison walls restored mobility to people who continued to spend nearly all of their waking hours outdoors, but who were now confined to prison.

The national council adopted manual-labor training and public works strategies to convert felons into productive citizens, but labor was not the only proposed method of reform. In 1878, the *Cherokee Advocate* proposed that churches and benevolent societies should not only play a role in the reform of prisoners while they were incarcerated but also should aid prisoners' transitions back into society. In the writer's opinion, all the convicts discharged "should be attached to some church" where Christians offered "sympathy and encouragement." Churches, in the author's opinion, offered former prisoners "a welcome among the ranks of worthy people . . . protected from the danger of relapse to evil ways." The writer also proposed that the council employ chaplains so that prisoners could "realize the benefits of religious instruction."[103] The Nation's recognition of its Christian denominational diversity and its traditional adherents may have been the reason it failed to employ a chaplain, but the council later authorized the purchase of Bibles for those prisoners who desired to use them and required the high sheriff to grant ministers access to the prisoners at "seasonable and proper times."[104] National leaders chose not to privilege denominational teachings or subject prisoners to religious teachings they had not chosen.

While there was little concern that the employees were undermining institutional goals at the orphanage, the prison employees were another story. The Nation's authorities used institutional structures to promulgate and exert economic and social coercion to control not only the prisoners but the guards as well. As an 1879 case attests, while teachers met annually at the teacher's institutes to give speeches decrying intemperance or debate the decline of Cherokee masculinity as a result of the exclusively academic instruction provided to men at the Cherokee Male Seminary, alcohol-related offenses not only landed prisoners in jail but cost at least one guard his job.[105] Prison rule changes published by High Sheriff Jesse Mayes reiterated what had already become clear to one guard: any guard who allowed a convict to escape "through neglect . . . [would] be discharged at once."[106] Over time, prison laws and rules governing prisoners increasingly policed the actions of the guards.

Guards operated as the gatekeepers to freedoms, literally and figuratively. If guards turned their heads, slept on the job, or passed out from drink, prisoners could simply walk away. Guards also engaged in activities that men incarcerated in the prison enjoyed. An 1888 rule forbade anyone from playing cards anywhere in the vicinity of the prison.[107] Assuming this law was reactive, guards and prisoners benefitted from the idle pursuits cards provided until it took effect (and probably after). Guards' actions toward prisoners could subvert institutional aims, but they could also fulfill them.

Throughout the prison's existence, guards forged the daily relationships and performed the care that matrons, stewards, teachers, and farmers provided for residents of the orphanage and the asylum. They accompanied prisoners on work projects, guarded the cells at night, and served as interpreters when necessary. The released inmates received a new suit of clothes and a five-dollar cash payment.[108] In 1886, as a result of a prison budget shortfall, Deputy Charley Poorbear, whose wife Nellie was the cook at the prison, provided each of three inmates released five dollars, an amount equal to a month's salary as a guard.[109] Deputy Poorbear did not have to produce the money; but rather than allowing the prisoners to leave empty-handed, he personally fulfilled the financial obligation of the Nation.[110] He and his wife had taken care of the inmates on a daily basis before their release, and that obligation to care for others may have motivated his gesture.

When sentences expired, the Nation and individual Cherokees tried to ensure that released prisoners left with more than what they had when they entered. The law required that all personal effects confiscated from the prisoner to be returned. Through manual-labor training, the Cherokee Nation imparted skills to its prisoners that extended beyond their sentences. Upon release, they received their suit and their cash payment.[111] The obligation to prisoners was so strong that when financial difficulties made it impossible for the Nation to pay, Charley Poorbear did. Whether he felt it was his duty as a guard or as a fellow Cherokee or because he knew he would be repaid by the Nation at a later time, he offered the funds so that the released men could reenter society with some financial resources. Charley Poorbear's actions were not public except to prison administrators and the prisoners who received the money; other events at the prison were far more public.

The question of race played a public role in discussions of Cherokee social policy. The Cherokee Nation was a Native nation surrounded in Indian Territory by other Native nations, all of which had passed racially discriminatory laws before the war. In the post–Civil War era, each of the Five Tribes continued to grapple with their racialized pasts, presents, and futures.[112] Each enacted policies that impacted their African Indian citizens differently, and for the Cherokee Nation this was most obvious in the courts. For example, the Cherokee Nation impaneled exclusively African Cherokee juries to handle cases involving freedmen for a period of time after the Civil War. In 1876, it impaneled a "colored jury" to hear the "case of

Cherokee *Nation v. Chas Buffington*, charged with robbery."[113] In this case, the jury found Buffington not guilty. The use of African Cherokee juries may have been modeled after practices of the freedmen's bureau, or it may have reflected recognition on the part of some Cherokees from their experiences with federal and state courts that *justice* was wanting when juries and judges were not their peers. On at least one occasion in 1876, when a jury of African Cherokees delivered a guilty verdict in a murder case and sentenced the condemned to hang, officials muted the final words of one of its African Indian citizens. The press noted the execution of an African Cherokee, but "no reporter being present we shall not vouch for what he said."[114] African Cherokees, like other Cherokees, participated in nearly all facets of the judicial system. They could file complaints, but they relied on Cherokee juries to adjudicate these writs.[115] The Nation incarcerated African Indians in the prison as it did other Indians. After being convicted of larceny in 1879, for example, African Creek Jeff Marshall served time in the national prison.[116] Littlefield notes that at least one editor of the *Advocate* expressed concerns, however, that African Indians faced more severe penalties than did Indians.[117]

Outside critique may have played a role in the fact the Cherokee Nation, despite the widespread practice in the South, never used chain gangs to terrorize blacks and enforce a racial hierarchy, but other economic conditions existed that could easily explain its absence. In 1877, Cherokee John Wolfe "made a crop" with prison labor in the penitentiary's second year of operation.[118] Until 1890, the Cherokee Nation experimented with a variation of the convict lease system, but the Nation never turned its prisoners over to private contractors without the presence of prison officials. As other southern states understood, the convict lease system represented a means of generating income for the prison while occupying prisoners in labor. The high sheriff on occasion rented prisoners supervised by guards to Cherokees who needed labor, but there is no evidence to suggest that race played any role in whom he chose to participate in work projects. However, the inability of lessees to pay their fees in a reasonable amount of time resulted in new prison rules. Rule number four established that if "anyone hires jail labor, it must be settled at once, as soon as the work is done."[119]

Another factor that limited the rise of the convict lease system to exploit the labor of Cherokee inmates was the presence of white laborers. The New Codes permitted Cherokees to apply for one-year work permits to employ white tenant farmers, laborers, mechanics, and sharecroppers. The law required a $250 bond per laborer.[120] In exchange for their labor, whites were able to rent homes and reap the benefits of small farms of their own. However, the land they occupied remained the Nation's communal property.[121] The prison labor system at its height in the late 1870s and early 1880s dwindled within a decade and the high sheriffs reported few additional projects by lessees. The Cherokee Nation preferred a state-use system, whereby the Nation exclusively benefitted from the products and services of convict labor.[122]

By contrast, when reconstruction officially ended and with it federal oversight in the South, southern states used their prison systems to re-create the economic conditions provided by slavery. In the period before the war, 90 percent of prisoners in the South were white; from the Civil War through 1900, 90 percent were black. States across the South turned to convict leasing to provide a reliable labor stream for private industries, many of which had previously relied on enslaved labor. In 1886, the former president of Mercer University in Georgia defended Georgia's use of the leasing system and argued that it was harder on whites because they were not used to the labor conditions that African Americans were; further, he stated, the clothing and food provided to African Americans was better than what they would have otherwise.[123] As it had before the Civil War, the South resisted expanding the use of prisons. Instead, in the postwar period the states turned prisoners over to private industries with minimal, if any, state oversight. The results were damning.

With or without a brutal convict lease system, incarceration and coerced labor of any kind resulted in escape; this was true in the United States and in the Cherokee Nation. From 1873 to 1875, escapes hovered around 4.5 percent of the total Georgia lease population.[124] In 1874, seven prisoners escaped Fort Smith; five were recaptured, one was killed, and the fifth, a preacher, remained at large.[125] An 1882 report revealed that 1,100 men from southern states successfully escaped between 1880 and 1882.[126] In 1884, the *Cherokee Advocate* reprinted the following vignette from another paper outside the Nation to demonstrate how widespread and comedic escape had become: "A lawyer some time since asked a judge to charge the jury 'that it was better for ninety-nine guilty men to escape than for one innocent man to be punished.' 'Yes,' said the judge, 'I will give that charge; but it is the opinion of the court that the ninety-nine guilty men have already escaped.'"[127]

Prisoners who escaped often sought refuge in other jurisdictions, including Indian Territory. U.S. marshals policed western portions of Arkansas as well as the entirety of Indian Territory, an area of 74,000 square miles. To police this area, the federal court employed two hundred deputy marshals, a number insufficient to police an area of that size. Marshals often traveled two hundred to three hundred miles to retrieve prisoners. Many of those in custody escaped the officers tasked with their return.[128]

Incarcerated Cherokees' escapes occurred under similar conditions to those happening in the United States. In 1877, two years after the Cherokee National Prison opened, officials added the fence around the perimeter to discourage escape.[129] The fence provided both an additional barrier and a new expense of $150 annually to keep it in good repair.[130] Based on the number of escapes that followed, the fence probably did more to prevent theft from the prison grounds than it did to deter escape. In 1878, Big Bullet escaped from his guards in the Flint District.[131] The following year, four prisoners escaped from the prison.[132] Escapes increased during the 1880s. In 1882, Dosh Bennet, Isaac Dougherty, and William Pastel escaped from their work duty at the asylum.[133] Three years later, Stealer escaped from a seminary work project.[134] Looney Griffin and Dick Hays escaped while "on trust."[135] In 1886, the *New York Times* reported the "daring and successful" escape of Thomas Ross, an African Cherokee, and Cornelia Hendricks from the Cherokee penitentiary. Ross left a stuffed dummy in his cell. Hendricks feigned illness, which granted her more mobility.[136] They scaled the prison fence and, much to the chagrin of High Sheriff Charles Starr, stole "two fine horses" from the prison stables.[137]

Despite the prevalence of prisoner escape regardless of the sovereign authority responsible for the confinement of prisoners, speculators and territorializers capitalized on the perception that Indian Territory harbored dangerous criminals and argued that Native nations were incapable of policing their lands. This misrepresented the responsibilities that treaties designated the federal government fulfill and those that treaties forbade Native nations from instituting. For example, Cherokee officials lacked the right to police or adjudicate non-Indians in their midst.

In order to avoid looking ineffectual, Cherokee officials took numerous steps to prevent escape. Even before escapes became a serious problem, officials mandated that prisoners begin wearing striped uniforms in 1877.[138] In 1879, the act that also dismissed guards for intoxication authorized the high sheriffs to keep guards available for emergencies and required guards on the outside and inside of each cell "in order to prevent [prisoners] from plotting escape or other mischief." Anyone who escaped had his sentence doubled, and, if the escape resulted from a guard's dereliction of duty, the guard lost his job. To encourage district sheriffs to aid in the apprehension of escaped prisoners, High Sheriff William McCracken sent the local sheriffs a list of escaped prisoners broken down by district. The sheriff made sure to note rather smugly, "In justice to [himself], all escaped before [he] became High Sheriff."[139] Three months later, three prisoners escaped on McCracken's watch.[140]

The brand-new building of the 1870s limited escapes, but over time the prison's deteriorating conditions and constrained budgets aided prisoners' escape attempts. In 1893, High Sheriff McCracken described in detail the prison conditions that made escape possible: "The Jail as it now stands is in a terribly dilapidated state. The floors in the same being rotten—especially from one room to another— where a prisoner only has to dig under the partitions in order to get out into the hallways of the same."[141] Within fifteen years of its construction, the prison was in decline. The prison was the one institution unfunded by treaty provisions, which required its allocations to come from the general fund. Budget constraints made upkeep difficult, even when the result of neglect was prison breaks.

Even though officials justified the introduction of a prison as a means to eliminate escapes from justice, the transport involved in moving convicted prisoners from districts to Tahlequah added opportunities for escape. Both before and after the Nation built the prison, sheriffs and deputies had to guard prisoners awaiting trial. In 1878, though Big Bullet managed to escape his guards, he was apprehended a short time later.[142] Six years later, Tom Griffin gained access to one of his guard's guns and stole his guard's horse to make his escape. To his credit, he discarded the gun and returned the horse after getting away.[143]

In many ways the stealth required for escape and the hunting of escapees that followed had become an important rite of passage for a sizeable minority of Cherokee men; it also provided financial incentives to private male citizens to support the efforts of the prison. By the early 1880s, the council offered ten dollars for the return of an escaped inmate to the prison.[144] High Sheriff McCracken, embarrassed by the escapes on his watch, offered fifty dollars for the return of two escapees, more than double the normal rate.[145] Private citizens, like Nelson Hicks and D. H. Williams, also captured and returned escapees for compensation.[146] Guards took advantage of these opportunities and supplemented their prison salaries by apprehending escaped inmates. In June of 1882, the national treasurer paid Cull Thorne, a guard who later became high sheriff, ten dollars for hunting escaped convicts.[147] Bounties became a lucrative means for men to generate income, but another expense for the Nation was tied to prison administration. On at least one occasion, prisoners expected returned escapees to abide by traditional community ethics. Upon Bear Toater's return in 1884, the other prisoners imposed a communitarian ethic and redistributed his tobacco among all the prisoners; even they received a reward upon an escaped prisoner's return.[148]

Although its administrative practices and the centralized location of the national jail where executions were performed were new, execution rituals had changed little since before removal. In 1828, John Huss had translated the final words of a Cherokee man executed for murder near the Chickamauga courthouse in the old Cherokee Nation in the East. The man addressed his "uncles," encouraging them to abandon alcohol and "follow that which is good."[149] Sixty-five years later and seven hundred miles west, a "crowd had assembled to witness the execution of Sam Mayes. With Henry Dick as interpreter, he confessed to having committed the crime, though it was not premeditated murder. He gave advice to young boys not to carry pistols, get drunk and be tough and to obey their parents."[150] Instead of deferring to his uncles as matrilineal family systems required, Dick deferred to his parents, which was indicative of Cherokee families' shifting family configurations.

The Cherokee Nation's rejection of reforms opposing capital punishment set them apart from the views of eastern reformers, but placed them squarely within western approaches to capital punishment. As Durwood Ball argues, for territories that sought statehood, reigning in the behavior of unruly wild men was a crucial step. Hangings offered those men's bodies up for the civilizing efforts. The perception that the West needed to be tamed through law and order connected directly to the overwhelming presence of Indian peoples, especially Indian men.

In Ball's assessment of masculinity in the West, execution rituals provided men a final opportunity to become civilized and at the same time, the state maintained and exercised its state power.[151] The pattern was fairly consistent. Courts issued a verdict and sentenced the men to die. For seven to ten days after sentencing, jail keepers maintained a constant watch over the men and provided them access to clergy to encourage their spiritual redemption. The death proclamation and procession to the gallows reaffirmed the power of civil society's institutions to onlookers. Once on the gallows, men had the opportunity to make confessions and claim their brief place in civilized society by unemotionally admitting wrongdoing, professing their Christianity, offering a warning to others who might be tempted to follow in their footsteps, and then accepting their fate.[152]

Whereas western territories developed with statehood as a likely end goal, the vast majority of Cherokee people opposed statehood. Cherokee officials performed similar public rituals as other governments in the West, but the rituals also advertised the sovereignty of the Cherokee Nation. The execution rituals worked to assert its status as a sovereign equal *and* to affirm the humanity of Cherokee people, especially its men. Some men rode to the gallows on top of their coffins.[153] Just as it had done when it passed laws acknowledging the rights of Cherokee people to an insanity defense in criminal wrongdoing, the Nation used executions as symbolic rituals affirming Cherokee masculinity and human dignity to nonnatives.

The Cherokee Nation's emphasis on community obligations, kin, and family also set it apart from many other western spaces. On the morning of Dirt Seller's execution at the Cherokee National Prison in October of 1877, his wife and three children visited him. On the scaffold, "he called for his three children, the oldest seven or eight, with whom he affectionately parted by shaking hands with them."[154] He informed the minister he was ready to die, "shook hands all around," "prayed for about a half a minute to himself," and in ten minutes "Dirt Seller was pronounced dead."[155] Legal historian Rennard Strickland recorded an instance of a Cherokee family picnicking together immediately before the man's hanging.[156] The Nation continued to offer prisoners freedom to get their affairs in order and the executive time to hear any potential appeals. For instance, Principal Chief Dennis Bushyhead issued Stover a thirty-day respite before his execution in 1885.[157] Execution procedures provided prisoners the chance to fulfill their obligations to families, file appeals, and make final statements to the larger community.

As in other municipalities, responsibility for carrying out the death penalty rested with the high sheriff, although the guards sometimes performed the execution. High Sheriff John Hawkins and the guards led Spade Sunshine to the gallows in 1887, put the rope over his neck, placed a black cloth over Sunshine's face, and pulled the rope connected to the trap door.[158] In 1893, Wash Mayes served as high sheriff when his nephew was executed. Rather than perform the execution, he locked himself in his office the entire day and let the undersheriff carry out the deed. John Duncan, Walter Adair Duncan's only living son, who served as the Cherokee Nation's last high sheriff from 1895 to 1900, never "sprang the trigger on a single man." Instead, he assigned the job to guard Cale Starr, who had served as the high sheriff before him.[159] One official often tied the rope and another pulled the trigger. Regardless of the symbolic purposes the execution rituals served for the Nation, the executions were "sad day[s]" for the families of those executed.[160]

The Cherokee Nation's gallows, ca. 1898–1901. Courtesy A. Heye Foundation Collection, photographs, box 1, Research Division of the Oklahoma Historical Society, Oklahoma City.

After the men were executed, families often claimed their kin and buried them in their community cemeteries.[161] In 1891, when the Nation executed the Dunawas brothers together, their mother, a traditional Cherokee healer, walked beside the wagon carrying her sons' coffins to the family cemetery. She stayed with them for seven days after their burials.[162] Burial, in a palpable way, restored men to their communities and families forever.

Restoration of residents to their community was the ultimate goal of the orphanage and the prison. When it opened in 1875, restoration was also the goal of administrators for the individuals who entered the Asylum for the Deaf, Dumb, Blind, and Insane. Officials had justified the asylum's existence based on its ability to provide a home and care to (dis)abled and indigent pensioners while reducing the national costs of that care. Chronic illness presented an economic, medical, and social challenge to restoration and to the Nation's ability to provide a home to residents.

Individually and communally, the administrators at the asylum had far fewer professional and personal experiences to draw from relative to their institutional counterparts. Orphan care in the Nation had developed over thirty-four years, and several plans were devised before the orphanage actually opened. Duncan had been thinking about education, orphan care, and manual labor long before he was tapped to run the institution. The prison had been debated for over two decades before it was actually built. In the late 1870s, (dis)ability provisions were new and other than managing guardianships and aiding pension acquisitions, the Nation had yet to seriously consider how to provide care for residents with a range of physical and mental health needs.

The New Codes tasked the asylum's board of trustees with management of the facility and creation of its bylaws. They required the appointed steward to see to the facility's operation and daily care of residents. The codes permitted the board to contract with a physician until a permanent medical superintendent was hired. The laws also established two paths for resident admission. The first was social need. In order to be admitted, "a person must have cause, be destitute, and [have] no relatives able or willing, to be burdened with his support."[163] At least some of the patients had care before they arrived at the asylum. "Blind Cherokee Sam," who arrived at the asylum in 1877, had been living with Mrs. C. M. Beck in the Choctaw Nation for the previous twelve years.[164] The need for medical care alone did not make a person eligible for services: the failure on the part of kin to provide care made one eligible. Embedded in the admissions policy was a needs-based requirement based on the inability of families to meet the basic needs of (dis)abled Cherokee people. What remained less clear was whether the Nation could fulfill those needs.

The second admissions procedure applied solely to people who were mentally ill. "If friends or relations of any lunatic" neglected or refused to put their relatives in the asylum, a sheriff armed with the "petition of a citizen" could place an individual there. The asylum board then evaluated the individual and made a final determination of the appropriateness of institutionalization.[165] The presence of the asylum and the alternative admissions procedures for those living with mental health conditions signified far more developed public health procedures than those established by the 1826 law that provided for an insanity defense in criminal proceedings. With a national asylum, the responsibility to manage the troublesome insane shifted from the local community to the Cherokee Nation.

Recipients of national pensions became the most likely candidates for asylum residency. The need for financial assistance from the Nation was evidence that families were unable to provide for individuals, the primary criterion for admissions. From the Nation's perspective, the asylum was a more efficient means of distributing aid than cash payments. When the asylum opened its doors for residents in 1875, the Nation suspended all pension payments and repealed its pension laws.[166] Henceforth, if former pensioners needed support, they had to become residents of the asylum. Despite the suspension of pension payments, pensioners did not flock to the institution for services. In 1877, Dr. E. Poe Harris, the second physician assigned to the institution, reported the presence of six residents, four blind, one rheumatic, and one paralytic, despite a list of dozens of pensioners published in the *Advocate* in the early 1870s.[167]

The asylum attempted to provide care to patients who were served in separate institutions in many regions of the country. In 1877, the steward reported the presence of eleven blind inmates and three labeled "insane" or "idiots" (probably the hearing and speech impaired), out of a total of twenty-two.[168] The asylum also housed several amputees. Cherokee families' needs and expectations from the asylum and their general ideas about care and treatment shifted over time for reasons not entirely different than those outside the Cherokee Nation.

Despite the large number of blind residents at the asylum, the Nation did not provide the kind of education or treatments increasingly available to the visually impaired throughout the United States. Even before removal, the Cherokee press had covered advances in the treatment and education of the blind.[169] The *Advocate* continued to cover and highlight advancements in Braille education and the prosthetics available to amputees.[170] Cities in the Northeast, including Boston, Philadelphia, and New York, had opened schools for the blind during the 1830s and 1840s. In 1860, Arkansas established its first such institution in Arkadelphia; the school relocated to Little Rock eight years later.[171] Most schools for the blind in the United States provided literacy skills, weaving and sewing, woodworking, and music classes. Some provided college preparatory training. But none of this translated into additional social provision allocations for the (dis)abled by the Cherokee Nation. In 1877, four blind residents left the asylum. At least one of those residents sought the services of another doctor. One woman, Nellie Peacheater, a monolingual Cherokee speaker, requested a leave to visit family; yet she took all of her clothes with her when she left.[172] The asylum did provide residents access to an organ and hymnals, but never employed a music teacher.[173] In 1882, Mrs. Alberty, the steward's wife, helped inmates produce two hundred yards of rag carpeting. Manual-labor opportunities and training were the only education inmates received and that largely depended on the staff, or more specifically on the steward's wife, who used her skills and position to benefit some residents.[174]

Education for the hearing impaired in the United States had advanced in the same way as that offered to the blind.[175] The institution geographically closest to the Cherokee Nation was the Arkansas Deaf-Mute Institute, opened in Little Rock in 1867.[176] Despite the education many people with (dis)abilities received at these schools, few graduates were able to overcome prejudices that the visually and hearing impaired were lazy, incapable of learning, and unable to earn their way in the world. Regarded as inefficient workers and relegated to underpaid manual-labor work, many were unable to support themselves, so they returned to institutions and exchanged services for room and board.[177]

Within the Cherokee Nation, however, people did not necessarily view blindness and other (dis)abilities as deficiencies. The deficiencies rested with family members unwilling to fulfill their kinship responsibilities. Families with sufficient means accommodated family members who were differently abled. When her aging grandmother was thrown from a horse and injured right after the Civil War, for example, Emma Blythe Sixkiller returned home from the Moravian mission school she had attended to help care for her. When her grandmother later lost her sight and her hearing, Sixkiller and her children assisted her in the final seven years of her life. In 1887, male seminary graduate Harvey Wirt Courtland Shelton left Dartmouth College to return to the Cherokee Nation to care for his sick aunt who had raised him.[178]

The Nation increasingly reported, described, and responded to incidents of moral insanity among Cherokees. Moral insanity was the idea that external conditions in the world could lead to insanity. In 1887, the *Advocate* reported the suicide of former High Sheriff Samuel Sixkiller's nephew. In response to a sudden bout of insanity, the young man threw himself into the path of an oncoming train.[179] Ten years later, a Cherokee writer to the *Advocate* argued the moral legitimacy of suicide as a legal right of self-defense against the "opposing force of the world"; put another way, the writer argued that suicide offered a legitimate treatment for moral insanity.[180] The paper also reported numerous high-profile cases involving insanity defenses in the United States, several of which involved assassinations of elected officials, including President Garfield's assassin.[181] These cases, in addition to being sensational, probably resonated with Cherokees. Cherokee leaders were willing to link Cherokee criminal behavior to insanity. By the late nineties, the asylum employed male "sick nurses" who had previously been employed as prison guards probably to monitor the criminally insane.[182]

Gadugi required that Cherokee people accommodate the needs of their (dis)abled family and community members instead of asking those family members to adapt to them or earn their keep. Cherokee society had long shown the ability to adapt to human difference.[183] In 1877, asylum residents Sah sah, who was blind, and Creek Killer, who was crippled, "formed a 'cooperative association' using each other's strengths to visit the 'ladies seminary.'"[184] Margaret Galcatcher, a blind resident at the asylum in the 1880s, "did lots of work at the Asylum" according to the matron. When U.S. resident Benjamin Stone arrived in the Cherokee Nation in the 1890s, he met the Kerby Smith family. Although Mrs. Kerby Smith was blind and deaf, the family had devised a system of hand shaking to communicate. The Smiths perhaps drew upon the system used by Cherokees who did not have physical (dis)abilities but who lacked English language skills to communicate, a method that Stone also witnessed in the Bunch family.[185]

Functioning family systems, adequate resources, and gadugi protected (dis)abled Cherokee Nation citizens from the prejudices many
(dis)abled citizens in the states faced including the view that a
(dis)ability was something the individual had to overcome as opposed
to the view that the community bore the responsibility to accommodate difference.[186]

Within the Cherokee Nation, individual Cherokees' attitudes toward
care were diverse, like those outside the Nation. However, the diagnosis, treatment, and legal protections offered by professionals to
white U.S. citizens were not the same as those available to Cherokees,
other Indians, and African Americans. This was in part due to conclusions drawn by medical professionals decades earlier. In the first
issue in 1844 of the *Journal of Insanity*, the precursor to the *Journal of
Psychiatry*, a scholar concluded that Cherokees and Africans were
incapable of suffering from insanity.[187] As evidence of his claim related
to the Cherokees, he cited a medical missionary to the Cherokees
who recorded no cases of insanity during or following removal.
Rather than assume that the community's violence that had followed
removal was in any way a legitimate psychological response to the
trauma induced by U.S. policy and individual states' actions, missionaries and medical professionals came to the conclusion that Cherokees were exempt from insanity. This conclusion—that repressive
policies produced no long-term psychological consequences for which
the United States or its citizens needed to atone through social welfare policies—provided legal and moral indemnity for policies and
actions committed by individuals, local, state, and national governments. At the 1863 meeting of the Association of Medical Superintendents of American Institutions during the Civil War, doctors
accepted the legitimacy of moral insanity, but worried that it might
be used as an excuse for "legal and social implications."[188] If medical
superintendents continued to apply the professional standards
established decades earlier that established racial exemptions to
those capable of experiencing insanity, neither African Americans
nor Cherokees could ever hope for a diagnosis of moral insanity to
explain criminal behavior.

As medical science and training took hold in the United States,
ideas about insanity were changing, but the changes in attitudes

toward the insane remained uneven. U.S. medical professionals advocated medical explanations for insanity, even as many in the middle
class continued to understand insanity through their religious worldviews.[189] In 1874, Chicago neurologists began publishing the *Journal
of Nervous and Mental Diseases*, and, a year later, the American Neurological Society formed. Physicians began to question the ability
to cure mental illness while they increasingly debated the causes of
insanity as physical as opposed to moral.[190]

Cherokees' interactions with their own institutions and the ideas
coming from outside the Cherokee Nation led to changes in care
within the Nation. In 1884, the *Advocate* received a copy of a book
written by the former president of the Board of Charities to the State
of Pennsylvania George L. Harrison.[191] His book compiled and assessed
the states' and territories' legislation related to insanity and provided
recommendations to aid "that most to be pitied class of humanity."
The *Advocate* encouraged "Cherokee lawmakers . . . our executive
. . . and all . . . [in] official positions" to read it, but especially the
preface called "Legislation on Insanity."[192]

In the 1870s and later, the Cherokee Nation's efforts to professionalize its own institutional staff to care for institutional residents
affected men and women differently at the professional and care
level. Most of the leadership roles created at institutions benefitted
Cherokee men who had received advanced education in the United
States. The lack of access to professional training for women in the
United States impacted all women, including Cherokee women.

In 1879, the young woman who would become the first female
doctor in Indian Territory graduated from the female seminary.[193]
Isabel Cobb would go on to pursue an advanced medical degree,
receiving her MD in 1892 from the Women's Medical College in Pennsylvania, founded by Elizabeth Hopewell. Despite having almost
exclusive rights to obstetrics and gynecology (also known as mid-
wifery) before the American Revolution, women at the end of the
nineteenth century constituted only 5 percent of the doctors with
medical degrees. The systematic denial of women to medical schools
led to this underrepresentation. The numbers dropped even more
when nursing schools were established to divert women into a sub-
sidiary role to aid male doctors.[194]

The Women's Medical College directly benefitted Indian women and contributed to the presence of institutionally trained female doctors in Indian Territory.[195] After finishing her degree at the college, Isabel (Belle) Cobb spent six months interning in the Staten Island Nursery and Child's Hospital and then returned to the Cherokee Nation. However, when she applied to serve as the medical superintendent to the seminaries, prison, and asylum, she was passed over in favor of Dr. Richard Fite, an intermarried white citizen who had served the institutions before.[196] The Cherokee Nation's principal chiefs, who were responsible for institutional appointments, tended to subscribe to patrilineal family systems that privileged men as economic providers in families and viewed women as managers of the domestic space. Cobb suspected that they were not ready for a woman to serve in the position.[197] Cherokee women continued to serve as local healers, but that was not what Belle Cobb was trained to be. Her assessment fails to consider the importance of gadugi. Cobb's family did not move to the Cherokee Nation until the 1870s. As a result, she did not share the same history with most Cherokee people and had limited interactions with Cherokee people over time. It is possible that this played a role in her not receiving the position. Regardless of the reason, Cobb, like other early female doctors, benefitted from a shortage of doctors in the West. Over time she built a successful practice among the very patients male Cherokee medical school–trained doctors were ill-equipped to handle from the perspective of a traditional social welfare system—women.[198] Women's specific conditions, pregnancy and menstruation, required the care of other women.

U.S. citizen Elizabeth Hopewell's success at providing women's medical education implicates the Cherokee Nation in its exclusion of women from professional social welfare positions. The inability of Cherokee officials to imagine institutional medical care administered by a female doctor coupled with the limits of institutional budgets to adequately staff facilities meant that medical superintendents were not prepared to meet the needs of menstruating or pregnant residents at the asylum—nor should they have been by traditional social welfare standards. Historically, menstruating Cherokee women isolated themselves in special women's houses, ate from special dishes, and bathed in fresh water before resuming their places in the community.[199] Kinship obligations ensured that other women in the household brought food, and that both men and women took responsibility for fulfilling her duties.[200] Within a Cherokee worldview, blood belonged inside the body, and when it flowed outside the body, it had the power to affect the health of the entire community.

Cherokees who held to traditional beliefs prevalent in the early nineteenth century about care of the sick, mentally ill, or infirm believed that contact with menstruating or pregnant women could undo any treatment provided. Ceremonial leaders forbade menstruating and pregnant women as well as their husbands from participating in ceremonies because of the power imbalances their presence created. Nonetheless, the superintendents' descriptions of women's conditions at the asylum remained relatively vague. Thus, as late as 1906 Cherokee people continued to worry about the power of women's specific conditions. For example, when Nick Cummingdeer treated John Ragsadale's wife for a snakebite, he specifically told Mr. Ragsdale not to permit any pregnant women to visit or the medicine would not be effective. Out of feelings of hospitality and neighborliness, Ragsdale allowed a pregnant neighbor to look in on his wife. Immediately after her visit, his wife took a turn for the worse that required Cummingdeer to return and repeat the treatment.[201] The public acknowledgment and sequestering of such women was normal, as was their social interaction when they were not menstruating.

Gender-specific concerns that related to the power of bodily fluids pervaded traditional ideas about care; when these ideas converged with professional medical training and fiscal limitations, it resulted in the neglect of women at the asylum. If the Cherokee Nation had in fact been committed to traditional ideas about medical care or even to adequate but gendered care of its patients, employing a male and a female doctor made perfect sense. The closest it came to an effort of this kind were the medical superintendent's annual requests for funds to hire a female nurse from the late 1880s through the early 1890s for the five or six female residents who "do not appear to realize the propriety of personal cleanliness—the idea of attending to nature's demands unaided never enters their minds."[202] Despite being trained to "treat" patients, superintendents resisted providing the less appealing labor necessary for patients' care. Instead, care of female patients fell to the steward's wife, if he was married, or to other female patients.

Without women to care for other women, their care suffered. Satiza Tucker entered the asylum in 1887 with a diagnosis of insanity. She required constant care and did not "attend to nature's demands." Tucker's sister visited her, and what she found "was deficient in every respect." Tucker had lost ninety pounds, was scantily clad, and her hands were covered in what appeared to be dry feces. Charlotte, another inmate, was the only person available to respond to Tucker's sister's requests while she was visiting. Immediately after Tucker's sister filed the complaint, board member Looney Gourd requested funds for a female nurse, though it appears that the board never hired one.[203]

The medical superintendent's education and training led officials at the asylum to pursue treatments common throughout the United States. In 1877, expenditures included the purchase of an "electrical apparatus" for use by Dr. Harris.[204] The use of electrotherapeutics was common throughout the nineteenth century; even the basement of the U.S. Capitol contained a room with an electrical apparatus that officials used to stimulate themselves after lengthy sessions or long speeches.[205] Professionals and the public embraced the possibilities of electrotherapeutics as restorative and medicinal. Psychiatrists touted its use for the treatment of rheumatism, hysteria, neurasthenia, dyspepsia, and constipation. Although the asylum purchased the device, no evidence indicates how or on whom Dr. Harris used it. Electrotherapeutics was both cutting-edge and controversial; the Indian Territory Medical Association expelled at least one of its members because of his association with an "electric physician."[206]

Although not used in the 1870s, restraints were adopted by asylum medical practitioners in the 1880s, another practice that generated debate in the United States. U.S. asylum officials faced the practical reality of managing a soaring patient population at facilities built and staffed for smaller numbers. Most medical practitioners agreed that restraints presented a practical solution when a patient presented a danger to him or herself or others.[207] However, restraints also became a substitute for attendants. In the 1880s, Cherokee asylum officials justified the purchase of six straightjackets and two metal cages not only for inmate safety but also for economic reasons. The trustees reported to Principal Chief Bushyhead that it had become "necessary during the past two years to have two substantial wooden cages constructed . . . for the safe-keeping of the more unruly and unmanageable inmates . . . to restrain them from harm."[208] The cages also provided additional "protection to the plastering on the walls which had become injured and defaced."[209] The purchase implies the failure of the asylum staff to keep pace with the changing resident demographics. It also suggests that Cherokee Nation institutions faced many of the same budgetary constraints that led to declining conditions and care over time in many state and private institutions.[210]

In the late 1870s, the asylum encouraged the freedom and independence of residents both on and beyond its grounds. In 1877, seminary students visited the asylum and spent time with residents.[211] Residents regularly made appearances in Tahlequah to voice serious grievances or simply make their presence known. Four years later, Old Goose, an asylum resident, "made a speech in the Council Chamber." Goose "wanted to draw his part of the money out and go home and live."[212] Although he was unable to get his share, he did leave the asylum. Six years later, Lum Langly "paid the Capital a flying visit and broke the monotony of the town with his comical ways and exchange of peculiar with the boys."[213] Residents also solicited leaves of absence from the asylum. Officials granted Josephine Rider a four-month leave and Arley Osage time away to visit with friends.[214] These leaves did not always end well; Osage met an untimely death "while with some of her friends on 14 Mile Creek."[215] Such tragedies preceded stricter standards of release. In recognition of the difficulties many residents faced outside, asylum officials occasionally bent rules to readmit those who had left without authorization. Five years after his speech to the council, Goose returned to the asylum after he had "forfeited his rights by leaving." Instead of turning the old man away, the asylum admitted him illegitimately. He later died and was buried at the expense of the asylum.[216]

A community beyond the asylum offered the most successful means of discharging patients from the institution. In 1877 when

Nellie Peacheater left (with all of her belongings) for a visit to her family, it was her family who continued to care for her. In 1900, her sister Sallie Manus enrolled with the Dawes Commission on behalf of Nellie who was in Manus's care.[217] In 1882, after Rachel Cornsilk ran away, her neighbors reported that "she had greatly improved and that she would not return to the Asylum as an Inmate." Tahlequah District judge Faulkner married George Washington Hughes "late of the Insane Asylum" to Josephine Redden of Arkansas.[218] Five years later, asylum resident Little George courted a neighbor's daughter, and with her mother's approval, they married and he left the asylum. Dr. Adair reported to the council that Little George was able to find a home and "a person able, and willing to be burdened with his support."[219]

George Washington Hughes, Little George, and Rachel Cornsilk owed their departures from the asylum to traditional social services, not institutional treatment. The asylum, on paper, supported the residents' return to their communities. After learning of Cornsilk's improvement, asylum officials, "let her go and [wished] joy be with her." Adair called "attention" to "a pleasing first" when Little George was able to sever his institutional ties. To Little George, the board and officials said, "Go in peace, and joy go with you"; they blessed the union and "plac[ed] him upon a level with his neighbors."[220] Institutional officials did not "release" these individuals because they had cured them. Instead, individuals had established relationships—Cornsilk with her community and Little George with his wife—that made the institution unnecessary. The lack of or failure to form relationships jeopardized the ability of residents to be restored to their community.

Instead of encouraging community ties, however, the asylum tightened its control over the residents. Less than two months after Goose's speech before the council in 1881, the *Advocate* published an opinion "that the Insane Asylum was fixed for putting and keeping people in it, when they were sent there declared by the Judge to be insane." Letting people out who were deemed insane by the courts undermined the Nation's guardianship decisions. In 1890, the asylum board of trustees took steps to limit residents' ability "to roam around the country as ha[d] been practiced in the years past."[221] These measures may have been for resident safety, but the change limited community interaction as well as the freedom of residents. Without access to the outside world, residents stood little chance of being released or reunited with family. Many of them consequently met their end at the asylum, succumbing to a host of illnesses. In 1877, Annie Young and Nelson Boston, for example, died of consumption.[222] Seven years later, William Patrick, who was blind and insane, "wasted away with general debility." Another resident died from "congestion of the Brain and complication of the bowels and spine."[223] In 1897, Charles Carr died of heart failure.[224] Unable to help them further, the asylum provided coffins and a burial. Continued community interaction benefitted the lives and well-being of residents.

The imprecision of medical diagnosis led to reports with vague causes of death as well as a wide range of symptoms associated with insanity. Some of the diagnoses reflected those common throughout the United States—fevers, acute mania, and epilepsy, which fell into the category of insanity throughout the nineteenth century.[225] In 1884, asylum medical superintendent Dr. Adair reported the death of Ellen Garret, a Shawnee citizen of the Cherokee Nation, who was "insane and affected with Epileptic Spasms."[226] Some patients fell into a general category of "insane" with little description or definition provided. The *Advocate* reported that one of the inmates at the asylum "amuses himself by imitating the crowing of a rooster, which he begins at early dawn and keeps . . . up until day." To the *Advocate* editor, the "poor man [was] hopelessly insane."[227] Victorian psychiatrists often linked women's mental health to women's reproductive systems, including menstruation, pregnancy, childbirth, and menopause.[228] U.S. doctors regularly diagnosed women with hysteria, but none of the women at the Cherokee asylum ever received this diagnosis.

As professional psychiatrists in the United States worked to divorce ideas about medical care of the insane from the grips of theology, Cherokees applied their own worldviews to this process. In the 1880s, an intermarried white man, Jim Connally, repeatedly entered the asylum. Connally lived in Vinita on a piece of land long associated with the ghosts of two horse thieves who made sounds resembling crashing dishes and pounding noises. Even more powerful evidence of these ghosts was the dinner plate–sized white lights that appeared at the horizon, moved mysteriously across the land, and then dipped out of sight.[229]

Local Cherokees and medical professionals agreed that he was insane, but they likely came to that conclusion for different reasons. Rather than learn to live with the presence of the spirits, as Cherokees who resided in the vicinity had, Connally responded to the ghosts by menacing his neighbors; he chased one young woman, lurked about another's house, and caused a third woman to hide with her children in an inner room until he departed.[230] His behavior led to his repeated incarceration in the asylum. While there, he showed improvement, but after returning home, his condition recurred. After one release, Connally had no sooner returned home than he began to chop down small trees on the property to barricade his road from intruding spirits. Once he finished with the small trees, he moved on to his orchards. To Cherokee people, cutting down a food source and harassing women and children was evidence of insanity, seeing ghosts was not. Local Cherokees credited Connally's insanity to his unacceptable responses to ghosts, not to his imagining their existence. Most Cherokees accepted that they shared their world with ghosts. Seeing ghosts meant that Connally needed to placate them, not enter an asylum.[231] But as an intermarried white man, Connally could be expected to behave irrationally even in the face of an accepted occurrence. In any case, he soon disappeared.

Despite agreement that Connally was insane, traditional Cherokees' ideas about care diverged from those of professional medical practitioners providing institutional services. Traditional Cherokee social welfare required holistic care and did not necessarily distinguish between mental and physical illnesses or the cures appropriate for them. Some healing required the entire community's participation, and a community ethic required everyone to participate. Consequently, the asylum often took on the appearance of a hospital. Cherokee people expected the medical superintendents to provide medical services to nonresidents for fevers, bowel complaints, sore eyes, sore throats, pneumonia, and bronchitis.

In response to these requests, superintendents asked for economic and bureaucratic guidance. One, for example, wrote that "persons lame with old chronic ulcers of the leg frequently apply for admission . . . and we have doubts . . . as to whether persons of this class are entitled under the law to a home in this Asylum."[232] At other times, need for treatment was immediate, and the asylum provided emergency medical care. The *Cherokee Advocate*, for example, reported the amputations of B. T. Will's leg in 1877 and fourteen-year-old Will Irons's foot in 1888 at the asylum.[233] Alex Coon, sane and otherwise able-bodied, arrived with "one of those indolent ulcers" and died eight days later, a situation that obligated the asylum to pay for his burial in its graveyard.[234] As a result of the additional burden such cases placed on the facility, the medical superintendent repeatedly called for clarification from the board for the admittance policy for patients with medical conditions who did not fall under the specific categories of (dis)abled and indigent.[235] Regardless of its official designation, however, Cherokees recognized the asylum as an institution intended to address public health, a designation that they interpreted broadly.

Even though the Cherokee Nation never explicitly infringed on the rights of traditional Cherokee doctors and their presence remained ubiquitous into the twentieth century, the rise of institutionalized medicine began to displace traditional practices, especially in bigger towns where doctors who attended medical school were more likely to reside. Even though it was more isolated, children who grew up in the orphan asylum as opposed to their local communities became accustomed to institutionally trained doctors. When children became ill, the medical superintendent was their primary doctor, although matrons occasionally provided care.

Most seminary students' families preferred western-trained physicians. In 1893, when the council debated cuts to its medical superintendent services, a strong case was made that seminary families would send their children elsewhere if a doctor were not readily available to their daughters. The council rejected this position. It argued that seminary students' families could afford to pay for a doctor's services if their daughters required care, unlike families of those residing at other institutions.[236] As the council had when it debated cuts to the public schools and the seminaries before the Civil War, it privileged the funding for the services provided to those with less individual wealth. The council maintained the medical super-intendent services for the orphanage, but decided that the asylum, seminaries, and prison, all located in the Tahlequah and Park Hill area, could share the services of a medical superintendent.

Medical superintendents exercised the most control at the asylum, though this developed over time. The prisoners, who were able-bodied men, exercised the most choice in their medical treatment. In 1887, when John Stover was shot during an escape, Hog Shooter, a traditional medical practitioner, treated him.[237] The medical super-intendent's authority at the insane asylum eventually surpassed the steward's, and the rules that followed further restricted outside visitation. This left treatment that for some may have included electrotherapeutics in the hands of the medical superintendent.

Over time, the Nation granted medical superintendents and doctors trained in medical schools more authority over death. Death that occurred at institutions threatened to supplant the traditional social welfare responsibilities Cherokees had to one another and to poten-tially disrupt larger balances in the world. Through the late 1870s, many Cherokees forbade anyone who had handled a corpse from entering their gardens for four days, and traditional doctors con-tinued to store medicines outside the home.[238] Given the likelihood that those responsible for tending to the dead were also responsible for farm work, it seems unlikely that institutions were able to continue these practices even if they had desired to do so. Traditional Chero-kees believed that the Ravenmocker, a witch, preyed on the sick, intending to rob them of their lives.[239] When a family member was sick or dying, families and neighbors kept watch all day and night. This may have led to decisions by the extended family members of orphans to bring them home when they were ill, even though they chose not to educate and attend to them on a daily basis.

Each of the institutions reflected the Nation's engagement with reform efforts in the United States. Administrators and professionals tapped to run the institutions subscribed to many of the same per-sonal beliefs as the middle-class, Protestant reformers in the Northeast. However, many were also Cherokee people whose families had felt the brunt of the coercive, exploitative, and sometimes violent good-will of U.S. and state reformers and agents bent on the denigration of Cherokee sovereignty and the community's core values. This led Cherokee leaders to privilege a community ethos that modeled the behaviors they saw as ideal, but avoided the "benevolent repression" thrust on so many groups deemed deviant who were placed in institutions in the United States. Despite its commitment to a community ethos, language, race, class, and gender impacted access to and experiences at all of the institutions.

As a result, daily life within the Nation's social welfare institutions varied widely. Cherokees, young and old, prized freedom of movement and autonomy. The more it was denied, the more they sought it. Positive associations of and within the institutions related directly to its interactions with the larger community. Through its public events and church services, the orphan asylum promoted interaction with all classes of Cherokee society and as a result received the least resistance from the community. This more than likely aided its continued funding when other institutions went without, which in turn enabled it to provide a continuity of care to children over time. Both the orphanage and the prison benefitted from debates over several decades as to the purposes and merits of the institutions and suffered far less from community confusion over their mission and intent.

The asylum, the least populated institution relative to its capacity, was the least vetted institution prior to its establishment. The asylum's total numbers for deaf, mute, blind, and mentally ill patients peaked in 1890–91 at thirty-two, but by 1894 dropped to seventeen.[240] As a consequence, the community's and the administrators' understandings of its purposes often diverged. Because the asylum did not offer the education that other facilities of its kind did, Cherokee people who saw their family members as individuals who needed to improve their skills and abilities created institutions or turned to other institutions to accomplish those ends. In its first years of operation, blind residents opted out in large numbers, in part because they were "well supplied with both friends and relatives."[241] Twenty years later, another option was the school for the blind that Laura Rowland opened at Fort Gibson, to which the Cherokee Nation provided three hundred to six hundred dollars annually for its support.[242] Some Cherokee citizens would opt to send their blind family members to this institution rather than to the Nation's asylum, where attention increasingly turned to the care of those suffering from mental or chronic illness.[243] Cherokee George Lowery, who was blind, attended the school founded by Rowland and later married her.

Once the institutions opened, Cherokee institutions were in a position to live up to or disappoint Cherokee people's expectations. Communal landholdings and federal pensions aided Cherokee people in achieving a level of economic and social stability in the early years of the institutions. If kinship obligations and gadugi were intact, no (dis)abilities existed. If kinship obligations suffered, the (dis)ability belonged to the family and community, not the individual. For those less connected to kinship systems, institutions became increasingly important for fulfilling social welfare obligations. Early institutional administrators, including Walter Adair Duncan and Samuel Sixkiller, set the standards for and modeled institutional procedures, but both men also faced challenges that preexisted national institutions. Cherokees continued to discuss ways to improve the institutions and their understandings of what the institutions provided or failed to provide. These debates marked a continuation of the community debate about national social policy that began decades before removal. However, just as the Cherokee Nation started to engage with these internal questions, the allotment era began in earnest. This new policy, aimed at dividing Native nations' communal landholdings, impacted the stability and the budgets necessary to bring about internal reform amenable to most Cherokee people. As the pressures to allot Cherokee lands and force Indian Territory to become a state increased in the late 1880s and early 1890s, social services became the battleground for tribal sovereignty again—a battle that Walter Adair Duncan and other institutional leaders were prepared to wage.

CHAPTER 6

"We Will Solve the Indian Problem," 1880–1893

In 1879, non-Indian reformer Richard Henry Pratt founded the Carlisle Indian School in Pennsylvania to extend his Indian educational "experiment." His experiment began in 1875 with American Indian prisoners in Florida and shifted to a new group of Native American wards, children.[1] Carlisle became the first in a series of off-reservation boarding schools supported by federal funds in an attempt to assimilate Native American children into American society. Unlike the Cherokee Nation's institutions, these institutions were outside of the purview of the families, communities, and Native nations whose children they took.

Although Pratt only makes brief references to the specific inspiration for his experiment in his memoirs, nearly his entire education related to Indian people came from "talking with the Indians [in Indian Territory]" and his service in the region. It was this professional education that provided him the credentials to launch Indian educational reform onto the U.S. national agenda. In the years following the Civil War, Pratt had commanded African American troops and American Indian scouts in Texas and within Indian Territory, including an assignment at Fort Gibson in the Cherokee Nation. The army also assigned Pratt to Fort Arbuckle within the boundaries of the Chickasaw Nation and in close proximity to the Choctaw Nation, where many Cherokees sought refuge during the war, including bilingual former superintendent of the Cherokee Board of Education and Presbyterian minister Stephen Foreman.[2] The Chickasaws had also established a public school system and funded a manual-labor school, an academy for Chickasaw girls, and an educational institute run by the Methodist Episcopal Church South.[3] The Choctaws supported similar types of educational facilities. From 1870 to 1875, during the same years the Cherokee Nation was opening its national prison, asylum, and orphanage in Tahlequah and Salina, Pratt was moving back and forth with Indian scouts from the Five Tribes between Fort Sill, Indian Territory, Fort Supply in the Cherokee Outlet, and Fort Griffin in northern Texas, all posts providing support to the federal government's efforts to put down Indian resistance to westward expansion.[4] During his time in Indian Territory, he "learned that most [Indians] had received English education in home schools conducted by their tribal government. Their intelligence, civilization and common sense was a revelation, because [he] had concluded that as an army officer [he] was there to deal with atrocious aborigines."[5]

Pratt's attitudes and beliefs typified those held by the majority of U.S. reformers during the last two decades of the nineteenth century. Pratt joined a cadre of former military men who had interacted with Indians and freed people and had come to the realization that groups different from themselves were competent and intelligent. Yet, like other Progressive reformers, this revelation did not translate into a trust in the group's abilities to design social policy and administer services equal to what the reformers believed they could create. Instead, reformers often minimized the accomplishments of the very people who enabled their discoveries and then marketed their personal expertise as social reformers for elevated positions and prominence.

The Civil War era had ushered in a new phase of federal Indian policy that led to a legal reimagining of the ward/guardian relationship. The Reservation Policy, which Cherokee people had escaped, crippled many of the tribes subjected to the policy economically, socially, and legally and manipulated their coercion if they did not comply with the will of federal officials. Allotment threatened to dissect the Five Tribes' communal land bases and thereby destroy the sovereignty Native nations exercised, which enabled individuals and families to fulfill their community social welfare responsibilities to one another. Social policy had always been at the heart of Cherokee nationhood

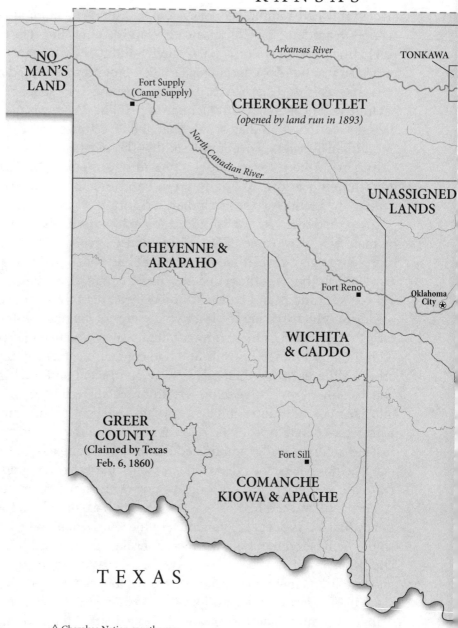

KANSAS

NO MAN'S LAND

Arkansas River

TONKAWA

Fort Supply
(Camp Supply)
■

CHEROKEE OUTLET
(opened by land run in 1893)

North Canadian River

UNASSIGNED LANDS

CHEYENNE & ARAPAHO

Fort Reno
■

Oklahoma City ✺

WICHITA & CADDO

GREER COUNTY
(Claimed by Texas
Feb. 6, 1860)

Fort Sill
■

COMANCHE KIOWA & APACHE

TEXAS

△ Cherokee Nation courthouses
■ Military forts or camps
• Existing communities

Indian Territory and the Cherokee Nation. Map by Carol Zuber-Mallison. Copyright © 2016 by the University of Oklahoma Press.

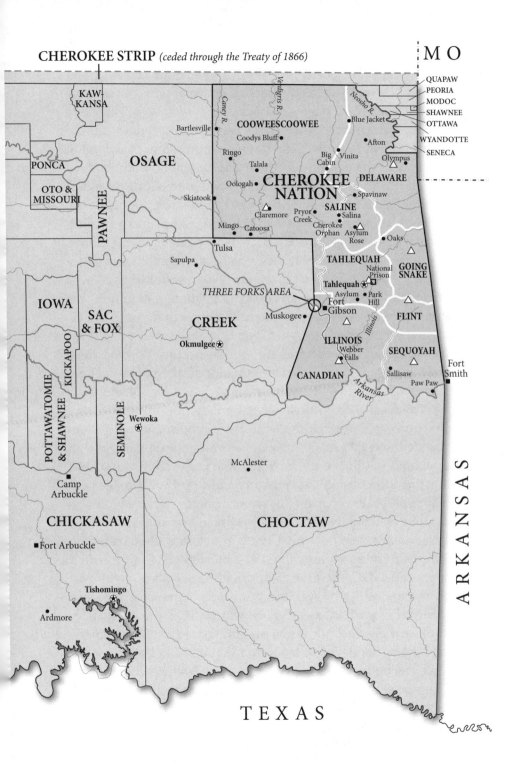

M O

QUAPAW
PEORIA
MODOC
SHAWNEE
OTTAWA
WYANDOTTE
SENECA

KAW-KANSA

Bartlesville

Caney R.

Verdigris R.

Neosho R.

Blue Jacket

COOWEESCOOWEE

Coodys Bluff

Afton

PONCA

OSAGE

Ringo

Talala

Big Cabin

Vinita

Olympus

DELAWARE

OTO & MISSOURI

Oologah

Skiatook

CHEROKEE NATION

Spavinaw

PAWNEE

Claremore

Pryor Creek

SALINE

Salina

Asylum Rose

Oaks

Mingo

Catoosa

Cherokee Orphan

Tulsa

Sapulpa

THREE FORKS AREA

TAHLEQUAH

National Prison

GOING SNAKE

IOWA

SAC & FOX

CREEK

Muskogee

Tahlequah

Asylum

Park Hill

Fort Gibson

FLINT

KICKAPOO

Okmulgee

ILLINOIS

Webber Falls

Illinois R.

SEQUOYAH

Sallisaw

Fort Smith

CANADIAN

Paw Paw

Arkansas River

POTTAWATOMIE & SHAWNEE

SEMINOLE

Wewoka

McAlester

Camp Arbuckle

CHICKASAW

CHOCTAW

A R K A N S A S

Fort Arbuckle

Tishomingo

Ardmore

T E X A S

and everyday Cherokee people's defense of sovereignty. By the 1880s, the Cherokee Nation had already stocked its social provision arsenal and anticipated the next wave of attack.

This chapter examines the changes occurring in federal Indian Policy from 1880 to 1893, the year Dawes commissioners arrived in Indian Territory to negotiate allotment and statehood with the Five Tribes, and how the Cherokee Nation responded to efforts to undermine the exercise of its sovereignty. Over the previous eighty years, the Cherokee Nation had designed and chosen to implement an alternative system of social welfare based on its assessment of its citizens' demands, needs, and identifiable problems, but one of the most pressing problems was not Indians or communal landholdings; it was the United States' desire to void its treaty obligations and undermine the efforts of Cherokee people to administer their own social policy. Rather than see this period as an attack on Cherokee families or Cherokee government in order to free up lands—though both of these happened—the attacks threatened to dismantle an alternative national and viable social welfare policy that prioritized the needs of an Indian citizenry. The Cherokee Nation's social policy not only belied the claims by advocates of territorialization and allotment that Indian people needed non-Indians to provide for and educate them or that communal landholdings were incompatible with "civilization" but also maintained the Nation's sovereignty and thereby Cherokee people's abilities to fulfill responsibilities to one another. The Nation was a social policy enacted by Indian people, in and of itself.

Pratt and others were not only Civil War veterans; they were also known for their efforts as Indian fighters. In late 1875, Pratt escorted Cheyenne, Arapaho, Comanche, Caddo, and Kiowa people who participated in the Red River War, but who were sentenced to prison without a trial from Fort Sill to Fort Marion in Saint Augustine, Florida.[6] Once there, he launched a preliminary educational experiment with the prisoners at Fort Marion that included many of the educational elements common to the Cherokee Nation's institutions: English-language education, manual-labor training, outings, and art instruction. Pratt's original contribution to the experiment was to impose militarized and regimented discipline and an outing system that placed Indians in jobs in the local community.[7] In reality, Pratt tested the conclusion that the Five Tribes took for granted and that Enlightenment-era missionaries had already reached eighty years earlier—Indians were able to be educated.

To extend his experiment, Pratt arranged in 1878 for seventeen of the released prisoners to attend Hampton Institute, a manual-labor school for African Americans run by General Samuel Chapman Armstrong, a former Freedmen's Bureau agent. Politicians and reformers visited Hampton and Carlisle in the early 1880s to marvel at the educational progress of Indian pupils. This spawned national discussions of Indian educational reform among reformers including politicians, university presidents, women's groups, former Freedmen Bureau employees, social reformers, philanthropists, and Christian missionaries (in particular Protestant evangelicals), who began meeting annually at the Lake Mohonk Conference in New Paltz, New York. Calling themselves the "Friends of the Indian," they met to devise solutions to the "Indian problem." The 1884 annual conference of the National Education Association's session on the Education of Indians featured Pratt and Armstrong as speakers: "Educated and uneducated Indians [were] present as an object lesson."[8] It was at an annual conference on public charities that Pratt offered his infamous advice that "all the Indian there is in a race should be dead. . . . Kill the Indian in him to Save the Man."[9] President Chester A. Arthur embraced Pratt's message and suggested extending state and territorial laws and courts over all tribes, allotment of tribal lands, and expansion of Indian education for children.[10]

The extension of state laws over Indian people no doubt raised tremendous anxiety for citizens of the Five Tribes whose families had lived through the extension of Georgia's, Alabama's, and Tennessee's laws over Indian people. From the Five Tribes' perspective, history had demonstrated that the extension of state laws was not a social service benefit to better protect Indian people; it was a tool of coercion and intimidation. In the pre-removal era, the vast majority of Cherokee people had tacitly consented to nation building in order to maintain a system that enabled them to care for their families, protect communal landholdings, and maximize their ability to fulfill a community ethic. Arthur's new iteration of "civilization" policy threatened nearly all Cherokees' interests again.

During a period that historian Rose Stremlau describes as one that included "debating" between Cherokees and U.S. officials and reformers, Cherokee leaders launched a public education campaign on Cherokee social policy directed at U.S. residents.[11] In January of 1882, Daniel H. Ross, the editor of the *Cherokee Advocate*, published an article titled the "Hypocritical Friendship for the Indians," which blasted the efforts of Congress to pass legislation, including the Oklahoma Bill and the U.S. Court Bill promoted by Missouri senator George Vest, to dismantle tribal autonomy. Ross pointed out that the legislators who crafted these bills deployed "stereotypical" language that suggested the bills were "for the better protection of Indian rights" to convince an "unsophisticated" American public of their morality. He instead countered that these bills did little more than distort history and misrepresent Indian people's legal rights to their lands. The lands the Five Tribes occupied were not charity given to Indian people out of kindness or pity. In the Five Tribes' case, Indian peoples bought and paid for those lands and held title to them. In most instances, the United States had not yet paid in full. Further, he stated, the United States had received "a hundred times more" than what was given to Indian peoples in exchange. The editor cast blame on land speculators' efforts to carry out frauds "more indelible than hell itself." Ross deplored legislators to carefully examine these measures, recognize their supporters' true intents, and not to rob the Nation under the "garb of friendship." As for the "Indian question," which U.S. officials increasingly used as a rhetorical catchall to attack Native peoples' and Native nations' educational practices, legal systems, family systems, and communal landholdings, Ross asserted, "We will solve the Indian problem."[12]

By 1880, Cherokees had been developing, tweaking, and debating national social services for three-quarters of a century. The Nation housed a mix of types and levels of educational and institutional services. For instance, in 1880, with the Cherokee Nation's financial support, Baptist missionary Almon Bacone sponsored and opened the Indian University in Tahlequah, what is today Bacone College located in Muskogee, which served students from the Five Tribes as well as non-Indians.[13] To counteract the bills and the criticism of Cherokee institutions, in 1882, the *Globe Democrat*, a Saint Louis paper that

Cherokees, including Chief Dennis Bushyhead, corresponded with often, published an article in response to attempts to establish a territorial court for all residents of Indian Territory, stating, "Now the Indians of the Indian Territory do not want any United States Court, and they do not need any. They have efficient courts of their own."[14] The Nation had administrators who had been engaged in the day-to-day work of administering social provisions to and in collaboration with Cherokee people for decades. It had people like Walter Adair Duncan, who, despite lacking a clan, had been educated in the importance of communal landholdings and gadugi.

In its efforts to preserve this sovereignty, the Nation was up against formidable and well-funded opposition. To railroad corporations, territorializers, and land speculators, the "Indian problem" was the inability to run roughshod over the property rights of Native nations to gain access to land. Treaties and fee simple rights to the land secured communal landholdings.[15] U.S. Indian educational reform provided cover for the railroads and speculators to lobby for legislation to advance their economic interests in Indian Territory. In order for those monied interests to gain access to the lands, "greedy cormorants," as Chief Bushyhead described them, had to convince U.S. citizens and politicians that the treaties made in good faith with Native nations were voidable and that the Five Tribes were just like all the other Indians, who in most American minds were defeated, dependent, and in need of paternalistic guardianship.[16] President Grant's 1870 Peace Policy had introduced a means to bring about the first condition when it ended the practice of treaty making. By discontinuing that practice, a generation of U.S. citizens viewed treaties as relics of the past. The congressional debates over the Peace Policy broadcasted politicians' views on treaties and left Native nations to lobby treaty rights behind the scenes in Washington and seek redress in the U.S. press.

As Five Tribes officials had anticipated, when railroads arrived in the early 1870s, whites had streamed into Indian Territory hoping to capitalize on the economic opportunities railroads offered. Because Congress had blocked its proposal to collaborate with the Union Pacific Southern Division (UPSD), the Cherokee Nation relied on railroad corporations and their employees to act ethically and abide by the legal agreements forged between the United States, the railroads, and the Cherokee Nation. Almost as soon as railroad construction began in 1868, railroads violated agreements by failing to pay for timber used to make railroad ties. Intruders profited from illegally selling timber to railroads. Some Cherokees who resented the economic exploitation of railroads, and many non-Cherokees, trafficked in illegal timber as well. As expected, towns and temporary camps emerged to serve the material and social needs of railroad employees.[17] This included the development of hotels and stores and an increase in the number of laborers, dentists, doctors, whiskey peddlers, and prostitutes. All of this escalated crime in Indian Territory. Treaties required that the federal government manage its criminal class, but the federal government left the federal court in Fort Smith, Arkansas, without the material or human resources to adequately do so. This enabled territorialists to argue that Indian Territory was a lawless place, inadequately policed by Native nations and in need of state and federal oversight.

Railroad promoters and territorializers collaborated with Five Tribes' citizens who shared their views to undermine the majority position of the communities. For example, in 1875, when Cherokee citizen Elias Cornelius Boudinot, treaty signer Elias Boudinot's son, and intermarried white doctor E. Poe Harris, former medical superintendent at the asylum, had established a pro-territorialization paper at Muskogee, the Creek Nation shut it down and assumed control. Boudinot reestablished his paper in Vinita, a town he had helped incorporate in anticipation of railroads arriving there. Boudinot and non-Cherokees understood that publishing the papers in Indian Territory gave the appearance to U.S. citizens and officials outside of Indian Territory that Indian peoples desired a U.S.-controlled territory, that they themselves opposed communal landholdings, and that they worried about their government's capacities to manage their own affairs.[18] Cherokees and Creeks, regardless of their positions on railroads, deployed the press to articulate their claims to the United States.

To defend its sovereignty, the Cherokee Nation had to meet arguments of territorializers and Friends of the Indian head on. The Five Tribes needed to, as Alexandra Harmon argues, "reduce the dissimilarities" perceived to exist between Indians and U.S. citizens at a time when both U.S. citizens and Cherokees were "hypersensitive to the differences."[19] Cherokee leaders argued that the Nation's social provisions performed the same functions and produced similar outcomes to other social states' social provisions. The Nation's officials worked to put poverty and deviance and the solutions proposed to end them in perspective. The Nation needed to demonstrate to U.S. officials and citizens that no one had devised a perfect system to solve all social ills. Finally, it had to convince the U.S. public that communal landholdings served a social welfare function superior to those provided by the private property ownership that severalty imposed. It had to do all of this as it engaged in internal debates about the ways it could improve its social policy as changing federal policies produced new allegations of the Five Tribes' supposed incompetence, particularly allegations of lawlessness aided by monolithic stereotypes of "the Indian" as uneducated, savage, and uncivilized.[20] By the 1880s, social policy emerged as the battleground for Native nationhood.

Because of the perception held by many U.S. citizens and promoted by Five Tribes leaders that the Five Tribes had obtained "civilized" status through education, constitutional governance, economic pursuits, and Christianity, the Indian problem described by reformers appeared to many non-Indians as a slightly different problem to solve. Whereas the so-called Indian Wars that coincided with and followed the Civil War in the West convinced many U.S. citizens of the "savagery" and lack of civilization among western tribes, inducing U.S. citizens to believe that the Five "Civilized" Tribes were part of the problem proved to be more difficult. In 1877, the *National Teacher's Monthly*, an education journal published in New York, wrote in support of Pratt's efforts at Fort Marion. In it, the article's author acknowledged the "civilization" accomplished by the Cherokees, Choctaws, and Creeks. Given this progress, the author argued that it was only fair that Comanches and Kiowas should receive the same "privileges and endowments" that the Five Tribes had received forty years earlier.[21] What the *Teacher's Monthly* misunderstood or refused to acknowledge was that the Five Tribes asserted their rights to manage and oversee educational opportunities within their nations and communities as a result of negotiated treaties, no longer a viable means for Kiowas and Comanches to negotiate endowments. Further, the federal government imposed the privileges that the *Teacher's Monthly* witnessed among the Kiowa and Comanche on prisoners who were incarcerated at Fort Marion in Florida, hundreds of miles from their communities and families. Incarceration compromised the Kiowas' and Comanches' collective abilities to control or direct the education and so-called privileges they received.

Cherokee people were fully aware of what federal and state officials meant by solutions to the Indian problem, which were increasingly espoused by reformers previously associated with antislavery movements and the Freedmen's Bureau.[22] Whether driven by ethnocentrism or racism, reformers often believed that the policies that worked for one race would also work for others even in light of evidence to the contrary. For example, the *Advocate* reprinted portions of Rutgers College president Merrill Gates's paper, "Land and Law as Agents in Education." In it, Gates argued that the "spirit" of Kansas settlement, including its free state status and its supposed embrace of its African American citizens, could be revived as a model to solve the "Indian problem." For Gates, if the United States granted Indians citizenship and distributed private property to them, the "Indian problem" would be solved. Although *Advocate* editor Daniel Ross could have easily called upon Cherokee people's experiences with the allotment provisions contained in the Treaties of 1817 and 1819, he drew his rebuttal from more recent Indian policy. Ross asked, "Where are these [Kansas] Indians today—the Delawares, Shawnees, Pottowatomies, Kaws, Osages, and others," who were promised so much by Kansas? Most, Ross answered, relocated to Indian Territory after suffering abuses and "undisguised violence" from the "laymen and missionaries" who grew tired of their Indian neighbors. Cherokee people understood the implications of private property ownership and U.S. citizenship, and the vast majority rejected it.[23] As they had during the removal era, allotment schemes left Indians subject to states governed by whites who were unwilling to protect the social and economic rights of Indian people.[24] Instead of allotment, Ross proposed that the government provide tribes with "ample lands . . . ample school and agricultural and stock raising facilities—and leave the rest to time and the Indians themselves."[25]

The federal court at Fort Smith had already served as a preliminary introduction to what non-Indian administration of justice meant
for Cherokee people. If Cherokees became subject to non-Cherokee
laws as territorializers proposed, all prisoners faced incarceration
outside the Nation. Because the federal district court offered no
appeals upon conviction, the only way to overturn a conviction was
through executive clemency. Cherokee people often submitted petitions for clemency on behalf of their family members.[26] Despite some
improvements in the administration of justice after Judge Isaac Parker
took the bench in 1875, Cherokees remained suspicious of its equity.[27]
In 1878, Walter Adair Duncan's brother DeWitt Clinton Duncan had
attacked the actions of federal marshals who "scour[ed] Indian Territory hunting down Cherokee citizens and dragging them off to be
tried in a foreign country by jurymen of a strange race and by judges
that are by nature biased against the Indian."[28] In 1882, Cherokee
R. B. Harris pointed out the continued discrimination of federal
marshals in the country, where "great sinners go free" and small
ones face punishment. As evidence of the injustice, Harris decried
a two-year sentence handed down against Cherokee George Lowery
for bringing a quart of whiskey into Indian Territory. In contrast,
men from Chicago, who were arrested the same year by a federal
marshal for illegal hunting in Indian Territory and for bringing twenty-
five gallons of whiskey, were released and allowed to continue
hunting.[29] After visiting Fort Smith, Anna Dawes, Progressive reformer
and daughter of Senator Henry Dawes of Massachusetts, published
a scathing critique of the federal prison there in 1886, calling it
"Hell on Earth."[30] Echoing Anna Dawes's positions, DeWitt Clinton
Duncan critiqued the "stinking dungeons of civilization" at Fort
Smith and the "tyrannical incarceration" that prisoners faced there.
When released, the men were often "broken in health" as a result
of the prison conditions.[31] Cherokees argued, in contrast, that Cherokee social policy provided a barrier to the gross inequities present
in other social policies.

If Cherokee prisoners became subject to neighboring states' laws,
the prospects were equally grim. In 1887, the *Cherokee Advocate* editor
reminded readers that, given the way white juries applied the laws,

Cherokees might as well "live in England instead of Arkansas." White juries "despise[d] an [Indian's] color and don't know his language."[32] After an Arkansas scandal in the early 1870s involving prison finances, which revealed that the state paid businesses to take control of its prisoners at a significant financial loss to the state, Arkansas moved to a convict-leasing system resembling the systems in other southern states that were throwing off the oversight Reconstruction had imposed.[33] Arkansas passed laws that severely criminalized minor theft, and the prison populations of African Americans in particular and, to a lesser degree, poor whites, soared. Several years after Dawes excoriated Fort Smith, a penitentiary physician discovered an inmate's body at Coal Hill, a prison-leasing operation. This discovery led to an investigation in 1888 that revealed additional atrocities, including prisoners being murdered, tortured, and forced to fight to the death. No one affiliated with the leasing company, the prison boards, or the state ever faced prosecution, though the warden served five years—not at a prison camp, but in a penitentiary.[34]

An equally foreboding prospect for federal prisoners convicted at Fort Smith was incarceration in prisons outside Arkansas, including those at Leavenworth, Kansas, and Detroit, Michigan. Whereas Cherokee prisoners incarcerated at Fort Smith may have returned home weak or ill and later died there, those sentenced to serve prison terms far from home often died away from their families, their communities, and their Nation. In 1886, during his two-year sentence at Detroit, Cherokee George Lowery passed away. The next year, Taylor Parris died while serving time in Detroit.[35] After his release from prison in Little Rock, Arkansas, Cherokee Alex Teehee reported witnessing state prisoners being beaten to death. In contrast, authorities punished federal prisoners, by "confin[ing them] in a dark dungeon on bread and water." Teehee served approximately 160 days in solitary confinement after he refused to work when he was sick.[36]

It was not only those subjected to the criminal justice system who were at risk; the educational reforms being imposed on Native nations threatened to undo the almost century-long social policy efforts of the Cherokees. Individual Cherokees had sought and the Cherokee Nation had advocated for and provided education to boys and girls since educational efforts began in the Nation in 1800. While early U.S. educational reformers like Horace Mann had struggled to generate the public will for local taxation to fund common schools during the 1830s and 1840s, the Cherokee Nation used its treaties to secure funds for and control of educational services.[37] It devised its universal common school system and established its seminaries before most states.[38] The off-reservation boarding schools introduced by Pratt threatened to remove children from their families and the Nation. Such a move would affect boys and girls differently, given that some federal officials, including Indian commissioner E. A. Hayt, opposed funding the education of female students at federal boarding schools.[39]

Beginning in the removal era, the Cherokee Nation used the press as a means to deploy comparative evidence of its investment in social services to meet internal and external concerns; it did so again to fight allotment and education of its children beyond the community. In 1878, the Cherokee Nation provided educational services to 69 percent of its school-aged population. These numbers did not include children privately served in mission schools run by the various denominations. Arkansas, in contrast, provided public education to 7 percent of its children the same year.[40] All of the Cherokee Nation's new institutions modeled and required labor from physically able residents. The *Cherokee Advocate* analyzed the educational expenditures per child and overall number of pupils served in Missouri, Kansas, and Texas and asserted that the Cherokee Nation's educational services and expenditures exceeded all of them.[41] In contrast to its regional neighbors and some states in the Northeast, the Cherokee Nation assumed primary responsibility for funding and administering education. It did not rely on families and private schools to provide the bulk of its educational opportunities to its children. As late as 1895, the *Advocate* published an educational report from Connecticut highlighting widespread absenteeism of students, unqualified teachers, varied lengths of school years, and high rates of illiteracy.[42] Even though the Cherokee Nation's educational efforts more closely resembled those in the North than the far less universally available public education provided by its regional neighbors in the South and West, northern reformers scrutinized Native nations more closely as a result of allotment efforts.

The annual teacher's institutes, which included discussions, debates, and essay presentations, demonstrated an engagement with educational reforms in the Northeast, yet maintained the Cherokee Nation's longer educational policies that infused gadugi.[43] For example, by the 1880s, more than one hundred teachers attended the annual events. Local officials, including Chief D. W. Bushyhead and Dr. Walter Thompson Adair, paid for and hosted banquets to close the events.[44] At one institute, president of the Cherokee Board of Education Duncan reminded teachers that their decorum contributed to a teacher's ability "to win the confidence and the esteem of those he offers to serve, viz; the whole people."[45] At the 1884 institute, officials illustrated the normal methods, which aimed to establish professional teaching standards for everyone entering the field of public education. The same year, the annual meeting of the National Educational Association included a session on the "Principles and Methods of Elementary Education," which discussed the standard classes that properly trained teachers, most often adherents of a normal method, should be able to provide to students.[46] Both meetings reflected an active engagement by its members with efforts to standardize and professionalize teaching.

Given the attention paid to institutional economy within and outside the Nation, the Nation used fiscal records to support the value of the services it provided. In 1881, the *Advocate* answered a letter from a Fort Gibson subscriber who asked the editor to verify the comparative daily cost of orphan care per pupil at the New Haven Orphan Asylum in Connecticut and the Cherokee Orphan Asylum and to detail the Cherokee Orphan Asylum's funding sources. The article used published data from the annual budgets ($12,596 in Connecticut versus an average of $20,000 from 1876 to 1880 in the Cherokee Nation) to verify the numbers used by the subscriber to determine that the Cherokee orphanage spent on average eight cents less per pupil than the Connecticut orphanage.[47]

The Cherokee Nation also used institutional hospitality to try to convince U.S. officials and reformers and Cherokee people of the Nation's institutional merits. The orphanage, during its public exams and opening and closing ceremonies, and the prison hosted non-Cherokees who visited the Nation. In 1884, the *Advocate* reported,

"Mr. J. W. Parker of the Chickasaw Nation and Mr. J. A. Manning of the United States . . . took in our prison and other places of interest."[48] In addition, in the 1880s, two U.S. travel writers, A. M. Williams and George Foster, author of the book *Sequoyah*, published travel accounts based on their visits to the Cherokee Nation and its places of interest.

Cherokee people welcomed U.S. citizens into the Nation if they believed it provided an opportunity to advertise their social policy accomplishments and the Nation's sovereignty. A bilingual Cherokee served as Williams's guide, and a district sheriff opened his four-room log home to Williams for lodging. The sheriff shared that all of his children had attended the national schools and made their living as public schoolteachers. Both writers' articles described the Nation's institutions, including its schools, orphan asylum, and seminaries. Foster's piece included a drawing of the asylum and listed the total numbers of prisoners incarcerated and executions carried out at the national prison. For Williams, it was a form of government "modelled upon the State formation in the Union." The churches were led by "native preachers," schools were taught by "Cherokee young men and women," and the orphanage provided a "home and education" to every orphan who exemplified "all the outward signs and institutions of a civilized people." Foster declared, in reference to the Cherokee Male Seminary, what most Cherokees already felt: "Well may this Indian people be proud of this and other kindred institutions."[49] What Williams described was a success of the civilization policy, but not because it "modelled" the United States. It was a success, to borrow the language of Bonnie Sue Lewis from her discussion of Christian missionization among the Dakotas and the Nez Perces, because Cherokees remained Cherokees and "incorporated their cultural and behavioral patterns" into their self-chosen institutions.[50]

As it had with federal pensions, the *Advocate* aided the Nation's efforts to advertise its engagement with U.S. reforms. It published and reprinted articles on institutional and social reform efforts in the states as well as those happening in the Nation. In 1884, the same year the Cherokee Orphan Asylum sent children in their new kindergarten program to the Indian Agricultural Fair in Muskogee, the *Advocate* printed an article supporting the merits of kindergarten education, which argued that children should begin formal study at an earlier age. It also provided "Rules for Home Education," which encouraged children's obedience, parents' appeals to their children's reason, and punishment for disobedience.[51] The paper followed international cholera outbreaks and inoculation efforts.[52] An editorial outlining the history of Cherokee judicial reforms called for an expansion of "prison labor in the way best adapted to this Nation" and suggested that the prisoners could assist in operating the mill on Dry Creek.[53] The *Advocate* reprinted a variety of articles on the use of Braille and artificial limbs.[54] All of these articles indicate that Cherokee officials and Cherokee people, but especially readers of the *Advocate*, continued to discuss and make informed choices about the social provisions available and those they might decide to demand.

Walter Adair Duncan mustered his familial, communal, and institutional resources to launch his own counteroffensive to the Friends of the Indian. After he acquired the printing press in 1881, Duncan distributed the *Orphans' News* to reformers employed as foreign missionaries and to boarding schools aimed at African American and Indian residents. These publications commended Sequoyah's invention of a written Cherokee language, provided evidence of the Cherokee Nation's civilized institutional social services, advertised the Nation's functioning political systems, and simultaneously celebrated the intellectual and physical beauty of Indian children. These testaments stood in contrast to the statements produced by the Indian children attending Carlisle, who disparaged their Native languages and lauded the beneficence of whites.

Cherokee leaders also argued that communal landholdings prevented widespread poverty and made homelessness impossible. In an 1881 piece, Chief Bushyhead emphasized that communal landholdings, like the "air and waters, is the heritage of Cherokee people." He further asserted that communal landholding was a superior system for Cherokee people; it was a historically tested first line of defense against the social ills reformers railed against.

> If [common landholding ceased to exist], our domain would soon drift into the hands of a few, and our poor people in a few years would become like your poor people, most of whom, if they died to-morrow; do not own a foot of the earth's surface in which they could be buried.

If this is the phase of your civilization, to which you are at present so nervously inviting us, can you wonder if we pause to study the present tendencies and probable future of this fearfully anti-Republican system. Our people have been taught from remote ages to believe that the surface of the earth, apart from its use, is not chattel. We are neither socialists or communists; but we have a land system which we believe to be better than any you can devise for us. Individual rights are fully respected, but the rights of the whole people are not destroyed. Cannot you leave us alone to try our plan, while you are trying yours?[55]

In his statement, Bushyhead summarized the origins and development of the Cherokee Nation's hybrid social welfare system. The system balanced the rights of Cherokee citizens tied more closely to the newer national welfare system with the rights of the "whole people," including those who relied more heavily on a traditional system of social welfare guided by kinship responsibilities. It prevented individualism and personal greed from overwhelming the social welfare needs of the community, and it avoided repressive benevolence, a trait Bushyhead asked the United States to emulate. The Nation's social policy embodied a community ethic, and communal landholdings nourished it.

The two-pronged assault from business interests and reformers centered on the perceived economic and social welfare needs of Indian peoples. A war with two fronts required two advances. Cherokee principal chiefs were more often than not politicians and businessmen; they understood the economic arguments used by representatives from the railroad industry, speculators, and territorializers to attack the Nation. Even though many of these men were products of Cherokee educational institutions, they had not spent their adult lives engaged with and thinking about the daily concerns of middle-class Cherokees or those who most adhered to traditional social services. Most of them lacked the skills, expertise, and intimate knowledge of the Cherokee Nation's and the United States' social provisions to meet the reformers head on.

These elected officials shared and expressed similar anxieties as those articulated by U.S. citizens, but lacked the economic or political clout to get federal officials to act on their behalf as treaties required.

The federal government committed itself to policing and removing from the Cherokee Nation illegal intruders. However, federal officials lacked the will, Indian Territory judiciaries lacked the resources, and most federal marshals often personally lacked the desire to police illegal intruders. The crime committed by illegal intruders became representative of Indian lawlessness and Native nations' governmental weaknesses. Rather than supporting the removal of intruders, politicians and speculators in favor of allotment capitalized on the crime that occurred as a result of intruders as evidence of the weakness of Native nations to police Indian Territory.

The Cherokee Nation and its citizens resented the corporate intrusion from railroad corporations and illegal timber operations that infringed on tribal sovereignty and legitimized the illegal activities of U.S. citizens in Indian Territory. In 1882, Chief Dennis Bushyhead confronted a documented intruder to the Cherokee Nation who had threatened violence and armed resistance against Cherokee officials and railroad personnel if they tried to remove him from his land to make room for the railroad's right-of-way. The Cherokee Nation asserted that the man's claims to the improvements on his property were fraudulent by Cherokee law and therefore asked federal officials to remove him. Ultimately, the man agreed to give up his claims to his property if the U.S. commissioners for the railroad agreed to assess damages for his losses. They did and the man moved into the Creek Nation and staked another claim to property.[56]

This event represented the mutual concerns over illegal intruders and immigration policy shared by U.S. residents and Cherokees. In response to demands by U.S. citizens calling for federal immigration policy to manage the increases in immigration that taxed community resources, Congress had passed its first immigration policy in 1875. In irony certainly not lost on Cherokee people, the *Advocate* published the details of Chief Bushyhead's confrontation with the intruder the day before President Arthur signed the Chinese Exclusion Act into law in 1882.[57] Despite the Immigration and Chinese Exclusion Acts, U.S. immigration reformers pressed for more policies.

The *Cherokee Advocate* capitalized on U.S. citizens' nativist concerns about immigration to mock reformers' advocacy of allotment to solve the "Indian problem." In 1889, the *Advocate* reprinted several pieces on U.S. immigration. One piece, "To Check Immigration," called on the federal government to end the "outrageous" abuses of Switzerland, Germany, and Great Britain that dumped their "paupers," "criminals," "idiots," "insane," and "undesirable folk" in Canada, who then crossed into the United States. Within "forty-eight hours" many immigrants wind up in "our almshouses." The writer called on the government to protect the United States from an "invasion which does not fertilize our institutions."[58] The same year, a *Saint Louis Globe Democrat* piece argued that Chinese and Europeans were "carrying off their earnings" by sending money to their relatives in their home countries rather than spending their earnings within the United States. Immigration reformers urged federal officials to draft laws to address this.[59] Concerns over U.S. immigration paralleled the demands by Cherokee officials that federal officials remove intruders from the Cherokee Nation. In 1892, the editor of the *Advocate* pointed to the obvious hypocrisy when he wrote, "How would the United States Government [like] to change her way of holding lands in order to keep foreign criminals from fleeing to her shores to escape justice? If the experiment proved effective the five civilized tribes would without a doubt be willing to try it."[60]

In 1892, Walter Adair Duncan echoed Chief Bushyhead's earlier defense of communal landholdings and U.S. concerns over social welfare obligations when he described in the *Advocate* why "the title in common to our lands is the strongest guarantee against the homelessness of many of our people." Duncan opposed allotment, not because he feared that backward or uncivilized Indians could not manage their affairs, but because he knew that "owning land in severalty has the effect to exclude so many people among the whites from the enjoyment of a home." The poverty white men, women, and children endured was not, in Duncan's opinion, something Cherokee people should risk by embracing private landownership.[61] When one considered prosperity in terms of equal access to food, clean water, and land on which to build a home and grow crops, in comparison to other rural communities, the Cherokee Nation was far from impoverished.

To the Cherokee Nation, the problem was not Indians or communal landholdings; it was U.S. policy. Cherokee leaders reminded

U.S. politicians and citizens of their culpability in the creation of
Cherokee poverty and deviance in the Cherokee Nation historically.
In 1881, Principal Chief Bushyhead wrote a letter to the editor of
the *Fort Smith Western Independent* under the headline "A Defense
of the Cherokee Indians" in response to an article it had published
by an alleged Cherokee citizen condemning the Nation. Bushyhead
reminded readers of the "violent removal" when "hundreds of Cherokees perished." Members of his own "father's household" became
"prisoners in their own dooryard" and were then carried away, victims of the "Georgia assailant" and its "reluctant . . . accomplice"
the U.S. government. Bushyhead described the Cherokees at the
time of removal, as "partially" civilized, but he added that "modes
of administering justice were crude, and often violent in many states."
He blamed "squatters," "railroad interests," "intruders," and "greedy
cormorants" ready to swoop down and consume whatever they could
for the attacks on Cherokee landholdings. He added that any government that denies the "sacred assurances" of its treaty obligations
and engages in "robbery, murder, and bad faith" does not have the
"blessing of God."[62] He turned the accusations of criminality against
Indian people on its head and accused those who broke treaties of
criminal behavior. For Bushyhead, a government that could not be
trusted to make agreements in good faith was deviant—exactly the
quality that Progressive reformers attacked American Indian communities for fostering.

Racial prejudice and ethnocentrism limited non-Cherokee officials'
abilities to fully endorse the Cherokee Nation's institutions as civilized or equal. In 1883, DeWitt Clinton Duncan scolded Indian agent
Nathan Reaves, who visited the Indian Territory with the assigned
purpose of adjusting Indian soldiers' pension claims. Rather than
expedite the claims and report his findings, which was his assigned
task, Reaves published an article, which Duncan described as one
that critiqued the "manners and customs of the [Cherokee Nation]."
Duncan pointed out that the

> Indian problem is a moral question; it has nothing to do with the
> subject of natural history. This inquiry is not how, or what, the Indians
> may eat, drink, or wear; nor yet what proportion of red, white, or

black blood may be in their veins; but what are the reciprocal rights, privileges, duties, and obligations that may exist. . . . We believe . . . readers . . . will say, "very well, sir; your story about the 'hot biscuit, fried pork, and hominy' is all entertaining enough; but we sent you to the Cherokee Nation in the service of a great principle; tell us something about how you executed your mission there."

DeWitt Clinton Duncan expected Agent Reaves not to produce a "backbiting critique" of the Cherokee Nation, but to do his job in justice to the "still unpensioned . . . loyal citizens."[63]

Unlike the Enlightenment-era late-eighteenth-century and early nineteenth-century civilization policy, when Christianity, education, and Euro-American notions of gendered labor were the keys to "civilized" status for tribes, race and phenotype had become crucial factors in determining who was or could become civilized and through what means. The *Western Recorder*, a newspaper published in Lawrence, Kansas, by John Waller, who benefitted from colonization efforts in Kansas, promoted stereotypical and misleading representations of Indian people. In a series of articles related to "Oklahoma" published in 1883 and 1884, the editor "hope[d]" that Oklahoma, "entirely occupied by Indians and colored people," would be "thrown open" to settlement. Oklahoma stood too close to "civilization to . . . remain in the hands of the Indians, who as an agricultural people; are a failure." As for the "colored people" who resided in Oklahoma, they were "the former slaves of Cherokee Indians," some of whom had become "very rich." The paper encouraged "colored men from the States to go there and settle down" as soon as settlement was possible because cotton could be produced and "there are no people better prepared to cultivate cotton . . . than the colored people."[64] These types of misrepresentations in the press encouraged attitudes and beliefs that supported the dispossession of Indian peoples in the region.

In addition to failing to differentiate among the thirty tribes with individual treaties guaranteeing their lands in Indian Territory, casting Indians as one homogenous group, all of whom were incapable of agriculture, and celebrating African Americans as naturally predisposed to growing cotton, the *Recorder* trumpeted the colonization efforts of David Payne, who led illegal colonization efforts to

Oklahoma. The paper also railed against treatment of "between twenty and thirty thousand colored people in the Indian Territory who have never been emancipated," whom the editor claimed were former slaves of the Five Tribes and former Union soldiers. This claim exaggerated the total number of former slaves in Indian Territory. The paper also applied a critique that U.S. officials lobbed at the Choctaw Nation for laws it had passed that limited the rights and protections of African Choctaws, to all of the Five Tribes. The editor called for the Indian Territory to be brought into "harmony" with the government of the United States.[65]

Race was part of the Indian problem; the Cherokee Nation had established inequitably funded segregated schools, bureaucratically blocked orphan services to African Cherokees, and denied African Cherokee students access to the seminaries. Individual Cherokees held racist beliefs. However, the problem was multifaceted and not simply one of race. The problem also stemmed from attitudes held by whites and African Americans outside Indian Territory as much as by intertribal race relations within Indian Territory. It also factored into nation-to-nation jurisdictional concerns. In 1880, officials of the district court at Fort Smith wrote Principal Chief Bushyhead to seek a pardon for Jeff Marshall, "a negro" convicted of larceny in 1879, so that he could testify in a federal case against "a gang of thieves" accused of robbing railroad company trains.[66] Without Marshall, the court had not been able to "procure sufficient proof to convict them." On its surface, this case was a routine bureaucratic negotiation between two sovereign bodies. Marshall was a Creek Nation citizen subject to the laws of the Cherokee Nation by virtue of an 1843 intertribal compact, but the federal court and railroad corporations needed his assistance.[67] Jeff Marshall fully understood the importance of his testimony and leveraged the U.S. court against the Cherokee Nation.

The Marshall case demonstrated to the Cherokee Nation that instances of perceived racial inequity within the Nation could be used as a catalyst to undermine its sovereignty. If the Nation desired to stave off external critique and earn the loyalty of African Indian citizens, it behooved the Cherokee Nation and its officials to act more civilly toward African Indian citizens. For their part, Marshall and his family members hedged their bets in order to determine which

Nation offered the best social service provisions. In which Nation would his life, property, family, and community be most protected? Not only did Marshall refuse to testify without the pardon from the Cherokee Nation, but his family members, who were also witnesses, agreed to testify in the federal court only if Marshall was released. Becoming desperate, the U.S. district court offered to exchange "twelve Creek negroes" accused of robberies in the Cherokee Nation and held at Fort Smith on other charges in exchange for Marshall's testimony.[68]

The court's offer followed two significant events. First, in 1878, the Senate Committee on Territories began holding meetings in Indian Territory to discuss territorialization. In order to bolster support from railroad officials and the few Indian Territory citizens in favor of territorialization, the committee chose to hold their meetings in railroad towns, infuriating Cherokee people and national officials. The location ensured the presence of a Cherokee minority in favor of territorialization, including Elias C. Boudinot. Railroads and territory measures increasingly went hand in hand. Most Cherokees felt no sympathy when individuals robbed the railroads. For some Cherokees, these minor losses paled in comparison to the collective losses that resulted from timber theft that supported the railroads and the even more threatening loss of all landholdings promoted by railroad companies and speculators.

The second event involved intertribal disputes over cattle theft between Creeks and Cherokees along the Cherokee-Creek border, where Jeff Marshall had lived. Many of the Cherokees involved were from the families of former slaveholding Cherokees and intermarried white men. At least one Cherokee was the direct descendent of a right of wife Cherokee who was admitted to citizenship in the early 1870s after relocating from southeastern Tennessee.[69] As the violence escalated on both sides, Cherokee vigilantes took direct aim at African Creek lighthorsemen. In 1880, Cherokees seized two African Creeks and lynched them. A gun battle followed, resulting in Cherokee men's deaths. Cherokee Nation citizens argued that the Creek Nation failed to police its border towns. Creek Nation residents worried that African Creeks could not possibly receive fair trials in the Cherokee district courts.[70]

Offered "twelve Creek negroes," possibly men affiliated with the crimes on the Cherokee-Creek border, the Cherokee Nation refused the swap. Instead, when Marshall's sentence expired on November 10, 1881, the Cherokee Nation released Marshall with his new suit of clothes and his five-dollar cash payment as it did for other Cherokee citizens.[71] Sarah Marshall, a woman who shared the same name as Jeff Marshall's mother and who served as a cook at the prison throughout Marshall's sentence, received forty-four dollars for her cooking services a month after Marshall was released. Given the lack of any other Sarah Marshalls in census and Dawes records, it is more than likely that Sarah Marshall was his mother.[72] Despite racial tensions between the Creeks and Cherokees, protecting tribal sovereignty and communal landholdings (and by extension social welfare for all of Indian Territory) trumped the interests of the federal courts doing the bidding of railroads. In this case, solving the Indian problem required careful negotiations between Native nations, bureaucratic processes between the federal government and the Cherokee Nation, management of racial tensions within the local communities, and, to an extent that is not completely clear, fulfillment of the social service demands of a single African Creek family.

By the early 1880s, the Five Tribes, all of which had former slaveholders and freed slaves in their communities, continued to grapple with their legal, social, and national obligations to freedmen and freedwomen in ways other former slaveholding states did not. For example, the federal government did not impose the citizenship of former slaves on states. Nor did southern states continue to experience the same level of scrutiny of its legal systems or social policies after Reconstruction ended in 1877. From 1865 to 1872, the U.S. Freedmen's Bureau had facilitated the distribution of social, educational, and legal services to freedmen, freedwomen, and poor whites throughout the South. A lack of executive will and Democrats' recalcitrance doomed the overall effectiveness of the bureau.[73] In Arkansas, bureau leaders encouraged schools and free labor and sought donations from northern benevolent societies, but privileged the planters' economic interests at the expense of freed people.[74] An ex-overseer, who served seven months as an agent in Arkansas, used his office to conduct blackmail, extract bribes, and force women to perform sex acts in exchange for the Freedmen's Bureau's services.[75] Texas residents killed bureau agents, burned numerous schools for freedmen, and harassed teachers.[76] Many white state residents actively thwarted the bureau's efforts during its brief existence. Although some situations were extreme, many agents openly expressed racist sentiments, and many others imposed their paternalism and moral judgments on freed people. Despite its contributions to stabilizing southern economies, providing educational opportunities for freed people, and distributing rations to the most destitute, black and white, the Freedmen's Bureau failed to provide most freed people with land, a key ingredient for long-term economic stability, but an economic salve that was offered, in theory, by opening up Indian Territory.

By the early 1880s, when Jeff Marshall leveraged the federal court against the Cherokee Nation, southern states had already curtailed many of the political gains realized by freed people under the Freedmen's Bureau's administration. They had also passed repressive poor laws that disproportionately impacted freed people and contributed to the expansion of convict leasing. The Choctaw Nation passed an 1883 law that prohibited intermarriage between Choctaws and anyone of African descent. Embracing racial segregation like the white South, the Cherokee Nation also resisted offering services to freed people in the same facilities established exclusively for other Cherokee citizens. In 1889, after a hotly contested election in which candidates had courted the vote of African Cherokee citizens, rather than admit descendants of freed people to the seminaries, the Cherokee Nation established a separate high school for African Cherokees.[77] Despite the fact African Cherokee citizens disagreed over other political issues in the Nation, African Cherokee citizens agreed that the Cherokee Nation blocked access to its social service institutions.[78]

Even though some Five Tribes' citizens shared the racist views of their southern counterparts, other factors complicated race relations in Indian Territory. The Creek, Cherokee, and Choctaw Nations had all passed repressive laws toward slaves in the antebellum era, but the Creek Nation failed to police those laws to the degree that its Choctaw and Cherokee counterparts did. This laxity in enforcement of slave laws in the years leading up to the Civil War had led those in neighboring slave states to advocate for territorialization of Indian

Territory. Arkansas papers had warned of the refuge Indian Territory offered to fugitive slaves.[79] In the post–Civil War period, territorializers' rhetoric seemingly interchanged the word "criminals" for "fugitive slaves" to argue against tribal sovereignty and for territorialization.

Cases like Jeff Marshall's brought the fluidity of racial boundaries in Indian Territory into the purview of federal officials and complicated the ability of Native nations to oversee their national social provisions. In the early 1870s, the federal agent to the Creeks had worked to have African Creeks classed as non-Indians under the Indian Intercourse Acts in order to have them tried for crimes against other Creeks in the federal courts. The Creek Nation's principal chief, whose sympathies were not necessarily with Creek freed people, but who viewed the issue as significant to national sovereignty, protested this action, arguing that the Creek Nation's court had jurisdiction over these cases.[80] For Cherokee and Creek governments, the ability to administer the Nation's laws to its citizens was a sovereign right, regardless of the race of those citizens.

Racism and inadequate state and federal institutional services often left the mentally ill in a vulnerable position, and this was no less true in the Cherokee Nation. In 1893, Principal Chief C. J. Harris requested that the state of Missouri take responsibility for a demented man found near Echo, Indian Territory, on the grounds that he was a former citizen of Missouri. The governor of Missouri denied any responsibility for the man on the basis that previous presumed residency in his state did not make the man a citizen.[81] Four years later, W. D. McBride, a hotel owner in Fort Gibson, requested information from Principal Chief Samuel H. Mayes to determine the "proper authority" to deal with a "crazy Negro" named William Biggs, whom McBride's wife and daughter had awakened to find standing in their bedroom. Given the sensitivity of the situation, McBride worried that another episode could bring "fatal" consequences. McBride wrote that Biggs "was a state negro" (in other words a state resident), but he wondered if authorities at Fort Smith could take charge of him.[82] Under Cherokee law and treaties, the Cherokee Nation could not. The Cherokee Nation knew that it bore no responsibility for non-Cherokee citizens and that the federal government had a responsibility to remove them. Resenting the continued exploitation of its resources by noncitizens, the Nation sought remedies from state and federal authorities for U.S. citizens who threatened the sustainability of the Nation's social welfare services.

Regardless of the fact that states and the Cherokee Nation often proved unwilling to provide care for those they denied legal residency to, leaving freed people particularly vulnerable, the federal government and reformers used the Cherokee freedmen's accusations of racial discrimination in the Cherokee Nation as a pretext to advance allotment. In 1883, the same year that the *Western Recorder* encouraged African Americans to settle Oklahoma as soon as possible, Senator Henry Dawes arrived in Indian Territory to investigate Cherokee freedmen's claims of discrimination. Rather than continuing to contest the freedmen's claims entirely, the Cherokee Nation allocated $75,000 to be distributed pro rata among the freedmen. As officials had chosen to do during the Treaty of 1866 negotiations, the Cherokee Nation focused on the greater threats—allotment and territorialization.

Despite the Five Tribes' lobbying efforts, Congress passed the Dawes General Allotment Act in 1887, sometimes referred to as the "Indian Emancipation Act." Hampton officials arranged a celebration, though whether students personally found the day celebratory is less clear.[83] The act itself granted "heads of household" 160 acres of land, 80 acres to each adult member of the family, and 80 acres to "orphans" under the age of eighteen. Children received forty acres. Each person received a patent, and additional provisions required the land to be held in trust by the federal government for twenty-five years. The act also provided U.S. citizenship to Indians who took allotments.[84] The Five Tribes were not able to stop the Dawes Act. The Cherokee Nation successfully negotiated its exclusion from the Dawes Act based on articles in the removal treaty and the Treaty of 1866 that secured ownership of Cherokee lands in fee simple. The treaties stipulated that Cherokees could only allot lands "when the National Council shall request it."[85]

This did not fully satisfy reformers. Dawes had argued that, despite the progress of the Five Tribes, members could not develop any further because they lacked private ownership of land; they lacked "selfishness," which he argued was the foundation of civilization.[86]

Dawes and others assailed the basic features of the Cherokees' traditional social welfare system, especially kinship systems that privileged the place of elders, especially women, and extended family. If allotment happened to bring down the social welfare systems' non-Indian reformers promoted in the process, so be it.[87] Those who favored allotment blasted communal landholdings, communitarian ethics, and shared resources and argued the superiority of individualism.

Increasingly, the reformers played on the U.S. citizens' middle-class anxieties and framed the Indian problem as a public health crisis. Communal lands were "a fever infected hospital . . . in league with the powers of death."[88] Friends of the Indian described Indian peoples as a "disturbing element of society," a deviant population that allotment and education could save.[89] In 1889, two years after the Dawes General Allotment Act passed and the Five Tribes had successfully argued for their exemption, "Friend" Charles Painter attacked the policy's restrictions that prevented Indian allottees from selling their lands for twenty-five years. For Painter, this "handicapped" and "manacled" Indian peoples, sending them on a path straight for "our" almshouses and jails.[90] Yet, the Cherokee people most in favor of allotment had argued that these very protections should be in place.[91]

Poverty, vice, and deviance preoccupied late nineteenth-century northeastern reformers, and it was through this lens that reformers viewed all Indian peoples. During Reconstruction, northern Republicans had celebrated the work ethic of all black people in the South to combat the Democrats' claims that all former slaves were lazy.[92] Northern reformers promoted an industrious work ethic as a cure for poverty, regardless of race. Beginning in the late 1860s, Horatio Alger's stories flourished. He celebrated work and perseverance as the path out of poverty. *Harper's Weekly* featured weekly biographies of men's rags-to-riches stories. Northern reformers often contrasted the urban poverty suffered by recent European immigrants, many of whom were more likely to support the Democratic Party, against the poverty suffered by hardworking rural black southerners. Publications like *Frank Leslie's Popular Monthly*, one of the few publications drawing attention to the Five Tribes' positions on allotment, published exposés describing the squalid conditions of cities. By 1880, nondenominational religious societies operated thirty agencies in city slums in the United States.[93] Most people believed that poverty was self-inflicted and indicative of moral failings. If this was the case, then educating and reforming the poor, particularly children, could offer a prescription for the poverty and public health concerns that plagued U.S. cities.[94] Reformers' unwavering commitment to free labor in the South, their hostility toward the northern urban poor, and their unwillingness to address racism and ethnocentrism as a factor that limited upward mobility blinded them to situations—like those in the Cherokee Nation—that defied reformers' arguments.

Reformers also sought to redefine how guardianship responsibilities should be administered. Children's ward status, non-Indian or not, subjected them to the experimental whims of Gilded Age and Progressive Era reformers. Operating from the 1850s through the 1920s, orphan trains relocated hundreds of thousands of poor urban youths to families who needed help to settle the West, yet reformers applied the opposite logic to Indian children.[95] In their view, they needed to be sent to the East to become civilized under the tutelage of former Indian fighters turned Indian-education reformers, though over time federal officials opened boarding schools in the West. This paternalism impacted everyone who was not white, middle-class, English-speaking, Protestant, and U.S.-born. African Americans had faced similar experiences with the agents of the Freedmen's Bureau.[96]

Tribal sovereignty prevented these whims from subjecting Cherokee children to similar coercive efforts without the permission of their families and also protected adults from the overwhelming intrusions into their private lives that urban poor and immigrant non–English speaking families faced in the East. The inability to assert social control over Indian people frustrated reformers and led them to more extreme positions than their civilization-touting counterparts eighty-five years earlier. In 1885, Merrill Gates, president of Rutgers College and a member of the Board of Indian Commissioners, stated his position: "We must not only give them law, we must force law upon them. We must not only offer them education, we must force education upon them."[97]

As territorializers and reformers continued their two-pronged offensive, Walter Adair Duncan received reinforcements from his family. DeWitt Clinton Duncan had returned to the Nation permanently by 1880. With his Dartmouth credentials, his public service record, and his multilingualism, DeWitt Clinton Duncan served in a variety of official capacities. In 1882, he served as a prosecuting attorney on behalf of the Cherokee Nation in the federal court against David Payne, the illegal intruder who led a colonization group to an area of Indian Territory not open for settlement.[98] Duncan's legal win positioned him as a defender of traditional social welfare and national interests. In the 1890s, he and his wife both served as editors for the *Indian Chieftain* in Vinita, a position that provided editorial reinforcement so his brother could focus his efforts on reformers' and U.S. officials' arguments for dissolution of the Nation.

Reformers posed one challenge to Cherokee sovereignty, but changes in federal policy that opened up Indian Territory to U.S. settlement prompted a series of other challenges. In 1889, the federal government authorized a land run on two million acres, land it had obtained from the Cherokees in the Treaty of 1866. It was an area of land roughly equivalent to three-fourths the size of Connecticut, located right in the middle of what is today Oklahoma.[99] Two more land runs followed in 1891 and 1893. A deluge of landless whites and freed people, homesteaders, railroad employees, and government officials washed over Indian Territory into the region to claim 160-acre parcels. Overnight, thousands of people poured into the region, traversing the lands occupied and governed by Native nations, which received no additional resources to manage this kind of demographic crisis. As Oklahoma historians Dale and Wardell describe the process of Oklahoma settlement, it was greed coupled with speed.[100] The 1889 land run led directly to the organization of the western half of Indian Territory into the Oklahoma Territory in 1890. The Organic Act of 1890 imposed the laws of Nebraska on the Oklahoma Territory, but made no financial provisions for social services or law enforcement. The act left local counties in control of schools, and all of them established segregated schools. The Oklahoma Territory paid Kansas to house its prisoners. It did assign lands for schools, which Oklahoma Territory officials leased to add to its coffers.[101]

In 1889, with membership reinvigorated by the surging demands for medical care created in Indian Territory as a result of illegal

DeWitt Clinton Duncan. Courtesy the Thomas Lee
Ballenger Papers, 1730–1968, photographs, ca. 1866–ca.
1904, box 3, folder 34, Newberry Library, Chicago.

settlement and squatting, the Indian Territory Medical Association
(ITMA) reorganized. To handle the increased presence of unlicensed
"doctors" in the Cherokee Nation, the Cherokee Board of Health
passed more aggressive policies toward the illegal practice of medicine in Indian Territory. Some of the physicians who arrived in the
region at this time worked for the railroads; many others were seeking free land. These new arrivals lacked the same professional relationships with the Cherokee Nation as did the physicians who had
originally organized the ITMA in 1881. As it had since 1878, the
Cherokee Nation continued to require all doctors to provide proof

of medical credentials and to submit themselves for evaluation to its Board of Examiners. By the middle of the 1880s, officials worked to remove those individuals who entered with labor permits but then overstayed their permits and engaged in quackery. During the same period, the Choctaw Nation published its laws, and the Creek Nation established its first rules regarding physician licensure.[102] By the early 1890s, the Cherokee Nation and the Choctaw Nation provided clear licensing procedures for those seeking to practice medicine in the two Nations. The Cherokee Nation distributed its guidelines to other states and territories, advertised the dates and locations of licensing boards, and printed the names of noncitizens illegally practicing medicine in the Cherokee Nation without a license.[103] In 1893, the year of the third land run, the Oklahoma Territory formed its own medical association; this group's members, unlike their ITMA counterparts, were little beholden to the policies and practices of the Five Tribes.[104] The reorganization of the ITMA in 1889 and the establishment of the OTMA four years later added a new wave of legal and professional challenges to the Cherokee Nation's and Indian Territory's abilities to administer social provisions based on the needs of communities.

As thousands of non-Indians flooded into Indian Territory and Oklahoma Territory as would-be homesteaders, the "Indian problem" remained the talking point for reformers. Cherokees refused to assimilate into American society by acquiescing to allotment and continued to assert their rights to care for each other based on the merits of Cherokee social service systems.[105] In response, Congress established another commission through its 1893 Indian appropriation bill and sent commissioners to Indian Territory to negotiate allotment agreements with the Five Tribes. Despite a clear rejection of allotment collectively, "no" did not mean "no" to the federal government. The Five Tribes faced continued charges that their governments were dysfunctional and should be dissolved based on the perceived lawlessness of Indian Territory. The Cherokee Nation's sovereignty and its social service delivery system were bound together. If one was under attack, the other was as well. Despite these increasingly difficult conditions, Cherokee Nation continued to look inward to discuss and debate its social service policy and needs.

CHAPTER 7

Talking Back to Our
Civilized Nation, 1893–1898

In 1893, the same year Walter Adair Duncan spelled out the reasons he was not prepared for U.S. citizenship, Congress formed a commission that traveled to Indian Territory to negotiate allotment among the Five Tribes.[1] Because many of the stereotypes non-Indians held about "the Indian" failed to match the discourse circulated about the Five Tribes, territorializers, speculators, and reformers had to change their tactic. Additionally, regardless of the fact that the federal government had ceased making treaties, it still had to abide by the legal precedents of preexisting treaties and uphold the land rights treaties guaranteed to the Cherokee Nation.[2] As Connecticut's *Hartford Courant* asserted, the Senate was "for giving the Indians further opportunity for reflection . . . and [the opportunity to] yield to the force of these arguments," or they might "continue to show themselves deaf, blind, and stubborn." The article quoted Senator Dawes's statement that the Five Tribes were no longer "safe" under their treaty, given Congress's and the executive's ability to tear up a treaty, to which the paper asked how the "thing is to be done honestly and with a good conscience?"[3] It took Congress another five years to pass the Curtis Act, which subjected the Five Tribes to allotment. In the interim, allotment gripped Cherokee people's attention; in their minds (and clearly in the mind of the *Hartford Courant* editor), social welfare policy and allotment were connected. Allotment threatened to dismantle key features of traditional and national Cherokee social welfare policy and to disable Cherokee people metaphorically and legally if necessary. Unfortunately, defending the Cherokee Nation's sovereignty to journalists and politicians and, by extension, to the American public drained the Nation of financial resources it could have used, and it diverted the attention of Cherokee people best suited to improve its institutions away from social policy discussions and delivery.[4]

This chapter examines the conversations Cherokee people had with one another about social welfare policy as they simultaneously worked to stave off allotment and statehood. It covers the period from 1893, when the Dawes commissioners arrived, through 1898, when Congress passed the Curtis Act subjecting the Five Tribes to allotment and unilaterally imposing U.S. law on the Cherokee Nation. Throughout these years, Cherokee elected officials and administrators remained answerable to the "ultimate sovereigns," as Walter Adair Duncan described them, Cherokee people. Cherokee people continued to participate in and debate features of the civic life of the Nation. Regardless of the national instability that the allotment era fostered, Cherokee elected leaders continued to carry out the Nation's responsibilities as a sovereign state, and the community continued to negotiate and debate the merits of its hybrid social welfare system. The weight of settler colonialism continued to inform the kinds of changes that Cherokee institutional service providers could implement, and over time, the Nation aligned its institutional practices more closely with those advocated by northeastern reformers in order to better defend itself against outside critics. By the 1890s, race, class, gender, and preference for traditional or institutional social welfare systems informed many of the internal renegotiations of social welfare expectations with the Nation. At a time when the future of national social provisions remained tenuous, leading men often expressed their anxieties over granting individuals and some groups' institutional access to social welfare provisions. This came at a high cost for everyday Cherokee people, including women, who lacked external channels for their views, but even more so for those living, incarcerated, or working within social welfare institutions, and those with the least access to traditional social welfare provisions.

When federal officials formed the Dawes Commission to negotiate allotment among the Five Tribes in 1893, elected tribal officials opposed the federal government's efforts.[5] By the 1880s, nearly all of the leading men and many Cherokee women had benefitted from the educational institutions in the Cherokee Nation. The common schools and seminaries provided their educations in advance of any college education they received in the United States. As a result of the Cherokee Nation's support of the American Baptist Mission Indian University, some Cherokee people remained within the Nation for their college education.[6] However, many of them also started and advanced their professional careers in the Nation's institutions. Both men and women had taught in the public schools and had served as teachers and administrators at the orphanage and seminaries. Numerous graduates practiced as attorneys in the courts or served as superintendents of the facilities. Countless others sold their crops and provided services to institutions. Though not expressed as a loss of professional opportunities, as early as 1872 Walter Adair Duncan had warned that the misinformation spread about Indians in the United States led people to argue "that because the Indians are this way, they ought to have their houses and lands taken away from them."[7] If Cherokees' lands and homes could be taken, by extension their economic livelihoods could be too. Therefore, they meant to defend the Nation's sovereignty and its institutions.

Although Walter Adair Duncan shared the Cherokee Nation's opposition to allotment, his perspective was slightly different. By the 1890s, Duncan was approaching seventy years of age. He was part of a dwindling generation born before removal. He was an expert witness to the trials and tribulations and *successes* of nation building; he was an original beneficiary of the citizenship offered by the Nation. Duncan had not actively pursued a political career. He had instead devoted the bulk of his adult life in service to and working with people largely underrepresented at the national level—women, children, rural farmers, monolingual Cherokee speakers, and Cherokee citizens without family supports. The Cherokee people he knew and cared for relied on the communal land base and each other to make a life in the Cherokee Nation. They were the majority, and allotment did not represent their best interests, nor was it, in Walter Adair Duncan's view, in the best interests of the Nation.

U.S. citizens and Cherokee people expressed similar anxieties related to land monopolies and their impact on everyday people. Beginning during the Civil War, the federal government began disbursing federal lands (much of it occupied by other Indian nations) to homesteaders in order to settle the West. By the 1880s, speculators and cattle companies controlled much of the land dispersed to homesteaders, often amassed through unscrupulous and exploitative means. These entities used tenant farmers and ranch hands to maintain vast tracts of lands. Both the United States and the Five Tribes passed laws to limit wealthy entities from enclosing large spaces in the late 1880s and 1890s.[8] In 1881, DeWitt Clinton Duncan had pointed out the "waspish petulance of Civilization." Civilization's representatives critiqued Indian people as "uncivilized" for opposing railroads yet failed to acknowledge the shared concerns of groups in the United States including the Greenback Party, an anti-monopoly party concerned with agrarian issues, with those of the Cherokee Nation.[9] In 1895, when Robert B. Ross would accept the nomination for principal chief of the National Party, he described monopoly as a "fatal evil in itself if unchecked." He added that, in the Cherokee Nation's case, monopoly provided the "enemies of our government with an effective weapon to attack [the Nation]." For that reason, he argued, the problem of monopoly "must be met and settled . . . for the safety of the nation." Although monopoly concerned groups in the United States and the Cherokee Nation, politicians and corporations were not calling for the dissolution of the United States because monopolies existed.[10]

By the early 1890s, territorializers and reformers adjusted their attacks on the Five Tribes by targeting the overstated inequities created by monopolies within the Cherokee Nation relative to the monopolies in the United States. From 1892 to 1896, the *Cherokee Advocate* provided a venue for Cherokee "Prominent Men" to debate the issue of land monopolies. This preference for leading men implied a hierarchy of voices eligible to speak for the Nation and eliminated a host of voices from the discussion. U.S. reformers had attacked communal landholdings as spaces that prevented Indian advancement and discouraged greed. The presence of land monopolies in the Cherokee Nation defied this argument and provided clear evidence of greed. Territorializers and U.S. reformers adjusted their arguments to attack this practice as exploitative of "full-bloods" and "the poor." Many Cherokee people shared concerns over monopolies, but only a few favored allotment as a solution to the problem. Beginning in 1892, Christopher Columbus Robards wrote editorials to pro-allotment papers attacking Walter Adair Duncan's refusal to see the poverty created by monopoly in the Nation. He had lived outside the Cherokee Nation in Arkansas for many years. It was only after Robards's attacks on Walter Adair Duncan began and after a per capita distribution was to be made to Cherokee citizens that he returned to the Nation in 1894.[11] John Lynch Adair, who had traveled to California during the gold rush in the late 1840s and early 1850s, and who later served on the committee to build the prison, joined Robards in opposing Duncan in the early 1890s.[12] They both favored allowing the federal government to survey the land and argued that this did not necessarily lead to allotment.[13] Both men resented the large land-holdings of the wealthiest Cherokee men. But they also pitied those selling seed corn on the open market at deflated prices, merchants unable to pay freight costs, and the falling interests on bonds.[14] The men pitied the poor, but the "poor" they described were those people eager to participate in market economies; they ignored the concerns of those committed to osdv iyunvnehi.

Within the Nation, race baiting fueled the debate over land monopolies. Robards attempted to rouse support against land monopolies by charging that African Cherokee Jeff Foreman had "colonized one hundred worthless negroes." Instead of attacking Cherokees or inter-married white men who exploited communal landholdings and monopolized far greater tracts than had Foreman, he honed in on Foreman's anomalous case and suggested that this was the norm. In another article, he eliminated Foreman's name entirely, stating, "A colored man (adopted citizen) has four thousand acres improved, on which he has one hundred intruders, not one fourth of whom even pay a permit." He preyed on legitimate Cherokee fears over intruders and their concerns over laborers failing to pay work permits. Robards "wonder[ed] if that is what Bro. Duncan calls preserving our 'sacred institutions,'" a reference to communal landholdings.[15] Calling Walter Adair Duncan "brother" as a means of manipulating ideas about family and kinship ignored the social welfare protections that community landholdings and gadugi extended to all Cherokee people, regardless of race. Walter Adair Duncan's defense of communal landholdings as a sacred institution, whether he intended it to or not, did protect African Cherokees and Shawnee and Delaware citizens' economic and social welfare to a degree.[16]

Robards's rhetorical sleight of hand coupled racist ideology with anti-intruder sentiment to advocate for "poor" individuals who he claimed lacked access to land. The people Robards worried about were who those eager to benefit financially from the market; Walter Adair and DeWitt Clinton Duncan advocated for a different constituency. In the *Cherokee Advocate*, Walter Adair Duncan "beg[ged] the Cherokee people . . . chiefly those who do not read english" to study the issues before them so they could "talk in a friendly way about the best interests of our country."[17] In contrast to most Cherokee people, DeWitt Clinton's education and experiences beyond the Nation more closely resembled those of the men who "roast[ed]" his brother in local papers. Yet, those same experiences also provided him with the perspective to provide counterarguments to those in favor of surveying Cherokee lands and who offered the ills of monopoly as a reason to favor allotment.[18] But DeWitt Clinton also understood the Cherokee language; this enabled him to add to the debate the voices of monolingual Cherokee speakers whose opinions men like Robards liked to seem informed about, but whom they regularly dismissed as ignorant and blind.[19] DeWitt Clinton attacked "native statesmen . . . who have been educated out of 'touch' with the poor, down-trodden tribesmen from whom they themselves originally sprang . . . ever ready to march right along with civilization without a question as to the moral nature of the banner under which they are moving."[20] Although DeWitt Clinton avoided any overtly gendered statements, he reprimanded men like Robards whose education and lives outside the Nation led them to parrot the social welfare policy advocated by the United States and not the one that protected their grandmothers, mothers, and sisters and their matrilineal kin.

Even though DeWitt Clinton advocated a social welfare policy that benefitted women economically, it was still well-educated, middle-class, and affluent leading men who controlled many of the debates not only about land monopolies but also about social provisions within the Nation. Yet, these conversations also reveal an equally vital and important aspect of sovereignty often left out of discussions by scholars about it—the activities of the "ultimate sovereigns," as Walter Adair Duncan described them, the Cherokee people collectively. This included women. As Cherokee citizens continued to make clear to their national government, they could consent to, withhold consent from, renegotiate the terms of, or actively oppose the services provided and administered by institutional officials.

The pardon process for those convicted of crimes within the Cherokee Nation highlights one of the ways Cherokee people communicated their expectations of the legal system with the Nation. In 1895, Cherokee petitioners sought an "unconditional pardon" for James Peacock, who was convicted by the Cherokee courts of attempted murder. Applications for pardon usually came from a single community group on behalf of an incarcerated individual. In the James Peacock case, however, competing appeals arrived at the executive branch. The petitioners for pardon invoked arguments that favored families headed by economically independent men. Petitioners argued that Peacock needed to care for his blind wife and child and attend to his farm. He headed his family, his wife and children were dependent on him, and he was solely responsible for their livelihood. Another group of citizens presented a petition that "respectfully asked that no clemency be shown to James Peacock, a convict in the National Prison" for what they described as one of "the most treacherous and atrocious crimes ever committed in the Cherokee Nation by a human by attempting to steal the lives of a man and wife while peacefully sleeping in their own house, by chopping them with an axe and then leaving them for dead."[21] The circumstances of the case were in fact quite different from other cases. Most attempted murder and murder cases involved whiskey and/or money. This case involved neither.

The competing arguments framed by the petitioners revealed the extent to which families who adhered to traditional social welfare practices tenuously supported the Nation's newer criminal justice system. Petitioners who objected to Peacock's pardon invoked older systems of community responsibilities that favored the wronged party above the wrongdoer and provided protection to its members. They asked "in justice to our laws, and to his victims" that Peacock be denied a pardon. They supported the current system of justice because Peacock's conviction performed the function of a traditional social service system. If that system failed, they feared, "neighborhood trouble" could arise. The veiled threat implied that the older system of blood vengeance could and would be employed if the national system of courts, juries, jails, and pardons failed.

Petitioners opposing Peacock's pardon also described the use of gadugi to protect its members. Peacock's wife, they said, had "always" called upon her "friends for protection," which implied that kinship and reciprocity supported the woman more than her husband. The petitioners suggested that her husband was actually a threat to her; they insisted that she would need even more assistance if the executive granted clemency. Her community, not her husband, provided her care and protection. The community, therefore, consented to the Cherokee Nation's institutional social services based on the Nation's ability to uphold and support traditional social service principles, including a community's responsibility to protect its members.

Throughout the nineteenth century, U.S. citizens' requests for and the president's use of the executive pardon had increased. In 1896, 64 percent of all federal prisoners received a pardon, some of whom had not even applied for one. Some of this is explained by the limited use of parole or probation as options for release. The absence of federal facilities and the need to house federal prisoners in state institutions offers another reason for its prevalence.[22]

Both Cherokees and U.S. citizens regularly used the executive pardon process throughout the nineteenth century; however, U.S. legal provisions traced the pardon's origin and use to different strains of philosophical thought. By the late nineteenth century, many Cherokee leaders articulated similar rationales for pardons based on principles of justice and rights. Some Cherokee leaders certainly saw public executions and the statements that accompanied them as a means to assert sovereignty and Cherokee personhood. But others articulated the Cherokee peoples' use of the pardon as one that extended from their traditional social service system and a different philosophical worldview than those reflected in U.S. legal systems.[23] Traditional social services functioned at their best when they achieved restorative balance, not retributive justice.[24] The sheer number of pardon applications reveal the willingness of Cherokee communities to excuse convicted criminals, yet they also reveal the debates within the communities over who could be restored and who could not and under what conditions.[25]

Almost universally, Cherokees embraced the use of an executive pardon, but how they navigated the process reflected their everyday reliance on national versus traditional social service systems. Traditional Cherokee jurisprudence, administered widely into the early nineteenth century, incorporated and annually mandated social redemption.[26] The first written law in 1808 extended a pardon to officers of the Nation for homicides committed while carrying out their official duties. An 1810 law criminalized the killing of one brother by another, whereas older law granted clans the ability to pardon a brother. Both of these laws attempted to shift how Cherokees conceived of pardonable offenses. Crimes were no longer matters that impacted clans and communities; they were crimes that harmed the Nation and challenged its national authority.

In the aftermath of removal and civil war, the Cherokee Nation used amnesty in the Treaty of 1846 to reconcile the Treaty Party, the National Party, and the Old Settlers. It granted general amnesty and pardon for all "offenses and crimes committed by a citizen or citizens of the Cherokee Nation against the nation, or against an individual or individuals." It invited those who had left the Nation to return to their homes so that they could "unite in enforcing the laws against all future offenders."[27] Amnesty provisions in Treaty of 1866 that followed the Civil War had performed a civil and international function between the Cherokee Nation and the United States.[28] The internal use of amnesty that followed Cherokee civil war included some of the functions previously provided by annual ceremonies, but amnesty distorted the once-egalitarian processes by excluding women, elders, and children and modified other features of annual ceremonies. Amnesty, in theory, made homicide a pardonable offense on a massive scale. The New Codes adopted in the 1870s maintained a newer provision that granted the principal chief and the executive council the ability to pardon or commute sentences, even for murder, based on "such conditions and restrictions as [the executive] may think proper."[29] The centralization of a pardon process with the executive and its applicability to murder was certainly new, but gadugi had long dictated the responsibilities of the community to set aside ill will toward those who committed a wrong in order to reestablish balance.

Cherokee people adapted the use of a pardon process to conform to their particular social service worldviews, but how Cherokee people applied for pardons within the community adhered to gendered patterns, some of which they deployed outside the Cherokee Nation as well. Most petitions for pardon came from men in the community who sought to correct some legal error. The second most common appeal came from attorneys on behalf of women who sought pardons for family members. Cherokee men and women utilized the pardon process based on the social service needs of their families and communities.

In their appeals for pardons, men tended to challenge the legality of trials, points of law, and unethical or problematic actions of jurors. The people who presented such appeals often included the signatures of hundreds of men from the appellants' community to support their claims.[30] Petitions from leading men did not guarantee one's release. In October of 1893, for example, the *Advocate* reported that "a strong petition was presented to the Chief for commutation of the sentence of Sam Mayes who was hung yesterday."[31] But such petitions often succeeded. For example, chief clerk of the Senate L. B. Bell visited Principal Chief Oochalata with a petition for executive clemency on behalf of John Still.[32] The courts had convicted Still of the murder of Edwin Downing and had sentenced him to seven years of hard labor. The petition carried by Bell claimed that juror Moses Fields was "not of lawful age." Therefore, the court had convicted Still based on an illegal trial. Jennie Stinson, an adoptive mother who "raised the said Moses Fields from infancy," testified that he was between the age of nineteen and twenty at the date of the trial rather than twenty-one, the age required of jurors.[33] Based on her affidavit and a petition from "a large number of responsible citizens," the executive council "unanimously advised the unconditional pardon of the said John Still." Less than eight weeks after his conviction, Principal Chief Oochalata Charles Thompson set John Still free.[34]

Despite nineteenth-century changes that had excluded Cherokee women from political office and service on juries, women used the pardon to appeal to forms of justice that existed before written laws, modern courts, and the use of a prison. Women used appeals much as they had petitions during the removal era; they invoked their matrilineal rights as mothers and sisters, but applications for pardon also reflected the willingness of many women to advocate for their husbands. In 1882, the wife of Sam Beaver told Principal Chief Bushy-head that her husband, who was serving time in prison and was crippled, could "only be a burden on the prison keepers."[35] For Beaver, imprisonment did not provide justice. To achieve justice, traditional Cherokee people sought a restoration of balance. The jailors, in a sense, were being punished for Beaver's crime; this did not achieve balance. A wrongdoer must pay for his crimes, but not at the expense of another.

William Grapes's mother combined older interpretations of Chero-kee legal thinking with the newer goals promoted by reformers when she argued for her son's pardon. During his arrest, he was "shot several times and crippled for life." For his mother, this was "punishment enough" and "such a severe lesson that he would be a reformed man if given another chance."[36] Traditionally, Cherokee people did not seek punishments; they sought a restoration of both temporal and cosmic order. The injuries of these men balanced their crime; the addition of prison terms amounted to overkill.

As women advocated for the prisoners' release, superintendents of the various social service institutions struggled to clarify admis-sions criteria and determine which citizens and residents were legally entitled to admission and long-term care. Funded by the Cherokee Nation, the asylum was presumably open to all Cherokee citizens, but not to noncitizens. In 1893, the asylum steward drew Principal Chief C. J. Harris's attention to two "unauthorized inmates" and requested action to "relieve the Institution of the[ir] care and custody." The first was Perry Lee, a white U.S. citizen, an intruder "with no claims to citizenship whatsoever."[37] Principal Chief Harris asked the U.S. agent to remove Lee from the asylum and place him in a federal facility. The agent replied that no such facility existed, that the agency lacked the resources to provide for the man's care, and that he had contacted Lee's brother to encourage him to seek citizenship for Lee in Kansas, where an asylum operated. The agent then requested that the Cherokee Nation, "as an act of humanity," permit Lee to remain until his family could make other arrangements.[38] The Cherokee Nation responded humanely and continued his care. Like many Cherokee citizens who found care there, Perry Lee died at the asylum.[39] It is unclear what would have happened to Lee had the Nation denied him services.

The second "unauthorized" asylum resident was "Jonas, the colored adopted Cherokee freedman who is at the Asylum without 'due course of law.'"[40] In Lee's case, the issue of rights to services was clear—he had none—but Jonas's case was more ambiguous. "Without due course of law" suggests a legal explanation for why his presence created a problem. An official admitted Jonas to the facility, so his initial admittance seems proper, but his eligibility for permanent residency appears to have raised questions. Questions over Jonas's eligibility for asylum care coincided with efforts of the Cherokee Nation to exclude intermarried whites and freedmen from future claims to Cherokee land.[41]

Because Cherokee officials and citizens feared allotment, the national council passed legal measures meant to limit some groups' future economic claims to land. It had also struggled to retain its sovereign right to determine citizenship and resented the federal government's imposition of a commission to determine which freedmen were entitled to inclusion. This commission to investigate the freedmen's claims in 1884 had been led by Senator Henry Dawes, a proponent of allotment. Citizenship rights and per capita distributions related to freedmen had nothing to do with allotment, but it was not a coincidence that the officials advocating for freedmen's rights and allotment were the same. The Cherokee Nation was reluctant to acknowledge the citizenship of individuals who appeared before that commission rather than follow Cherokee procedures. The influx of African Americans to the region based on colonization efforts and individual hopes for homesteads and intermarriage with Cherokees complicated the Cherokee Nation's task to determine its rightful claimants to citizenship. These national concerns and constrictions left individuals in need of care in vulnerable situations.

There is no evidence that Jonas had personally aroused animosity or suspicion, but his commitment occurred in a particularly charged racial climate. Jonas's initial admission to the asylum represents recognition by Cherokees and African Cherokees that national services extended to African Cherokees, but it also points to the continued ambivalence of institutional officials to deliver those services as they would to other Cherokees and intermarried whites, or, in at least one case, an illegal intruder.

The orphanage excluded freedmen as well, though officials offered different reasons. Despite the orphanage's willingness to aid Cherokee citizens who adhered to a variety of family configurations and the Nation's willingness to debate the merits of educational opportunities and the outcomes of its young men, it did not extend the same considerations to all of its citizens.[42] This had been the case for some time. In 1873, the orphanage's second year of operation, Cherokee freedmen complained to missionaries that it failed to serve their children. A year later, they petitioned the council "to provide support and education of our Orphan Children."[43] The Cherokee Nation pointed out that so many children had needs that the orphanage could not possibly serve them all, but the council did make plans for a separate building for the children of freedmen at the orphanage's permanent location in Salina.[44] The effort stalled when the council and the board of education deadlocked over who bore responsibility for the orphans of freedmen.[45] Neither entity took responsibility.

Many Cherokee citizens either ignored or feigned ignorance of the need for orphan care for the children of freedmen and freedwomen. Hearings conducted in 1885 by the federal government to evaluate the Cherokee Nation's fulfillment of its treaty obligations asked pointed questions about orphan care of Cherokee witnesses.

Q: Is there an asylum in the Cherokee Nation for colored people?
A: I do not think there is.
Q: Are there colored people in your asylums?
A: I do not think there are.
Q: They do not have any orphans, do they?
A: I do not know.
Q: What becomes of their orphans?
A: I cannot say.[46]

Social services developed to meet the needs of families who lacked access to traditional social service systems. The Cherokee Nation extended citizenship to freedmen, but resisted extending the traditional principles of community hospitality to the children of freedmen that it offered to other Cherokees at its institutions. Unless freed people had matrilineal kin or a community willing to provide for them, they were locked out of either social welfare system. National officials steeped in the primacy of men's property rights, many of whom had owned slaves, shared the racist views of many of their southern neighbors. Cherokee officials reconciled the new demands of citizenship by meeting the minimal needs of freed people through segregated services. In the 1880s, the Cherokee Colored High School opened to serve freed people within the Cherokee Nation. In 1895, twenty-three years after the freedmen's initial request for orphan services, the Colored High School, underfunded in comparison to the Cherokee schools, established a residential primary department to provide a home and education to the orphaned and indigent children of former slaves and their descendents.[47]

Cherokee leaders and public servants remained attuned to the accusations, including mistreatment of freed people, lobbed by reformers at its social welfare system to promote allotment, yet Cherokees continued to debate the purpose of social welfare institutions, improvements to them, and social provisions offered to Cherokee people. In 1893, Walter Adair Duncan suggested that a portion of the monies from the sale of the Cherokee Strip be set aside for school funds. Duncan argued that the growth of the school system, the need for schools in rural areas, and the need for an expanded board of education to aid the superintendent in overseeing schools warranted additional funds. The same year, at the teacher's institute, Duncan presented on "The Object of Education."[48] In 1898, just a month before the adoption of the Curtis Act, the teacher's institute showed that the discussions over how best to serve monolingual Cherokee speakers were still ongoing after several years. One discussion planned for the event reflected the Nation's self-awareness on issues relating to allotment: "How Our Educational System Appears to an Outsider."[49] Walter Adair Duncan had long been a proponent of manual-labor training for all Cherokee men based on the practical realities of making a living in rural Indian Territory. At the same time, he looked for ways to introduce skills to educational settings that expanded students' opportunities beyond the orphanage, the best example being the addition of the printing press to the orphanage.

By the late 1880s, the push for manual labor overwhelmed many of the debates surrounding education. Education for the masses, especially education of the poor, immigrants, and people of color, focused on producing malleable workers capable of meeting the labor needs of industries. As U.S. reformers, known as child savers, attacked the overcrowded, unsanitary, and economically inefficient conditions at orphanages, they nevertheless began to see institutions as the ideal location to educate Indian children.[50] In 1882, the Indian Rights Association (IRA) formed, later calling themselves the "Friends of the Indian." The IRA sought to remove children from what reformers saw as the destructive influence of their backward families and to place them under the tutelage of benevolent Protestant mentors to train them for productive lives. It was within this broader context as well as the realities of rural life in Indian Territory that debates over manual labor took place in the Cherokee Nation.

Cherokee debates over manual labor extended to its prisoners but focused on their interactions with the rest of the community. In 1886, a year after a prisoner escaped while digging a well at the seminary, Walter Adair Duncan argued that labor projects afforded prisoners too much freedom and placed others in the Nation, especially the women and girls at the seminaries, in particular moral peril.[51] He "[had] seen young ladies and little girls working on the yard with the convicts." Although Duncan was a proponent of manual labor at the orphanage and the prison, he worried that the character of the prisoners might rub off on the students at the female seminary and normalize criminal activity.[52] For example, he suggested that prisoners chop wood elsewhere, and then it could be brought to the seminaries. His position aligned with penology reformers in the United States who were attempting to use reformatories to classify criminals in order to accomplish what prisons had not. The goal was to keep hardened criminals away from petty criminals and all criminals away from everyone else.[53]

However, Walter Adair Duncan's criticisms revealed ideas about class, gender, and criminality that the majority of Cherokees did not adhere to. All women attending the seminary, regardless of economic means, labored daily to maintain the institution.[54] All children at the orphanage worked, and those who were able worked at the asylum. Gadugi guided both national responsibilities and neighborliness. George Welch provided his home as a guardhouse for prisoners awaiting trial and opened his home to known outlaws. Moses Welch, George Welch's son, described his father as a "peace-loving citizen [who] refused to meddle in matters in which he had no interest."[55] Guard John Parris, who served High Sheriffs George Roach and Zeke Parris in the 1890s, described outlaw (and lawman) Zeke Proctor as "a bad man in some ways and a good man in some ways."[56] Figure 12 documents enough of a comfort by at least one Cherokee prison guard with his prison community to include his young child in the photograph. Walter Adair Duncan's concerns over the moral influence of Cherokee prisoners did not match the way most Cherokees reconciled national law and community obligations, nor did it reflect the razor-thin line between law abider and criminal that most Cherokee people, as Samuel Sixkiller's arrest demonstrated, walked. If community members turned away from wrongdoers, they violated their kinship obligations and gadugi. Breaking the law did not negate the community's responsibility to interact with that individual.[57]

Confessions from the gallows in the Cherokee Nation provided one of very few means for prisoners to express their support for or discontent with national social service systems. National goals for public confessions and traditional social service expectations merged in the public rituals surrounding execution. Nineteenth-century newspapers inside and outside the Cherokee Nation published gallows confessions, and very often editors used the confessions to convey moral lessons and affirm the legitimacy of state authority.

Some Cherokees used their gallows statement to publically challenge the judicial equity of the Nation. The courts convicted Spade Sunshine of the murder of Long John in the Sequoyah District. On the day of his execution in 1887, Sunshine bid farewell to his wife, children, and friends before ascending the gallows, where he admitted to shooting the wrong man. Sunshine then accused the principal chief and the executive branch of accepting bribes in exchange for pardons. His application for pardon had called into question the competency

Cherokee Nation prisoners, ca. 1900. Courtesy Cherokee Nation Cultural Tourism Division.

of three jurors. As a poor man, Sunshine said he could not afford the bribes necessary to secure his pardon.[58]

The *Advocate* dismissed his accusations as bitter mudslinging from the previous election: "To the impartial and those who respect the law Sunshine's own statement of the manner of the killing will be sufficient reason why he was not pardoned."[59] Despite the *Advocate*'s insistence to the contrary, some Cherokees believed that justice in the Cherokee Nation was only available to those who could afford to pay for it. Long John's family likely agreed with the *Advocate*.

The concept of prolonged incarceration was new to Cherokee people and escape or aiding escape offered a means of rejecting national social services and/or privileging the local community's ability to adjudicate crime. On several occasions, prisoners chose not to escape when given the opportunity. When a large group of prisoners managed to use a knife and shovel to cut a wood joist in two and make their escape, six prisoners chose to stay behind. One cited the cold winter weather as a reason; most said they would rather take their chances with the pardon process.[60] Randolph Hummingbird escaped with Blossom after his application for a pardon was rejected and his sentence was commuted to ten years.[61] Frustration over not receiving his pardon likely prompted his escape.

Returning from an escape suggests that prisoners accepted responsibility for their wrongdoing and reconciled themselves to their fate, but increasing anxiety over allotment may have encouraged prisoners to return. Two years before the Curtis Act passed, several escaped prisoners voluntarily returned to the Nation. If they had not returned and allotment had occurred, they would have been excluded from land distributions. Whether these decisions were motivated by concerns over allotment is unclear, but within a week of one another, Hummingbird, who had escaped ten years earlier, returned, as did Dick Catcher.[62] Both men completed their sentences. Dick Catcher was released in 1897.[63]

Because most Cherokees regarded institutions as belonging to them and because they adhered to a community ethic, they visited residents frequently and expected institutions to extend hospitality to visitors. Cherokee people refused to stay away from institutions and their friends and neighbors who resided there, despite numerous attempts by institutional officials to limit their access. The prison reined in its visitors by setting visiting hours and by requiring guests to obtain permission from the executive.[64] In 1878, asylum officials requested that students from the seminaries discontinue their "frequent and unnecessary" visits to the asylum. Officials also discouraged family and friends of patients from visiting. They reminded citizens that, though the "institution was built with the public funds of the Nation," it was not a "public house where they can come and eat and lounge at pleasure."[65] Attesting to its effectiveness (or lack thereof), in 1886, the national council passed an act forbidding anyone without an "official connection" to the asylum from receiving meals or lodging at the facility. It added that the steward "will show due respect and courtesy to persons visiting . . . but shall not encourage such to remain longer than [necessary]."[66] This rule exposes the difficult decisions administrators faced as they continued to try to fulfill traditional social service expectations. Cherokee people demanded that institutions exhibit a community ethic, an ethic that institutional officials continued to exercise despite national rules aimed at economy.

Limiting visitors was common at many asylums for the mentally ill. Some early nineteenth-century reformers, including Dr. Benjamin Rush, whom many considered the father of psychiatry in the United States advocated the complete isolation of residents from friends or family as a part of the patient's treatment. Later reformers, including the Quakers, who subscribed to a "home" setting for the mentally ill, rejected complete isolation from visitors.[67] The Cherokee Nation did not isolate residents, but they did discourage visits that risked residents' treatment. The institution also limited visitors in order to rein in spending on the food that a hospitality ethic required the institution to provide.

The medical superintendents providing treatment to patients at institutions received their education and training at medical schools in the United States. As a result, new medical practices in the United States infiltrated the Cherokee Nation's institutional care. Increasingly, they failed to match the beliefs and practices of everyday Cherokee people, especially as it pertained to understandings of gender. Conditions and treatments at asylums in the United States tended to be gendered throughout the nineteenth century. In 1878, following practice in the United States, the Cherokee staff divided the building into two wards, one for men and one for women, and required residents to seek permission to visit with the opposite sex. In the steward's next report, he "regretted to say, that against these resolutions, there was a general rebellion." For Cherokees, normalcy included interaction and even intimacy between men and women, except when women were menstruating.[68]

Doctors' scientific approaches to bodies increasingly offended the sensibilities of traditional Cherokee people. According to the Dunawas family, a white doctor approached Chawayukee to purchase her sons' bodies after their double execution in the 1890s to use as medical cadavers. Five doctors attended the execution, including James A. Thompson, Joseph M. Thompson, Ross, Treadwell, and Fite. The latter two were intermarried whites.[69] This was the largest number of doctors the *Advocate* had ever recorded being present at an execution. As the medical superintendent for the prison at the time, officials required Joseph M. Thompson to attend the execution and pronounce the deaths. As a result of the offer to purchase her sons' bodies, Chawayukee feared that their bodies might be stolen, so she refused to leave them. She watched them being taken from the gallows, she dressed and groomed their bodies before they were placed in the coffins, and she accompanied their bodies on the thirty-mile journey to the Lacie Cemetery. Then she had a chair placed by their gravesides, where she stayed day and night. Family and friends provided food and company during the day. After seven days, a sacred number to Cherokee people, she returned home. Before she departed, she used her skills as a traditional healer to curse anyone who might try to remove the bodies. For Chawayukee, doctors trained in medical schools had become the Ravenmocker, intent on stealing the bodies of her boys.[70] Professionalized medicine not only introduced a health care system intent on divorcing the physical from the spiritual and communal but also reintroduced a system that placed monetary value on the bodies of dead Cherokee people.[71]

By the mid-1890s, Cherokee institutions were in their second decade and were in need of significant repairs. As Walter Adair Duncan pointed out in his 1893 article, school growth and expanded educational services required more investments in education. At the same moment the Nation needed to build additional schools and its residential facilities required significant repairs, the Nation had to spend an inordinate amount of time, energy, and money on public relations campaigns in the press and delegations to Washington to fight allotment. In his 1895 annual report, High Sheriff George Roach called attention "to the seriously leaky condition of the iron roof [of the prison] . . . which is damaged to such an extent as to allow rains to run down on inside walls."[72] In a series of articles in 1895, the *Cherokee Advocate* threatened to publish an exposé on the conditions at the asylum if there were not immediate efforts to improve conditions for the inmates. After being attacked by another paper for its potentially libelous claims, the *Advocate* editor wrote, "We called attention to the facts. . . . By so doing we not only did our duty as the editor . . . but we did the officers of that Institution a friendly turn. The inmates are part owners of this paper, and it is the duty of the *Advocate* to make their defense."[73] As the editor made clear, institutions answered to the people and confinement to an institution did not diminish the mutual obligations Cherokee people had to one another.

The need for repairs coincided with the need for significant increases in spending in order to fund delegations to Washington and mount legal and public relations campaigns to defend the Nation's land base and its right to function as a governing entity. Walter Adair Duncan's insight into social welfare policies, coupled with his intellectual abilities, likely led the Cherokee Nation to choose Duncan and Joseph Franklin Thompson, Duncan's successor as superintendent at the orphanage, to serve on its 1894 delegation to Washington to object to the Dawes commissioners' allotment efforts. In his testimony to the Dawes Commission, Duncan chided the commissioners' intentions and questioned the sincerity of their aims. If, on the commissioner's 1893 visit, they were engaged in diplomatic visits to Indian Territory to negotiate for statehood, why, Duncan asked, did they return to "accuse, arraign, and prosecute the Indians and Indian governments?" The only good things the commissioners reported on were the "coal mines, mineral lands, marble quarries, rich soils, good timber, and beautiful sky." Why, he asked, did the report fail to mention the Cherokee Nation's self-sufficient institutions, "our colleges, schools, churches, industries?" He challenged the report's claim that the "'permission' to govern ourselves has 'proved a failure.' It is not simply a 'permission' to govern ourselves. . . . It is a 'right'" upheld by the Supreme Court and a right that preexisted the United States.[74] Walter Adair Duncan chastised the commission for ignoring the humanity of Cherokee people in favor of tallying the economic resources the Nation possessed and speculators and territorializers coveted.

The commission's focus on the Nation's resources was not the only problem. In 1896, Henry Dawes, speaking to the Senate about what he saw as the Five Tribes' recalcitrance, argued for the continuation of salaries to allotment commissioners, who he admitted did not need the income for their livelihoods. On their behalf, he pointed out the difficulties of dealing with the "character of men who refuse to see what is the best thing for them. . . . The worst feature of the Indian service is that the Indian sometimes does not know what is best for him."[75]

To combat the cultural superiority and paternalism espoused by officials in the United States and strengthened by scientific racism that informed politicians' and reformers' ideas about their "guardian-ship" responsibilities to Indian peoples, Cherokee leaders like Walter Adair Duncan offered their institutions as the physical and intel-lectual testimony of the Nation's continued right to exist and its function as a guardian to Cherokee people. The Nation had long been debating paternalism and guardianship responsibilities. Osdv iyunvnehi coupled with the previous detrimental federal policies had cemented social policy as the nation's raison d'être for nearly all Cherokee people whether by clan or citizenship. As Walter Adair Duncan had stated in 1885, it did not "comport well with [his] dig-nity" to let others "act as his guardian and the guardian of his children." In his twelve years as the orphanage superintendent, he had gained responsibility for hundreds of Cherokee children, whom he was obligated to protect based on his understandings of care and gadugi.[76] It was the Nation's job to act as a guardian to Cherokee people. Reformers bastardized the legal relationship that existed between the federal government and tribes. It was not reformers' jobs to protect individual Indian people; it was the Native nation's responsibility to do so.

In 1897, when the Dawes commissioners arrived in Indian Territory to meet with Cherokee people to discuss allotment, DeWitt Clinton Duncan interviewed the "Real People" and printed their responses to the commissioners in the pages of the *Indian Chieftain*. The men he interviewed rejected allotment, and they did so based on their preference for their current social service system and their fears for the social services that Cherokee men, in particular, would be offered by the United States. As one man said, "We have laws, and we have courts of justice. When one of our men commits a crime, we can try and punish him." Another man expressed similar anxieties related to the legal system:

> We know the white men; they are a proud and overbearing race.
> . . . Their laws are too many . . . and in a language, too, which we
> cannot understand. We shall never know when we are violating their
> laws until we are arrested and dragged away to trial. Your judges,
> too, will be white men; they will not be able to talk to us. When on
> trial, we shall be at the mercy of the white men; when convicted, we

shall not know the nature of our offense; and when punished, we shall not know whether we have been punished according to the law or against it.[77]

The "Real People" (the word DeWitt Clinton Duncan used and which is a translation of *Aniyunwiya*, the word Cherokee speakers call themselves as a people) worried, as their ancestors had when the hunting grounds were sold almost a hundred years earlier, what this new system would mean for Cherokee men and women who adhered to traditional social welfare practices.

Despite this testimony and the Cherokee delegation's best efforts, Congress passed the Curtis Act in 1898, subjecting the Five Tribes to allotment. The Curtis Act unilaterally dissolved the governments of the tribes and seized the treasury of the Cherokee Nation, forcing Cherokee officials to petition the secretary of the Interior to approve expenditures and release funds. This act not only compromised social service institutions but left the Nation unable to expedite relief when national emergencies arose. The preoccupation of U.S. reformers with care of the poor, the non–English speaking, and peoples of color had proven to be a moral smoke screen used by land speculators and railroad magnates who sought to clear a way for their economic interests in Indian Territory. Cherokee officials had urged the federal government to respect the treaties and let Cherokee people fulfill their responsibilities to one another. Even though threats of allotment distorted and constricted the conversations Cherokee people might have had related to reform, Cherokee people continued to engage with one another over the social welfare rights and responsibilities they had.[78] In response to the Dawes officials arrival in the Nation to enroll Cherokee people for allotments against the majority's will, Cherokees from all backgrounds chose to express their hostility and negotiate the process in a variety of ways.

AUTHOR'S ACKNOWLEDGMENT

I borrowed and modified the title of Frederick Hoxie's *Talking Back to Civilization* (2001) for this chapter's title. Hoxie's edited primary source reader includes the writings of numerous Indian people who "talked back" to Progressive reformers from 1893 to 1920 to protest myths of the "vanishing Indian" and the hypocritical and self-serving policies advanced by reformers and politicians. Hoxie admits that his work is limited by documents produced by English-speaking Indians. Since the Cherokee Nation adopted institutions, many of which were promoted by U.S. reformers, the conversations within the Cherokee Nation over those social service institutions accomplishes what many scholars fail to see as an equally and vital exercise of sovereignty—the debates and interactions that Native nations and people continue to have with one another regardless of the pressures they face from external bodies. It is not only during these moments of external pressure that sovereignty matters; it matters to Cherokee people every day. Individual interactions with national institutions provide a richer and more textured understanding of what sovereignty means. Nearly all of those executed in the Nation were Cherokee speakers who required a translator. Institutions collectively served (or failed to serve) every part of Cherokee society, women and men. Cherokee people's conversations with each other provide a more intimate picture not only of their concerns but also of the limitations placed on the conversations and debates Cherokee people could have as a result of another colonial policy—allotment.

CHAPTER 8

Social Services and Tribal Sovereignty, 1898–1907

Writing less than a month after the adoption of the Curtis Act, DeWitt Clinton Duncan predicted the future:

> Our Cherokee laws regulating the relation of the sexes are not only repealed by this vandalic Curtis law, but they are swept away into annihilation for all the past, as well as the future. . . . The nefarious, tyrannical Curtis law dishonors the social life of our people; it invades the domestic circle, abolishes the institution of marriage; it stigmatizes our happy homes as mere places of brutal cohabitation, it bastardizes our children, and reduces all the noble fathers and mothers of our country to the moral condition of pimps and prostitutes.[1]

DeWitt Clinton foretold a more graphic situation than the one foreshadowed by his brother in 1893 when Walter Adair Duncan expressed his concerns over Cherokee people being classed as "the poor" in the United States.

The Duncan brothers recognized that it did not matter whether they were subjected to state or federal social welfare policies; the attitudes and beliefs held by the vast majority of non-Indians who would be selected to enact the policies that impacted them would denigrate Cherokee families and regard them as dysfunctional. Within these systems, most Cherokee families would be perceived as deviant—an overwhelming percentage of Cherokees would be classified as orphaned, incapacitated, or (dis)abled; indeed, their resistance to allotment and commitment to communal landholdings had already rendered them blind, deaf, and imprisoned, according to reformers. The Cherokee Nation and its officials used their positions to advocate for those connected to social welfare institutions based on their professional and community responsibilities. Institutions had not provided the permanence John Ross had imagined in 1857, but they did provide a staging ground for the Cherokee Nation to wage another campaign to secure the continuation of social provisions for Cherokee people.

This chapter investigates the Cherokee Nation's continued resistance to allotment and Oklahoma statehood, which occurred in 1907, with a specific emphasis on the social welfare fallout created by the passage of the Curtis Act in 1898. I examine how national officials, social welfare administrators, and recipients of national social provisions responded to the social policy crisis created by allotment and statehood. The responses to allotment were certainly not uniform; but taken together, they do represent an overwhelming commitment on the part of Cherokee people to osdv iyunvnehi. Examining the actions of those closely connected with national social policy debunks assumptions about class divisions in the Nation and reveals an endless capacity for creative resistance to a process Cherokee people almost unanimously rejected and an equally creative ability to generate solutions to the social welfare crises that the Curtis Act produced.

In addition to distributing equal parcels of land to individual Cherokees, the Curtis Act nullified treaties and dissolved the Cherokee courts. Once the process was complete, individuals would be subject to the laws of the new state and granted U.S. citizenship. As Cherokee people were well aware, and as Walter Adair Duncan stated regularly, U.S. citizenship did not ensure Cherokee people protection or security. Quite the opposite. The process required the redistribution of the wealth, institutions, and human resources the Cherokee Nation had fostered over the previous one hundred years. The primary beneficiaries would be the future state and its non-Indian residents. Statehood became a central concern to Cherokee people, but one that also presented new social welfare possibilities. As they had before, Cherokee leaders worked to manage and design social welfare systems that might benefit Cherokee people.

Over the previous twenty years, the Cherokee delegations had actively resisted an allotment process it neither solicited nor wanted by dragging out bureaucratic negotiations. By 1898, the delegations had drafted resolutions to solve problems related to the sale of national property. Many of the provisions discussed the distribution of annuities, buildings, and national finances, but an entire section was devoted to "Educational and Charitable Institutions." Once again, Cherokee guardians focused their efforts on social welfare obligations. The Cherokee agreement of 1902 distributed all lands not set aside for railroads, town sites, cemeteries, churches, schools, public institutions, and public buildings into equal shares for "each citizen." It stipulated that only fathers, mothers, or guardians could make selections for minors. Prisoners could select agents to act on their behalf, and guardians or some "suitable person akin to them" were to select allotments for "incompetents." The Cherokee Nation donated the orphanage, the asylum, and the school for the blind established by Laura Lowery to the state so long as the facilities continued to provide care for Cherokee people.[2] It did this in order to continue protecting the well-being of Cherokee people and to ensure that Cherokee people remained close to their communities and families.

Although the Curtis Act severely curtailed the authority of the Cherokee national government, officials continued to look after the social welfare of the Cherokee Nation's citizens, and Cherokee people continued to look after each other. Walter Adair Duncan could have easily concluded that allotment was in his best personal interest. He had the skills, acumen, and financial resources to successfully weather the storm. But his education as a Cherokee person residing in the Nation included mastering another curriculum not written in textbooks or instilled through the domestic arts. He believed in Cherokee national sovereignty, "inherent with us before Columbus touched the New World." He may have trumpeted the merits of certain elements of civilization, including Christianity and the use of English as the language of education, but he rejected individualism and personal greed as a means to incapacitate the poor and diminish the power of Native nations to direct the changes that were in their best interests. In the United States, Duncan observed, there were "many a man smart enough to be President, and many a woman as great as Queen Victoria, who by the attritions of society there, have been ground down as if in the teeth of a nether millstone." He refused to vote for allotment "based on information gathered up in a long lifetime of observation, reading, and reflection."[3] Leaders including Duncan continued to negotiate, debate, and creatively contest a process that disregarded their sovereignty and their collective will.

Institutional social service leaders had obligations to fulfill. They used the legal and social authority attached to those positions to best represent Cherokee people's social well-being in the years that followed the passage of the Curtis Act. In addition to his service as a delegate, Walter Adair Duncan officially contested the boundary line established in Fort Smith during the allotment process to point out additional problems with the survey process that ultimately hurt Cherokee people. Duncan attempted to select his allotment on the contested land in order to force federal officials to correct the boundary.[4] Another group of Cherokees opposed to allotment who prioritized communal landholdings and gadugi above all else attempted to negotiate communal landholdings in Mexico so that they could adhere to osdv iyunvnehi as they understood it.[5]

Even though the Curtis Act extended federal legal jurisdiction over all persons who committed crimes in the Cherokee Nation and dissolved the Cherokee Nation's courts, it did not spell out what to do with prisoners or those in the process of being adjudicated in the legal system. As a result, the prison continued to operate much as it did before. Guards remained employed. The Cherokee treasury maintained the prison, but with the budgetary oversight of the federal government. The last high sheriff appointed in 1895, John Duncan, Walter Adair's only living son, continued to supervise the facilities, order supplies, and hire local citizens to provide various services.

Despite a series of congressional measures, political conundrums, and the jurisdictional confusion created by the pressures leading up to the Curtis Act, the Cherokee Nation continued to assert its rights to criminal jurisdiction. On August 8, 1896, the Cherokee Nation executed Bob Talton, the last execution it would ever perform. This case was mired in controversy after Talton appealed to federal courts contesting the legality of the Cherokee grand jury after the Cherokee

Nation passed new grand jury rules in line with the federal court's. The Cherokee Nation prevailed.[6] What the case laid bare, and the *Advocate's* headline "A Matter of Justice" implied, was the Cherokee Nation's continued belief that its ability to administer protection and punishment to its citizens was an essential feature and duty inherent to its sovereignty. For Talton, self-preservation trumped Cherokee national sovereignty.

The Curtis Act, referred to by U.S. officials as the "act for the protection of the people of the Indian Territory," subjected Cherokee citizens to trial and incarceration in one of the three additional federal courts established in Indian Territory in 1895. In 1898, the *Indian Sentinel*, a newspaper published in Tahlequah, printed an article under the headline "Indian Territory Jails" with highlights from a federal investigation on the conditions of the federal jails. Investigators reported that the jails lacked proper "sanitary arrangements," and that conditions were "crowded," which left prisoners "compelled to sleep on the floor." Although diminished budgets in the Cherokee Nation created similar basic conditions at its prison, Cherokee prisoners received more than "two meals a day," food that was not "condemned," and "medical attendance" that was ranked better than "very poor."[7]

In a final act of its sovereign authority over the Cherokee Nation's prisoners, Chief Mayes used his executive authority to pardon all eighteen of the Cherokee Nation's prisoners and send them home to their friends.[8] By 1900, the Cherokee Nation and the federal government had reached an impasse over what to do about the Cherokee National Prison. The federal government broadly criticized the prison's operations, from its architecture to its budget, but offered no concrete solution to these problems. Despite the president's disapproval, on January 18, 1900, Principal Chief Samuel Mayes granted an "absolute and unconditional pardon to all persons who have been heretofore convicted in the courts of the Cherokee Nation of a violation of Cherokee law." The pardon also extended to "all other persons . . . convicted or indicted by the courts of the Cherokee Nation" the restoration of their "full rights of citizenship."[9]

Whether the prison fostered new communities among the inmates or brought together old friends, once freed, former prisoners aided one another. In 1902, Sam Squirrel, pardoned two years earlier, enrolled with the Dawes Commission. His parents had died, and he did not have any family members with him. With Henry Ross acting as an interpreter, Sam Squirrel provided the Dawes enrollment personnel with numerous family connections to verify his rights since his name did not appear on the 1880 census. Mose Fields, who was pardoned at the same time, acted as a witness to confirm that Squirrel was living in the Cherokee Nation at the time of the 1880 roll. Despite being able to name a number of living extended family recorded on the 1880 census, the lengthy questioning suggests that it was the 1896 prison roll coupled with his former cellmate's testimony that secured his rights to an allotment.[10]

With the prisoners restored to society, the building stood empty. The physical structure, located a block from the capitol in the governmental heart of the Cherokee Nation, remained a point of contention between Cherokee and U.S. officials. The Cherokee Nation and the federal government agreed to rent the structure to private individuals, but finding a responsible tenant was not easy; too many people were like Jake Parris, upon whom, the chief learned in 1902, "there is no use depending . . . for rent in the future."[11] In his 1903 annual message, Principal Chief William C. Rogers posed the "paramount" question of what should be done with surplus lands, if any remained from allotment, and "with our public buildings."[12] These negotiations extended the life of the Cherokee Nation's government and its ability to continue administering social services.

At the same moment federal reports condemned a lack of adequate medical care in the federally administered Indian Territory jails, the medical establishment was expanding its influence in Indian Territory and Oklahoma Territory. This occurred in tandem with the national growth and professionalization of the medical field. Although it had been in existence since 1847, the American Medical Association (AMA) in 1901 reorganized and devised a universal code of ethics and practices for the entire country.[13] Many doctors joined the association, and many more subscribed to the association's journal.[14] In 1900, all fourteen Indian Territory members of the AMA received the journal. From 1901 to 1902, the AMA gained sixty-eight subscribers from Indian Territory and fifty-five from Oklahoma Territory.[15] As statehood loomed, the numbers decreased in Indian Territory but swelled in the surrounding states and Oklahoma Territory. Medical professionals were cormorants of another kind; they entered Indian Territory or swarmed the region, prepared to align their professional attachments with the territorial polities able to assure their professional futures.

Allotment and the Americanization goals officials sought to achieve provided an opportunity for non-Indians to usurp professional medical opportunities and control from Native nations and their citizens, but it also forced reconsiderations of the care available to Indians diagnosed with mental illness. The Cherokee Nation had an asylum and staff responsible for mentally ill patients, yet the Curtis Act made no accommodations for their care. However, the same year as the Curtis Act, the Senate passed a bill allocating $75,000 to build an asylum for mentally ill Indian patients to be located in Canton, South Dakota. Canton's inaccessible location and the staff it employed severely curtailed the ability of Native nations or families to challenge culturally and spiritually violent treatments or offer alternative causes of mental illness. In 1904, the *Chelsea Commercial* reported that a "deal [had] been made" to provide care for the "white people of Indian Territory" in Norman; "insane Indians" were to be sent to Canton, with the paper adding, "There are very few Indians, however, who lose their minds."[16] The presence of an institution in the United States to treat mentally ill Indians served to debunk the position promulgated by U.S. medical professionals since the 1850s that Cherokees were incapable of suffering from insanity, but it did not undo the pervasiveness of those ideas more broadly.

Instead of advocating for the rights and sovereignty of the Cherokee Nation, the Indian Territory Medical Association (ITMA) undermined the efforts of the Cherokee Nation to defend its sovereignty. The ITMA's Committee on Medical Legislation promoted a congressional bill as early as 1896 that sought to apply Arkansas medical statutes to all of Indian Territory because, its members claimed, "we can expect little from the tribal governments and the sooner the matter can be placed with federal authorities the better."[17] The association increasingly ignored the efforts of the Cherokee Nation to provide public health services to its citizens. Instead, it called for institutions of its own making in Indian Territory. This included a push in 1900 to obtain congressional legislation to build an insane asylum and establish boards of health in Indian Territory.[18]

Allotment and the push for statehood provided inducements for opportunistic Cherokee citizens, including many intermarried whites, to abandon the Nation's community ethic in favor of the economic interests of a narrowing group of professional men. At least one long-term member of its own board of health shrewdly calculated his support of Cherokee national sovereignty based on his economic and professional aims, not necessarily those of the Nation. In 1899, the *Indian Chieftain* reprinted an article from the *Tahlequah Republican* that pointed out that Dr. Fortner, secretary of the Cherokee Board of Health, "believes [Cherokee medical laws] are excellent and should be strictly enforced" because they prevented professional competition. But in his capacity as director of the National Bank at Vinita, Fortner was more than willing to actively work against the enforcement of Cherokee revenue laws after the Curtis Act passed because it hurt his "friends'" finances. Dr. Fortner's hypocrisy did not lead to his dismissal from the Cherokee Board of Health. It is likely that the Cherokee Nation was more concerned with impeding the efforts of the Dawes commissioners than with Fortner's ability to smash "the jewel of consistency into smithereens."[19]

Because the Cherokee Nation failed to sanction Dr. Fortner as a member of the Board of Health in 1899 and because the Curtis Act had enabled Vinita to incorporate under Arkansas law, a year later he was able to do what Daniel Ross had refused to do almost one hundred years earlier.[20] When a smallpox outbreak hit Vinita in 1900, Drs. Fortner and Bagby, with funds solicited from the federal government, quarantined Vinita. Quarantines also took place on the Grand River. With the cooperation of the Vinita School Board, doctors required all children to produce a certificate of health from a local physician and proof of vaccination in order to return to school.[21] Two years later, a smallpox outbreak occurred at the Cherokee Male Seminary. This resulted in a quarantine of sick students on the third floor and compulsory vaccinations of all other students and staff. Bill Meeks, a student at the seminary, refused the vaccination. The newly appointed non-Cherokee superintendent selected by federal officials threatened to have the older boys hold Meeks down while officials forcibly

vaccinated him. Bill Meeks ran away rather than be vaccinated. Cherokee E. C. Alberty, a teacher at the school, contracted smallpox during
the outbreak. The superintendent isolated Alberty in a small house
by the cemetery. Needless to say, Alberty "did not like this arrangement" and "escaped." He walked to his home in Claremore, a distance
of over fifty miles, and returned to his position after the crisis had
passed.[22] One hundred years after the variolation debate, some Cherokee people, even those who attended or worked at one of the pre-
miere educational institutions in the Nation, resented and resisted
outsiders imposing public health policies on them that violated
their autonomy and ignored the importance of community input
and concerns.

Alberty's and Meek's responses, like the response of the Cherokee
community in the East in 1806, came at a moment when federal
policy assumed the inferiority of Cherokee people's governing systems, lifeways, community values, and competency. In this context,
Alberty's and Meek's responses may not simply have been resistance to quarantine next to a cemetery or a compulsory vaccination.
These types of policies were not new. In fact, the Cherokee Nation
had adopted vaccination laws over a decade earlier. Perhaps, theirs
was a (sub)conscious response to a deaf United States unable to hear
the voices of Cherokee people defending their sovereign nation's
treaty rights and their inherent ability to carry out policies that
impacted them.

At a moment when the Cherokee people's professional capacities were called into question (in the name of helping them become
competent professionals), the Curtis Act created opportunities for
non-Indians to professionally and economically benefit from the
Cherokee Nation's losses. For example, the Curtis Act led to the
creation of the first superintendent of schools in Indian Territory, a
position appointed by federal officials. When non-Indian John D.
Benedict arrived to serve in the post, he "enumerated various defects
in the territory's schools, including incompetent supervision, irregular attendance, financial mismanagement, and neglect in teaching
the English language."[23] Benedict admitted that he knew nothing
about Indian Territory or its educational systems before he was
offered the job.

When he arrived in Indian Territory in 1899, Benedict sensed hostility from tribal leaders.[24] In an interview he gave in the 1930s, Benedict speculated that the hostility he felt emanated from a financial clause in the Curtis Act being used by federal officials to usurp administrative control of the Five Tribes' schools and institutions. Benedict also reported that officials at the Five Tribes' boarding schools could not even speak English. Although it is possible that some of the staff did not speak English, the superintendents in the Choctaw, Creek, and Cherokee Nations did, which suggests some combination of Benedict lying or bilingual superintendents refusing to speak English as a sign of resistance to his presence.[25] In conjunction with his time as supervisor of schools, Benedict served as a director with the Bradley Real Estate Company. In 1903 Bradley Real Estate published a manual of statistical information and valuations for each of the Five Tribes' institutions, real estate, and types of mineral resources, all of which were of interest to settlers and speculators.[26] Benedict aimed to personally profit from allotment though his position as supervisor of schools and through the real estate transactions that followed. It was in his economic interest for the Five Tribes to appear incompetent and for allotment to move forward.

Cherokee officials at every level defied efforts by the federal government to limit and control their educational endeavors. In 1899, the annual report from the Board of Education submitted to the federal government highlighted higher-than-usual expenses at the orphanage "on account of the United States authorities withholding our funds for some time, which were appropriated for their support."[27] Under the 1898 Curtis Act, the control of funds shifted from the Cherokee Nation to the secretary of the Interior. Instead of disbursing the funds as Cherokee National Council acts required, the Department of the Interior withheld the funds, forcing the schools to operate on credit and pay additional interest. A debate ensued between Principal Chief Mayes, the school supervisor, and the Department of the Interior. Chief Mayes argued that the "Secretary [of the Interior] has no more authority over funds than the Cherokee treasurer formerly had. . . . The Secretary is the Nation's banker and must disburse the Nation's money in accordance with tribal law."[28] Despite Chief Mayes's written and verbal "deliberation[s]" of the Curtis Act with federal officials and the Choctaw Nation's heated debates with Supervisor of Schools Benedict and the federal government to maintain their school projects, it became clear that federal officials intended to use features of the Curtis Act to further undermine the Five Tribes' ability to administer social provisions to their people.[29]

Politicians were not alone in their political resistance to the take-over of educational administration. While the federal government and its officials robbed and fleeced the Cherokee Nation—as DeWitt Clinton Duncan had described the process in 1898—Cherokee people staged acts of resistance together and individually.[30] In 1902, Dawes commissioners attended the Annual Teacher's Institute. The program advertised a "fullblood choir," but it failed to appear. At the same event, an official evaluating a Cherokee candidate for a teaching position asked what the products of Indian Territory were. The candidate answered, "Seed ticks, the Dawes Commission, and Kansas Carpetbaggers."[31] In 1907, when John Benedict required the Chero-kee Female Seminary teachers to record the "race and tribe" of only those students entitled to allotments in addition to other data pieces needed about all students, some teachers recorded all the data in detail except race and tribe.[32]

On November 17, 1903, fifteen miles from the nearest railway station and fifty miles northwest of Tahlequah, a fire engulfed the Cherokee Orphan Asylum. The inferno threatened the lives of the 149 orphans, many of whom were feverish and bedridden from mea-sles. Despite the dire situation, every person in the building survived, though the fire displaced the children and staff. Extended family housed some of the children. The Cherokee Nation arranged for the Whitaker Orphan Home, a private orphanage for white children run by a North Carolina Cherokee who had received Cherokee Nation citizenship in 1881 and located at Pryor Creek, to take those children without extended family able to do so. They transported the children by wagons. Unwilling to accept the "strange" location and officials, "nine or ten boys" walked back to Salina, "swam in the river," and "went to live with different Indian families in the area."[33] Whether it was the emergency created by the fire or the unwillingness of officials to acknowledge or call upon Salina residents who were obviously guided by a community ethic to foster the children,

Cherokee Orphan Asylum ruins, destroyed by fire, Salina, 1903. Courtesy the Thomas
Lee Ballenger Papers, 1730–1968, photographs, ca. 1866–ca. 1904, box 4, folder 76,
Newberry Library, Chicago.

children at the orphanage clearly had preexisting ties to the larger
community. The shadow of allotment and statehood may have also
guided the community's embrace of the children.

The Whitaker Orphan Home only provided a temporary solution,
and Cherokee officials acted quickly to provide another facility. Less
than two weeks after the fire, Cherokee officials decided to move
the small number of residents of the asylum into the empty prison so
that the children could move into the larger structure. The national
council appropriated funds to make both buildings more habitable
for the patients and children.[34] Because the orphanage was under-
insured, the building's destruction added further financial strain to
its operation. Although federal authorities did take total control of
the facility in 1914 and the militarization of its regimen followed, the
Cherokee Orphan Asylum has operated continuously since 1872.

As U.S. officials continued to press for statehood with or without
the Five Tribes' consent, Five Tribes' political leaders banded together
to create another social welfare institution to defend their interests—
the state of Sequoyah. The political question emerged whether the
Oklahoma Territory and Indian Territory would enter the United
States as a single state or two different states. Most Cherokee people

(and their Oklahoma Territory counterparts) did not want to enter the United States as a single entity. Throughout the early 1890s, the Cherokees had pointed out Oklahoma Territory's inadequacies to bolster its resistance to statehood and allotment. In 1890, the *Advocate* had documented reports that "there [were] thirty thousand people, more or less, hanging on the ragged edge of starvation." A year later it reported "the number of insane persons in Oklahoma" at two hundred, yet the Oklahoma Territory lacked any "provisions for taking care of the demented in her borders."[35] Oklahomans harbored tremendous resentment toward the Indian Territory, which they viewed as standing in the way of progress (and blocking colonization efforts by white settlers). The incongruity of this attitude became apparent during hearings debating single or double statehood. When questioned in 1902 about turning over Oklahoma Territory institutions to the proposed state, Thomas H. Doyle, member of the Oklahoma statehood executive nonpartisan committee, responded, "We have no State Capitol, we have no penitentiary. . . . We have no blind asylum."[36] It became clear to Five Tribes' officials that their nations had developed an array of social provisions for Indian people that stood in contrast to those of Oklahoma Territory. Oklahoma's social policy inadequacies and its residents' attitudes toward Indian people did not bode well for Indian people if single statehood proceeded.

Certainly attuned to the individual political and economic power that they might lose if single statehood moved forward, the chief executives of the Five Tribes in 1903 met in Muskogee to discuss calling a constitutional convention comprised of representatives from their Native nations. Two years later, the town of Muskogee hosted the Sequoyah constitutional convention to draft a constitution and to elect delegates to represent the state of Sequoyah. As expected, delegates and alternates included many of the wealthiest individuals from the Choctaw, Creek, and Cherokee Nations. However, African Creeks and monolingual Cherokee, Creek, and Choctaw speakers also served as delegates. Despite the conspicuous absence of women, delegates represented some aspects of the racial, lingual, and class diversity present in Indian Territory. From the Cherokee Nation, Walter Adair and DeWitt Clinton Duncan both served as alternates. The question facing the delegates and alternates was how to best protect the interests of the citizens of their respective Native nations and how to incorporate the U.S. residents illegally and legally residing in Indian Territory.

The push for separate statehood failed. President Roosevelt favored single statehood. Congress refused to consider either of the bills brought forward. Republicans worried that forming two new western states meant two new states favoring the Democratic Party.[37] Politics prevented those in power from imagining and supporting a new state fashioned on the ideals and concerns of Native nations, but it still represented a "path not taken . . . the alternative possibilities that existed in the development of U.S. colonialism."[38] The attempt, however, produced a constitution that provided a template for what became the Oklahoma Constitution.

One of the final expenditures before the Cherokee Nation's dissolution was poor relief. In the midst of efforts to stall the incorporation of the Cherokee Nation into the state of Oklahoma, the Nation faced an "almost unprecedented drought," leaving the "class of [Cherokee] people who have always relied upon corn crops for sustenance" face to face with the possibility of starvation.[39] In an attempt to fulfill the Nation's responsibility to its citizens, Principal Chief Thomas Buffington traveled to Washington in 1902 to "secure aid" for the "Cherokee fullbloods, many of whom are in want."[40] Chief Buffington discovered "that nothing could be done as the governmental red tape could only be unwound by having a request for help come from the Cherokee council."[41] From April 15, 1902, to June 8, 1902, the U.S. agent to the Cherokees traveled to eighteen communities in the Cherokee Nation to distribute funds to heads of households. A total of 4,189 people received money.[42] Although federal oversight of those funds weakened the Cherokee Nation's exercise of sovereignty and federal agents once again acted as gatekeepers to the Nation's social provisions, the money distributed came from the Cherokee Nation's coffers.

The Dawes enrollment process, which began in 1896 and continued until 1914, was not meant to ensure that state and federal officials fulfilled community and social welfare obligations to a new group of citizens. It was an economic and political transaction meant to redistribute the collective land wealth of the Cherokee Nation and all of its members to individuals in a manner that reinforced nuclear families with male heads of households.[43] Federal officials intended to sell surplus land, institutional structures, and national buildings and to provide access to the nation's mineral resources to non-Indians. By dismembering the land base and the structures that governed institutions and appointed national caregivers, the federal government usurped the rights of Cherokees to appoint social service providers and more effectively fulfill their kinship and community obligations to one another.

In the short term, Cherokees' institutional skills ensured an ongoing place for Cherokee people in support positions. Over time, the administrative opportunities, the educational attainments and expectations, and the social and economic mobility of all Cherokee people suffered, particularly those racially, economically, and linguistically classed as individuals with more Indian blood and therefore (in the view of non-Indians) less competent.[44] Federal supervisor of schools John Benedict could not see the educational and professional potential of monolingual Cherokee people that Walter Adair Duncan and Charley Poorbear did. Rather than creating a system of independent, hard-working individual U.S. citizens, the allotment process ensured an expansion of those classed as the "poor" and "dependent" and in legal and economic need of non-Indian guardians. Allotment and statehood silenced a sovereign voice that expected more from the United States, reminded individual states of their social service limitations, and modeled the ability of a government similar to its own to incorporate the participation of non–English speaking, nonwhite, and non-Christian citizens. Officials failed to acknowledge that gadugi and a degree of mutual dependency formed a more powerful and sustainable social service system than the individualistic approach offered by allotment and statehood.

Conclusion

Walter Adair Duncan walked into a meeting with the Dawes commissioners in the late 1890s, wearing his hat. One of the commissioner's assistants, a man probably half his age, ordered him to remove it. Duncan refused and responded, "Well, young man, you come and take it off." Duncan kept his hat on, and, by doing so, he symbolically showed his contempt for a process he neither accepted nor respected.[1]

In 1902 my great-great-grandfather Keetoowah leader Redbird Smith "stood up for [his] rights." He was arrested for refusing to comply with the allotment process, nearly lynched by a mob, taken to prison in Muskogee, and forced to enroll for an allotment under the Curtis Act.[2] Five years later, he sought "help and protection" from Congress. Through an interpreter, Smith informed the committee that he was "suffering from the infraction of [our treaties]"; he showed federal officials a picture of the treaty and the Cherokee Nation's land patent. Smith expressed concern that he would lose the land where he had lived, farmed, and made improvements for the last twelve years—lands that were not his allotment. Senator Henry Teller condescendingly asked Smith if he had taken his allotment. Smith responded that he had not. Teller warned him that if he did not accept his allotment, "after a while he won't have any land at all." To this Smith responded, "I can't stand and breathe and live if I take this allotment. . . . The Indian can't live on allotments." Speaking to the interpreter, and not Smith, Teller said, "Tell him that the law has passed and can't be changed and that it won't be changed—that is final and positive—and he must accept his allotment unless he wants to go without any land at all."³ Undeterred, Smith continued to advocate for a "full-blood commonwealth" and worked to purchase a large tract of land that Cherokee "full-bloods" could farm communally and use the profits from to make interest-free loans to each other when needs arose.⁴

Despite his statement to the contrary, Redbird Smith did continue to stand and breathe and survive the initial impact of allotment and statehood, but Walter Adair Duncan did not. On Friday, October 17, 1907, exactly one month before Oklahoma became the forty-sixth state, Walter Adair Duncan, "patriot and statesmen," died at his home before becoming a citizen of the United States.⁵

In many ways, Duncan and Smith were nothing alike. Their differences paralleled those of John Ross and Sequoyah a generation earlier. Duncan, like Ross, advocated the importance of Christianity, English-language education, citizenship, and key aspects of Progressive reforms. Smith, like Sequoyah, spoke Cherokee, belonged to a clan, adhered to traditional religious practices, and remained committed to cooperative agricultural practices. And yet despite their differences, Duncan and Smith both bitterly opposed allotment through official and local channels. They expressed sentiments held by Ross and Sequoyah that communal landholding was an essential component to life, living, and the ability to fulfill social welfare responsibilities to other Cherokee people.

The Cherokee Nation was not simply an institution built to protect the financial interests of a growing elite class of Cherokee men. Cherokee people consented to state building because, first and foremost, it ensured a governmental structure attuned to the voices of Cherokee people. Cherokee people consented to a Nation because it better ensured their ability as Cherokee people to continue to provide osdv iyunvnehi by embedding a communitarian ethic and the protection of a communal land base into its national institutions.

Differences aside, Duncan, Smith, Sequoyah, and Ross shared a commitment to Cherokee people and Cherokee self-determination even as they imagined, governed, debated, and disagreed on the specific adaptations national institutions might adopt moving forward. Ross and Duncan were more open to religious educational institutions, and Sequoyah and Smith tended to favor locally controlled secular schools. They all contributed to building a Nation with courts, delegations, and an executive branch that cumulatively employed interpreters in multiple Native languages. The public schools made uneven efforts to discuss bilingual education and accommodate monolingual Cherokee speakers by employing bilingual Cherokee teachers. Legislative, executive, and educational policies affirmed multilingualism. Acceptance of lingual diversity ensured less restricted access to social provisions, employment opportunities, and elected office. It also ensured those more likely to adhere to osdv iyunvnehi could continue to communicate their expectations and needs to one another. Ross, Sequoyah, Duncan, and Smith collaborated with other Cherokee people to construct a nation that promoted an alternative social welfare policy than what was offered by states and the federal government—one that privileged the needs and interests of Indian people.

From the Removal era through the Civil War, osdv iyunvnehi that required and offered services to all clan members gave way to a hybrid national social policy based on racialized citizenship laws. Traditional social policy, controlled by matrilineal clans and local communities, and the egalitarian rights it engendered increasingly privileged bilateral family structures. Osdv iyunvnehi had provided Euro-Americans, free blacks, and enslaved people an opportunity for inclusion in the traditional social safety net. As the Nation centralized, enslaved peoples increasingly lacked the clan connections necessary to access traditional social provisions and protections. Citizenship laws based on race and laws against intermarriage that existed until the Civil War left enslaved people and their families locked out of its national system entirely. By way of contrast, the Duncan family benefitted from the Nation's earliest citizenship laws privileging white Cherokee families and accrued significant benefits from national social provisions over time.

Removal and the Civil War both produced conditions that compromised traditional social welfare policy. In both instances, however, Cherokee sovereignty ensured the continued existence of a space, on communal landholdings, which enabled Cherokee people to reconstitute traditional elements of its previous social policy. It was for this reason that Cherokee people had initially consented to nation building and continued to defend it over time.

The Treaty of 1866 ushered in a new era of national social policy and yet again produced uneven distributions of provisions. The Nation introduced more coercive social policies stemming from the Treaty of 1866, including its first nationally administered census and the introduction of residentially administered social provisions. Leaders soon discovered that the support for institutions depended in large part on their ability to foster a community ethic that resisted coercion. Once the institutions opened, hundreds, if not thousands, of Cherokee people participated with institutions through the economic transactions necessary to keep the goods and services supplied. Institutional needs tied people's livelihoods to the Cherokee Nation in ways they had never been before.

The Cherokee Nation's compromised sovereignty as a result of its participation in the Civil War benefitted new groups of citizens including former slaves, but it also secured the conditions and monies necessary to continue fulfilling its responsibility to protect Cherokee people. The Duncan family provides a useful demonstration of whom the Nation extended social welfare protections to through its citizenship laws and how those benefits and protections amassed over the course of generations. Through this demonstration, it becomes even more apparent how nation building acts as an expanded social safety net for some Cherokee families, while denying those protections to others, especially in regard to families made up of Cherokees and individuals of African descent.

The Nation's success at institution building, its ongoing consent from the community, and its long-term care of its residents remained tied to its ability to integrate traditional social welfare features into its institutions and avoid coercive social control. National sovereignty provided Cherokees with a space to contest their policies and provided them with the means to fix those policies.

Cherokee social welfare institutions were not perfect; none were or are. Threats of territorialization and allotment placed severe restrictions on the types of institutional reforms Cherokees could pursue in the short term, but they in no way limited their commitment to having intense debates over their social service policies. Cherokees guided the birth, lives, funding, and missions of their institutions. Cherokee actions, not the policies of non-Indians, readied the Nation and its citizens to defend their interests to "Friends of the Indian," who joined speculators and territorializers in attacks on Cherokee sovereignty and nationhood after the Civil War.

Walter Adair Duncan and Redbird Smith both opposed allotment, not because they uniformly agreed on the merits or faults of all aspects of national social policy, but because they agreed that Cherokee people were ten times better than non-Indians to prepare to direct, limit, and debate the changes to institutions that served Cherokee people. The two men remained committed to a social service system that fostered a hospitality ethic supported by communal landholdings. They believed the Cherokee Nation, not the United States or its agents, had a sovereign right and a community duty to respond to the needs and interests of the larger body of Cherokee people. Neither man passively resisted, though each chose different strategies to express their anger, frustration, and hostility to the process.

When Walter Adair Duncan refused to remove his hat and Smith faced arrest; both men spoke the same language. They communicated the value of Cherokee peoplehood and the importance of Cherokee nationhood. They articulated what it meant to be Cherokee based on the inherent right and responsibility of Cherokee people to care for one another, acknowledged by the United States through treaties and both literally and symbolically represented in social service institutions.

Epilogue

Statehood and allotment could not extinguish gadugi. Gadugi continues to thrive in Sycamore, Vian, Salina, and Colcord, Oklahoma. Families and communities just became more creative under increasingly austere conditions in order to meet the needs of their immediate and extended families.

Oklahoma Territory had offered little in the way of social provisions to the future state while the Cherokee Nation relinquished not only the land that it had governed but also the institutions Cherokee people had built and that had protected most Cherokee citizens. After statehood, Cherokee County, Oklahoma, used the national prison as a county jail. The federal government assumed control of the Cherokee Orphan Asylum, which became a Bureau of Indian Affairs boarding school. Today, it once again operates under the control of the Cherokee Nation. As for those battling mental illness, the 1907–1908 Oklahoma state legislature established the "Jim Crow" Eastern Oklahoma Hospital for the Insane in Vinita, a town formerly located in the Cherokee Nation's limits.[1] The hospital's first board of trustees included two former members of the Indian Territory Medical Association, Oliver Bagby and Courtland L. Long, both non-Indians who began their medical careers in Indian Territory, but who moved on to banking and trade.[2]

Institutional alumni navigated statehood in a variety of ways. Former administrators and teachers tended to do so successfully. A significant number used their institutional skills and their comfort with institutional processes to immortalize the accomplishments of the Cherokee Nation and Cherokee people. Mary Riley, who had contributed her article "Trees" to the *Children's Playground* in 1881, published an article, "Cherokee Orphan Asylum Was Established in Year 1873" in the *American Indian* in 1929. The article recounted a brief history of the Cherokee Orphan Asylum from its opening at the Salina location until it burned down in 1903.[3] Her first experiences with a printing press and journalism almost certainly occurred at the orphanage, and those experiences provided her with skills that served her beyond her years there. She also conducted numerous interviews with Cherokee people for the Indian Pioneer Project through the New Deal WPA projects.[4] One of her interviews recorded the location of the resting place of Jim Stearns, the cook who made sure runaway orphans had food.[5] In 1930, the *American Indian*, possibly with the aid of Mary Riley, reprinted an article written by DeWitt Clinton Duncan before his death, which discussed education reform.[6]

The local controls built into the Oklahoma Constitution ensured a place for many Cherokee people in the new state. Baby Ella Mae Covel, whose first teeth were recorded in the *Orphans' News*, taught in the segregated Indian Schools immediately after statehood. She later edited the *Tahlequah Arrow*. In 1912, she delivered a talk to the Federated Women's Clubs of Nowata, in which she said, "To write a sketch of Tahlequah is to write the history of the Cherokees from 1835 to 1906."[7] In 1919, she became the first woman elected to office in Tahlequah and one of the first women elected to office in Oklahoma. Tahlequah elected her to the office of city clerk; and, with the exception of one term, she held that office until her retirement in 1951. She never married.[8] On the day of her retirement, she swore in the new mayor, who in turn swore in the new officials; she then headed to Northeastern State University for the one-hundredth anniversary of the Cherokee Female Seminary.[9] In May of 1912, former high sheriff Cale Starr served as the sheriff of Cherokee County, Oklahoma. Cherokee James Sanders served as the undersheriff.[10]

In 1908, several of the residents, still housed in the former prison-turned-asylum, relocated to the asylum built in Norman.[11] On at least one occasion, a traditional Cherokee healer accompanied family members of a Cherokee patient to an asylum to provide traditional treatment. After the treatment, the patient recovered and returned

Cherokee Orphan Asylum graduates. Courtesy Cherokee Heritage Center Archives, Tahlequah, Oklahoma.

home.[12] Another woman was moved to Canton far away from her family and her community.

Despite the clear discrimination freed people faced in universally accessing every institutional service, the process of allotment inadvertently assured at least some Indian freedmen documentation on the Dawes rolls. In 1900, Cherokee citizen, genealogist, and historian Emmet Starr submitted applications for numerous individuals

Ella Mae Covel. Courtesy the Thomas Lee Ballenger Papers,
1730–1968, photographs, ca. 1866–ca. 1904, box 3, folder 33,
Newberry Library, Chicago.

listed as residents or inmates at the Cherokee Nation's social welfare
institutions based on census rolls and institutional documents. One
of those applications was for African Creek Jeff Marshall, featured
in the bureaucratic standoff between federal, Cherokee, and Creek
officials over his testimony at the federal court at Fort Smith. Starr
did not question Marshall's rights to an allotment. However, the non-
Indian commissioners investigated further. Dave Alberty, a Cherokee
freedmen, testified that he knew Marshall. Alberty informed officials that Marshall resided in the Creek Nation and that Alberty understood Marshall's land and citizenship rights to be rooted there.[13]
Marshall did receive his allotment in the Creek Nation, as did three
of his children. Ironically, incarceration in the Cherokee Nation's
prison provided an extra layer of protection for his rights to land.

As Cherokee men like the Duncan brothers predicted, allotment
and statehood led non-Cherokees to minimize the contributions and
skills of Cherokees. For example, in the eyes of certain contempo-
raries, some Cherokee people formerly associated with social welfare
institutions who continued to fulfill their social service responsibilities "seemed unable to adopt [themselves] to the changed conditions
of statehood." John Henry Covel (Sah le koo ge), Ella Mae's father,
taught for twenty-five years in the Cherokee Nation and regularly

served as an interpreter. In 1914, at the age of sixty-five and after "a long and useful life . . . spent in the service of his country," including "a hobby . . . advising and befriending the poor ignorant full bloods," John Henry Covel died.[14] The article announcing his death suggested that his continued service and advocacy on behalf of those Cherokees labeled "the poor and ignorant" provided the evidence of his inability to adjust to statehood. I disagree. John Henry Covel's advocacy was not evidence of a failure to adjust; it was evidence of the continuation of gadugi regardless of divides attributed to race, class, educational attainments, and language that allotment and statehood intensified.

Other alumni of social welfare institutions defied non-Cherokee expectations and continued to serve Cherokee people. William Drew, a graduate of the orphanage, found work in a restaurant in Tahlequah at the time of allotment, but he and other former residents also bridged lingual divides among Cherokee people. Drew, like many who attended the orphanage, was bilingual. On several occasions, he served as an interpreter for the Dawes Commission.[15] Located in the Newberry Library in Chicago is a speech, written in syllabary, given by Cherokee George Lowery in 1839. Will Sevier, who also attended the orphanage, translated the speech into English in 1915 for Principal Chief John Ross's nephew Joshua Ross, who, even though he could sign his name in syllabary, was not able to translate the entire speech.[16] As a result of the men's bilingualism and biliteracy and an institution that provided English language skills, but never sought to smother the Cherokee language, a more permanent and secure record exists of the institutions and people who supported and defended their right to exist.

John E. Duncan, the last high sheriff of the Cherokee Nation, kept watch over state social welfare institutions. In his papers at the Talbot Library and Museum in Colcord, Oklahoma, are numerous articles clipped from papers on Oklahoma's social welfare institutions. I suspect that John Duncan, Walter Adair Duncan's son, never ceased believing that the Cherokee Nation's social policy was ten times better for Cherokee people.

Notes

ABBREVIATIONS

ARCIA	*Annual Report of the Commissioner of Indian Affairs*
CHN	Cherokee Nation Records
CLCN (1875)	*Constitution and Laws of the Cherokee Nation*, 1875
CLCN (1881)	*Compiled Laws of the Cherokee Nation*, 1881
CNP	Cherokee Nation Papers, WHC
IPP	Indian-Pioneer Papers, WHC
ITMA Collection	Indian Territory Medical Association Collection, WHC
LCN (1839–67)	*Laws of the Cherokee Nation*, 1839–67
LCN (1852)	*Laws of the Cherokee Nation*, 1852
NARA	National Archives and Records Administration
RCIA	*Report of the Committee on Indian Affairs*
WHC	Western History Collections

A NOTE ON LANGUAGE

1. Debo, *And Still the Waters Run*, 61–125.
2. Reyhner and Eder, *American Indian Education*, 132–57.
3. Noah Webster, *An American Dictionary of the English Language* (Springfield: George and Charles Merriam, 1850), 80.

INTRODUCTION

1. *Cherokee Advocate*, 14 October 1893.
2. *History of Rev. W. A. Duncan*, MS 154, folder 16, Duncan Collection, Cherokee Heritage Center Archives, Tahlequah, Oklahoma (hereafter *History of Rev. W. A. Duncan*).

3. *Cherokee Advocate*, 14 October 1893.

4. Ibid.

5. Anthropologist Robert K. Thomas built on Frederick Gearing's discussions of a "harmony ethic" to conclude that a "conservative" Cherokee value system produces one of the most "highly developed 'social security systems' in the world." Robert K. Thomas, "Cherokee Values and Worldview," North Carolina Collection, Wilson Special Collections Library, University of North Carolina, Chapel Hill.

6. Hudson, *Southeastern Indians*, 184–202; Perdue, *Cherokee Women*, 24.

7. Adair, *Adair's History of the American Indians*, 434–41.

8. Reid, *Law of Blood*; Perdue, *Cherokee Women*, 41–59.

9. Hudson, *Southeastern Indians*, 260–69; Perdue, *Cherokee Women*, 19–40.

10. Perdue, *Cherokee Women*, 19–40, 72–73; Hill, *Weaving New Worlds*, 72–78.

11. Women received the title beloved woman after reaching menopause or, in more isolated cases, after distinguishing themselves in battle. The title elevated their political status within the community. Perdue, "Nancy Ward"; Gearing, *Priests and Warriors*.

12. Perdue, *Cherokee Women*, 19–40, 72–73.

13. Strickland, *Fire and the Spirits*, 35–36.

14. For a list of deviations and their penalties broken down by spiritual, community, and clan offenses, see Strickland, *Fire and the Spirits*, 35–39.

15. Hudson, *Southeastern Indians*, 367–70.

16. Mooney, "How the World Was Made," 239–40.

17. Mooney, *Myths and Sacred Formulas*, 243–44

18. Ibid., 250–52, 319–24.

19. Hudson, *Southeastern Indians*, 179.

20. Kilpatrick and Kilpatrick, *Run toward the Nightland*, 127.

21. Hudson, *Southeastern Indians*, 174.

22. Mintz, *Huck's Raft*, 27–47.

23. Cherokees experienced two major outbreaks, the first in 1738–39, which led to a mass suicide of traditional healers to restore the balance, and the second, coupled with measles, in 1759–60. Thornton, *Cherokees*, 29; McLoughlin, *Cherokee Renascence*, 17–18.

24. Perdue, *Cherokee Women*, 70–80, 134–37.

25. White, *Roots of Dependency*, xv, 71, 84. White describes this process within Choctaw society. The English wanted Indians to increase their consumption of European trade goods for the purpose of bringing "Indian resources, land, and labor into the market." Colonial officials hoped to replace the Choctaw's system of reciprocal gift exchange, which was central to forming trade relationships, and instead to "educate Choctaws in trade, market values, and hard-bargaining." Traders short-weighted deerskins or downgraded their quality and brought large amounts of liquor to aid in their chicanery and increase Choctaw debt. By 1770, officials estimated that 80 percent of the trade to the Choctaws was liquor.

26. McLoughlin, Conser, and McLoughlin, "Cherokee Anomie," 8–9.

27. McLoughlin, *Cherokee Renascence*, 34–40.

28. Ibid.

29. Ibid., 67–68.

30. Colonial New Englanders credited Indian violence during King Philip's War as a cause of poverty. Colonists also conflated the causes of poverty with vice. Indian peoples engaged in cultural and social practices unfamiliar to colonists, and from the perspective of colonial settlers' ethnocentrism, Indian peoples' everyday lives were filled with vice and were completely impoverished. Trattner, *From Poor Law to Welfare State*, 22–24. Early poor laws provided welfare to the most deserving "whites who were aged, in male-headed families, and widows"; based on these criteria, Indian people would never deserve aid. Handler and Hasenfeld, *Moral Construction of Poverty*, 19–20, 34. In *The Poorhouse*, Wagner uses the following vignettes to describe what circumstances led individuals to need poor relief in the colonial era: "If Mrs. Jones found herself widowed because her husband was killed in battle with Indians or if Mr. Smith was too old to work his farm and had no children to work it, both would submit themselves to the will of the overseers of the poor." Wagner, *Poorhouse*, 7. Berkowitz and McQuaid ignore the role of treaties and take the strongest dependency stance as it relates to American Indians and national welfare administration. Berkowitz and McQuaid, *Creating the Welfare State*. Less than a year after Berkowitz and McQuaid published their work, Gary C. Anders argues that "colonialism and the imposition of White control over Native institutions undermined the social, cultural, political and economic basis of the tribe's solidarity." He briefly summarizes the Cherokee Nation's post-removal accomplishments and concludes, "The establishment of their own corporate/community structures strongly indicates that when left to their own initiative, Native peoples still have the capacity to innovate, and that economic development need not preclude preservation of their cultural values." I agree with his overall assessment, but his work makes no attempts to understand the successes and failures of their efforts and simply suggests that they were capable of further innovation. Anders, "Reduction of a Self-Sufficient People," 225–37. Seth Rockman makes clear that U.S. policy conceived of Republican citizens in very specific ways (i.e., adult white male heads of households). This definition left Native Americans as groups dependent upon those men. Rockman, *Welfare Reform in the Early Republic*, 8. Jensen's recent work challenges scholars of selective entitlements to look earlier, but still presupposes that Indians were an obstacle that provoked an expansion of entitlements. Jensen, *Patriots*, 12.

31. Usner, "American Indians and Welfare," 312–26.

32. Genetin-Pilawa, *Crooked Paths*; Cahill, *Federal Fathers*.

33. Bruyneel, *Third Space*.

34. Shoe Boots was a veteran of the Red Stick War who fathered children by his slave Doll. Despite the Cherokee Nation's increasingly racialized citizenship laws, the family successfully petitioned for three of the children's citizenship. The removal era created additional legal vulnerabilities for Doll and her children. After Shoe Boots's death in 1829, his children were re-enslaved. Miles, 123–43. For a full discussion of

the impact of race and slavery covered by recent scholars, see Miles, *Ties That Bind*; Miles, *House on Diamond Hill*; Yarbrough, *Race and the Cherokee Nation*; and Naylor, *African Cherokees*.

35. Usner, "American Indians and Welfare," 312–26.

36. Usner, *Indian Work*, 71.

37. Usner, "American Indians and Welfare," 319–20.

38. The first work to take a more comprehensive view of boarding schools as total institutions is Adams, *Education for Extinction*. Szasz's 1988 *Indian Education in the Colonies* argued that although the larger goals of Indian education were consistent across the colonies (Christianize and civilize), each colony operated under different conditions and approached these goals differently, resulting in uneven outcomes.

39. Several works that responded to Adams and Szasz include Child, *Boarding School Seasons*; Lomawaima, *They Called It Prairie Light*; and Cobb, *Listening to Our Grandmother's Stories*. All of these works focus on specific boarding schools and highlight Indian students' and their families' responses to the second civilization policy that accompanied allotment in the late nineteenth and early twentieth centuries.

40. Lomawaima and McCarty point out that, despite the stated assimilation policies governing boarding schools, staff at the institutions permitted students the opportunities for "acting out" traditional life at the schools. Officials did not intervene despite intervention being the goal of assimilation policies. The authors argue instead that boarding schools created "safety zones" that "neutralized" and "contained" the power of what children and their respective communities created. These images and practices provided evidence to an American public that Indians had in fact been domesticated and were safely contained. Lomawaima and McCarty, *"To Remain an Indian,"* 1–4.

41. Denson, *Demanding the Cherokee Nation*, 159.

42. Cahill, *Federal Fathers*, 17, 24–25, 222–23; Burch, "'Dislocated Histories,'" 141–42.

43. Applying Foucault's approach from *Madness and Civilization*, social historian David Rothman promotes the former. David Grob argues for the latter. Cited in Katz "Origins of the Institutional State," 6–22.

44. Malinda Maynor Lowery makes a similar argument in *Lumbee Indians in the Jim Crow South*. Lumbees used local institutions as a means to project and protect identity yet maintain traditional community values and goals. Lowery, *Lumbee Indians*.

45. Stremlau, *Sustaining the Cherokee Family*, 9.

46. Chang, *Color of the Land*, 9.

47. Adair, "Indian Territory in 1878," 269.

CHAPTER 1

1. Pathkiller to Friend Colonel Meigs, 17 February 1806, MS-2033, Penelope Johnson Allen Collection, Special Collections University of Tennessee, Knoxville (hereafter Allen Collection).

2. The Glass to Return J. Meigs, 5 March 1806, box 1, folder 43, Allen Collection.

3. Waterhouse, *Prospect of Exterminating the Small-pox*.

4. Jenner, *Instructions for Vaccine Inoculation*.

5. Daniel Ross to Return J. Meigs, 24 March 1806, MS-2033, Allen Collection.

6. The Glass to Return J. Meigs, 5 March 1806, box 1 folder 43, Allen Collection.

7. Daniel Ross to Return J. Meigs, 24 March 1806, MS-2033, Allen Collection.

8. Ibid.

9. Payne and Butrick, *Payne-Butrick Papers*, 4:220–33.

10. Mooney, "Myths of the Cherokee," Mooney, History, Myths and Scared Formulas of the Cherokees, 242–252, 316–19.

11. Gambold and Gambold, *Moravian Springplace Mission* (2007), 1:354.

12. Ibid., 2:56. Often healers used bones or teeth to cause an individual to bleed and then searched for the cause of the illness in the blood. Healers also scratched a person's skin before he or she went to water, or bathed, as part of a purification ritual. This may have been the ritual performed on Dawzizi. Mooney, "Myths of the Cherokee," 230, 334.

13. Zogry, *Anetso*, 3; Mooney, "Cherokee Ball Play," 125–32.

14. Phillips and Phillips, *Brainerd Journal*, 503n1.

15. Moulton, *John Ross*, 5.

16. Ibid.

17. Hoig, *Cherokees and their Chiefs*, 126.

18. Alice Taylor-Colbert, "John Ross (1790–1866)" *New Georgia Encyclopedia*, 6 August 2014, http://www.georgiaencyclopedia.org/articles/history-archaeology/john-ross-1790-1866.

19. Payne and Butrick, *Payne-Butrick Papers*, 2:132–43.

20. Malone, *Cherokees of the Old South*, 156; Foreman, *Sequoyah*

21. Payne and Butrick, *Payne-Butrick Papers*, 2:143. These accusations came just a few years before Cherokee people questioned the actions and intentions of Christian missionaries. In 1826, Cherokees near Etowah suspected Christian converts in their community of using hymns to perform witchcraft. Even more egregious to the community was the minister's discouraging congregants from participating in events at the council house. The community expressed similar anxieties related to community participation as those critics of Sequoyah's efforts. Perdue, "Traditionalism in the Cherokee Nation," 164–70.

22. McLoughlin, *Cherokee Renascence*, 350–54.

23. Gambold and Gambold, *Moravian Springplace Mission* (2010), 121.

24. Edward T. Luther, "Walden Ridge and Sequatchie Valley" *Tennessee Encyclopedia of History and Culture*, 25 December 2009, https://tennesseeencyclopedia.net/entry.php?rec=1449.

25. Wilkins, *Cherokee Tragedy*, 6–39.

26. Ibid., 23–27.

27. Payne and Butrick, *Payne-Butrick Papers*, 2:102–103.

28. In 1775, Henderson's purchase cost the Cherokees 27,000 acres of hunting grounds in what is today most of Kentucky. Many of the same young chiefs who

opposed this cession formed the leadership of the Chickamauga band, which continued to fight the United States and settlers long after the American Revolution ended and Cherokees signed treaties of peace. McLoughlin, *Cherokee Renascence*, 19–20, 26.

29. According to the account in the *Payne-Butrick Papers*, Vann's wife accompanied the party and hoped to carry out the execution herself. When Vann became sick on the trip, she tended to him and was unable to continue. The Ridge along with two other men proceeded with the task, but "without reference to the domestic quarrel, but merely as a Speculator upon the National Lands and no Friend to his Country" (2:104). McLoughlin interprets this event as Doublehead's clan's acceptance of the act as a "semiofficial political act taken by responsible chiefs for the good of the tribe and therefore outside the area of clan revenge." Theda Perdue suggests that the family failed to seek vengeance because Doublehead's death fulfilled clan vengeance of Vann's wife's family. McLoughlin, *Cherokee Renascence*, 121; Perdue, *Cherokee Women*, 49–51.

30. "Resolved by the Chiefs and Warriors in a National Council Assembled," 11 September 1808, *Laws of the Cherokee Nation*, 1852, 3–4. Hereafter *LCN* (1852).

31. Ibid.

32. Ibid.

33. Meserve, "Chief William Potter Ross," 23.

34. Presbyterian minister Gideon Blackburn hired Jonathon Blacke as a schoolmaster at Hiawassee, who benefitted from the unpaid services of his wife. She cooked, taught, sewed clothes, managed the female students who lived in the Blacke's home, and attended to her own young children. Blackburn recognized that wives provided free labor desperately needed in underfunded institutions. Bass, "Gideon Blackburn's Mission," 213–14.

35. McLoughlin, *Cherokees and Missionaries*, 239–66.

36. Phillips and Phillips, *Brainerd Journal*, 80.

37. Entry of 14 November 1818, Phillips and Phillips, *Brainerd Journal*, 92.

38. Perdue, *Slavery*, 52–53.

39. Return J. Meigs to William Crawford, Secretary of War, 4 November 1816, Allen Collection.

40. McLoughlin, Conser, and McLoughlin, "Cherokee Anomie," 24–30.

41. Abram, "Shedding Their Blood," 33; McLoughlin, *Cherokee Renascence*, 192.

42. Numerous Cherokees filed claims of losses of cattle, horses, crops, and hogs and reported these losses to Agent Meigs. Applicants of Claims taken at Turkytown, 1816, Correspondence and Miscellaneous Records, Records of the Cherokee Indian Agency, East, 1801–35, RG 75, M208 (hereafter Records of the Cherokee Indian Agency), roll 0008, record 1819, 189–200, National Archives and Records Administration (hereafter NARA).

43. Abram, "Shedding Their Blood," 37; McLoughlin, *Cherokee Renascence*, 189–98.

44. Here I am borrowing the language of Kristin Collins as she applies it to the expansion of "traditional war widows" regardless of their husbands' rank. Collins, "'Petitions without Number,'" 7–8.

45. Glasson, *History of Military Pension*, 58–60.

46. Cherokees who lived outside the boundaries of the Cherokee Nation did appeal to district courts. In 1837, Culscawee, aged sixty, applied to the Alabama District Court for a pension. Because of a gunshot wound to his right side, he claimed a permanent (dis)ability. The court rejected his claim on the grounds that his injury was not documented in the records. Culscawee, War of 1812 Pension and Bounty Land Warrant Application Files, compiled ca. 1871–ca. 1900, documenting the period 1812–ca. 1900, War of 1812 Pension and Bounty Land Warrant Application Files, RG 15, M208, NARA (hereafter War of 1812 Pension and Bounty Files).

47. 26 October 1815, Copies Of Accounts, Receipts, And Disbursements, 1801–1820, Fiscal Records, Records of the Cherokee Indian Agency, roll 0011.

48. Copies of Accounts, Receipts, And Disbursements, 1801–1820.

49. Other scholars have demonstrated how the federal government used marriage and social provision as a means to privatize care of women within families in the larger United States. Kristin Collins contends that antebellum widows' pensions moved women's care into public law and expanded the anemic federal bureaucracy. Collins's work challenges Theda Skocpol's chronology and argument that the growth of the United States' maternal welfare state, at odds with the systems developing in Europe, begins in earnest with Civil War pensions. Laura Jensen, also challenging Skocpol's assessment, argues that these selective entitlements "played a major role in the constitution of a distinctly American, exceptional state . . . organized around neither universal social provision nor even social provision per se." Collins, "Administering Marriage," 1092; Skocpol, *Protecting Soldiers and Mothers*; Jensen, *Patriots*, 12.

50. Hicks letter, 8 July 1819, Relating to pensions and children of Cherokee warriors, Correspondence and Miscellaneous Records, Records of the Cherokee Indian Agency, roll 0008.

51. Can naw e sos kee, a Cherokee Warrior killed in Battle 27 March 1814, 3 June 1819, Correspondence and Miscellaneous Records, Records of the Cherokee Indian Agency, roll 0008.

52. Hicks letter, 6 June 1819, Correspondence and Miscellaneous Records, Records of the Cherokee Indian Agency, roll 0008.

53. Hicks letter, 8 July 1819.

54. Guardianship—John Miller for orphan children, Correspondence and Miscellaneous Records, Records of the Cherokee Indian Agency, roll 0008.

55. Charles Hicks to Col. Return J. Meigs, 23 June 1819, Correspondence and Miscellaneous Records, Records of the Cherokee Indian Agency, roll 0008.

56. Charles Hicks letter about Paweskee [Paw yus skee], 8 April 1819, Correspondence and Miscellaneous Records, Records of the Cherokee Indian Agency, roll 0008.

57. Pension Accounts United States with Widows and Orphans of Cherokee Warriors, Correspondence and Miscellaneous Records, Records of the Cherokee Indian Agency, roll 0008.

58. Charles Hicks to War Dept, 6 June 1819; Michael Hildebrand, Richard Taylor, Gideon Morgans Bond Guardianship, 22 July 1819, both in Correspondence and Miscellaneous Records, Records of the Cherokee Indian Agency, roll 0008.

59. McLoughlin documents numerous instances of bribery or "inducements" paid to individual Cherokees and intermarried whites to gain signatures for treaties and land cessions. McLoughlin, *Cherokee Renascence*, 77, 89, 98, 106, 210, 305.

60. John D. Chisholm to Return J. Meigs, 22 July 1814, Correspondence and Miscellaneous Records, Records of the Cherokee Indian Agency, roll 0006.

61. "Whereas, fifty-four towns and villages have convened," 4–6. McLoughlin makes clear that these laws were in effect much earlier. McLoughlin, *Cherokee Renascence*, 220–25.

62. Ethan Allen Hitchcock recorded that by the 1840s upper Creek towns referred to members of their local councils as "lawyers," who disseminated legal information among the towns and "execute[d]" the laws. Hitchcock, *Traveler in Indian Country*, 121–22. Around the same time, whites dubbed bilingual Hallalhotsoot a Nez Perce leader "The Lawyer" for his skills at negotiation and argument. Josephy, *Nez Perce Indians*, 78.

63. Miles, "Narrative of Nancy," 59–80.

64. Pathkiller and John Lowrey [Lowery] to Friend Col. Meigs, 17 February 1806, Allen Collection.

65. Daniel Ross to Col. Return J. Meigs, 24 March 1806, Allen Collection.

66. McLoughlin, *Cherokee Renascence*, 331–32.

67. The Cherokees lost 4 million of their remaining 14 million acres through these cessions. McLoughlin, *Cherokee Renascence*, 256.

68. Treaty with the Cherokee, 1819, Article 3, in Kappler, *Indian Affairs*.

69. Cherokee Reservations, 6 June 1816–6 December 1819, Fiscal Records, Records of the Cherokee Indian Agency.

70. In 1809 Meigs hired George Barber Davis to conduct a census. Although the accuracy of his numbers is questionable, he counted the total number of intermarried white men at 113. It is likely this number was higher by 1817, but this still represents a significant portion of intermarried white men. McLoughlin, *Cherokee Renascence*, 168–70. Register of Persons Who Wish Reserves under the Treaty of July 8th, 1817, Cherokee Reservations, 6 June 1801–6 December 1819, Fiscal Records, Records of the Cherokee Indian Agency, roll 0013.

71. Bloomer and Bloomer, *Life and Writings*, 55–57.

72. Cherokee Women, Petition of 30 June 1818, in Perdue and Green, *Cherokee Removal*, 131–33.

73. "Resolved by the National Committee and Council," 10 November 1825, *LCN* (1852), 10.

74. Ibid., 2 November 1819, *LCN* (1852), 10.

75. Finger, *Eastern Band*, 10–11.

76. Ibid.

77. Davis, "Chaos in the Indian Country," 134–35.

78. Register of Persons Who Wish Reserves.

79. Starr, *History of the Cherokee Indians*, 441–42.

80. "Resolved by the National Committee and Council," 10 November 1825, *LCN* (1852), 57.

81. McLoughlin, *Cherokee Renascence*, 256.

82. Powell, "4 ᐁ Ꮨ Was Here"; McLoughlin, *Cherokee Renascence*, 351–52.

83. Treaty with the Cherokee, 1817, Article 6, in Kappler, *Indian Affairs*.

84. McLoughlin, *Cherokees and Missionaries*, 184.

85. Fay Yarbrough examines this event as one that also contributes to new racial criteria by which Cherokee men's children could receive the benefits of citizenship. Yarbrough, *Race and the Cherokee Nation*, 33, 39–41.

86. Miles sees this moment as one that begins a "fundamental shift" in Cherokee and black relations. Miles pointed out that this extension of citizenship to Shoe Boots's children was due, in part, to the goodwill the council felt toward Shoe Boots and because of legal loopholes, which the council addressed just two weeks after ruling on Shoe Boots's petition. Miles, *Ties That Bind*, 106–107, 113, 125–28.

87. A List of Claims, Cherokee Daybook, 18 October 1817–12 June 1821, Fiscal Records, Records of the Cherokee Indian Agency, roll 0012.

88. Copies of Accounts, Receipts, and Disbursements, 1801–1820, Fiscal Records, Records of the Cherokee Indian Agency, roll 0011.

89. McLoughlin, Conser, and McLoughlin, "Cherokee Anomie," 24–30. The Choctaw agent made similar payments to families when territorial courts failed to convict whites of murder. Usner, "American Indians on the Cotton Frontier," 312.

90. McLoughlin suggests that patrilineal and patrilocal structures became the "norm" in the early 1800s, though subsequent scholars, including Theda Perdue and Rose Stremlau, reject this position. Pension records provide further evidence that this was not the case. McLoughlin, *Cherokee Renascence*, 141.

91. Until this time, Cherokee legal theory made no official distinction between degrees of homicide, motives, or intent. Strickland, *Fire and the Spirits*, 27–28.

92. "Be it known, that this day," 10 April 1810, *LCN* (1852), 4.

93. Reid, *Law of Blood*, 90–91.

94. The Cherokees established a light horse in 1797 to preserve peace on the national borders. Major Ridge proposed the use of the light horse to police the law that forbid sale of lands by local chiefs. McLoughlin, *Cherokee Renascence*, 44–46.

95. Strickland, *Fire and the Spirits*, 57.

96. "Resolved by the National Committee and Council," 2 November 1820, 11 November 1824, *LCN* (1852), 15–19, 37.

97. "Resolved by the National Committee and Council, That the Circuit Judges . . . " 12 November 1822, *LCN* (1852), 28.

98. "Resolved by the National Committee and Council, That the law requiring the several Light Horse," 14 October 1825; "For the better security of the common property," 14 October 1825, both in *LCN* (1852), 44–46.

99. "22 October 1827 John Downing vs. Martin Downing & Mother," "23 October 1827 Betsey Walker vs. William Blythe," Entries from the Cherokee Supreme Court

Docket, 1823–1834, Allen Collection, University of Tennessee Special Collections, Hodges Library, Knoxville, Tenn. Digital Collection available at http://diglib.lib.utk.edu/dlc/tdh/index.html.

100. Martin, "Nature and Extent," 27–63.

101. "Resolved by the National Committee and Council," 10 November 1828, *LCN* (1852), 104.

102. Ibid.

103. Reid, *Law of Blood*, 94–95.

104. Rothman explores the embrace of institutions in the Jacksonian era as the best means to manage social ills. Reformers promised rehabilitation of wards and reassured citizens of the early republic of the new government's merits. Rothman, *Discovery of the Asylum*.

105. "Resolved by the National Committee and Council," 14 October 1826, *LCN* (1852), 78.

106. Return J. Meigs to the Secretary of War , 14 November 1819, Correspondence and Miscellaneous Records, Records of the Cherokee Indian Agency, roll 0008.

107. McLoughlin, *Cherokee Renascence*, 388–90; Perdue, "Traditionalism in the Cherokee Nation," 159–61.

108. "Resolved by the National Council," 9 November 1829, *LCN* (1852), 64–65.

CHAPTER 2

1. Foreman, *Indian Removal*, 229. McLoughlin, *Cherokee Renascence*, 438–39.

2. The Georgia court defended its right to try and execute Corn Tassel by denying the sovereignty of the Cherokee Nation within its boundaries using a states' rights argument. It also argued that those who had signed treaties with Indian tribes were wrong to do so. Norgren, *Cherokee Cases*, 95–98.

3. Through a series of legislation from 1827 to 1832, Alabama extended its laws over Creeks and Cherokees. They forbade hunting, trapping, and fishing and only allowed Indians to testify against other Indians. Green, *Politics of Indian Removal*, 146–47.

4. McLoughlin, *Cherokee Renascence*, 106–108, 126.

5. Ibid., 190–92.

6. Ibid., 188–98.

7. "Resolved by the National Committee and Council," 27 October 1821, *LCN* (1852), 19.

8. "For the better security of the common property of the Cherokee Nation," 15 June 1825, *LCN* (1852), 46.

9. "Resolved by the Committee and Council, in General Council Convened," 17 November 1828, *LCN* (1852), 113.

10. McLoughlin, *Cherokee Renascence*, 244–45, 428–31.

11. Ibid., 443–44; Martin, "Nature and Extent," 27–63; Bonner, "Georgia Penitentiary," 309.

12. Moulton, *John Ross*, 45; McLoughlin, *Cherokee Renascence*, 432.

13. McLoughlin, "Cherokees and Methodists," 44; *Cherokee Phoenix*, 19 March 1831.

14. Foreman, *Indian Removal*, 250–51.

15. McLoughlin, *Cherokee Renascence*, 432.

16. Green, *Politics of Indian Removal*, 147; McLoughlin, *Cherokee Renascence*, 272–74. Special Indian agent William Carroll viewed the subjugation of Indians to the civilized violence of southern courts as a precursor to inducing removal. In 1829, Carroll wrote, "They cannot bear the execution of our criminal laws. I was in South Alabama a short time since, when three or four Indians were tried and found guilty of horse-stealing in a county near Fort Strother. The sentence of the court was immediately carried into effect, and the red brethren gave abundant proof of their dislike to a whipping post and the laws of civilized society. I cannot but hope, that I can induce both the Creeks and Cherokees as directed by the Secretary of War to agree to hold treaties in which event, the means of success will be found in assailing the avarice of the chiefs and principal men." William Carroll to Andrew Jackson, 29 June 1829, Papers of Andrew Jackson Digital Edition, http://rotunda.upress.virginia.edu/founders/JKSN-01-07-02-0227.

17. McLoughlin, *Cherokee Renascence*, 428–33.

18. Ibid., 431–32.

19. Bonner, "Georgia Penitentiary," 309.

20. Moulton, *John Ross*, 69; Wilkins, "John Howard Payne," 2–11; Foreman, *Indian Removal*, 268.

21. Georgia also undermined Cherokees economically in other ways; theft, for example, went largely unpunished. Georgia's extension of its laws over Cherokees nullified treaties between whites and Indians, unless witnessed by two whites, and once gold was discovered on Cherokee lands, Georgia passed laws making it illegal for Cherokees to mine for it. Wilkins, *Cherokee Tragedy*, 209–10.

22. This was proposed by Wilkins, *Cherokee Tragedy*, 215.

23. Throughout the 1820s, the state legislature allocated lands and funds to academies already operating in the state to establish poor schools. In some counties, it allocated monies to county officials to distribute monies as they saw fit to educate the poor. For example, in 1820 Georgia passed legislation allowing a conveyance of land in Augusta to build a facility to house and educate poor children. An Act to make it lawful for the Trustees of Richmond Academy, 21 December 1820; An Act to Appoint Trustees for the Poor School Fund in the County of Irwin, 19 December 1827, both in Dawson, "1831 Dawson's Compilation." The only form of outdoor relief consistently protected and expanded during the period coinciding with rise of social welfare institutions were military pensions. Wagner, *Poorhouse*, 7–9.

24. Green, *Politics of Indian Removal*, 129.

25. Ibid., 129, 132, 138.

26. *Cherokee Phoenix*, 8 May 1830, and 11 September 1830.

27. Moulton, *John Ross*, 40–41.

28. McLoughlin, *Cherokee Renascence*, 238.

29. Green, *Politics of Indian Removal*, 146.

30. Foreman, *Indian Removal*, 107–10.

31. *Cherokee Nation v. Georgia*, 30 U.S. 1 (1831); *Worcester v. Georgia*, 31 U.S. 515 (1832).

32. *Webster's 1806 Dictionary: A Compendious Dictionary of the English Language*, s.v. "guardian," http://www.premierathome.com/library/Reference/Webster's%201806%20Dictionary.txt.

33. Deutsch, *Mentally Ill in America*, 137; *Webster's Dictionary 1828 Online*, s.v. "guardian," http://webstersdictionary1828.com.

34. Cherokee children who attended Worcester's missionary schools used Webster's spelling books throughout the 1820s. Boudinot ordered a set on behalf of the mission school on at least one occasion. It seems likely that elite Cherokee families who embraced education and Christianity, and who were institutionally educated themselves, were aware to some degree of Webster's efforts, especially those that directly impacted education and textbooks. Bass, *Cherokee Messenger*, 45, 47, 66; Jill Lepore, *A is for American*, 1–25.

35. Green, *Politics of Indian Removal*, 128–30.

36. Garrison, *Legal Ideology of Removal*, 187–88.

37. *Cherokee Phoenix and Indians' Advocate*, 23 July 1828.

38. Dale and Litton, *Cherokee Cavaliers*, 12.

39. The Five Tribes signed treaties in succession: the Choctaws in 1830, the Creeks and Seminoles in 1832, the Chickasaws in 1833, and finally the Cherokees in 1835. Foreman, *Indian Removal*, 28, 110–11, 193–95.

40. Dale and Litton, *Cherokee Cavaliers*, 4–5, 10–12.

41. Wilkins, *Cherokee Tragedy*, 235–41.

42. Ibid., 242–45.

43. The Cornwall community objected to these marriages through mob violence. After the second marriage, the school shut down. Demos, *Heathen School*, 153–87.

44. Wilkins, *Cherokee Tragedy*, 259–67.

45. In 1834, Treaty Party proponents negotiated a treaty that provided money to individuals for rifles, blankets, and kettles; $10,000 for schools; and $25,000 for general funds, but no payments for any of the personal property or improvements that would be lost in the East. Garrison, *Legal Ideology of Removal*, 200; Wilkins, *Cherokee Tragedy*, 259–61.

46. Garrison, *Legal Ideology of Removal*, 200.

47. Treaty with the Cherokee, 1835, in Kappler, *Indian Affairs*, 445.

48. Ibid., Article 10, in Kappler, *Indian Affairs*, 443.

49. Treaty with the Choctaw, 1830 Article 20; and Treaty with the Creeks, 1832, Article 2 and Article 13, both in Kappler, *Indian Affairs*.

50. Treaty with the Cherokee, 1835, Preamble, in Kappler, *Indian Affairs*.

51. Treaty with the Choctaw, 1832; and Treaty with the Chickasaw, 1832, Preamble, both in Kappler, *Indian Affairs*.

52. Foreman, *Indian Removal*, 28, 110–11, 193–95.

53. Ibid., 97.

54. Gibson, *Chickasaws*, 158–75.

55. Reverend Cephas Washburn reported bilious fever, mosquitoes, and ague among the Old Settlers. Other groups faced cholera outbreaks as they traveled. Howard, "Cherokee History to 1840," 71–82.

56. Agent Meigs included Ross's name and those of his immediate family members on the list of individuals who agreed to take reserves under the Treaty of 1817. McLoughlin suggests that he was simply protecting land his father owned and left to him, though I am skeptical of that conclusion. McLoughlin, *Cherokee Renascence*, 267. Moulton points out that Ross proposed U.S. citizenship as a viable option for remaining in the South, although this may have been a tactic to stall the process. Moulton, *John Ross*, 70–71; Ross, *Papers of Chief John Ross*, 1:1–20. Wilkins asserts that Ross intended to remain in the East and accept citizenship. Wilkins, *Cherokee Tragedy*, 260–61.

57. Cherokee Nation, *Memorial and Protest of the Cherokee Nation*.

58. Walker, *Torchlight to the Cherokees*, 301.

59. Here I borrow the language of the Declaration of Independence.

60. Mulholland and Morgan, "Illuminating Cherokee Removal," 24–37 (underlined in original).

61. Norgren, *Cherokee Cases*, 136.

62. Major General Winfield Scott's Order No. 25 Regarding the Removal of the Cherokee Indians to the West, 17 May 1838, Letters Received and Other Papers of Major General Winfield Scott Relating to the Cherokees, 1838–1838, Records of U.S. Army Continental Commands, 1817–1947, RG 393, NARA.

63. Perdue and Green, *Cherokee Nation*, 123, 124; Wilkins, *Cherokee Tragedy*, 320–24.

64. McLoughlin, *After the Trail*, 7.

65. Howard, "Cherokee History to 1840," 71–82.

66. Vick, "Cherokee Adaptation," 394–405.

67. Perdue and Green, *Cherokee Nation*, 126.

68. Demographer Russell Thornton generally accepts approximately four thousand deaths, but he argues that the numbers have to include the numbers lost because of the disruption to normal family life cycles. Cherokee population was on an upswing before removal. Removal, therefore, took the lives not only of those who died but also of those who should have been born had removal and the civil war that followed not disrupted their parents' and grandparents' lives. Thornton, *Cherokees*, 47–78. John Ross lost his wife, Quatie, from pneumonia during removal. Wilkins, *Cherokee Tragedy*, 327–28. The Beaver, a (dis)abled War of 1812 pensioner died during removal. Beaver, War of 1812 Pension and Bounty Files.

69. United States, *Right of President to Withhold Papers*, 13–26, 126–29.

70. Ross, *Papers of Chief John Ross*, 1:35.

71. "Laws of the Old Settlers or Western Cherokees," *LCN* (1852), 152–79.

72. Daniel, "From Blood Feud," 113–14.

73. Wilkins, *Cherokee Tragedy*, 334–39.

74. Daniel, "From Blood Feud," 113–14.

75. "Act of Union Between the Eastern and Western Cherokees," 12 July 1839, *LCN* (1852), 3–4.

76. "Constitution of the Cherokee Nation," 6 September 1839, *LCN* (1852), 5.

77. Ishii, *Bad Fruits*, 96–97.

78. "An Act to Prevent the Introduction and Vending of Ardent Spirits," 28 September 1839, *LCN* (1852), 32.

79. "An Act Prohibiting the Introduction of Spirituous Liquors," 25 October 1841, *LCN* (1852), 57–58.

80. Littlefield and Underhill, "Slave 'Revolt,'" 121–31.

81. Gaines, *Confederate Cherokees*, 5.

82. Mrs. John E. Duncan, interview by James R. Carselowey, 18 May 1937, 26: 217–27, Indian-Pioneer Papers, Western History Collections (hereafter WHC), University of Oklahoma Library, Norman, Oklahoma (hereafter IPP).

83. "An Act prohibiting the Sheriff from boarding Prisoners or Guards at the Public Houses during the session of the National Council," 25 December 1843, *LCN* (1852), 103.

84. In 1879, Mrs. Jennie Sixkiller boarded guards during the annual session. "An Act Making an Appropriation for the Benefit of Mrs. Jennie Sixkiller," 17 December 1881, in Cherokee Nation, *Laws and Joint Resolutions 1881–2–3*, 33.

85. Wardell, *Political History*, 95.

86. McLoughlin, *After the Trail*, 88.

87. McLoughlin, "Cherokee Anti-Mission Sentiment," 361–70.

88. "An Act Relative to Schools," 26 September 1839, *LCN* (1852), 30–31.

89. McLoughlin, *Cherokees and Missionaries*, 190–95.

90. H. D. Reese to Colonel George Butler, 4 September 1855, in U.S. Commissioner of Indian Affairs, *Annual Report of the Commissioner of Indian Affairs* (hereafter *ARCIA*), (1855).

91. No Moravians participated in forced removal. McLoughlin, *Cherokees and Missionaries*, 320–28.

92. "An Act Relative to Public Schools," 16 December 1841, *LCN* (1852), 59–61.

93. "An Act for Public School Appropriation," 23 December 1842, *LCN* (1852), 76–77; P. M. Butler to T. Hartley Crawford, Commissioner of Indian Affairs, Letters Received by the Office of Indian Affairs, 1824–1880, 30 September 1843, M234, reel 87, frames 49–72, NARA.

94. "Enacted by the National Council," 22 November 1847, *LCN* (1852), 165; "An act making appropriation for the support of Public Schools for the year 1849 and for other purposes," 10 November 1848, *LCN* (1852), 186.

95. McLoughlin, *After the Trail*, 88–92.

96. McLoughlin, *Champions*, 210–13.

97. W. A. Duncan to George Butler, 25 September 1856, *ARCIA* (1857), 690–94.

98. Smith, *Capture These Indians*, 29–32.

99. Babcock and Bryce, *History of Methodism*, 99–100.

100. "A Bill on the Subject of an Orphan School," 19 December 1842, *LCN* (1852), 75.

101. O'Sullivan, "Missionary and Mother," 452–65.

102. Elizur Butler to P. M. Butler, 19 June 1843, Cherokee Agency, 1836–1880, Letters Received by the Office of Indian Affairs, 1824–1880, RG 75, M234, reel 87, frames 81–82, NARA.

103. The army oversaw the first three removal detachments. When significant deaths occurred, Principal Chief John Ross successfully requested that Cherokees take control of their own removal. He selected Cherokee men to lead each of the detachments; these men were also referred to as conductors. Detachment leaders distributed provisions, directed the personnel (wagon masters, physicians, commissaries), and accounted for costs.

104. "An Act for the Benefit of John Benge—for $24.00," 19 December 1843, *LCN* (1852), 101; "An Act for the Benefit of Michael Waters," 8 January 1844, *LCN* (1852), 105.

105. "An Act Further to Amend an Act Relative to Public Schools," 23 December 1843, *LCN* (1852), 101–102.

106. Ibid.

107. "An Act Relative to Guardians," 18 November 1847, *LCN* (1852), 164–65.

108. H. D. Reese to Colonel George Butler, 4 September 1853, *ARCIA* (1855), 330.

109. "An Act for the Benefit of Big Dollar" 5 November 1849, *LCN* (1852), 198.

110. "An Act Authorizing the Appointment of Guardians for Insane Persons and Orphan Children," 12 October 1841, *Laws of the Cherokee Nation Passed during the Years 1839–1867*, 46–47. Hereafter *LCN* (1839–67).

111. Moore, *Brief History of the Missionary Work*, 26–28, 32–33, 36, 38–39, 62; Babcock and Bryce, *History of Methodism*, 93.

112. McLoughlin, *After the Trail*, 69–71.

113. "Message of the Principal Chief of the Cherokee Nation to the National Committee and Council," 5 October 1857, S. Doc. 35th Cong., 1st Sess. (1857–58), 506–11.

114. McLoughlin, *After the Trail*, 59–69.

115. "An Act to Reduce the Numbers of Orphans Attending Public Schools," 23 October 1856, 1830, CNP-6, frames 623–24, Cherokee Nation Papers, WHC (hereafter CNP).

116. Walter Adair Duncan to George Butler, 18 September 1857, *ARCIA* (1858), 505.

117. Ross, *Papers of Chief John Ross*, 2:408–409.

118. Ibid., 2:443.

119. Cheatham, "If the Union Wins," 158.

120. "Message of the Principal Chief," 506–11.

CHAPTER 3

1. E. F. Vann, interview by L. W. Wilson, 1938 March 10, IPP; Hicks, "Diary," 11, 13, 14.

2. Hicks, "Diary," 11, 13, 14.

3. Within this space, Bruyneel points out that tribes challenged attempts to limit their sovereignty, and they worked to "gain the fullest possible expression of political identity, agency, and autonomy." Bruyneel, *Third Space*, 13, 25.

4. Gaines, *Confederate Cherokees*, 7–10; Confer, *Cherokee Nation*; Hauptman, *Between Two Fires*, 41–65.

5. Gaines, *Confederate Cherokees*, 15.

6. Confer, *Cherokee Nation*, 42–52, 58–75.

7. McLoughlin, *After the Trail*, 206–1; Confer, *Cherokee Nation*, 79–82, 109, 206–10.

8. W. G. Coffin to W. P. Dole, 13 February 1862, *ARCIA* (1863), 289–91.

9. Ibid., 113–15.

10. Dale and Litton, *Cherokee Cavaliers*, 93–94.

11. Calloway, *Indian History of an American Institution*, available at http://www.dartmouth.edu/~library/digital/publishing/books/calloway2010/html/index.html#cho06. Duncan, "Story of the Cherokees," http://www.ualr.edu/sequoyah/uploads/2011/11/DunStor.htm#Too-qua-stee.

12. McLoughlin, *After the Trail*, 241.

13. Reed, "Postremoval Factionalism," 161.

14. Though specifically focused on the United States, Gilpin Faust argues that the scale and location of war-related deaths from battle as well as disease and infections transformed how all people understood, related to, ritualized, and managed death. Faust, *Republic of Suffering*.

15. McLoughlin, *After the Trail*, 207; Abel, *American Indian in the Civil War*, 328–29.

16. Franks, *Stand Watie*, 137.

17. Gaines, *Confederate Cherokees*, 124.

18. J. Harlan to E. Sells, 1 October 1865, *ARCIA* (1865), 468–70. Mary Nevins, interview by Breeland Adams, 22 February 1937, 66:352–53 and "Research of Elizabeth Ross," 108:333–36, both in IPP.

19. McLoughlin, citing Harlan, records the elderly and children suffering from dehydration, dysentery, and malnutrition. Pneumonia, smallpox, and malaria also took their toll. McLoughlin, *After the Trail*, 212–13.

20. Ibid., 219–21.

21. Ibid., 224–25.

22. Miner, *Corporation and the Indian*, 21–22.

23. James Parins acknowledges Boudinot's individual motivations, but also suggests that this railroad would "benefit . . . his own people." I disagree with this conclusion, unless by "his people," he means a few select individuals. This proposal was not made on behalf of Native nations. The name itself, which includes the word "Oklahoma," suggests even more nefarious purposes, given the fact that Oklahoma did not exist as a state or territory. In fact, the Cherokee Nation was actively working against Oklahoma bills. Parins, *Elias Cornelius Boudinot*, 109–14.

24. Treaty with the Cherokee, 1866, Articles 15–16, in Kappler, *Indian Affairs*, 947.

25. Ibid., Article 9, in Kappler, *Indian Affairs*, 944.

26. McLoughlin, *After the Trail*, 251–54.

27. Treaty with the Cherokee, 1835, Article 6, in Kappler, *Indian Affairs*, 442.

28. Although her work centers on the origins of U.S. social policy, Jensen describes the hotly contested debates surrounding short-term versus lifelong pension benefits

for indigent American Revolution veterans. Ultimately, she points out that these measures passed with bipartisan support because citizens demanded them. Jensen, *Patriots*, 40–79.

29. McLoughlin, *After the Trail*, 245–49.

30. McLoughlin, *Champions*, 440; McLoughlin, *After the Trail*, 244–47.

31. Meserve, "Chief Lewis Downing," 315–25.

32. Faust, *Republic of Suffering*, xi–xii.

33. National Home for Disabled Volunteer Soldiers Board of Managers, *Annual Report* (1968), 1–9.

34. Logue, "Union Veterans," 415.

35. Kelly, "Creating a National Home," 4–5. Orphan services were prominent before the Civil War, but their necessity exploded in the post–Civil War period. Zmora cites three Baltimore case studies including the Hebrew Orphan Asylum established in 1872, the Samuel Ready School, a Protestant-run facility opened in 1887, and the Catholic Dolan's Aid Society, founded in 1874. Zmora, *Orphanages Reconsidered*, 20, 26, 32. Dulberger traces trends in New York's State Board of Charities, which were developed in the 1860s. Dulberger, *"Mother Donit for the Best,"* 1–23.

36. Both Skcopol's and Jensen's works make clear that military pensions represented the only significant and ongoing federal social provision offered by the federal government until the New Deal. Skocpol, *Protecting Soldiers and Mothers*; Jensen, *Patriots*.

37. McClintock, "Civil War Pensions," 458.

38. Escott, "'Cry of the Sufferers,'" 228–40.

39. Green, "Protecting Confederate Soldiers," 1079–1104.

40. Foner and Mahoney, *America's Reconstruction*, 93.

41. Levine, "Single Standard," 52–77.

42. "An Act Authorizing the Principal Chief to appoint agents to take the Census of the Orphans," 10 December 1867, *LCN* (1839–67).

43. "Making an appropriation for the Support of the Public Schools for the year 1868," 14 December 1867, *LCN* (1839–67), 186.

44. Scott, *Seeing like a State*, 76–83.

45. *Cherokee Advocate*, 18 November 1876.

46. Freeberg, "Meanings of Blindness," 119–53.

47. "An Act for the Benefit of Persons Herein Named," 25 November 1872, in Cherokee Nation, *Laws and Joint Resolutions 1870–72*, 26.

48. "An Act for the Relief of Big Ellis, a Cripple, of Sequoyah District," 10 December 1867; "An Act for the Benefit of Goo-di-ee, a Cripple, Granting a Pension," 19 October 1866; "An Act Allowing Annual Pension to Charlotte," 18 November 1867; "An Act for the Relief of Cha car lac tah, A Blind Man of the Flint District," 22 November 1867; and "Act for the Benefit of Thomas Burtholph, A Blind Person," 10 December 1867, all in *LCN* (1839–67), 123, 146, 148, 172, 173.

49. "Resolution of Respect to Daniel Backbone," 26 November 1867, *LCN* (1839–67), 151; "An Act to Defray the Funeral Expenses of Wah la ne da," 8 December 1870, in Cherokee Nation, *Laws and Joint Resolutions 1870–72*, 28.

50. Blanket, Native Cherokee, War of 1812 Pension and Bounty Files.

51. William Barnes, War of 1812 Pension and Bounty Files.

52. Ross, *Papers of Chief John Ross*, 1:147–48.

53. The Beaver, a (dis)abled War of 1812 pensioner, died during removal. Beaver, War of 1812 Pension and Bounty Files.

54. Ross, *Papers of Chief John Ross*, 2:348–52.

55. For the impact of these rules on African Americans, see Shaffer, "'I Do Not Suppose,'" 132–47.

56. Stremlau describes this same situation in her work and discusses the challenges it creates for researchers. Stremlau, *Sustaining the Cherokee Family*, 12–13.

57. U.S. Congress. House Committee on Indian Affairs, *Alleged Frauds against Certain Indian Soldiers*, 12–16.

58. Ibid., 33.

59. Hogue and Blanck, "'Benefit of the Doubt,'" 377–99.

60. Shaffer, "'I Do Not Suppose,'" 138.

61. Skocpol, *Protecting Soldiers and Mothers*, 143–48.

62. Ibid., 139–41.

63. Ross, *Petition for the Relief of Certain Soldiers of the Indian Home-Guard*, 1–2.

64. U.S. Congress. House Committee on Indian Affairs, *Alleged Frauds against Certain Indian Soldiers*, 3–4.

65. "Bills and joint resolutions introduced in the United States Senate, first and second sessions, Forty-seventh Congress," 26 July 1882, S. Mis. Doc. 48, 47th Cong., 2nd Sess. (1882), Serial 2083, 101.

66. *Cherokee Advocate*, 14 January 1871.

67. Ibid., 13 September 1873.

68. "Pension claims, including correspondence, affidavits, and legal forms regarding the collection of pensions for veterans, 1878–1894," James R. Hendricks Papers, box H31, folder 16, WHC (hereafter Hendricks Papers).

69. U.S. Congress. House Committee on Indian Affairs, *Alleged Frauds against Certain Indian Soldiers*, 33.

70. Ibid.

71. "Pension claims, including correspondence, affidavits, and legal forms regarding the collection of pensions for veterans, 1878–1894," box H31, folder 16, Hendricks Papers.

72. James Shave Head, Indian Home Guard, Regiment 3, Company A, Case Files of Approved Pension Applications of Widows and Other Dependents of Civil War Veterans, ca. 1861–ca. 1910, RG15, NARA (hereafter Case Files of Approved Pension Applications).

73. Go ne chu squah le, Indian Home Guard, Regiment 2, Company K, Ske No Yah, Indian Home Guard, Regiment, 2, Company K, Indian Home Guard, Regiment 3D, Case Files of Approved Pension Applications.

74. George Downing, Indian Home Guard, Regiment 3, Company D, Case Files of Approved Pension Applications.

75. Big Talker, Indian Home Guard, Regiment 3, Company D, Case Files of Approved Pension Applications.

76. Treaty with the Cherokee, 1835, in Kappler, *Indian Affairs*, 2.

77. Moses Vann, Regiment 3, Company A, Indian Home Guards, Case Files of Approved Pension Applications of Widows and Other Dependents, RG 15, NARA.

78. William Bump, Company A, Regiment 3, Indian Home Guards, Case Files of Approved Pension Applications.

79. Crossing Tadpole, Company C, Regiment 3, Indian Home Guards, Case Files of Approved Pension Applications.

80. Jackson Rail, Company C, Regiment 3, Indian Home Guards, Case Files of Approved Pension Applications.

CHAPTER 4

1. John B. Jones to F. A. Walker, 1 September 1871, *ARCIA* (1872), 616–21.

2. Cahill, *Federal Fathers*, 18–20.

3. Emmet Starr, an early twentieth century genealogist, historian, and doctor included the Duncan Family genealogy in his papers. Duncan Family, box 8, folder 286, Genealogical Materials, 1793–1968, Thomas Lee Ballenger Papers, Newberry Library (hereafter Ballenger Papers). "Constitution of the Cherokee Nation: Formed by a Convention of Delegates at New Echota, July 1827," *LCN* (1852), 118–30.

4. *History of Rev. W. A. Duncan*.

5. McLoughlin, "Cherokees and Methodists," 63.

6. Babcock and Bryce, *History of Methodism*, 185, 343.

7. Ibid., 93.

8. Zmora, *Orphanages Reconsidered*, 9, 15; Hacsi, *Second Home*, 27.

9. Gordon, "Who Deserves Help?," 12–25; Dulberger, *"Mother Donit for the Best,"* 3–4.

10. For example, Pennsylvania authorized the creation of thirty-two facilities from 1864 to 1867. Paul, *Pennsylvania's Soldiers' Orphan Schools*. Another well-known orphanage was the Illinois Soldiers' and Sailors' Children's School, which opened in 1865. Cmiel, *Home of Another Kind*, 11–12.

11. Hacsi, *Second Home*, 4.

12. Ibid., 65–66; Dulberger, *"Mother Donit for the Best,"* 17, 23.

13. "An act authorizing orphan institutes," 23 October 1866, *LCN* (1839–67), 65; John B. Jones to F. A. Walker, 1 September 1871, *ARCIA* (1872), 616–21.

14. Littlefield and Underhill, "Trial of Ezekiel Proctor," 307–22.

15. *Cherokee Advocate*, 4 May 1872 (emphasis in original).

16. "An Act to Build a Jail," 23 November 1873, *Constitution and Laws of the Cherokee Nation*, 279. Hereafter *CLCN* (1875).

17. Strickland, *Fire and the Spirits*; Parins, *Elias Cornelius Boudinot*.

18. "An Act Adopting the New Code of Laws," 19 November 1873, *CLCN* (1875).

19. Ibid.

20. Ibid., 119, 120–21, 128.

21. Ibid., 124–25.

22. Matthew Walton James, interview by Pete W. Cole, 16 July 1937, IPP.

23. Burton, *Indian Territory*, 91.

24. Harring, *Crow Dog's Case*, 88–92; Benedict, *Muskogee and Northeastern Okla-homa*, 185; Alexander Spoehr, "Kinship System," 49; Mihesuah, *Choctaw Crime and Punishment*, 148–51.

25. The *Cherokee Advocate* advertised two public lectures delivered in Tahlequah on the subject of phrenology; students of phrenology argued that those predisposed to violence who witnessed an execution could be encouraged to commit violence rather than be deterred by it. The Semiprivate execution reflected the reform efforts of the era that moved executions from a public arena attended by hundreds, if not thousands in some places, to enclosed prison yards. Masur, *Rites of Execution*, 96, 99, 111, 117–59.

26. "An Act Relating to Executions," *CLCN* (1875), 148.

27. "An Act Authorizing the Board of Trustees of Orphan Asylum to Select Suitable Location, and Report to the Next Session of the National Council," 30 November 1872, *CLCN* (1875), 262–63; "An Act Authorizing the Locating Perma-nently of the Orphan Asylum, and the Home for the Insane, Deaf, Dumb, and Blind of the Cherokee Nation, and for Other Purposes," 29 November 1873, *CLCN* (1875), 263–64; The *Cherokee Advocate* discussed these legal and ethical controver-sies over several years. *Cherokee Advocate*, 20 December 1873; 19 August 1876.

28. McLoughlin, *Champions*, 468–71.

29. Deutsch, *Mentally Ill in America*, 248.

30. *Cherokee Advocate*, 29 November 1873.

31. Hicks, "Diary," 7–8.

32. Ibid., 22.

33. Nevins interview, 66:352–53; and "Research of Elizabeth Ross," 108:333–36, both in IPP.

34. Dary, *Frontier Medicine*, 55–68.

35. "Our history," American Medical Association, http://www.ama-assn.org/ama/pub/about-ama/our-history.page?.

36. In 1849, doctors presented information on a Cherokee treatment for sore eyes made by boiling bark. The following year, phrenologists—practitioners who believed an individual's or the average of a group's skull measurements bore a direct connection to their intellectual abilities—presented findings on the size of Native American skulls collected in the United States compared to those of Peru-vians and Mexicans. Of the 161 total skulls measured for all groups, Cherokee skull size ranked behind those of the Iroquois and the Lenapes, but ahead of that of the Shoshones. Whether the Cherokee Nation was aware of the American Medical

Association's interest in Cherokees and their intellectual capacity when Cherokee citizen Dr. Robert Ross, John Ross's nephew, began attending association meetings in 1855 is unclear. John Ross's second wife hailed from Philadelphia, where the organization was founded, and both Ross and the Cherokee Nation had established a track record of engaging with U.S. reform efforts. Moulton, *John Ross*, 91. Transactions of the American Medical Association, 1849; Transactions of the American Medical Association, 1850; and History of the American Medical Association, from its Organization up to January, 1855, all in Digital Collection of the Historical AMA Archives, http://ama.nmtvault.com/jsp/browse.jsp.

37. Transactions of the American Medical Association, 1856, 903; Transactions of the American Medical Association, 1857, 673; Transactions of the American Medical Association, 1858, 1023; Transactions of the American Medical Association, 1859, 720; Transactions of the American Medical Association, 1860, 926; and Transactions of the American Medical Association, 1864, 414, all in Digital Collection of the Historical AMA Archives, http://ama.nmtvault.com/jsp/browse.jsp.

38. Crockett, "Health Conditions," 33–34.

39. "Article XIV. Permits to Hire Citizens of the United States," *CLCN* (1875), 220–21. "Article XIV. Permits to Hire Citizens of the United States," in Cherokee Nation, *Compiled Laws of the Cherokee Nation*, 272–74.

40. *Cherokee Advocate*, 27 May 1874.

41. Martin and Howard, "Medical Organization," 58–62.

42. "Notice of D. W. Bushyhead," 29 Oct. 1879, Dennis Wolf Bushyhead Papers, box 53 folder 11, WHC (hereafter Bushyhead Papers).

43. S. W. Ross, interview by Elizabeth Ross, 25 October 1937, 78, IPP; Holland, *Cherokee Newspapers*, 368.

44. Benge, *1880 Cherokee Nation Census*.

45. Office of the Asylum Board of Trustees to Honorable Charles Thompson, 13 October 1877, reel 6, frame 684, CNP.

46. "In the Fall of 1885," MS 120, Emma Fleming Papers, Cherokee Heritage Center Archives, Tahlequah, Oklahoma (hereafter Fleming Papers).

47. Roberts, "Cherokee Orphan Asylum," 12.

48. "Whereas much inconvenience and expense," 26 October 1820, *LCN* (1852), 2–3.

49. McLoughlin, *Cherokees and Christianity*, 29–60.

50. Rachel Lane, interview by Nannie Lee Burns, 21 June 1933, IPP.

51. "The Cherokee Orphan Asylum: History of an Old School Now Extinct From Facts Gathered by James R. Carselowey," 102:416–22, IPP.

52. McLoughlin, *Champions* , 470–71.

53. Marcus H. Johnson, Indian Agent to Honorable George W. Manypenny, Commissioner of Indian Affairs, 1 October 1855, *ARCIA* (1856), 346–47.

54. Book Order from Robert D. Patterson & Co., 6 March 1878, reel 7, frame 713, CNP.

55. *Cherokee Advocate*, 6 July 1878.

56. J. T. Adair to Emma Dunbar, 9 October 1885, MS 120, Fleming Papers.

57. Mihesuah, *Cultivating the Rosebuds.*

58. John B. Jones to F. A. Walker, 1 September 1872, *ARCIA* (1872), 616–21.

59. "Payments totaling," 19 December 1876, reel 6, frame 658, CNP.

60. Adair to Dunbar, 9 October 1885.

61. Starr, *History of the Cherokee Indians*, 130, 133, 285, 293.

62. Littlefield and Parins, *Native American Writing*, 14; Robert Lynch, interview by Carl R. Sherwood, 17 November 1937, IPP.

63. Treaty with the Cherokee, 1835, in Kappler, *Indian Affairs*, 442.

64. "An Act to Build a Jail," 23 November 1873, *CLCN* (1875), 270; *Cherokee Advocate*, 4 July 1874; Harry Starr, interview by Breland Adam, 16 March 1837, 87:114–15, IPP.

65. *ARCIA* (1894), 331.

66. Bond for Samuel Sixkiller, 4 December 1875, National Prison and High Sheriff, RG 1, reel 31, frame 2889, CNP.

67. Starr, *History of the Cherokee Indians*, 146.

68. *Cherokee Advocate*, 7 June 1879.

69. Ibid., 25 November 1881.

70. Ibid., 22 August 1877.

71. Ibid., 11 April 1877.

72. "An Act making an appropriation to enable the Prison to become self-supporting," 7 December 1877, in Cherokee Nation, *Laws and Joint Resolutions 1876, 1877, and the Extra Session 1878*, 31–32.

73. *Cherokee Advocate*, 25 March 1876.

74. Ibid., 28 October 1876.

75. Ibid., 8 April 1877.

76. When Cherokee judge James Hendricks [Hendrix] attended court at Fort Smith in May of 1881, 1,017 cases were pending; most involved murder, larceny, and intent to kill. Correspondence, General, 1866–1906, box H30, folder 7, Hendricks Papers.

77. *Cherokee Advocate*, 31 August 1872.

78. McLoughlin, Conser, and McLoughlin, "Cherokee Anomie"; Perdue, *Cherokee Women*, 122–24.

79. Rand, *Kiowa Humanity*, 59, 67, http://site.ebrary.com/lib/alltitles/docDetail.action?docID=10217007.

80. McLoughlin, *After the Trail*, 345.

81. *Cherokee Advocate*, 29 August 1877.

82. On motion of Jesse R. Birds, 2 February 1879, reel 31, frame 2895, CNP.

83. Steen, "Home for the Insane," 404.

84. "An Act in Relation to the Asylum for the Blind, Insane, and Others," *CLCN* (1875), 196.

85. Ibid.

86. "Senate Bill No. 15," microfilm roll 66, Cherokee (Tahlequah)—Insane Asylum records, 1885 January 1–1910 February 16, Cherokee Nation Records, Oklahoma Historical Society (hereafter OHS), Oklahoma City (hereafter CHN 66).

87. Ibid.

88. "To the Honorable Senate and Council," 10 November 1879, B53 F11, Bushy-head Papers.

89. Steen, "Home for the Insane," 406–407.

90. "An Act in Relation to the Asylum for the Blind, Insane, and Others," *CLCN* (1875), 197–99.

91. These states included Massachusetts (1869), California and Virginia (1872), and the District of Columbia (1870). Deutsch, *Mentally Ill in America*, 14.

92. Deutsch, *Mentally Ill in America*, 14.

93. Ibid., 281.

94. "Report of Board of Trustees, 1891," CHN 66.

95. "An Act Providing for a Medical Superintendent for the Male and Female Seminaries, Insane Asylum, and National Prison," Cherokee Nation, *Compiled Laws of the Cherokee Nation*, 326.

96. S. W. Ross, interview by Elizabeth Ross, n.d., IPP.

97. Robert M. French Bond for High Sheriff, n.d., microfilm reel 31, frame 2903; Bond for Charles Starr, n.d., reel 31, frame 2911, both in CNP.

98. $34 for Guard Services of Blue Duck for J. Thompson, 3 March 1881; $74.50 for Guard Services of Sar Sar for J. Thompson, 14 March 1881; Senate Bill No. 8, 30 September 1882, all in microfilm roll 95, Cherokee (Tahlequah) Prison and High Sheriff records, 16 April 1880–20 March 1909, Cherokee Nation Records, OHS (hereafter CHN 95).

99. "An Act Making an Appropriation to defray current and contingent expenses of the Asylum for Insane Blind and Others from 30 September 1888–30 September 1889," CHN 66.

100. Mrs. John E. Duncan interview by James Carselowey, 18 May 1937, 36, IPP.

101. Third Annual Report of Honorable Charles Starr From High Sheriff Charles Starr to the National Council, 30 September 1886, f272–82, CHN 95.

102. Reports of 10 February 1881; 28 February 1881; Flora Hawkins Sewing; 23 April 1887, CHN 95.

103. The act allowing the sheriff to pay for services reads, "He may appoint such cooks, police force, and other assistants as shall be required from time to time." "An Act Relating to the National Prison," chap. 6, article 1, section 7, *Compiled Laws of the Cherokee Nation*, 182; hereafter *CLCN* (1881). Nellie Poorbear, whose husband was a guard, also served as a cook.

CHAPTER 5

1. Catcher Rock, interview by Gus Hummingbird, 12 June 1937, 77:293–301, IPP.

2. Ibid.

3. Mintz, *Huck's Raft*, 148–51.

4. Ibid., 143–44.

5. Denson, *Demanding the Cherokee Nation*, 158–59; Wagner, *Poorhouse*, 39. Here, I borrow the phrase "benevolent repression" from Alexander Pisciotta's book of the same title. Pisciotta examines the introduction and subsequent rise of adult reformatories to respond to the failures of prisons operating under either the Auburn model, which promoted complete silence of prisoners, or the Pennsylvania model, which sought complete prisoner isolation into individual cells with only a window to the outside, to achieve meaningful results. Beginning with the opening of Elmira in New York in 1876 and ending in 1920, Pisciotta uses the conditions at Elmira to compare and contrast the conditions at these institutions and argues that, despite attempts to use benevolent reform to produce civilized Christian men capable of complying with the labor demands of the age, the institutions were "ineffectual and brutal." Pisciotta, *Benevolent Repression*, 1–6.

6. Holt, *Orphan Trains*, 3–4; Mintz, *Huck's Raft*, 160–66.

7. W. A. Duncan to George Butler, 25 September 1856, *ARCIA* (1857), 692.

8. McLoughlin, *Champions*, 470–71; W. A. Duncan to George Butler, 25 September 1856, *ARCIA* (1857), 690–94.

9. John Henry Covel was fluent in both languages. W. A. Duncan understood Cherokee, but he was certainly not fluent. His son John was bilingual.

10. McLoughlin, "Cherokees and Methodists."

11. Mihesuah, *Cultivating the Rosebuds*, 80–84.

12. "The Cherokee at School," MS 120, Fleming Papers.

13. *Cherokee Advocate*, 12 August 1876.

14. "Letter to Grant Foreman Adds to Oklahoma History," *Tulsa World*, 16 December 1934.

15. The *Children's Playground* later changed its name to the *Orphans' News*, and it continued publication under Joseph F. Thompson until at least 1891. "Rare Four Page Leaflet Once Popular in Indian Territory," *Tulsa Daily World*, 18 November 1934.

16. "Rare Four Page Leaflet."

17. Cherokee Orphan Asylum Officers, *To the Men and Women of the Cherokee Nation*, Beinecke Rare Book and Manuscript Library, Yale University, New Haven, Conn. Prucha, *American Indian Policy*, 134.

18. *Orphan Asylum Press*, 7 October 1880, reel 7, frame 744, CNP.

19. *School News*, June 1880, vol. 1 no. 1, Carlisle Barracks, Pennsylvania, Ayer Collection, Newberry Library, Chicago.

20. Ibid., vol. 1., no. 11.

21. *Children's Playground*, 9 June 1881, Special Collections, Northeastern State University, Tahlequah, Oklahoma, 1–3.

22. Mihesuah, *Cultivating the Rosebuds*, 80–83.

23. These were the values endorsed by eastern philanthropists and taught to children at orphanages across the country. Rothman, *Discovery of the Asylum*, 210–14.

24. *Children's Playground*, 9 June 1881.

25. *Children's Playground* article quoted in "Rare Four Page Leaflet."

26. *Children's Playground*, 5 May 1881, MS 154, folder 15, Duncan Collection, Cherokee Heritage Center Archives, Tahlequah, Oklahoma; *Children's Playground*, 9 June 1881.

27. *Children's Playground*, 9 June 1881.

28. *Cherokee Advocate*, 24 August 1872.

29. Walter Adair Duncan, "Nature of the Cherokee Orphan Asylum," *Cherokee Advocate*, 12 August 1876.

30. By the mid-1820s, the number of Methodist converts far exceeded the numbers reported by Moravians and Presbyterians. McLoughlin provided the following numbers of increases in Methodist converts: 283 in 1825, 400 in 1827, and 1,028 in 1830. (In 1830 the Moravians reported 45; the Baptists, 90; and the Presbyterians, 167. McLoughlin, "Cherokees and Methodists," 49.

31. McLoughlin, *Champions*, 63–90.

32. Ibid., 63–93.

33. Ibid.; *Cherokee Advocate*, 23 June 1877, and 27 April 1878.

34. Hudson, *Southeastern Indians*, 365–75.

35. *Cherokee Advocate*, 22 July 1877, and 6 July 1878.

36. "Two Years with the Cherokees," MS 120, Fleming Papers.

37. Intermarried citizen James Paggett, who moved to the Cherokee Nation in 1881, described a seasonal custom of neighbors who butchered a hog and sent "his closest neighbors a mess of meat." James R. Paggett, interview by Wylie Thornton, 24 June 1937, 69:6, IPP.

38. *Indian Chieftain*, 1 June 1899.

39. *Cherokee Advocate*, 16 September 1876.

40. Ibid., 11 March 1876.

41. Ibid., 6 July 1878, 2 April 1886, 27 April 1887, and 7 October 1893.

42. Ibid., 6 July 1878.

43. *History of Rev. W. A. Duncan*.

44. *Annual Board of Education Report 1878*, 11 January 1878, reel 7, frame 715, CNP.

45. *Cherokee Advocate*, 1 March 1876. For a complete description and explanation of the International Fair, see Denson, *Demanding the Cherokee Nation*, 149–71.

46. Timmons, *Science and Technology*, 88–92.

47. Board of Trustees to Honorable Charles Thompson, 13 October 1877, reel 6, frame 684, CNP.

48. Office of the Board of Education to the Honorable D. W. Bushyhead, 6 April 1880, reel 7, frame 742, CNP.

49. Dolan, *Fruitful Legacy*, 4–8, http://babel.hathitrust.org/cgi/pt?id=pur1.327 54081199857;view=1up;seq=4.

50. Supply Expenses 120 days at Orphan Asylum, 31 January 1879, reel 6, frame 704, CNP.

51. Board of Trustees to Honorable Charles Thompson.

52. Estimates of expenditures, 30 September 1878, reel 6, frame 702, CNP.

53. "The Cherokee at School."

54. Mintz, *Huck's Raft*, 135–39.

55. *Children's Playground*, 9 June 1881.

56. *Children's Playground: Orphan Asylum Newsletter*, 5 May 1881.

57. "Two Years with the Cherokees."

58. Mintz, *Huck's Raft*, 148–49.

59. *History of Rev. W. A. Duncan*.

60. Garrett, *Cherokee Orphan Asylum*, 30–31.

61. "Only Baby Born in Old Cherokee Orphanage Still Lives in State," in Cherokee Orphan Asylum Vertical Files, Special Collections, Northeastern State University, Tahlequah, Oklahoma (hereafter Orphan Asylum Vertical Files).

62. *Cherokee Advocate*, 30 September 1876.

63. Ibid., 13 June 1877.

64. Ibid., 27 June 1877.

65. Ibid., 19 September 1877.

66. Ibid., 6 April 1878.

67. Ibid., 1 February 1879.

68. Ibid., 19 September 1874.

69. Ibid., 18 November 1876.

70. Ibid., 27 June 1877.

71. My Dearest Mother, 26 March 1878, Don Franklin Papers, privately owned document, Tahlequah, Oklahoma.

72. *Cherokee Advocate*, 30 November 1883.

73. In 1880, recently widowed Cherokee Narcissa Owen returned to the Nation after a thirty-year absence. Despite the fact that her husband had been a wealthy railroad president, his death left her in debt. To put her younger son through college, she took a position as a music teacher at the Cherokee Female Seminary. Her older son Robert and his wife returned to the Nation with her. In 1881, the Cherokee Orphan Asylum employed them both. Institutions provided a social service to the dependents of patriarchs who failed to meet their obligations of material protection.

74. Garrett, *Cherokee Orphan Asylum*, 27.

75. *Cherokee Advocate*, 20 December 1873, and 14 February 1874.

76. "The Cherokee at School."

77. By the 1840s, a variety of conditions including inadequate funding and surging populations in orphanages and houses of refuge led reformers to turn to reform schools to manage delinquency. Mintz, *Huck's Raft*, 160.

78. "The Cherokee at School."

79. Stremlau, *Sustaining the Cherokee Family*, 77.

80. William P. Ross Collection, box 2, folder 9, Cherokee Nation Papers, WHC.

81. U.S. Congress, Summary of the Cherokee Census, 1880, Table C, *Report of the Committee on Indian Affairs, United States Senate, on the Condition of the Indians in the Indian Territory*, S. Rpt. 1278, 49th Cong., 1st Sess., Serial 2362, 1886, 46 (hereafter *RCIA*).

82. "Tendency of the Times," *Cherokee Advocate*, 4 January 1893.

83. Mihesuah, *Cultivating the Rose Buds*; Mihesuah, "Out of the 'Graves,'" 507–10.

84. "In the Year 1885," Fleming Papers (underlined in original).

85. Gammon, "Black Freedmen," 357–64. For a more thorough discussion of the controversies and inequities surrounding education, citizenship, and per capita payments, see May, *African Americans and Native Americans*; and Naylor, *African Cherokees*.

86. Orphan Asylum annual report to the Board of Trustees, 13 October 1877, RG 1, Education, reel 6, frame 684, CNP.

87. Garrett, *Cherokee Orphan Asylum*, 34–35.

88. *Cherokee Advocate*, 15 July 1876.

89. Ibid., 5 February 1886.

90. Ibid., 5 January 1878.

91. Ibid., 15 June 1878.

92. October 1882 Purchases, CHN 95.

93. "An Act Relating to the National Prison," *CLCN* (1875), 150–55.

94. *Cherokee Advocate*, 24 June 1876.

95. October 1882 Purchases, CHN 95; "An Act Relating to the National Prison," in *Compiled Laws of the Cherokee Nation* (1881), 180–92.

96. *Cherokee Advocate*, 5 October 1878.

97. Ibid., 4 April 1884, and 30 May 1884. October 1882 Purchases, CHN 95. "Second Annual Report of the High Sheriff," *Cherokee Advocate*, 30 September 1893. "Annual Report of George Roach," *Cherokee Advocate*, 3 September 1895.

98. Strickland, *Fire and the Spirits*, 36.

99. Wahrhaftig, "More than Mere Work."

100. *Cherokee Advocate*, 30 May 1884, and 4 April 1884.

101. *Cherokee Advocate*, 21 December 1883.

102. "An Act Relating to the National Prison," 149–59.

103. *Cherokee Advocate*, 19 January 1878.

104. "An Act Relating to the National Prison," 220.

105. On motion of Jesse R. Birds.

106. "Rules of the National Prison," *Cherokee Advocate*, 26 September 1888.

107. *Cherokee Advocate*, 26 September 1888.

108. Ibid.; Letters Sent and Received and Other Documents, 10 September 1881, CHN 95.

109. Receipt for Monies Received Charles Starr to Charley Poorbear, 5 December 1886, CHN 95.

110. National Prison, Tahlequah, 5 December 1886, CHN 95.

111. "An Act Relating to the National Prison," 154; Letters Sent and Received and other Documents, 10 September 1881, CHN 95.

112. In his article, Saunt discusses how each of the Five Tribes grappled with race in similar and dissimilar ways during Reconstruction. Saunt, "Paradox of Freedom," 63–94.

113. *Cherokee Advocate*, 8 July 1876.

114. Ibid., 28 October 1876.

115. Ibid., 12 October 1887.

116. Ibid., 26 February 1879.

117. Littlefield, *Cherokee Freedmen*, 65.

118. *Cherokee Advocate*, 18 April 1877.

119. Ibid., 26 September 1888.

120. *CLCN* (1875), 220.

121. McLoughlin, *After the Trail*, 294–95.

122. Mancini, *One Dies, Get Another*, 15.

123. Ibid., 92.

124. Ibid., 85.

125. *Cherokee Advocate*, 20 March 1874.

126. McKelvey, *American Prisons*, 209.

127. *Cherokee Advocate*, 30 May 1884.

128. Shirley, *Law West*, 41.

129. *Cherokee Advocate*, 11 April 1877.

130. Estimate of Supplies for the use of the national Prison for the fiscal year ending 30th September 1883, CHN 95.

131. *Cherokee Advocate*, 9 March 1878.

132. Ibid., 19 February 1879.

133. Ibid., 21 July 1882, and 15 September 1882.

134. Ibid., 17 July 1885.

135. Ibid., 4 April 1888.

136. The incarceration of women was rare. In 1878, the Saline District sentenced a woman to a year in prison for the crime of larceny. The *Advocate* commented, "It looks bad to see a woman go to jail, but the law knows no distinction." *Cherokee Advocate*, 16 March 1878. Legislation later made distinctions, specifying that the prison provide separate cells for men and women. This move followed a larger trend in prison reform, but this had probably already occurred in the few occasions it was necessary. "Act Relating to the National Prison," *Constitutions and Laws of the Cherokee Nation*, 220.

137. "Escaped from the Cherokee Jail," *New York Times*, 7 March 1886, ProQuest Historical Newspapers, www.proquest.com.

138. *Cherokee Advocate*, 15 December 1877.

139. On motion of Jesse R. Birds; "To all Sheriffs of the Cherokee Nation," *Cherokee Advocate*, 16 January 1888.

140. *Cherokee Advocate*, 4 April 1888.

141. Ibid., 8 April 1893.

142. Ibid., 9 March 1878.

143. Ibid., 16 May 1884.

144. Ibid.

145. Ibid., 4 April 1888.

146. D. H. Williams $10 for Returning Escaped Convict, 6 June 1882; John Hawkins HS to Johnson Thompson, 13 July 1887, both in CHN 95.

147. For Hunting Escaped Convicts, 15 June 1882, CHN 95.

148. *Cherokee Advocate*, 30 May 1884.

149. Martin, "Nature and Extent," 54.

150. *Cherokee Advocate*, 7 October 1893.

151. Ball, "Cool to the End."

152. Ibid.

153. Walter Bigby, interview by Frank J. Still, 27 January 1937, IPP.

154. *Cherokee Advocate*, 17 October 1877.

155. Ibid.

156. Strickland, *Fire and the Spirits*, 174n33.

157. *Cherokee Advocate*, 16 October 1885.

158. Ibid., 14 September 1887.

159. Mrs. John E. Duncan, interview by James E. Carselowey, 18 May 1937, 26: 217–27, IPP.

160. George W. Mayes, interview by Amelie F. Harris, 21 July 1937, IPP.

161. *Cherokee Advocate*, 7 October 1893.

162. Dunawas Family Papers. Margaret Sixkiller Bagby, Cherokee Oklahoma Federation of Labor Collection, M452, box 5, folder 2, WHC.

163. "An Act in Relation to the Asylum for the Blind, Insane, and Others," chap. 11, *CLCN* (1875), 196–200.

164. *Cherokee Advocate*, 27 June 1877.

165. "Admission of Persons," art. 4, *CLCN* (1881), 287–88.

166. "An Act in Relation to the Asylum for the Blind, Insane, and Others," 200; Steen, "Home for the Insane," 402–406.

167. *Cherokee Advocate*, 11 April 1877.

168. Steen, "Home for the Insane," 402–406.

169. *Cherokee Phoenix*, 11 June 1828.

170. *Cherokee Advocate*, 22 June 1887.

171. Best, *Blind*, 323.

172. Steen, "Home for the Insane," 406.

173. "Expense Report 1878," reel 18, frame 1434, CNP.

174. *Cherokee Advocate*, 6 January 1882.

175. In 1817, the first permanent school for the deaf in the United States opened in Hartford, Connecticut. By the 1860s, the educated deaf provided a sizable number of the teachers for schools for the deaf. Brill, *Education of the Deaf*, 93–98.

176. U.S. Bureau of Education, *Report of the Commissioner of Education for the Year Ended June 30, 1912*.

177. Freeberg, "Meanings of Blindness," 134–35.

178. Calloway, *Indian History of an American Institution*, 108.

179. *Cherokee Advocate*, 9 March 1887.

180. Ibid., 27 March 1897. Although there are no records of Cherokee suicide rates historically, the act had a historical precedent. Eighteenth-century priests committed mass suicide when their efforts to combat epidemic disease failed. Priests may have believed their failures and therefore their lives would put the world back into balance. Adair, *Adair's History of the American Indians*.

181. *Cherokee Advocate*, 24 August 1881, 2 December 1881, and 28 March 1894.

182. Employee Pay, 1897, reel 18, frame 1499, CNP; Employee Pay, 1898, RG 1, subgroup 12, reel 18, frame 1501, CNP.

183. Perdue, *Cherokee Women*, 37–39.

184. *Cherokee Advocate*, 13 June 1877.

185. Mary Clark, interview by Frank Still, n.d., vol. 18, IPP; "Biography of Benjamin Franklin Stone," by Wylie Thornton, 1937, 90:505, IPP.

186. Nielsen, *Disability History*, 134.

187. Officers of the New York State Lunatic Asylum, eds. *Journal of Insanity* 1 (Utica: Bennett, Backus, and Hawley, 1844–45), 285–89.

188. Dain, *Concepts of Insanity*, 79.

189. Ibid., 58, 84.

190. Deutsch, *Mentally Ill in America*, 88–92, 95, 276.

191. *Cherokee Advocate*, 8 February 1884.

192. Ibid.

193. Kelly Brown, "Isabel Cobb," *Encyclopedia of Oklahoma History and Culture*, http://digital.library.okstate.edu/ENCYCLOPEDIA/entries/C/C0009.html.

194. Dary, *Frontier Medicine*, 229–31, 243.

195. Susan LaFlesche, a member of the Omaha Tribe, studied with Cobb at Women's Medical College. Due to an illness, LaFlesche graduated before Cobb and became the first Native American woman to receive an MD in the United States. "Cherokee Schools, copied from a manuscript loaned by Dr. Isabelle Cobb of Wagner," 104, IPP.

196. Mihesuah, *Cultivating the Rosebuds*, 90–91.

197. Ibid.

198. Dary, *Frontier Medicine*, 234–36; Brown, "Isabel Cobb."

199. Hudson, *Southeastern Indians*, 320–21.

200. Perdue, *Cherokee Women*, 29–30.

201. John P. Ragsdale, interview by Wylie Thornton, 24 June 1937, 74:116–29, IPP.

202. *Cherokee Advocate*, 16 October 1889, 27 November 1889, and 15 October 1890. "1890 Trustees Report," CHN 66.

203. "15 Nov 1888, Minerva Thomas Examined by the Committee," CHN 66.

204. "To Hon. Charles Thompson," July 1877, RG 1, subgroup 12, reel 18, frame 1428, CNP.

205. Kneeland and Warren, *Pushbutton Psychiatry*, xix.

206. "The Indian Territory Medical Association," Indian Territory Medical Association Collection, M310, I2, folder 3, WHC (hereafter ITMA Collection).

207. Deutsch, *Mentally Ill in America*, 215, 218–21.

208. Officer Boards Trustees of Asylum for Insane, Blind, & Others of the Cherokee Nation, 1 October 1885, CHN 66.

209. Ibid.

210. Rothman, *Discovery of the Asylum*.

211. *Cherokee Advocate*, 13 June 1877.

212. Ibid., 9 December 1881.

213. Ibid., 15 June 1887.

214. Quarterly Report Asylum for the Insane & Others Ending 30 September 1887; Officer Boards Trustees of Asylum for Insane, Blind, & Others of the Cherokee Nation, 1 October 1885, both in CHN 66.

215. Officer, Boards, Trustees of Asylum for Insane, Blind, & Others of the Cherokee Nation, 1 October 1885, CHN 66.

216. "Annual Report of the Blind and Insane Asylum for 1886," CHN 66.

217. Sallie Manus, 6365, RG 75, M1301, roll 0221, Applications for Enrollment of the Commission to the Five Civilized Tribes, 1898–1914, NARA (hereafter Applications for Enrollment to the Five Tribes).

218. *Cherokee Advocate*, 9 June 1882.

219. Quarterly Report Asylum for the Insane & Others Ending 30 September 1887, CHN 66.

220. Ibid.

221. *Cherokee Advocate*, 24 February 1882; "1890 Trustees Report," CHN 006.

222. *Cherokee Advocate*, November 1877. Insane Asylum, 1730–1968, bulk 1835–1968, Ballenger Papers.

223. "Annual Report, Office of the Medical Superintendent," 7 October 1884, CHN 66.

224. *Cherokee Advocate*, 13 February 1897.

225. By the late nineteenth century, doctors recognized two classes of epileptics, the "quiet and peaceable" and the "noisy and violent." Godding, "Recognition of Classes of the Insane."

226. "Annual Report, Office of the Medical Superintendent," 7 October 1884.

227. *Cherokee Advocate*, 9 February 1878.

228. McCandless, "A Female Malady?," 543–71.

229. Joe J. Rogers, an intermarried white who shared Jim Connally's story, witnessed the lights in the sky on the property. James J. Carselowey, the Indian Pioneer Papers fieldworker who interviewed Rogers, had "also seen the ball of fire in the sky" as late as 1937. Today, the lights are referred to as the Tri-State Spooklights, and every weekend people gather on a stretch of dirt roads in Ottawa County, Oklahoma, for a chance to see them. Joe J. Rogers, interview by James J. Carselowey, 11 August, 1937, 77:382–90, IPP.

230. Stella Evelyn Carselowey (Crouch), interview by James R. Carselowey, 20–21 June 1838, 22:128–57, IPP.

231. Rogers interview.

232. "Annual Report, Office of the Medical Superintendent," 7 October 1884.

233. *Cherokee Advocate*, 24 October 1877, and 26 September 1888.

234. "Annual Report of the Board of Trustees for Blind and Insane Asylum for years 1886 and 1887," CHN 66.

235. Report of the Trustees of the Insane Asylum Board, and Message to the National Council from Principal Chief Charles Thompson regarding Transmittal

of the Trustees' Report, 29 November 1878, "To Honorable C. Thompson," 31 September 1878, RG 1, subgroup 12, reel 18, frame 1437, CNP.

236. *Cherokee Advocate*, 25 November 1893, and 9 December 1893.

237. Ibid., 28 September 1887.

238. Paggett interview.

239. Mooney, *Myths of the Cherokee*, 401–403.

240. "1890 Trustees Report," "Report of Board of Trustees 1891," and "Annual Report of the Trustees of the Asylum for the Blind," 30 September 1894, all in CHN 66.

241. Steen, "Home for the Insane," 406.

242. Richards, *Oklahoma Red Book*, 198–99.

243. The Cherokee Nation appropriated funds to Rowland's facility because some of its citizens were attending school there. W. C. Rogers Collection, roll 34, folder 60, WHC (hereafter Rogers Collection).

CHAPTER 6

1. Pratt *Battlefield and Classroom* , 190–92, 215–20.

2. Ibid., x–xiii, 1–4; Foreman, "Reverend Stephen Foreman," 239.

3. Davis, "Education of the Chickasaws," 415.

4. Pratt, *Battlefield and Classroom*, 4–5, 40–103.

5. Ibid., 4–5.

6. Adams, *Education for Extinction*, 36–38; Lookingbill, *War Dance at Fort Marion*, 38–40; Pratt, *Battlefield and Classroom*, 109–12.

7. Pratt, *Battlefield and Classroom*, 118–20.

8. *Cherokee Advocate*, 30 May 1884.

9. Official Report of the Nineteenth Annual Conference of Charities and Correction (1892), 46–59, reprinted in Pratt, "Advantages of Mingling Indians with Whites," 260–71. Merrell Gates uses the rhetoric of "saving" Indians from themselves throughout his writings much earlier. For example, see Gates, "Land and Law," 49.

10. *Cherokee Advocate*, 16 December 1881.

11. Rose Stremlau describes the debates as an attempt by Cherokee leaders to "uplift Americans by nurturing them in the superior Cherokee culture." Stremlau, *Sustaining the Cherokee Family*, 69–104.

12. "Hypocritical Friendship for the Indians," *Cherokee Advocate*, 20 January 1882.

13. Ibid., 9 February, 1880, and 31 August 1881.

14. The *Cherokee Advocate* reprinted the piece on 6 January 1882.

15. Treaty with the Cherokee, 1835, Article 2; and Treaty with the Cherokee, 1846, Article 1, both in Kappler, *Indian Affairs*.

16. *Cherokee Advocate*, 3 March 1880.

17. McLoughlin, *After the Trail*, 67, 340.

18. Parins, *Elias Cornelius Boudinot*, 1–2, 120–30, 183–84.

19. Harmon, "Indians and Land Monopolies," 109.

20. "Law in the Territory," *Cherokee Advocate*, 6 June 1884; "Indian Problem," *Cherokee Advocate*, 16 October 1885.

21. Pratt, *Battlefield and Classroom*, 181–82.

22. Cahill, *Federal Fathers*, 28–30.

23. *Cherokee Advocate*, 16 October 1895. For a description of the Kansas Potawatomis' experiences with allotment during the period referenced by Ross, see Mosteller, "Place, Politics, and Property. Mosteller details the experiences of the Citizen Potawatomis, who accepted allotments in Kansas and U.S. citizenship through an 1861 treaty. As "citizens," they could not vote or testify in courts. Within ten years, most no longer held title to their lands. Mosteller, "Place, Politics, and Property," iv–v.

24. Harmon, *Rich Indians*, 133–69.

25. *Cherokee Advocate*, 16 October 1895.

26. Chief Bushyhead visited the president to seek a pardon for William Thompson, who was incarcerated in Detroit. *Cherokee Advocate*, 11 December 1885.

27. Burton, *Indian Territory*, 46–66.

28. *Cherokee Advocate*, 19 October 1878.

29. Benge, *1880 Cherokee Nation Census*; *Cherokee Advocate*, 15 December 1882.

30. Dawes, *United States Prison*.

31. *Cherokee Advocate*, 19 October 1878.

32. Ibid., 14 September 1887.

33. *Morning Republican*, 19 January 1871, 26 March 1873, 23 April 1873, 27 May 1873, 29 May 1873, 1 August 1873, 16 August 1873, and 26 August 1873. Mancini, *One Dies, Get Another*, 117–20.

34. Mancini, *One Dies, Get Another*, 120–23.

35. *Cherokee Advocate*, 26 February 1886, and 15 June 1887.

36. Ibid., 4 December 1889.

37. Nasaw, *Schooled to Order*, 53–66.

38. In 1860, after years of some U.S. reformers advocating the use of seminaries to train common schoolteachers based on the methods of the Prussians, only twelve states had adopted the system. Nasaw, *Schooled to Order*, 62. The Cherokee Nation opened its male and female seminaries in order to train teachers in 1851. Mihesuah, *Cultivating the Rosebuds*, 18–29.

39. Hill, *Weaving New Worlds*, 201.

40. "Progress of the Indian Tribes," 3 May 1878, *New York Times*, 8.

41. Ibid.

42. "Illiteracy in Connecticut," *Cherokee Advocate*, 13 February 1895.

43. Many of the topics reflected larger areas of interest throughout the Nation, but the best pedagogical practices related to Cherokee bilingual education were particular to the Cherokee Nation. Titles of institute offerings included "For the Good of the State, The School is Better than the Legislature," "The Relative Importance of Branches Taught in the Schools," "Responsibility of the Teacher," "Elocution,"

"The Best Method for Teaching Cherokee Children the English Language," and "The Best Method for Teaching Small Children Numbers." *Cherokee Advocate*, 23 May 1884, 8 June 1883, 4 July 1884, and 3 July 1885.

44. *Cherokee Advocate*, 23 May 1884, 8 June 1883, 4 July 1884, and 3 July 1885.

45. Ibid., 23 May 1884.

46. Ibid., 23 May 1884, and 30 May 1884.

47. Ibid., 1 August 1881.

48. Ibid., 14 March 1884.

49. Williams, "Among the Cherokees," 195; Foster, "Among the Cherokees," 231.

50. Lewis, *Creating Christian Indians*, xiii.

51. *Cherokee Advocate*, 16 May 1884, and 26 September 1884.

52. Ibid., 25 June 1890.

53. Ibid., 5 February 1886.

54. "The Wonder of Wonders," *Cherokee Advocate*, 1 May 1885.

55. *Cherokee Advocate*, 13 April 1881.

56. Ibid., 5 May 1882.

57. The Chinese Exclusion Act was signed into law on 6 May 1882.

58. "To Check Immigration," reprinted in *Cherokee Advocate*, 30 January 1889.

59. *Saint Louis Globe Democrat* article reprinted in *Cherokee Advocate*, 17 July 1889.

60. *Cherokee Advocate*, 21 December 1892.

61. Ibid., 5 October 1892.

62. D. W. Bushyhead, "A Defense of the Cherokee Indians," originally printed in the *Fort Smith Western Independent*, reprinted in the *Cherokee Advocate*, 7 April 1881.

63. "The Reaves Letter Again," *Cherokee Advocate*, 26 January 1883.

64. The push was ultimately successful. Catherine Adams points out that scholars have failed to acknowledge the scope of black migration to the Indian and Oklahoma Territories before statehood; 100,000 migrants went there before statehood. This resulted in thirty all-black towns. Adams notes that these numbers are significantly higher than the Exodusters who migrated to Kansas, but are far less studied. Adams, "Africanizing the Territory." *Western Recorder*, 5 April 1883, and 4 July 1884.

65. *Western Recorder*, 5 April 1883, and 4 July 1884.

66. To Hon. D. W. Bushyhead, 23 January 1880, microfilm roll 90, Cherokee (Tahlequah)—Pardons, 1877 September 23–1901 November 30, Cherokee Nation Records (hereafter CHN 90).

67. Ben Marshall, a mixed-descent Creek slaveholder, founded Marshalltown in the Coweta District of the Creek Nation in Indian Territory on the Cherokee Nation's border. He served as the interpreter at the 1843 convention. After the Civil War, Marshalltown remained an African Creek town. Jeff Marshall listed himself as the former slave of Lafayette Marshall, Ben Marshall's cousin. Tensions between Cherokee cattle herders and African Creeks increased when Cherokee citizens' cattle wandered across the line and were slaughtered for food. Cherokee Nation vigilantes armed themselves and attacked Creek lighthorsemen, killing a

number of African Creeks. Chang, *Color of the Land*, 29; Jeff Marshall, Creek Freedmen, Creek, Enrollment Cards, Enrollment Cards of the Five Civilized Tribes, 1898–1914, Records of the Bureau of Indian Affairs, roll 0086, M1186, RG 75, National Archives, Fort Worth, Tex.

68. 23 January 1880, to Honorable DW Bushyhead, CHN 90. This exchange was possible as a result of the compact negotiated between the Creeks, Osages, and Cherokees in 1843 that subjected Creek and Osage citizens "to the same treatment as if they were a citizen of [the Cherokee] Nation" if they committed serious crimes within the Cherokee Nation. "Compact Between the Several Tribes of Indians," 2 November 1843, *LCN* (1852), 87–89.

69. William Cobb, brother of Belle Cobb, first female doctor in Indian Territory, relocated to Indian Territory from Tennessee in the early 1870s. "Cherokee Schools, Copied from a Manuscript Loaned by Dr. Isabelle Cobb of Wagoner," vol. 104, IPP; Zellar, *African Creeks*, 132.

70. Zellar, *African Creeks*, 120–40.

71. 10 November 1881, CHN 90.

72. There is no record of a Sarah Marshall on the Cherokee, Cherokee Freedmen, Creek, or Creek Freedmen rolls. However, Jeff Marshall's Dawes card lists Sarah Marshall as his mother, though at the time of his enrollment in 1898 Sarah Marshall was no longer living. If she was his mother, it raises a number of interesting questions about her employ at the prison. Was she paid for her silence? Were they both living at the prison in order to keep them protected from reprisals from Cherokee people? How did prisoners interpret the daily presence of an African Creek prisoner's mother? What did it mean to the other prisoners and Jeff Marshall that his mother, Sarah Marshall, prepared the meals for all of them? Unnamed materials, 23 December 1881, CHN 95; Campbell, *Campbell's Abstract of Creek Freedman*, 56.

73. Cimballa and Miller, *Freedmen's Bureau*, xviii–xx.

74. Finley, "Personnel of the Freedmen's Bureau," 94–100.

75. Ibid.," 100.

76. Cecil Harper, Jr., "Freedmen's Bureau," *Handbook of Texas Online*, Texas State Historical Association, http://www.tshaonline.org/handbook/online/articles/ncf01.

77. Littlefield, *Cherokee Freedmen*, 55–57, 94.

78. Ibid.

79. Zellar, *African Creeks*, 32–33.

80. Ibid., 101–103.

81. "State of Missouri Executive Department City of Jefferson," 27 July 1893, CHN 66.

82. W. D. McBride, Proprietor of McBride Hotel, Ft. Gibson, IT, to PC Sam Mayes, 12 October 1897, CHN 66.

83. Stremlau, *Sustaining the Cherokee Family*, 90.

84. Otis, *Dawes Act*, 5–6.

85. Treaty with the Cherokee, 1866, Article 20, in Kappler, *Indian Affairs*, 948.

86. Otis, *Dawes Act*.

87. Stremlau, "'To Domesticate and Civilize.'"

88. Gates, "Land and Law," 52–54.

89. Schurz, "Present Aspects."

90. Painter, "Indian and His Property," 121.

91. *Cherokee Advocate*, 12 October 1892.

92. Richardson, *Death of Reconstruction*, 33.

93. Bremner, *Discovery of Poverty*, 58.

94. Richardson, *Death of Reconstruction*, 35–40.

95. Holt, *Orphan Trains*, 3–7.

96. Cimballa and Miller, *Freedmen's Bureau*.

97. Gates, "Land and Law."

98. "The Irrepressible Payne," *Cherokee Advocate*, 2 June 1882; "Advice to Payne's Followers," *Cherokee Advocate*, 16 February 1883.

99. Dale and Wardell, *History of Oklahoma*, 244. This area is referred to as the unassigned lands on the map.

100. Ibid., 10.

101. Dianna Everett, "Organic Act (1890)," *Encyclopedia of Oklahoma History and Culture*, http://www.okhistory.org/publications/enc/entry.php?entry=OR004; Balyeat, "Segregation in Public Schools."

102. *Cherokee Advocate*, 9 March 1893, and 12 March 1886. The Choctaw Nation required a certificate of diploma from its Board of Medical Examiners. Although the Creek Nation was listed as having no law in 1893, by 1894 it required a twenty-five-dollar annual licensing fee. "Resume of Medical Practice Acts in the Different States and Territories," *Medical and Surgical Reporter*, 21 January 1893; "Legal Requirements for the Practice of Medicine in the United States," *Medical and Surgical Reporter*, 17 March 1894.

103. "Resume of Medical Practice Acts"; "Legal Requirements for the Practice of Medicine"; *Cherokee Advocate*, 8 July 1891, 10 December 1890, 20 February 1892, 17 August 1892, 24 August 1892, 14 September 1892, and 22 April 1893.

104. Dianna Everett, "Medical Education," *Encyclopedia of Oklahoma History and Culture*, http://www.okhistory.org/publications/enc/entry.php?entry=ME004.

105. Stremlau, "'To Domesticate and Civilize,'" 265.

CHAPTER 7

1. Wardell, *Political History*, 312–20.

2. Genetin-Pilawa makes clear in his work that this was Ely Parker's intention when he served as an architect for the Peace Policy that ended the practice of treaty making with tribes. Genetin-Pilawa, *Crooked Paths*, 73–112.

3. *Hartford Courant* quoted in "Uncle Sam's Word and His Wards," *Cherokee Advocate*, 6 June 1894.

4. "Wolves in Sheep's Clothing," *Cherokee Advocate*, 24 February 1892.

5. Wardell, *Political History*, 312–20.

6. *Cherokee Advocate*, 31 August 1881.

7. Ibid., 24 August 1872.

8. Harmon, "American Indians and Land Monopolies," 115–22.

9. *Cherokee Advocate*, 9 December 1881.

10. Ibid., 8 May 1895.

11. Christopher Columbus Robards, roll 0214, Applications for Enrollment to the Five Tribes.

12. Littlefield, *Native American Writing*, 14–15.

13. *Cherokee Advocate*, 3 August 1892, 19 October 1892, and 9 October 1892.

14. Ibid., 3 September 1893.

15. Ibid., 27 July 1892, and 12 October 1892.

16. David Chang reaches a similar conclusion. Despite real racial divides in the Creek Nation, he points out the possibilities of "interracial nationhood" inherent in "indigenous soil." Chang, *Color of the Land*, 39–69.

17. *Cherokee Advocate*, 21 September 1892.

18. Ibid., 21 March 1894.

19. Ibid., 26 Wednesday 1892.

20. Ibid., 9 September 1897.

21. Petition for Pardon of James Peacock Confined in the National Prison, 6 March 1895, CHN 90.

22. From 1860 to 1900, the president granted 49 percent of the applications for pardon, but as the 1896 number indicates, it was much higher in that single year than over the previous forty-year average. Moore, *Pardons*, 49–54.

23. Philosophers Immanuel Kant, Jeremy Bentham, and G. W. F. Hegel all opposed the use of an executive pardon yet also provided exceptions to that position. Writing in the eighteenth century, Kant believed that a pardon was unnecessary in a properly functioning democratic system dedicated to liberty and equality for all. He did, however, accept that liberty and equality were not always achieved. He suggested that in order to correct an injustice, a ruling body or leader could use a pardon. Bentham, who wrote from the late eighteenth century through the early nineteenth century, laid out four conditions that might make a pardon necessary. He predicated three of these conditions on social service concerns, including (1) when punishment would not effectively deter crime (especially when it applied to infants, the insane, the intoxicated, and the incapacitated), (2) when it was groundless, the wrong could be repaired, or the wrong committed was for a greater good— for instance stealing bandages for someone's wound—and (3) when it was needless because education could correct the behavior. In most instances, education and social services could more effectively manage or deter the crime. The fourth condition included issuing pardons for amnesty during war. In this instance, punishment potentially created more harm than good. Hegel, Bentham's contemporary, defended his opposition to pardons based on the idea that criminals have a "right" to be punished; "punishing people implicitly acknowledge[d] them to be persons, moral agents making free choices." Moore, *Pardons*, 21–47.

24. John Phillip Reid makes this argument based on Cherokee legal codes of the eighteenth century. However, his work is not concerned with how Cherokees adapted their understandings of those codes within a national context. Reid, *Law of Blood*.

25. The high sheriff reported six pardons in 1888 and seven pardons and two commutations in 1894. *Cherokee Advocate*, 21 November 1888, and 13 November 1894.

26. Reid, *Law of Blood*, 86.

27. The treaty reads, "Amnesty is hereby declared by the United States and the Cherokee Nation for all crimes and misdemeanors committed by one Cherokee on the person or property of another Cherokee, or of a citizen of the United States . . . and no right of action arising out of wrongs committed in aid or in the suppression of the rebellion shall be prosecuted or maintained in the courts of the United States or in the courts of the Cherokee Nation." Treaty with the Cherokee, 1846, Article 2, in Kappler, *Indian Affairs*, 562.

28. Treaty with the Cherokee, 1866, Article 2, in Kappler, *Indian Affairs*, 942–43.

29. "Duties of the Principal Chief," *CLCN* (1875), 41.

30. It was not uncommon for sheriffs, judges, solicitors, jurors, and clerks to attach their names to these appeals. Honorable Dennis W. Bushyhead, 24 November 1879; To Honorable Chief of the Cherokee Nation 1881; To Honorable C. J. Harris, 15 October 1892, CHN 90.

31. *Cherokee Advocate*, 7 October 1893.

32. Ibid., 6 April 1878; Pardon of John Still, Oochalata Collection, box 021, folder 9.

33. "An Act Relating to the Judiciary," *CLCN* (1881), 96.

34. Pardon of John Still.

35. Letter from the Office of Boudinot, Jackson, and Morgan, 5 August 1882, CHN 90.

36. Petition for the Pardon of William Grapes [n.d.], CHN 90.

37. Office of the Steward to Hon. CJ Harris, 30 September 1893, CHN 66.

38. From Dew M. Wisdom, U.S. Indian Agent, to Hon. CJ Harris, 7 August 1893, CHN 66.

39. "Annual Report, Office of the Medical Superintendent," 7 October 1894, CHN 66.

40. Office of the Steward to Hon. CJ Harris, 30 September 1893, CHN 66. For a better understanding of the problems of intruders, see Sober, *Intruders*, 36–37.

41. For citizens, much of the debate centered on the rights of Delawares, Shawnees, and Freedmen to a share of the $300,000 payment for lands west of the Arkansas River. In 1883, the council voted to distribute the revenue from the sale of lands to "Cherokees by blood" only. Freedmen organized a protest to Congress. The Cherokee Nation argued that if these citizens contested their exclusion from the payment, their "lawful remedy" was "under the constitution of his own country" rather than through the federal government. The Cherokee Nation resented "citizens" who appealed to the federal authorities for redress that served to undermine the

Cherokee Nation's sovereignty. *Cherokee Advocate*, 27 June 1884. For an expanded discussion of the freedmen's appeal, see Littlefield, *Cherokee Freedmen*, 119–41.

42. Stremlau, "In Defense."

43. "To the Honorable Senate and Council in General Council Convened," 31 October 1874, reel 6, frame 635, CNP.

44. McLoughlin, *After the Trail*, 340–41.

45. Littlefield, *Cherokee Freedmen*, 55–56.

46. Investigation of condition of Indians in Indian Territory, *RCIA*, 38–39.

47. Littlefield, *Cherokee Freedmen*, 57–58.

48. *Cherokee Advocate*, 10 June 1893.

49. *Tahlequah Arrow*, 21 May 1898.

50. Carp, *Adoption in America*, 4–5.

51. *Cherokee Advocate*, 17 July 1885.

52. Ibid., 5 March 1886.

53. Pisciotta, *Benevolent Repression*, 81–103.

54. Mihesuah, *Cultivating the Rosebuds*, 82.

55. "The Early Life of Moses Welch," by Wylie Thornton, 13 August 1937, 96: 216–228, IPP.

56. John F. Parris, interview by Frank J. Still, 1937, 69:331–339, IPP.

57. In "Reading History: Cherokee History through a Cherokee Lens," Tom Belt and Heidi Altman use Cherokee linguistics to understand how Cherokee speakers interpreted key historical events. In the second half of the article, they focus on rescuing Cherokees Zeke Proctor and Ned Christie from negative portrayals by non-Cherokee speakers and positioning them as "catalysts for change" that helped late nineteenth-century Cherokees make choices to bring their world back into balance. I agree that they served this purpose, but "galvanizing Cherokee communities around the jurisdictional issues" was part of a larger process at work in the post–Civil War Cherokee Nation. As Cherokees had before, they asked themselves how to best fulfill their obligations to care for one another. Altman and Belt, "Reading History," 94–97.

58. *Cherokee Advocate*, 14 September 1887.

59. Ibid.

60. *Cherokee Advocate*, 4 January 1884, 22 February 1884, and 22 August 1896.

61. Ibid., 22 February 1884.

62. Ibid., 22 August 1896, and 29 August 1896.

63. Randolph Hummingbird, 7420, roll 0227, Applications for Enrollment to the Five Tribes.

64. *Cherokee Advocate*, 26 September 1888, Rules of the National Prison.

65. Ibid., 27 April 1878.

66. Ibid., 12 February 1886.

67. Deutsch, *Mentally Ill in America*, 85, 92–96.

68. "To Honorable C. Thompson," 31 September 1878, RG 1, subgroup 12, reel 18, frame 1437, CNP.

69. *Cherokee Advocate*, 22 April 1891.

70. Lamana S. Abraham, "A Chapter From Our Family History," Dunawas Family Papers, 4.

71. This was not the first time medical practitioners sought to use the bodies of executed Indians as a sacrifice in the name of "civilization" and medical science. In 1862, after Lincoln ordered the executions by hanging of thirty-eight Dakota men who attacked white settlers in Minnesota, their bodies were used as cadavers. This stands as the largest mass execution in the United States. Clapesattle, *Doctors Mayo*, 77–78.

72. *Cherokee Advocate*, 13 November 1895.

73. Ibid., 27 March 1895, 10 April 1895, 17 April 1895, 8 May 1895, and 29 May 1895.

74. The *Tahlequah Telephone* reprinted Duncan's testimony on 25 January 1895.

75. "Argument Made By Judge McKennon Before The Committee On Indian Affairs Of The House Of Representatives, Relative To Condition Of Affairs In The Indian Territory, Together With Other Papers, And Senate Document No. 12, Report Of The Commission Appointed To Negotiate With The Five Civilized Tribes Of Indians, Known As The Dawes Commission," 24 March 1896, 54th Congress, 1st Sess., Doc. 182.

76. *Cherokee Advocate*, 24 April 1885.

77. *Indian Chieftain*, 24 June 1897.

78. Rose Stremlau describes the allotment process and its impact on Cherokees in her book. In particular she focuses on how individual families, particularly adherents of a traditional social welfare system, navigated a degrading and economically exploitative process. Her work also provides a useful summary of the political negotiations specific to the Cherokee Nation. Stremlau, *Sustaining the Cherokee Family*.

Chapter 8

1. *Indian Chieftain*, 21 July 1898.

2. U.S. Congress, *Annual Reports of the Department of the Interior for the Fiscal Year Ended June 30, 1899*, 54–55. Agreement between Commission to Five Civilized Tribes and Cherokee Indians in Indian Territory, 16 April 1900, U.S. Department of the Interior. Commission to the Five Civilized Tribes, *Annual Report of the Commission to the Five Civilized Tribes*, 1899.

3. *Tahlequah Arrow*, 5 Saturday 1904.

4. Ibid., 10 September 1904.

5. Ibid., Saturday, 25 June 1904.

6. *Cherokee Advocate*, 18 March 1893, 13 February 1895, 30 May 1896, 6 June 1896, 1 August 1896, and 27 February 1897; *Indian Chieftain*, 30 January 1896, and 25 June 1896.

7. "Indian Territory Jails," *Tahlequah Indian Sentinel*, 28 January 1898.

8. Correspondence from U.S. Indian inspector J. George Wright to Principal Chief T. M. Buffington regarding U.S. presidential approval of various bills, Jan. 1900, reel 31, frame 2965, CNP. The prisoners pardoned included James Wolf, William Clark, William Linn, Dan Rogers, Lee Teehee, Will Wildcat, George Beck, Don Ross, James Shirley, Robert Austin, Keener Vann, Ross Benge, Mose Fielding [Fields], Jesse Rogers, John Watts, Will Sawnie, Sam Squirrel, and Walter Wofford. *Indian Chieftain*, 29 June 1899.

9. National Council act regarding criminal pardons. n.d., National Prison and High Sheriff, RG 1, reel 31, frame 2967, CNP.

10. Sam Squirrel, 7944, roll 0230, Applications for Enrollment to the Five Tribes.

11. J. T. Parks to T. M. Buffington, 9 January 1902, frames 1210–11, CHN 95.

12. First Annual Message of Hon. William C. Rogers, Principal Chief of the Cherokee Nation Tahlequah IT, 6 November 1903, R34 f 29, Rogers Collection.

13. Everett, *Medical Education in Oklahoma*.

14. In 1904, of the 718 physicians in Indian Territory, 146, or 21 percent, subscribed to the journal. In Oklahoma Territory, 195 of its 903 physicians subscribed to the journal, whereas only 13 percent of doctors in Arkansas did. House of Delegates Proceedings, Annual Session, 1904, Digital Collection of the Historical AMA Archives, http://ama.nmtvault.com/jsp/browse.jsp.

15. House of Delegates Proceedings, Annual Session, 1900, 1555; House of Delegates Proceedings, Annual Session, 1902, 1647; House of Delegates Proceedings, Annual Session, 1904, 12, all in Digital Collection of the Historical AMA Archives, http://ama.nmtvault.com/jsp/browse.jsp.

16. *Chelsea Commercial*, 2 September 1904.

17. "The Indian Territory Medical Association," M310 I2 F3, ITMA Collection.

18. Report of the Committee on Medical Legislation, box M310, folder 2, ITMA Collection; Clinton, "Indian Territory Medical Association," 27–28.

19. *Indian Chieftain*, 2 November 1899.

20. Craig County Genealogical Society, "Vinita," *Encyclopedia of Oklahoma History and Culture*, http://www.okhistory.org/publications/enc/entry.php?entry=VI009.

21. Crockett, *Origin and Development of Public Health*, 97; *Indian Chieftain*, 11 November 1900.

22. I Remember, Class of 1904, Commemorating the Fiftieth Anniversary of the Graduation Class of 1904, From the Cherokee National Seminaries at Tahlequah, Indian Territory, 1954, John E. Duncan Collection, Talbot Museum and Library, Colcord, Oklahoma.

23. Carolyn G. Hanneman, "Benedict, John Downing (1854–1946)," *Encyclopedia of Oklahoma History and Culture*, Oklahoma Historical Society, http://www.okhistory.org/publications/enc/entry.php?entry=BE016.

24. Ibid.

25. Wright, "John D. Benedict," 472–73.

26. C. M. Bradley, Bradley Manual of Statistical Information Pertaining to the Indian Territory and Rules and Regulations for the Sale of Land, Special Collections, DeGoyler Library, SMU, Dallas, Texas.

27. *Annual Report of the National Board of Education of the Cherokee Nation*, 13 October 1899, box 97.053, Ballenger Papers.

28. From Principal Chief S. H. Mayes to Hon. B. S. Coppock, School Supervisor, 22 June 1899, box 83–17, folder 1, John D. Benedict Papers, OHS.

29. Debo, "Education in the Choctaw Country," 388–90.

30. *Indian Chieftain*, 20 January 1898.

31. *Tahlequah Arrow*, 28 June 1902.

32. Daily Record of Attendance of Pupils for the Scholastic Year Beginning 1907, Ledger, Cherokee National Female Seminary, March 1907, Cherokee Schools: Female Seminary, 1905 July 1–1909 May, Cherokee Nation Records (CHN 90).

33. Fanny Whiteday, interview by J. W. Tyner, 19 February 1968, IPP.

34. An Act making an appropriation for the repair of the National Jail building for use and an Asylum for the Insane, 30 November 1903, Senate Bill 13, frame 1217, CHN 95.

35. *Cherokee Advocate*, 24 December 1890, and 27 May 1891.

36. Doyle, "Single Versus Double Statehood," 266–86.

37. "Sequoyah Convention," Oklahoma History Society online, http://www.okhistory.org/publications/enc/entry.php?entry=SE021.

38. Genetin-Pilawa, *Crooked Paths*, 2.

39. *Tahlequah Arrow*, 9 November 1901.

40. *Vinita Leader*, 13 November 1902.

41. "Editorial on T. M. Buffington," *Vinita Republican*, 21 February 1902.

42. Ibid.

43. Stremlau's book paints a beautiful and complex picture of how families in a single community weathered the storm of allotment. To better understand how adherents of osdv iyunvnehi navigated allotment, Stremlau examines the difficult choices made by families to fulfill their social responsibilities to one another without their communal landholdings. Stremlau, *Sustaining the Cherokee Family*.

44. Debo, "Education in the Choctaw Country," 388–90.

Conclusion

1. Life and Times of Thomas J. Parks, box 10, folder 315, Ballenger Papers.

2. *Indian Chieftain*, vol. 20, no. 30, ed. 1, Thursday, 20 March 1902; Stremlau, *Sustaining the Cherokee Family*, 147.

3. U.S. Congress, *Report of the Select Committee to Investigate Matters Connected with Affairs in the Indian Territory with Hearings*, 11 November 1906–9 January 1907, 59th Cong., 2nd Sess. (Washington, D.C.: GPO, 1907), 97–100.

4. Littlefield, "Utopian Dreams," 424–25.

5. *Tahlequah Arrow*, 26 October 1907.

EPILOGUE

1. *Tahlequah Arrow*, 18 April 1908.

2. Richards, *Oklahoma Red Book*, 218–19.

3. Roberts, "Cherokee Orphan Asylum," 12.

4. Alluwe; Further Facts about Nowata County; Nowata Settlers; When the Cherokees Moved West, all gathered by Mary Riley, vol. 107, IPP.

5. Fanny Whiteday, interview by J. W. Tyner, 19 February 1968, IPP.

6. *American Indian*, 1930.

7. *Tahlequah Arrow*, 30 May 1912.

8. Lorena Travis, "Early Cherokee Nation Receives Cultural Help from Covel Family," 23 October 1875, *Pictorial Press*, Orphan Asylum Vertical Files.

9. "Tahlequah's Woman City Clerk to Quit after 30 Years' Service," March 1951, Orphan Asylum Vertical Files.

10. *Tahlequah Arrow*, 30 May 1912.

11. Ibid., 9 May 1908.

12. Tom Belt, a bilingual Cherokee from the Rocky Ford community, recounted this story to me in conversation on 24 January 2010 at the American Indian Center at the University of North Carolina at Chapel Hill.

13. Jeff Marshall, R1186, Cherokee, Cherokee Freedmen, roll 0396, Applications for Enrollment to the Five Tribes.

14. *Cherokee County Democrat*, 28 May 1914.

15. *Cherokee Advocate*, 26 April 1902. Dollie Terrapin; and Nanyesah Hosey, roll 0267, both in Applications for Enrollment to the Five Tribes.

16. Joshua Ross to Honorable George N. Benge, box 7, folder 279, Ballenger Papers. William P. Sevier, 6248, roll 0220; and Joshua Ross, 36, roll 0174, both in Applications for Enrollment to the Five Tribes.

Bibliography

ARCHIVES AND MANUSCRIPT COLLECTIONS

Cherokee Heritage Center Archives, Tahlequah, Okla.
    Duncan Collection
    Emma Fleming Papers
DeGoyler Library, Southern Methodist University, Dallas, Tex.
    Special Collections
Don Franklin Collection, Tahlequah, Okla.
    Private Papers
Dunawas Family Papers, Tulsa, Okla.
    Private Papers
National Archives and Records Administration, Washington, D.C.
    Records of the Department of Veterans Affairs
        Case Files of Approved Pension Applications of Widows and Other
        Dependents of Civil War Veterans, ca. 1861–ca. 1910
        War of 1812 Pension and Bounty Land Warrant Application Files,
        ca. 1871–ca. 1900
    Department of the Interior. Office of Indian Affairs
        Letters Received by the Office of Indian Affairs, 1824–80. Cherokee
        Agency, 1836–80
        Letters sent by the Office of Indian Affairs, 1824–81
        Records of the Cherokee Indian Agency, East, 1801–35
    Finance Division (1849–1908)
        Records of Collections of the Five Civilized Tribes, compiled 1898–1906
National Archives and Record Administration, Fort Worth, Tex.
    Department of the Interior. Office of Indian Affairs.
    Office of the U.S. Indian Inspector for Indian Territory (1898–1907).
        Enrollment Cards of the Five Civilized Tribes, 1898–1914
        Letters Received, comp. 1900–1907

Applications for Enrollment of the Commission to the Five Civilized Tribes, 1898–1914
Office of the Commissioner of the Five Civilized Tribes.
Reports on Small Pox Epidemics, comp. 1900–1900
Records of Improvements Sold Relating to Intruders, comp. 1904–1904
Registers of Letters Received from the Union Agency, comp. 1906–1909
Letters and Telegrams Received, comp. 1903–14, documenting the period 1900–1914
Records of Children Enrolled by the Tribal Government, comp. 1897
Office of the Commissioner of Indian Affairs.
Letters Sent, comp. 1895–1914
Newberry Library, Chicago, Ill.
Ballenger Papers
Ayer Collection
Northeastern State University, Tahlequah, Okla.
Special Collections
Cherokee Orphan Asylum Vertical Files
Cherokee National Prison Vertical Files
Oklahoma Historical Society, Oklahoma City, Okla.
John D. Benedict Collection
Indian Archives Division
Cherokee Nation Records
Letters Sent and Letters Received, and Other Documents
Female Seminary, 1905 July 1–1909 May, CHN 99
Insane Asylum, 1885 January 1–1910 February 16
Orphan Asylum, 1890 May 20–1902 March 31
Pardons, 1877 September 23–1901 November 30
Prison and High Sheriff Records, 16 April 1880–20 March 1909
Oklahoma Historical Society, Tulsa, Okla.
Vertical Files
Talbot Library, Colcord, Okla.
John E. Duncan Collection
University of Oklahoma Library, University of Oklahoma, Norman, Okla.
Western History Collections
Virgil Berry Papers
Cherokee Nation Manuscript Collections
Frank J. Boudinot Papers
W. P. Boudinot Papers
Dennis Wolf Bushyhead Papers
Cherokee Nation Papers
James R. Hendricks Papers
Joel Bryan Mayes Materials
Joseph Samuel Murrow Papers

Oochalata Collection
Frank Phillips Collection
William Charles Rogers Collection
William P. Ross Papers
Cherokee Oklahoma Federation of Labor Collection
Doris Duke Collection
Indian-Pioneer Papers Collection
Indian Territory Medical Association Collection
Wheelock Seminary Collection
University of Tennessee Library, University of Tennessee, Knoxville, Tenn.
Special Collections
Penelope Johnson Allen Collection
Wilson Special Collections Library, University of North Carolina, Chapel Hill, N.C.
North Carolina Collection
Yale University Library, New Haven, Conn.
Beinecke Rare Book and Manuscript Library
To the Men and Women of the Cherokee Nation (Cherokee Orphan Asylum
Press, 1881)

PUBLISHED PRIMARY SOURCES

Adair, James. *Adair's History of the American Indians.* Edited by Samuel Cole Wil-
liams. Johnson City, Tenn.: Watauga Press, 1927.
Benedict, John Downing. *Muskogee and Northeastern Oklahoma.* Chicago: S. J. Clarke,
1922.
Bloomer, Amelia, and Dexter Bloomer. *The Life and Writings of Amelia Bloomer.* Boston:
Arena, 1895.
Campbell, Bert, comp. *Campbell's Abstract of Creek Freedman Census Cards and Index.*
Muskogee, Okla.: Phoenix Job Printing, 1915.
Dale, Edward Everett, and Gaston Litton, eds. *Cherokee Cavaliers: Forty Years of Chero-
kee History as Told in the Correspondence of the Ridge-Watie-Boudinot Family.* 1939.
Reprint, Norman: University of Oklahoma Press, 1995.
Dawes, Anna Laurens. *A United States Prison.* Philadelphia: Indian Rights Associa-
tion, 1886.
Dawson, William C. "1831 Dawson's Compilation" (1831). *Historic Georgia Digests and
Codes.* Book 29. Midgeville, Ga.: Grantland and Orme. Available at http://
digitalcommons.law.uga.edu/ga_code/29.
Duncan, DeWitt Clinton. "The Story of the Cherokees." American Native Press
Archives and Sequoyah Research Center, University of Arkansas at Little Rock.
Available at http://www.ualr.edu/sequoyah/uploads/2011/11/DunStor.
htm#Too-qua-stee.

Foster, George E. "Among the Cherokees." *Frank Leslie's Popular Monthly* 25 (1888): 231–37.

Gambold, Anna Rosina, and John Gambold. *The Moravian Springplace Mission to the Cherokees*. Vol. 1, *1805–1813*. Edited by Rowena McClinton. Lincoln: University of Nebraska Press, 2007.

————. *The Moravian Springplace Mission to the Cherokees*. Vol. 2, *1814–1821*. Edited by Rowena McClinton. Lincoln: University of Nebraska Press, 2007.

————. *The Moravian Springplace Mission*. Abbr. ed. Lincoln: University of Nebraska Press, 2010.

Gates, Merrill E. "Land and Law as Agents in Educating Indians." In *Americanizing the American Indians: Writings by the "Friends of the Indian," 1880–1900*, edited by Francis Paul Prucha, 45–56. Lincoln: University of Nebraska Press, 1978.

Godding, W. W. "Recognition of Classes of the Insane in Asylum Construction." *Alienist and Neurologist* 7 (July 1885).

Hicks, Hannah. "The Diary of Hannah Hicks." *American Scene* 13 (1972): 3–24.

Hitchcock, Ethan Allen. *A Traveler in Indian Territory: The Journal of Ethan Allen Hitchcock*. Edited by Grant Foreman. Cedar Rapids, Iowa: Torch Press, 1930.

Irving, Washington. *Three Western Narratives: A Tour on the Prairies, Astoria, The Adventures of Captain Bonneville*. New York: Library of America, 2004.

Jenner, Edward. *Instructions for Vaccine Inoculation, Commonly Called Vaccination*. Philadelphia, 1807.

Kilpatrick, Jack Frederick, and Anna Gritts Kilpatrick. *Run toward the Nightland: Magic of the Oklahoma Cherokees*. Dallas: Southern University Press, 1967.

Mooney, James. "How the World Was Made." In *History, Myths, and Sacred Formulas of the Cherokees*. Asheville, N.C.: Bright Mountain Books, 1992.

————. "Myths of the Cherokee." In *History, Myths, and Sacred Formulas of the Cherokees*. Asheville, N.C.: Bright Mountain Books, 1992.

Moore, F. M. *A Brief History of the Missionary Work in the Indian Territory of the Indian Mission Conference, Methodist Episcopal Church South*. Muskogee: Phoenix, 1899.

Mulholland, C. S., and Nancy Morgan. "Illuminating Cherokee Removal Again: Lucy Ames Butler to Harriet Nason Howe, December 20, 1838." *Journal of Cherokee Studies* 27 (2009): 24–37.

Otis, D. S. *The Dawes Act and the Allotment of Indian Lands*. Edited by Francis Paul Prucha. Norman: University of Oklahoma Press, 1973.

Painter, Charles C. "The Indian and His Property." In *Americanizing the American Indians: Writings by the "Friends of the Indian," 1880–1900*, edited by Francis Paul Prucha, 114–21. Lincoln: University of Nebraska Press, 1978.

Paul, James Laughery. *Pennsylvania's Soldiers' Oorphan Schools: Giving a Brief Account of the Origin of the Late Civil War, the Rise and Progress of the Orphan System, and Legislative Enactments Relating Thereto; with Brief Sketches and Engravings of the Several Institutions, with Names of Pupils Subjoined*. Philadelphia: Claxton, Remsen, and Haffelfinger, 1876.

Payne, John Howard. *Indian Justice: A Cherokee Murder Trial at Tahlequah in 1840.* Edited by Grant Foreman. Norman: University of Oklahoma Press, 2002.

Payne, John Howard, and D. S. Butrick. *The Payne-Butrick Papers.* 6 vols. Edited by William L. Anderson, Jane L. Brown, and Anne F. Rogers. Lincoln: University of Nebraska Press, 2010.

Perdue, Theda. *Nations Remembered. An Oral History of the Cherokees, Chickasaws, Choctaws, Creeks, and Seminoles in Oklahoma, 1865–1907.* Norman: University of Oklahoma Press, 1993.

Phillips, Joyce B., and Paul Gary Phillips, eds. *The Brainerd Journal: Mission to the Cherokees, 1817–1823.* Lincoln: University of Nebraska Press, 1998.

Pratt, Richard Henry. "The Advantages of Mingling Indians with Whites." In Prucha, Americanizing the American Indians, 260–71.

———. *Battlefield and Classroom: Four Decades with the American Indian, 1867–1904.* Edited by Richard Utley. New Haven, Conn.: Yale University Press, 1964.

Prucha, Francis Paul., ed. *Americanizing the American Indians: Writings by the "Friends of the Indian," 1880–1900.* Lincoln: University of Nebraska Press, 1978.

Ross, John. *The Papers of Chief John Ross.* Vol. 1, *1807–1839.* Edited by Gary E. Moulton. Norman: University of Oklahoma Press, 1985.

———. *The Papers of Chief John Ross.* Vol. 2, *1840–1866.* Edited by Gary E. Moulton. Norman: University of Oklahoma Press, 1985.

Ross, William P. *The Life and Times of William P. Ross.* Edited by Mary Jane Ross. Fort Smith, Ark.: Weldon and Williams Printers, 1893.

Starr, Emmet. *History of the Cherokee Indians and their Legends and Folk Lore.* Oklahoma City: Warden, 1921.

State of Oklahoma. *The Oklahoma Red Book.* Compiled by W. B. Richards and Seth Corden. Oklahoma City: Press of Tulsa Daily Democrat, 1912.

Waterhouse, Benjamin. *A Prospect of Exterminating the Small-pox, Being the History of the Variolae Vaccinae, or Kine-pox, Commonly Called the Cow-pox: As It Has Appeared in England: With an Account of a Series of Inoculations Performed for the Kine-pox.* Cambridge: Cambridge Press, 1800.

Webster, Noah. *An American Dictionary of the English Language.* Springfield: George and Charles Merriam.

Williams, A. M. "Among the Cherokees." *Lippincott's Magazine of Popular Literature and Science* 27 (February 1881): 195–204.

Woman's State Centennial Executive Committee (Wis.). *Centennial Records of the Women of Wisconsin.* Edited by Anna B. Butler, Emma C. Bascom, and Katharine F. Kerr. Madison, Wis.: Atwood and Culver, 1876.

NEWSPAPERS

Tulsa American Indian, 1929–30
Chelsea Commercial, 1906
Tahlequah Cherokee Advocate, 1844–1906

Cherokee County Democrat, 1912–30
New Echota Cherokee Phoenix, 1828–29
New Echota Cherokee Phoenix and Indians' Advocate, 1829–34
Fort Smith (Ark.) Western Independent, 1872–78
Vinita Indian Chieftain, 1882–1902
Tahlequah Indian Sentinel, 1895–1902
Lawrence (Kans.) Western Recorder, 1883–18[–]
Little Rock Morning Republican, 1877–1910
New York Times, 1870–1907
Orphan Asylum Press, 1880–81
Orphans' Home Journal, 1904–1908
Muskogee Our Brother in Red, 1882–98
Ontario Our Forest Children, 1887–90
Carlisle Red Man, 1910–17
School News, 1880–82
Tahlequah Arrow, 1896–1912
Tahlequah Telephone, 1887–88; 1890–1914
Tulsa Daily World, 1927–77
Vinita Leader, 1895–59
Vinita Republican, 1899–19[–]

PERIODICALS

Frank Leslie's Popular Monthly
Journal of Insanity
Lippincott's Magazine of Popular Literature and Science
Medical and Surgical Reporter

GOVERNMENT DOCUMENTS

Benge, Barbara, compiler and transcriber. *The 1880 Cherokee Nation Census Indian Territory (Oklahoma)*. Bowie, Md.: Heritage Books, 2000.
Cherokee Nation. *Compiled Laws of the Cherokee Nation*. 1881. Reprint, Wilmington, Del.: Scholarly Resources, 1973.
———. *Constitution and Laws of the Cherokee Nation*. 1875. Reprint, Wilmington, Del.: Scholarly Resources, 1973.
———. *Laws and Joint Resolutions of the Cherokee Nation Enacted during the Regular and Special Sessions of the Years 1881–2–3*. 1884. Reprint, Wilmington, Del.: Scholarly Resources, 1975.
———. *Laws and Joint Resolutions of the National Council Passed and Adopted at the Regular and Extra Sessions of 1870–72*. 1871. Reprint, Wilmington, Del.: Scholarly Resources, 1975.

————. *Laws and Joint Resolutions of the National Council Passed and Adopted at the Regular Sessions 1876, 1877, and the Extra Session 1878*. 1878. Reprint, Wilmington, Del.: Scholarly Resources, 1973.

————. *Laws of the Cherokee Nation: Adopted by the Council at Various Periods*. 1852. Reprint, Del.: Scholarly Resources, 1973.

————. *Laws of the Cherokee Nation Passed during the Years 1839–1867*. St. Louis: St. Louis, Democrat Print, 1868.

————. *Memorial and Protest of the Cherokee Nation: To Accompany Bill R.H. No. 695: Memorial of the Cherokee Representatives, Submitting the Protest of the Cherokee Nation against the Ratification, Execution and Enforcement of the Treaty Negotiated at New Echota in December, 1835*. Washington, D.C., 1836.

Kappler, Charles J., comp. and ed. *Indian Affairs: Laws and Treaties*. Vol. 2. Washington, D.C.: Government Printing Office, 1904.

National Home for Disabled Volunteer Soldiers Board of Managers. *Annual Report of the Board of Managers of the National Home for Disabled Volunteer Soldiers*. Washington, D.C.: Government Printing Office, 1868.

Ross, William P. *Petition for the Relief of Certain Soldiers of the Indian Home-Guard Regiments*. Washington, D.C.: Government Printing Office, 1874.

United States. *Right of President to Withhold Papers; Frauds on Indians: Message from the President of the United States, Transmitting the Report of Lieutenant Colonel Hitchcock, Respecting the Affairs of the Cherokee Indians, &c*. Washington, D.C., 1843.

U.S. Bureau of Education. *Report of the Commissioner of Education for the Year Ended June 30, 1912*. 2 vols. Washington, D.C.: Government Printing Office, 1913. Available at http://babel.hathitrust.org/cgi/pt?id=coo.31924097879682;view=1up;seq=7 and http://babel.hathitrust.org/cgi/pt?id=coo.31924097879690;view=1up;seq=5.

U.S. Commissioner of Indian Affairs. *Annual Reports of the Commissioner of Indian Affairs*. Washington, D.C.: Government Printing Office, 1854–1872, 1894–1900.

U.S. Congress. *Annual Reports of the Department of the Interior for the Fiscal Year Ended June 30, 1899*. H. Doc. 5/4, Serial 3916. Washington, D.C.: Government Printing Office, 1899.

U.S. Congress. *Bills and Joint Resolutions Introduced in the United States Senate, First and Second Sessions*. S. Mis. Doc. 48, Serial 2083. Washington, D.C.: Government Printing Office, 1883.

U.S. Congress. House Committee on Indian Affairs. *Alleged Frauds against Certain Indian Soldiers, June 8, 1872*. Washington, D.C., 1872.

U.S. Congress. Senate Executive Documents. *Report of the Board of Indian Commissioners*. 33rd Cong., 2nd Sess., 1853–55. 47th Cong., 2nd Sess., 1882–83. 49th Cong., 1st Sess., 1886, Serial 2363

U.S. Congress. Senate Executive Documents. *Report of the Committee on Indian Affairs, United States Senate, on the Condition of the Indians in the Indian Territory*. 49th Cong., 1st Sess., Serial 1278, 1886

U.S. Congress. Senate Executive Documents. *Report of the Select Committee to Investigate Matters Connected with Affairs in the Indian Territory with Hearings,* November 11, 1906–January 9, 1907. 59th Cong., 2nd Sess., 1907

U.S. Department of the Interior. Commission to the Five Civilized Tribes. *Annual Report of the Commission to the Five Civilized Tribes to the Secretary of the Interior.* Washington, D.C.: Government Printing Office, 1899.

U.S. Office of Indian Affairs. *Annual Report of the Commissioner of Indian Affairs.* 53rd Cong., 3rd Sess., Serial 3306. Washington D.C.: Government Printing Office, 1894.

SECONDARY SOURCES

Abel, Annie Heloise. *The American Indian in the Civil War.* 1919. Reprint, Lincoln: University of Nebraska Press, 1992.

Abram, Susan M. "Shedding Their Blood in Vain: Cherokee Challenges after the Red Stick War." *Journal of Cherokee Studies* 28 (2010): 31–59.

Adair, William Penn. "The Indian Territory in 1878." *Chronicles of Oklahoma* 4 (September 1926): 255–72.

Adams, Catherine L. "'Africanizing the Territory': The Contemporary Imagination of Black Frontier Settlements in the Oklahoma Territory." Paper presented at the Annual Meeting of the Western History Association, Newport Beach, Calif., October 14–18, 2014.

Adams, David Wallace. *Education for Extinction: American Indians and the Boarding School Experience, 1875–1928.* Lawrence: University of Kansas Press, 1995.

Altman, Heidi M., and Thomas N. Belt. "Reading History: Cherokee History through a Cherokee Lens." *Native South* 1 (2008): 90–98.

Anders, Gary C. "The Reduction of a Self-Sufficient People to Poverty and Welfare Dependence: An Analysis of the Causes of Cherokee Indian Underdevelopment." *American Journal of Economics and Sociology* 40 (July 1981): 225–37.

Babcock, Sydney Henry, and John Y. Bryce. *History of Methodism in Oklahoma: Story of the Indian Mission Annual Conference of the Methodist Episcopal Church, South.* Oklahoma City: Times Journal Publishing, 1937.

Ball, Durwood. "Cool to the End: Public Hangings and Western Manhood." In *Across The Great Divide: Cultures of Manhood in the American West,* edited by Matthew Basso, Laura McCall, and Dee Garceau, 97–108. New York: Routledge, 2001.

Ballenger, T. L. "Joseph Franklin Thompson: An Early Cherokee Leader." *Chronicles of Oklahoma* 30 (Fall 1952): 173–99.

Balyeat, Frank A. "Segregation in Public Schools of Oklahoma Territory." *Chronicles of Oklahoma* 39 (Summer 1961): 180–92.

Bass, Althea. *Cherokee Messenger.* Norman: University of Oklahoma Press, 1936.

Bass, Dorothy C. "Gideon Blackburn's Mission to the Cherokees: Christianization and Civilization." *Journal of Presbyterian History* 52 (Fall 1974): 203–26.

Berkowitz, Edward, and Kim McQuaid, *Creating the Welfare State: The Political Economy of Twentieth-Century Reform*. New York: Praeger, 1988.

Best, Harry. *The Blind: Their Condition and the Work Being Done for Them in the United States*. New York: Macmillan, 1919.

Bonner, James C. "The Georgia Penitentiary at Milledgeville, 1817–1874." *Georgia Historical Quarterly* 55 (Fall 1971): 303–28.

Bremner, Robert H. *The Discovery of Poverty in the United States*. 1956. Reprint, New Brunswick: Transaction Publishers, 1992.

———. *The Public Good: Philanthropy and Welfare in the Civil War Era*. New York: Knopf, 1980.

Brill, Richard G. *Education of the Deaf : Administrative and Professional Developments*. Washington, D.C.: Gallaudet College Press, 1974.

Britton, Wiley. "Some Reminiscences of the Cherokee People." *Chronicles of Oklahoma* 5 (June 1927): 180–84.

Bruyneel, Kevin. *The Third Space of Sovereignty: The Postcolonial Politics of U.S.-Indigenous Relations*. Minneapolis: University of Minnesota Press, 2007.

Burch, Susan. "'Dislocated Histories': The Canton Asylum for Insane Indians" *Women, Gender, and Families of Color* 2 (Fall 2014): 141–62.

Burton, Jeffrey. *Indian Territory and the United States, 1866–1906: Courts, Government, and the Move for Oklahoma Statehood*. Norman: University of Oklahoma Press, 1995.

Cahill, Cathleen. *Federal Fathers and Mothers: A Social History of the United States Indian Service, 1869–1933*. Chapel Hill: University of North Carolina Press, 2013.

Calloway, Colin G. *An Indian History of an American Institution: Native Americans and Dartmouth*. Hanover, N.H.: University Press of New England, 2010.

Carp, E. Wayne. *Adoption in America: Historical Perspectives*. Ann Arbor: University of Michigan Press, 2009.

Champagne, Duane. *Social Order and Political Change: Constitutional Governments Among the Cherokee Choctaw, Chickasaw, and Creek*. Stanford: Stanford University Press, 1992.

Chang, David. *Color of the Land: Race, Nation, and the Politics of Landownership in Oklahoma, 1832–1929*. Chapel Hill: University of North Carolina Press, 2010.

Cheatham, Gary L. "If the Union Wins, We Won't Have Anything Left: The Rise and Fall of the Southern Cherokees of Kansas." *Kansas History* 30 (Autumn 2007): 154–77.

Child, Brenda. *Boarding School Seasons*. Lincoln: University of Nebraska Press, 2000.

Cimballa, Paul, and Randall Miller, eds. *The Freedmen's Bureau and Reconstruction: Reconsiderations*. New York: Fordham University Press, 1999.

Clapesattle, Helen. *The Doctors Mayo*. Rochester, Minn.: Mayo Foundation for Medical Education and Research, 1969.

Clinton, Fred S. Clinton "The Indian Territory Medical Association." *Chronicles of Oklahoma* 26 (1948): 23–55.

Cmiel, Kenneth. *A Home of Another Kind: One Chicago Orphanage and the Tangle of Child Welfare*. Chicago: University of Chicago Press, 1995.

Cobb, Amanda J. *Listening to Our Grandmother's Stories: The Bloomfield Academy for Chickasaw Females, 1852–1949*. Lincoln: University of Nebraska Press, 2000.

Coleman, Michael C. *American Indian Children at School, 1850–1930*. Jackson: University Press of Mississippi, 1993.

Collins, Kristin A. "Administering Marriage: Marriage-Based Entitlements, Bureaucracy, and the Legal Construction of the Family." *Vanderbilt Law Review* 62, no. 4 (2009): 1085–1168.

———. "'Petitions Without Number': Widows' Petitions and the Early Nineteenth-Century Origins of Public Marriage-Based Entitlements." *Law and History Review* 31, no. 1 (2013): 1–60.

Confer, Clarissa. *The Cherokee Nation in the Civil War*. Norman: University of Oklahoma Press, 2007.

Conley, Robert. *A Cherokee Encyclopedia*. Albuquerque: University of New Mexico Press, 2007.

———. *The Cherokee Nation: A History*. Albuquerque: University of New Mexico Press, 2005.

Crockett, Bernice Norman. "Health Conditions in the Indian Territory From the Civil War To 1890." *Chronicles of Oklahoma* 36 (1958): 21–39.

Cumfer, Cynthia. *Separate Peoples, One Land: The Minds of Cherokees, Blacks, and Whites on the Tennessee Frontier*. Chapel Hill: University of North Carolina Press, 2007.

Dain, Norman. *Concepts of Insanity in the United States, 1789–1865*. New Brunswick, N.J.: Rutgers University Press, 1964.

Dale, Edward Everett, and Morris L. Wardell. *History of Oklahoma*. Englewood, N.J.: Prentice Hall, 1948.

Daniel, Michelle. "From Blood Feud to Jury System; The Metamorphosis of Cherokee Law from 1750 to 1840." *American Indian Quarterly* (Spring 1987): 97–125.

Dary, David. *Frontier Medicine: From the Atlantic to the Pacific, 1492–1941*. New York: Knopf, 2008.

Davis, Caroline. "Education of the Chickasaws, 1856–1907." *Chronicles of Oklahoma* 15, no. 4 (December 1937): 415–48.

Davis, Kenneth Penn. "Chaos in the Indian Country, 1828–35." In *The Cherokee Indian Nation: A Troubled History*, edited by Duane H. King, 129–47. Knoxville: University of Tennessee Press, 1979.

Debo, Angie. *And Still the Waters Run: The Betrayal of the Five Civilized Tribes*. 1940. Reprint, Princeton, N.J.: Princeton University Press, 1973.

———. "Education in the Choctaw Country after the Civil War." *Chronicles of Oklahoma* 10 (September 1932): 383–91.

Demos, John. *The Heathen School: A Story of Hope and Betrayal in the Age of the Early Republic*. New York: Knopf, 2014.

Denson, Andrew. *Demanding the Cherokee Nation: Indian Autonomy and American Culture, 1830–1900*. Lincoln: University of Nebraska Press, 2004.

Deutsch, Albert. *The Mentally Ill in America: A History of Their Care and Treatment from Colonial Times.* New York: Columbia University Press, 1949.

Dodge, L. Mara. *Whores and Thieves of the Worst Kind: A Study of Women, Crime, and Prisons, 1835–2000.* DeKalb: Northern Illinois University Press, 2002.

Dolan, Susan. *Fruitful Legacy: A Historic Context of Orchards in the United States, with Technical Information for Registering Orchards in the National Register of Historic Places.* Washington, D.C.: National Park Service, Olmsted Center for Landscape Preservation, Pacific West Regional Office, Cultural Resources, Park Historic Structures and Cultural Landscapes Program by Government Printing Office, 2009.

Doyle, Thomas H. "Single Versus Double Statehood." *Chronicles of Oklahoma* 5 (1927): 18–41.

Dulberger, Judith A. *"Mother Donit for the Best": Correspondence of a Nineteenth-Century Orphan Asylum.* Syracuse, N.Y.: Syracuse University Press, 1996.

Duncan, James W. "Interesting Ante-Bellum Laws of the Cherokee Nation." *Chronicles of Oklahoma* 6 (June 1928): 178–80.

Escott, Paul D. "'The Cry of the Sufferers': The Problem of Welfare in the Confederacy." *Civil War History* 23 (September 1977): 228–40.

Everett, Mark R. *Medical Education in Oklahoma: The University of Oklahoma School of Medicine and Medical Center, 1900–1931.* Norman: University of Oklahoma Press, 1972.

Faust, Drew Gilpin. *This Republic of Suffering: Death and the American Civil War.* New York: Vintage, 2009.

Finger, John R. *The Eastern Band of Cherokees, 1819–1900.* Knoxville: University of Tennessee Press, 1984.

Finley, Randy. "Personnel of the Freedmen's Bureau in Arkansas." In *The Freedmen's Bureau and Reconstruction: Reconsiderations*, edited by Paul Cimballa and Randall Miller, 93–118. New York: Fordham University Press, 1999.

Foner, Eric, and Olivia Mahoney. *America's Reconstruction: People and Politics after the Civil War.* Baton Rouge: Louisiana State University Press, 1997.

Foreman, Grant. *The Five Civilized Tribes: Cherokee, Chickasaw, Choctaw, Creek, Seminole.* Norman: University of Oklahoma Press, 1972.

———. *Indian Removal: The Emigration of the Five Civilized Tribes of Indians.* 1932. Reprint, Norman: University of Oklahoma Press, 1982.

———. *Sequoyah.* Norman: University of Oklahoma Press, 1938.

Foreman, Minta Ross. "Reverend Stephen Foreman, Cherokee Missionary." *Chronicles of Oklahoma* 18 (September 1940): 229–42.

Foucault, Michel. *Discipline & Punish: The Birth of the Prison.* New York: Vintage, 1995.

———. *Madness and Civilization: A History of Insanity in the Age of Reason.* New York: Random House, 1965.

Franks, Kenny A. *Stand Watie and the Agony of the Cherokee Nation.* Memphis: Memphis State University Press, 1979.

Freeberg, Ernest. "The Meanings of Blindness in Nineteenth-Century America." *Proceedings of the American Antiquarian Society* 110 (2000): 119–53.

Gaines, W. Craig. *The Confederate Cherokees: John Drew's Regiment of Mounted Rifles.* Baton Rouge: Louisiana State University Press, 1989.

Gammon, Tim. "Black Freedmen and the Cherokee Nation." *Journal of American Studies* 2 (1977): 357–64.

Garrett, Kathleen. *The Cherokee Orphan Asylum.* Stillwater: Oklahoma Agricultural and Mechanical College, 1953.

Garrison, Tim Alan. *The Legal Ideology of Removal: The Southern Judiciary and the Sovereignty of Native American Nations.* Athens: University of Georgia Press, 2009.

Gearing, Fred O. *Priests and Warriors: Social Structures for Cherokee Politics in the 18th Century.* American Anthropological Association 93. Menasha, Wis.: American Anthropological Association, 1962.

Genetin-Pilawa, C. Joseph. *Crooked Paths to Allotment: The Fight over Federal Indian Policy after the Civil War.* Chapel Hill: University of North Carolina Press, 2012.

Gibson, Arrell M. *The Chickasaws.* Norman: University of Oklahoma Press, 1971.

Glasson, William Henry. "History of Military Pension Legislation in the United States." PhD diss., Columbia University, 1900.

Goins, Charles Robert, and Danney Goble. *Historical Atlas of Oklahoma.* 4th ed. Norman: University of Oklahoma Press. 2006.

Gordon, Linda. *Pitied but Not Entitled : Single Mothers and the History of Welfare, 1890– 1935.* Toronto: Free Press, 1994.

———. "Who Deserves Help? Who Must Provide?" *Annals of the American Academy of Political and Social Science* 577 (September 2001): 12–25.

———, ed. *Women, the State, and Welfare.* Madison: University of Wisconsin Press, 1990.

Green, Elna C. "Protecting Confederate Soldiers and Mothers." *Journal of Social History* 39 (Summer 2006): 1079–1104.

Green, Michael D. *The Politics of Indian Removal: Creek Government and Society in Crisis.* Lincoln: University of Nebraska Press, 1985.

Hacsi, Timothy A. *Second Home: Orphan Asylums and Poor Families in America.* Cambridge: Harvard University Press, 1997.

Handler, Joel F., and Yeheskel Hasenfeld. *The Moral Construction of Poverty: Welfare Reform in America.* Newbury Park, Calif.: Sage Publications, 1991.

Harring, Sidney L. *Crow Dog's Case: American Indian Sovereignty, Tribal Law, and United States Law in the Nineteenth Century.* 1994. Reprint, New York: Cambridge University Press, 1999.

Harmon, Alexandra. "American Indians and Land Monopolies in the Gilded Age." *Journal of American History* 90 (June 2003): 106–33.

———. *Rich Indians: Native People and the Problem of Wealth in American History.* Chapel Hill: University of North Carolina Press, 2013.

Hauptman, Laurence M. *Between Two Fires: American Indians in the Civil War.* New York: Free Press, 1995.

Hill, Sarah. *Weaving New Worlds: Southeastern Cherokee Women and Their Basketry.* Chapel Hill: University of North Carolina Press, 1997.

Hirsch, Adam Jay. *The Rise of the Penitentiary: Prisons and Punishment in Early America.* New Haven, Conn.: Yale University Press, 1992.

Hogue, Larry M., and Peter Blanck, "'Benefit of the Doubt': African-American Civil War Veterans and Pensions." *Journal of Interdisciplinary History* 38 (2008): 377–99.

Hoig, Stanley W. *The Cherokees and their Chiefs: In the Wake of Empire.* Fayetteville: University of Arkansas Press, 1998.

Holland, Cullen Joe. *Cherokee Newspapers, 1828–1906: Tribal Voice of a People in Transition.* Edited by James P. Pate. Norman: University of Oklahoma Press, 2014.

Holt, Marilyn Irvin. *The Orphan Trains: Placing Out in America.* Lincoln: University of Nebraska Press, 1994.

Howard, R. Palmer. "Cherokee History to 1840: A Medical View." *Journal of Oklahoma State Medical Association* 63 (February 1970): 71–82.

Hoxie, Frederick E. *Talking Back to Civilization: Indian Voices from the Progressive Era.* Boston: Bedford/St. Martins, 2001.

Hudson, Charles. *The Southeastern Indians.* 1976. Reprint, Knoxville: University of Tennessee Press, 2007.

Ishii, Izumi. *Bad Fruits of the Civilized Tree: Alcohol and the Sovereignty of the Cherokee Nation.* Lincoln: University of Nebraska Press, 2008.

Jackson, Joe C. "Church School Education in the Creek Nation, 1898–1907." *Chronicles of Oklahoma* 46 (June 1968): 312–30.

Jensen, Laura. *Patriots, Settlers, and the Origins of American Social Policy.* Cambridge: Cambridge University Press, 2003.

Johnson, N. B. "The Cherokee Orphan Asylum." *Chronicles of Oklahoma* 44 (March 1942): 55–61.

Josephy, Alvin M. *The Nez Perce Indians and the Opening of the Northwest.* Boston: Houghton Mifflin, 1997.

Kann, Mark E. *Punishment, Prisons, and Patriarchy: Liberty and Power in the Early American Republic.* New York: New York University Press, 2005.

Katz, Michael B. *In the Shadow of the Poorhouse: A Social History of Welfare in America.* New York: Basic Books, 1986.

——— "Origins of the Institutional State." *Marxist Perspectives* (Winter 1978): 6–22.

———. "Was government the solution or the problem? The role of the state in the history of American social policy." *Theory and Society* 39 (May 2010): 487–502.

Keith-Lucas, Alan. *A Legacy of Caring: The Charleston Orphan House, 1790–1990.* Charleston, S.C.: Wyrick, 1991.

Kelly, Patrick Joseph. "Creating a National Home: The Postwar Care of Disabled Union Soldiers and the Beginning of the Modern State in America." PhD diss., New York University, 1992.

Keve, Paul W. *Prisons and the American Conscience: A History of U.S. Federal Corrections.* Carbondale: Southern Illinois University Press, 1991.

King, Duane H., ed. *The Cherokee Indian Nation: A Troubled History.* Knoxville: University of Tennessee Press, 1979.

Kneeland, Timothy, and Carol A. B. Warren. *Pushbutton Psychiatry: A History of Electroshock in America.* Westport: Praeger, 2002.

Knepler, Abraham E. "Education in the Cherokee Nation." *Chronicles of Oklahoma* 21 (December 1943): 378–401.

———. "Eighteenth Century Cherokee Educational Efforts." *Chronicles of Oklahoma* 20 (March 1942): 55–61.

Leahy, Todd. "The Canton Asylum: Indians, Psychiatrists, and Government Policy, 1899–1934." PhD diss., Oklahoma State University, 2004.

Levine, Daniel. "A Single Standard of Civilization: Black Private Social Welfare Institutions in the South, 1880s–1920s." *Georgia Historical Quarterly* 81 (Spring 1997): 1–26.

Lewis, Bonnie Sue. *Creating Christian Indians: Native Clergy in the Presbyterian Church.* Norman: University of Oklahoma Press, 2003.

Littlefield, Daniel F., Jr. *The Cherokee Freedmen: From Emancipation to American Citizenship.* Westport, Conn.: Greenwood Press, 1978.

———. "Utopian Dreams of the Cherokee Fullbloods: 1890–1934." *Journal of the West* 10 (1971): 404–27.

Littlefield, Daniel F., and James W. Parins, eds. *Native American Writing in the Southeast: An Anthology, 1875–1935.* Jackson: University Press of Mississippi, 1995.

Littlefield, Daniel F., and Lonnie E. Underhill. "Slave 'Revolt' in the Cherokee Nation, 1842." *American Indian Quarterly* 3 (Summer 1977): 121–31.

———. "The Trial of Ezekiel Proctor and the Problem of Judicial Jurisdiction." *Chronicles of Oklahoma* 47 (Fall 1969): 298–311.

Logue, Larry M. "Union Veterans and Their Government: The Effects of Public Policies on Private Lives." *Journal of Interdisciplinary History* 22 (Winter 1992): 411–34.

Lomawaima, Tsianina. *They Called It Prairie Light: The Story of Chilocco Indian School.* Lincoln: University of Nebraska Press, 1995.

Lomawaima, Tsianina, and Teresa L. McCarty, eds. *"To Remain an Indian": Lessons in Democracy from a Century of Native American Education.* New York: Teacher's College Press, 2006.

Lookingbill, Brad D. *War Dance at Fort Marion: Plains Indian War Prisoners.* Norman: University of Oklahoma Press, 2006.

Lowery, Malinda Maynor. *Lumbee Indians in the Jim Crow South: Race, Identity, and the Making of a Nation.* Chapel Hill: University of North Carolina Press, 2010.

Malone, Henry Thompson. *Cherokees of the Old South: A People in Transition.* 1956. Reprint, Athens: University of Georgia Press, 2010.

Mancini, Matthew J. *One Dies, Get Another: Convict Leasing in the American South, 1866–1928.* Columbia: University of South Carolina Press, 1996.

Martin, J. Matthew. "The Nature and Extent of the Exercise of Criminal Jurisdiction by the Cherokee Nation Supreme Court: 1828–1835." *North Carolina Central Law Review* 32 (2009): 27–63.

Martin, Richard E., and R. Palmer Howard, M.D. "Medical Organization in the Cherokee Nation, 1870–1900." *Bulletin of the Southern Medical Association* 57 (1969): 58–62.

Masur, Louis P. *Rites of Execution: Capital Punishment and the Transformation of American Culture, 1776–1865.* New York: Oxford University Press, 1989.

May, Katja. *African Americans and Native Americans in the Creek and Cherokee Nations, 1830s to 1920s: Collision and Collusion*. New York: Garland, 1996.

Meserve, John B. "Chief Dennis Wolfe Bushyhead." *Chronicles of Oklahoma* 14 (September 1936): 349–359.

———. "Chief Lewis Downing and Chief Charles Thompson (Oochalata)." *Chronicles of Oklahoma* 16 (September 1938): 315–25.

———. "Chief Thomas Mitchell Buffington." *Chronicles of Oklahoma* 17 (June 1939): 135–140.

———. "Chief William Charles Rogers." *Chronicles of Oklahoma* 17 (June 1939): 140–146.

———. "Chief William Potter Ross." *Chronicles of Oklahoma* 15 (March 1937): 21–29.

———. "The Mayes." Chronicles of Oklahoma 15 (March 1937): 56–65.

McCandless, Peter. "A Female Malady? Women at the South Carolina Lunatic Asylum, 1828–1915." *Journal of the History of Medicine* 54 (1999): 543–71.

McClintock, Megan J. "Civil War Pensions and the Reconstruction of Union Families." *Journal of American History* 83 (September 1996): 456–80.

McFadden, Marguerite. "Intruders or Injustice?" *Chronicles of Oklahoma* 48 (Winter 1970–71): 431–49.

McKelvey, Blake. *American Prisons: A History of Good Intentions*. Montclair, N.J.: Patterson Smith, 1977.

McLoughlin, William G. *After the Trail of Tears: The Cherokees' Struggle for Sovereignty, 1839–1880*. Chapel Hill: University of North Carolina Press, 1993.

———. *Champions of the Cherokees: Evan and John B. Jones*. Princeton, N.J.: Princeton University Press, 1990.

———. "Cherokee Anti-Mission Sentiment, 1824–1828." *Ethnohistory 21* (Fall 1974): 371–70.

———. *The Cherokee Ghost Dance: Essays on the Southeastern Indians, 1789–1861*. Macon, Ga.: Mercer University Press, 1984.

———. *Cherokee Renascence in the New Republic*. New Haven, Conn.: Yale University Press, 1986.

———. *The Cherokees and Christianity, 1794–1870: Essays on Acculturation and Cultural Persistence*. Edited by Walter H. Conser, Jr. Athens: University of Georgia Press, 1994.

———. "Cherokees and Methodists." *Church History* 50 (March 1981): 44–63.

———. *Cherokees and Missionaries, 1789–1839*. New Haven, Conn.: Yale University Press, 1984.

McLoughlin, William G., Walter H. Conser, and Virginia Duffy McLoughlin. "Cherokee Anomie, 1794–1910: New Roles for Red Men, Red Women, and Black Slaves." In *The Cherokee Ghost Dance: Essays on the Southeastern Indians, 1789–1861*. 3–37. Macon, Ga.: Mercer University Press, 1984.

Mihesuah, Devon A. *Choctaw Crime and Punishment, 1884–1907*. Norman: University of Oklahoma Press, 2009.

———. *Cultivating the Rosebuds: The Education of Women at the Cherokee Female Seminary, 1851–1909*. Urbana: University of Illinois Press, 1993.

————. "Out of the 'Graves of the Polluted Debauches': The Boys of the Cherokee Male Seminary." *American Indian Quarterly* 15 (Autumn 1991): 503–21.

Miles, Tiya. *The House on Diamond Hill: A Plantation Story*. Chapel Hill: University of North Carolina Press, 2010.

————. "The Narrative of Nancy: A Cherokee Woman." *Frontiers: A Journal of Women Studies* 29 (2008): 59–80.

————. *Ties That Bind: The Story of an Afro-Cherokee Family in Slavery and Freedom*. Berkeley: University of California Press, 2005.

Miner, H. Craig. *The Corporation and the Indian: Tribal Sovereignty and Industrial Civilization in Indian Territory, 1865–1907*. Columbia: University of Missouri Press, 1976.

Mintz, Steven. *Huck's Raft: A History of American Childhood*. Cambridge: Harvard University Press, 2004.

Mooney, James. "The Cherokee Ball Play." *American Anthropologist* 3, no. 2 (April 1, 1890): 105–32.

————. *Historical Sketch of the Cherokee*. New Brunswick, N.J.: Transaction, 2005.

Moore, Kathleen Dean. *Pardons: Justice, Mercy, and the Public Interest*. New York: Oxford University Press, 1989.

Morgan, Omer L. "The Saline County Courthouse Massacre." *Chronicles of Oklahoma* 33 (Spring 1955): 202–37.

Mosteller, Kelli. "The Cultural Politics of Land: Allotment among the Citizen Potawatomi in Kansas and Indian Territory, 1861–1887." Master's thesis, University of Texas, 2008.

————. "Place, Politics, and Property: Negotiating Allotment and Citizenship for the Citizen Potawatomi, 1861–1891." PhD diss., University of Texas, 2013.

Moulton, Gary. *John Ross, Cherokee Chief*. Athens: University of Georgia Press, 1978.

Nasaw, David. *Schooled to Order: A Social History of Public Schooling in the United States*. New York: Oxford University Press, 1981.

Naylor, Celia E. *African Cherokees in Indian Territory: From Chattel to Citizens*. Chapel Hill: University of North Carolina Press, 2008.

Nielsen, Kim. *A Disability History of the United States*. Boston: Beacon Press, 2012.

Norgren, Jill. *The Cherokee Cases: Two Landmark Federal Decisions in the Fight for Sovereignty*. Norman: University of Oklahoma Press, 2004.

O'Sullivan, Meg Devlin. "Missionary and Mother: Jersuha Swain's Transformation in the Cherokee Nation, 1852–1861." *Chronicles of Oklahoma* 83 (Winter 2005–2006): 452–65.

Parins, James W. *Elias Cornelius Boudinot: A Life on the Cherokee Border*. Lincoln: University of Nebraska Press, 2006.

Pascoe, Peggy. *Relations of Rescue: The Search for Female Moral Authority in the American West, 1874–1939*. New York: Oxford University Press, 1990.

Perdue, Theda. *Cherokee Women: Gender and Culture Change, 1700–1835*. Lincoln: University of Nebraska Press, 1998.

———. "Nancy Ward (1738?–1822)." In *Portraits of American Women from Settlement to Present*, edited by G. J. Barker-Benfield and Catherine Clinton, 83–100. New York: Oxford University Press, 1998.

———. *Slavery and the Evolution of Cherokee Society, 1540–1866*. Knoxville: University of Tennessee Press, 1979.

———. "Traditionalism in the Cherokee Nation: Resistance to the Constitution of 1827." *Georgia Historical Quarterly* 66 (Summer 1982): 159–70.

Perdue, Theda, and Michael D. Green. *The Cherokee Nation and the Trail of Tears*. New York: Viking, 2007.

———, eds. *Cherokee Removal: A Brief History with Documents*. Boston: St. Martin's, 1995.

Pisciotta, Alexander W. *Benevolent Repression: Social Control and the American Reformatory-Prison Movement*. New York: New York University Press, 1996.

Porter, Roy. *Madness: A Brief History*. New York: Oxford University Press, 2002.

Powell, Eric A. "ᏎᏉᏯ Was Here." *Archaeology* 62 (July/August 2009): 9.

Prucha, Francis Paul. *American Indian Policy in Crisis: Christian Reformers and the Indian, 1865–1900*. Norman: University of Oklahoma Press, 1976.

———. *The Churches and the Indian Schools, 1888–1912*. Lincoln: University of Nebraska Press, 1979.

Rand, Jacki Thompson. *Kiowa Humanity and the Invasion of the State*. Lincoln: University of Nebraska Press, 2008.

Reed, Gerard. "Postremoval Factionalism in the Cherokee Nation." In *The Cherokee Indian Nation: A Troubled History*, edited by Duane H. King, 148–63. Knoxville: University of Tennessee Press, 1979.

Reid, John Phillip. *A Better Kind of Hatchet: Law, Trade, and Diplomacy in the Cherokee Nation During the Early Years of European Contact*. University Park: Pennsylvania State University Press, 1976.

———. *A Law of Blood: The Primitive Law of the Cherokee Nation*. New York: New York University Press, 1970.

Reyhner, Jon Allan, and Jeanne M. Oyawin Eder. *American Indian Education: A History*. Norman, University of Oklahoma Press, 2006.

Richardson, Heather Cox. *Death of Reconstruction: Race, Labor, and Politics in the Post–Civil War North, 1865–1901*. Cambridge, Mass.: Harvard University Press, 2001.

Riney, Scott. "Power and Powerlessness: The People of the Canton Asylum for Insane Indians." *South Dakota History* 27 (1–2): 41–64.

Roberts, Mary Riley. "Cherokee Orphan Asylum Was Established in Year 1873." *American Indian* (November 1929).

Rockman, Seth. *Welfare Reform in the Early Republic: A Brief History with Documents*. Boston: Bedford/St. Martins, 2002.

Rothman, David J. *The Discovery of the Asylum: Social Order and Disorder in the New Republic*. Boston: Little, Brown, 1971.

Royce, Charles C. *The Cherokee Nation of Indians*. Chicago: Aldine, 1975.

Rutkow, Ira. *Seeking the Cure: A History of Medicine in America*. New York: Scribner, 2010.

Saunt, Claudio. "The Paradox of Freedom: Tribal Sovereignty and Emancipation during the Reconstruction of Indian Territory." *Journal of Southern History* 70, no. 1 (February 2004): 63–94.

Schurz Carl. "Present Aspects of the Indian Problem." *North American Review* 258 (Winter 1973): 45–54.

Scott, James C. *Seeing like a State: How Certain Schemes to Improve the Human Condition Have Failed*. New Haven, Conn.: Yale University Press, 1999.

Shaffer, Donald R. "'I Do Not Suppose that Uncle Sam Looks at the Skin:' African-Americans and the Civil War Pension System, 1865–1934." *Civil War History* 46 (2000): 132–47.

Shirley, Glenn. *Law West of Fort Smith: A History of Frontier Justice in the Indian Territory, 1834–1896*. New York: Henry Holt, 1957.

Skocpol, Theda. *Protecting Soldiers and Mothers: The Political Origins of Social Policy in the United States*. Cambridge, Mass.: Harvard University Press, 1992.

———. "A Society without a 'State'? Political Organization, Social Conflict, and Welfare Provision in the United States." *Journal of Public Policy* 7, no. 4 (October 1, 1987): 349–71.

Smith, Tash. *Capture These Indians for the Lord: Indians, Methodists, and Oklahomans, 1844–1939*. Tucson: University of Arizona Press, 2014.

Sober, Nancy Hope. *The Intruders: The Illegal Residents of the Cherokee Nation, 1866–1907*. Ponca City, Okla.: Cherokee Books, 1991.

Spoehr, Alexander. "Kinship System of the Seminole." *Anthropological Series* 33, no. 2 (1942): 29–113 .

Starkey, Marion L. *The Cherokee Nation*. New York: Knopf, 1946.

Steen, Carl T. "The Home for the Insane, Deaf, Dumb, and Blind of the Cherokee Nation." *Chronicles of Oklahoma* 21 (December 1943): 402–19.

Stratton, Ray. *The Cherokee National Insane Asylum*. Topeka, Kans.: Menninger Foundation, 1983.

Stremlau, Rose. "In Defense of 'This Great Family Government and Estate': Cherokee Masculinity and the Opposition to Allotment." In *Southern Masculinity: Perspectives on Manhood in the South Since Reconstruction*, edited by Craig T. Friend, 65–82. Athens: University of Georgia Press, 2009.

———. *Sustaining the Cherokee Family: Kinship and the Allotment of an Indigenous Nation*. Chapel Hill: University of North Carolina Press, 2011.

———. "'To Domesticate and Civilize Wild Indians': Allotment and the Campaign to Reform Indian Families, 1875–1887." *Journal of Family History* 30 (July 2005): 265–86.

Strickland, Rennard. *Fire and the Spirits: Cherokee Law from Clan to Court*. Norman: University of Oklahoma Press, 1975.

———. *The Indians in Oklahoma*. Norman: University of Oklahoma Press, 1980.

Szasz, Margaret Connell. *Indian Education in the American Colonies, 1607–1783*. Lincoln: University of Nebraska Press, 2007.

Thomas, Robert K. "The Origin and Development of the Redbird Smith Movement." Master's thesis, University of Arizona, 1953.

Thornton, Russell. *The Cherokees: A Population History.* Lincoln: University of Nebraska Press, 1992.

Timmons, Todd. *Science and Technology in Nineteenth-Century America.* Westport, Conn.: Greenwood Press, 2005.

Trattner, Walter I. *From Poor Law to Welfare State: A History of Social Welfare in America.* 4th ed. New York: Free Press, 1989.

Travis, V. A. "Life in the Cherokee Nation A Decade After the Civil War." *Chronicles of Oklahoma* 4 (March 1926): 16–30.

Usner, Daniel. "American Indians and Welfare in the United States." *European Contributions to American Studies* 37 (September 1996): 312–26.

———. "American Indians on the Cotton Frontier." *Journal of American History* 72 (September 1985): 297–317.

———. *Indian Work: Language and Livelihood in Native American History.* Cambridge, Mass.: Harvard University Press, 2009.

Vick, R. Alfred. "Cherokee Adaptation to the Landscape of the West and Overcoming the Loss of Culturally Significant Plants." *American Indian Quarterly* 35 (Summer 2011): 394–405.

Wagner, David. *Ordinary People: In and Out of Poverty in the Gilded Age.* Boulder: Paradigm Publishers, 2008.

———. *The Poorhouse: America's Forgotten Institution.* Lanham, Md.: Rowman and Littlefield, 2005.

Wahrhaftig, Albert L. "More than Mere Work: The Subsistence System of Oklahoma's Cherokee Indians." *Appalachian Journal* 2, no. 4 (July 1975): 327–31.

Walker, Robert Sparks. *Torchlight to the Cherokees: The Brainerd Mission.* 1931. Reprint, Johnson City, Tenn.: Overmountain Press, 1993.

Wardell, Morris L. *A Political History of the Cherokee Nation, 1838–1907.* Norman: University of Oklahoma Press, 1977.

White, Richard. *The Roots of Dependency: Subsistence, Environment, and Social Change among the Choctaws, Pawnees, and Navajos.* Lincoln: University of Nebraska Press, 1988.

Wilkins, Thurman. *Cherokee Tragedy: The Ridge Family and the Decimation of a People.* Norman: University of Oklahoma Press, 1986.

———. "John Howard Payne." *Columbia Library Columns* 12 (1961): 2–11.

Wright, Muriel H. "John D. Benedict: First United States Superintendent of Schools in the Indian Territory." *Chronicles of Oklahoma* 33 (1955): 472–508.

Yarbrough, Fay. *Race and the Cherokee Nation: Sovereignty in the Nineteenth Century.* Philadelphia: University of Pennsylvania Press, 2008.

Zellar, Gary. *African Creeks: Estelvste and the Creek Nation.* Norman, University of Oklahoma Press, 2007.

Zmora, Nurith. *Orphanages Reconsidered: Child Care Institutions in Progressive Era Baltimore.* Philadelphia: Temple University Press, 1994.

Zogry, Michael J. *Anetso, the Cherokee Ball Game: At the Center of Ceremony and Identity.* Chapel Hill: University of North Carolina Press, 2010.

Index

Page numbers in italics indicate illustrations.

Abercrombie, Elizabeth, 49
academies, Indian Mission Conference, 86
Act of Union, 76
Adair, John Lynch, 132, 133, 233
Adair, Walter Thompson, 126, 127, 141, 162, 210, 234
Adair, William Penn, 22
administrators, 273–74
adonisgi. See healers
adoption, 40–41
African Americans: in Arkansas, 208, 220–21; Cherokee Nation laws and, 51–52, 222; in Cherokee society, 16, 47; enslaved, 11, 79; in Oklahoma, 223, 312n64; during Reconstruction, 102–103. See also various African Indian groups
African Cherokees, 122; on Dawes Commission rolls, 275–76; discrimination against, 165–66, 218–19, 221, 240–41; on juries, 170–71; professional opportunities for, 103–104; race baiting and, 233, 234
African Choctaws, 218
African Creeks, 171, 219, 222, 312n67, 312n72
African Indians, 218–19
African Seminoles, 79
agriculture, 37, 94; at Cherokee Orphan Asylum, 129–30, 164; communal, 7–8; scientific, 159
Akego, 109
Alabama, 73, 285n46, 288n3, 289n16; and Creek relocation, 67–68
Alberty, Dave, 276
Alberty, E. C., 261
alcohol abuse, removal and, 77, 78–79
Allbones, 44

allotment, 61, 197, 223, 246, 259, 260, 266–67, 271, 311n23; Walter Adair Duncan on, 255–56; Five Tribes and, 228, 229; and Indian problem, 214, 224; opposition to, 234, 250–51; resistance to, 254, 268–69; rights to, 275–76
AMA. See American Medical Association
American Baptist Mission Indian University, 131
American Board of Commissioners for Foreign Missions, 36
Americanization, 259
American Medical Association (AMA), 125, 258
American Neurological Society, 140, 184
American Public Health Association, 140
American Revolution, 12–13
amnesty, 237, 316n27
animals, and disease, 10, 27
annuity, distribution of, 65, 66–67
Arkadelphia, school for the blind at, 181
Arkansas, 22, 92, 208, 209; federal court in, 120, 134; freedmen in, 220–21; removal to, 45, 50–51, 65; school for the blind, 180–81
Arkansas Cherokees. See Old Settlers
Arkansas Deaf-Mute Institute, 181
Armstrong, Samuel Chapman, 18, 201
Arthur, Chester A., 201, 214
assaults, punishment of, 55–56
Association of Medical Superintendents of American Institutions, 183
asylums: for (dis)abled, 115; for mentally ill, 259, 274–75
attorneys, 44, 46, 286n62

Bacone, Almon, 202
Bacone College (Indian University), 202